*Immigration Policy
in the Age of Punishment*

Studies in Transgression

Editor: David Brotherton
Founding Editor: Jock Young

The Studies in Transgression series will present a range of exciting new crime-related titles that offer an alternative to the mainstream, mostly positivistic approaches to social problems in the United States and beyond. The series will raise awareness of key crime-related issues and explore challenging research topics in an interdisciplinary way. Where possible, books in the series will allow the global voiceless to have their views heard, offering analyses of human subjects who have too often been marginalized and pathologized. Further, series authors will suggest ways to influence public policy. The editors welcome new as well as experienced authors who can write innovatively and accessibly. We anticipate that these books will appeal to those working within criminology, criminal justice, sociology, or related disciplines, as well as the educated public.

Terry Williams and Trevor B. Milton,
The Con Men: Hustling in New York City

Christopher P. Dum,
Exiled in America: Life on the Margins in a Residential Motel

Mark S. Hamm and Ramón Spaaij,
The Age of Lone Wolf Terrorism

Peter J. Marina,
Down and Out in New Orleans

Immigration Policy
in the Age of Punishment

Detention, Deportation, and Border Control

Edited by David C. Brotherton and Philip Kretsedemas

COLUMBIA UNIVERSITY PRESS

NEW YORK

Columbia University Press
Publishers Since 1893
New York   Chichester, West Sussex
cup.columbia.edu
Copyright © 2017 Columbia University Press

Library of Congress Cataloging-in-Publication Data

Names: Brotherton, David, editor. | Kretsedemas, Philip, 1967– editor.
Title: Immigration policy in the age of punishment : detention, deportation,
    and border control / edited by David C. Brotherton and Philip Kretsedemas.
Description: New York : Columbia University Press, [2017] | Includes index.
Identifiers: LCCN 2017024007 (print) | LCCN 2017027009 (ebook) | ISBN 9780231545891 |
    ISBN 9780231179362 (hardcover : alk. paper) | ISBN 9780231179379 (pbk.)
Subjects: LCSH: Emigration and immigration law. | Emigration and immigration—
    Government policy. | Asylum, Right of—Government policy. | Deportation. |
    Deportees—Legal status, laws, etc. | Human rights.
Classification: LCC K3275 (ebook) | LCC K3275 .I485 2017 (print) | DDC 325/.1—dc23
LC record available at https://lccn.loc.gov/2017024007

Columbia University Press books are printed on permanent and
durable acid-free paper.
Printed in the United States of America

Cover design: Jordan Wannemacher
Cover image: © J. Emilio Flores/Contributor/Getty Images

CONTENTS

*Immigration Policy
in the Age of Punishment*

1. INTRODUCTION

Immigration Policy in an Age of Punishment

PHILIP KRETSEDEMAS, UMASS BOSTON

DAVID C. BROTHERTON, JOHN JAY COLLEGE, CUNY

Over the past several decades, the U.S. government has increased its immigration enforcement powers to unprecedented levels. Annual deportations exceeded historic highs in the early 1990s, when they climbed above forty thousand per year.[1] But this was just the beginning of an escalation that has continued unabated to this day. U.S. deportations exceeded 300,000 per year by the end of the George W. Bush presidency and climbed even further—to over 400,000 per year—under the Obama administration.[2] These statistics do not even account for border enforcement actions, which used to make up the lion's share of U.S. immigration enforcement actions.[3]

The escalation of deportations has been matched by enforcement practices that have created a new class of criminalized noncitizens. The war on drugs, which used to be the focus of federal law enforcement, has been joined by what seems to be a new "war" on noncitizens. Over the past two decades, immigration-related offenses—mostly for legal status violations—have become a growing share of federal convictions. In recent years, prosecutions for immigration violations actually exceeded—and are now on par with—arrests for drug convictions.[4] As a result, Latinos have overtaken non-Latino blacks as the largest segment of the federal prison population.[5] And since the early 2000s, hundreds of state and local governments throughout the United States have enacted their own enforcement-oriented immigration laws and signed on to enforcement partnerships with the federal government.[6]

Although these trends can be explained in light of a policy history that is specific to the United States, they are not unique to the country by any means. The national obsession with controlling immigration and securing borders has become a global phenomenon. There are striking continuities running through complaints about unwanted Roma migrants in Slovenia, unwanted Turkish migrants in Greece, unwanted flows of West and Central African migrants in South Africa, and the tide of anti-immigrant sentiment that contributed to the UK's Brexit vote as well as the electoral victory of Donald Trump in the United States.[7]

The title of this book offers one way of thinking about the scale of these transformations. The punitive public culture that has come to define immigration policy can be understood as the emblematic feature of an age, a zeitgeist of the times. The idea of an age of punishment suggests a transformation on a scale that is much broader than a punitive turn in immigration policy. Immigration laws have not just become tougher; there has been a paradigm shift in the workings of the global migration regime. In order to come to grips with this transformation, it is necessary to look beyond the social fact of mass deportations and consider the broader changes that help explain why mass deportations and massive spending on border control can be rendered legible as a reasonable response to the challenges posed by international migration and that highly political construction known as "border security."

To begin with, the present-day migration regime is distinguished by its global scale. The migration flows of the current era are more fluid and circular than they were in the early twentieth century.[8] They are shaped by social networks and economic forces that do not operate simply on a national or an international scale—in other words, being limited to interactions between a "sending" and a "receiving" nation.[9] Moreover, the quotidian subject of the current migration regime is now the guest worker, not the permanent settler.

The United States, for example, is still admitting more international migrants than any other nation on earth, but the vast majority of these new entrants are now issued temporary visas.[10] And although many other nation-states are still attached to the narrative that they are "nations of immigration," permanent settlement is increasingly viewed as a long-term expense, contributing to the national fiscal deficit.[11] It would appear that arguments about the impracticality of replacement migration as a solution to the growing fiscal burden of aging populations have given way to migration schemes that supplement the national economy through their productivity and temporality. As some scholars have observed, the ideal migrant for many Western industrialized nations is skilled, is in the prime of his or her life, has few attachments (i.e., is unmarried or has no children), and has plans to return home—or go elsewhere—before he or she reaches retirement age.[12] One example of such a migrant is the legal resident who is deported for a minor criminal infraction and, on repatriation, loses the right to Social Security despite having paid into the system for years. Another example is the high-skilled guest worker who spends a decade or more shifting from one temporary visa to another, living under the constant threat of deportation (and leaving the country before this threat is realized). These examples illustrate how deportation can be used to police and shape the behaviors of an expendable noncitizen population. This situation, in which the "integration" of noncitizens is conditioned by their expendability and in which even the most "desirable" migrants are not spared from the hazards of legal precarity, also provides a good introduction into how neoliberal economic priorities have changed the way that immigration works today.

The neoliberal restructuring project was first implemented in the nations of the global North and was extended to developmentalist policies that have been applied to the nations of the global South.[13] Among other things, this restructuring project has been concerned with shrinking social welfare expenditures, incorporating a business model of fiscal management into the public sector, and boosting supply-side growth strategies that reduce restrictions on the flow of investment capital and make labor markets more flexible and amenable to the needs of entrepreneurs.

One consequence of these transformations is that the costs and benefits of all things are assessed on an increasingly restricted time frame and according to how well individuals can adapt to their immediate circumstances. Welfare assistance becomes geared toward putting people immediately back to work—even if this means placing them in low-wage jobs that keep them trapped in a cycle of welfare recidivism.[14] Economic restructuring in the industrialized West has also created a new stratum of precarious labor that is temporary, non-benefited, low paying, and typified by freelance or work-from-home arrangements. These labor market conditions, which are experienced by citizens and noncitizens alike, have been accompanied by a new kind of legal precarity that is specific to noncitizens. The rise of visa admittances and the growth of the unauthorized migrant population coincide with the shift toward labor market casualization and the escalation of public sector downsizing from the 1980s onward.[15]

It may seem ironic that this drive to reduce public expenditures and control the "fiscal burden" of the noncitizen population has culminated in the largest publicly funded immigration enforcement apparatus in modern history (both in the United States and transnationally).[16] This is an area of study that needs to be much better incorporated into work on the political economy of security; however, David Harvey's analysis of neoliberalism offers some helpful insights.[17]

Harvey insists that neoliberalism has, on balance, been more concerned with devising coercive strategies for capital accumulation than with the utopian goal of creating an "open society" (which entails the free flow of migrant labor, among other things). Harvey, along with other scholars of neoliberalism, also notes that neoliberal capitalism is distinguished by its reliance on a more proactive and interventionist mode of state regulation.[18] Although neoliberal restructuring is geared toward downsizing public spending and social services for lower-income populations, it also channels unprecedented levels of public resources into state-corporate partnerships and securitization strategies, which are used to expand the reach of market forces. The end result is a unilaterally structured market economy that is backed by the authority of a strong state. As it concerns immigration policy, this means that migrants can be recruited in large numbers while also being policed by a state-funded enforcement apparatus that removes noncitizens who are deemed unproductive or deleterious to economic growth. But the means–ends rationality guiding this process is also prone to excess and cruelty, and it's not unusual for the goal of securitizing migration flows to clash with the relentless drive for maximizing profit and productivity. This is one reason why get-tough immigration policies are often blamed for undermining the economic benefits of immigration. But as many immigration scholars have pointed out, get-tough enforcement practices have evolved from the same paradigm of economic growth that has been guiding immigration policy for the past several decades.

Kitty Calavita has traced this relationship between immigration enforcement and pro-growth immigration policies to the 1940s, focusing on the first temporary labor arrangement brokered by the U.S. and Mexican governments. Her groundbreaking account of the Bracero program treats immigration enforcement as a strategy for regulating legal flows of temporary migrant labor and the flows of undocumented migration that grew alongside them.[19] Calavita explains how border enforcement operations of the Bracero era were adapted to fluctuations in the labor market supply of migrant workers, with removals increasing when there was a perceived surplus of laborers, and removals decreasing during periods of employer demand for this labor. Katherine Donato and Douglas Massey offer another insight into the way employers can benefit from get-tough enforcement.[20] Their research on the outcomes of the Immigration Reform and Control Act (1986) has shown that "employer sanctions," intended to discourage the hiring of unauthorized migrants, actually enhanced the control of employers over these workers, without effecting a decline in the numbers of these migrant workers. In contrast, King, Massoglia, and Uggen have argued that unemployment rates of native-born citizens have more to do with immigration enforcement trends than with the size of the surplus noncitizen population, suggesting that native workers, not employers, are the primary beneficiaries of these practices.[21]

Nicholas De Genova has provided a different explanation, which suggests that it is too limiting to think about deportation as a "reward" for native workers, a "benefit" for employers, or even a punishment for "bad" immigrants.[22] De Genova's work focuses on the mechanics of deportability (the real but unactualized potential to be deported) and not just on the sociopolitical fact of deportation (i.e., the tally of those who are actually deported). He argues that deportations exert a disciplinary pressure on the "good" immigrants who are still living and working in the host nation, reminding them of their potential to be deported. Other scholars have offered complementary explanations of how immigration enforcement is used as a public theater to send signals to a broader citizen and noncitizen audience.[23] But it is worth emphasizing that deportability describes a regimen that is more concerned with managing the subjectivity of the migrant than it is with managing public opinion. Consistent with a Foucauldian understanding of disciplinary power, the aim is to cultivate a new (more productive, self-regulating) kind of person. Jonathan Inda offers a supporting analysis when he explains how immigration enforcement inculcates a prudential mind-set in the migrant, which is intended to encourage law-abiding behavior but can also discourage the migrant from exercising his or her legal rights (e.g., choosing not to participate in a vote for a union bargaining unit or press complaints about workplace safety violations).[24] Whereas earlier theories explained how immigration enforcement adapts to the ebb and flow of labor market demands or political pressures (including moral panics[25]), theories of deportation as a disciplinary regimen describe a mode of coercion that acts on its subjects continuously—because its aim is the transformation of subjectivity itself.

David Brotherton and Luis Barrios offer another insight into these enforcement priorities with their description of immigration policy as a case of social bulimia.[26] The bulimic's anxious relationship to food offers a template for thinking about the mainstream policy discourse on immigration, which appears to simultaneously want and fear migrants—and which controls the thing it wants with a politics of fear. Tanya Golash-Boza has also explained how these anxieties are epitomized by the treatment of black and brown racial minorities, who make up the overwhelming majority of the deportation caseload in the United States (and in many other nations).[27]

These observations offer insights into how the rational–disciplinary imperatives of immigration policy can spiral into the nativistic racism theorized by Robert Chang or the Latino threat discourse examined by Leo Chavez.[28] Under the grip of these impulses, the punitive excesses of neoliberal disciplinarity can become detached from the goal of cultivating orderly and compliant subjectivities and be overtaken by a generalized fear of the alien, which tilts in the direction of population control and mass expulsion.[29] As a result, the disciplinary imperatives of the contemporary migration regime can careen back and forth between moments of racist xenophobia and a quieter, "more rational" kind of racism that creates stratified employment niches of "white," "black," and "brown" jobs—as documented by Roger Waldinger and Lisa Catanzarite.[30]

PROBLEMATIZING THE AGE OF PUNISHMENT

The prior discussion touched on several key factors identified by critical research on immigration enforcement—the regulation of migrant labor markets, neoliberal growth strategies, the deepening links between criminal and immigration enforcement, tactics of discipline and control, and racism and nativism—and offered some insights into how they interlock within our present-day age of punishment. This list of factors is not exhaustive by any means, and we do not pretend to have arrived at a definitive explanation. Our modest aim has been only to introduce a number of issues that will be explored in greater depth by the book's authors and to provide a context for understanding how the themes of their chapters interrelate.

This book can also be read as an update on all the issues that were examined in the earlier book we coedited, *Keeping Out the Other: A Critical Introduction to Immigration Enforcement Today,* published in 2008.[31] Although a number of important works on immigration enforcement had been published before *Keeping Out the Other* (some of which we have already cited), to our knowledge it was the first book-length compilation of its kind to be published since the United States enacted the 1996 immigration reform laws.[32]

In the vein of publications that are self-consciously burdened by the mantle of being "the first," *Keeping Out the Other* offered an urgent report from the field—which ended up being an account of immigration enforcement in the final years of the George W. Bush administration. *Immigration Policy in an Age of Punishment* offers up another urgent report, in this case focusing on the final years of the Obama administration. The timeliness of this book is underscored by the election of Donald Trump, which has made the immigration debate a headline issue for public discussion, both in the United States and globally.

The electoral victory of Donald Trump—when viewed in tandem with the Brexit vote—appears to signal a political sea change on a transnational scale. The U.S.-UK alliance was a driving force behind the acceleration of economic globalization from the mid-twentieth century onward.[33] The rise of popular nationalism in both of these nations may not signal the end of globalization, but it does at the very least signal a new defensive posture in which globalization is increasingly viewed as a "threat to the West" by growing sectors of the electorate.[34]

Although our work on this book was started before the election of Donald Trump, we realize that its contents will be read in light of the immigration politics of the Trump era. This is why we think it is important to provide a discussion of how to read our analysis of late-Obama-era immigration policy with an eye toward the emerging immigration policy agenda of the Trump administration.

IMMIGRATION POLICY FROM THE OBAMA TO TRUMP ERA: WHAT HAS (AND HAS NOT) CHANGED?

It may seem odd to describe this book as documenting Obama-era policy when almost half of its contents are focused on national contexts besides that of the United States. Nevertheless, "the Obama era" works as a broad description of a global policy paradigm, for the same reason that we can speculate on the global significance of the Trump presidency. Both eras are described by immigration policy priorities that are articulated with an agenda for market-based growth, global and domestic security, and international diplomacy, all of which are used by the U.S. government to influence the policy agendas of other nations as well as international and transnational governing bodies.

This account does, admittedly, offer a U.S.-centric perspective on the global policy terrain, the assumption being that the United States is a global agenda setter—for immigration policy in particular. But the global attention given to the U.S. 2016 presidential race does lend credence to the "agenda setter" thesis. Where else but in the United States could the results of a national election spark protests across the global North and South?[35] The scale of this reaction indicates that multitudes across the world see a relationship between the changing tide of U.S. politics and the fortunes of their nations. The electoral victory of Donald Trump sent a message that something had fundamentally changed. If the world's leading immigration nation appears to have lost faith in its own national mythology on immigration, what does this portend for the global migration regime?

Keeping this context in mind, the main message this book sets out to deliver about the Obama era is a cautionary one. We should resist the temptation to treat the Obama era as a golden age of progressive immigration policies. The draconian overtones of Trump-era immigration policy—epitomized by its controversial travel ban targeting Arab Muslim nationals—certainly invite this way of framing things.[36] But the differences in Obama- and Trump-era policies, which are not inconsequential by any means, also operate within a continuum.

At the time of this writing, the Trump administration has distinguished itself, most apparently, in the overall scale of its enforcement actions. As of May 2017, arrests by Immigration and Customs Enforcement were up by 37.6 percent over arrest rates during the same period in 2016.[37] Immigration judges are also issuing deportation orders more frequently. As of May 2017, the proportion of deportation hearings ending in a final order of deportation was approximately 10 percent higher than the year-end average for 2016.[38] These enforcement trends are consistent with the objectives laid out by the executive orders on immigration that were issued by president Trump in January 2017.[39] Of special significance is the order titled "Enhancing Public Safety in the Interior of the United States," which expands the discretionary authority of immigration enforcement to arrest and detain noncitizens that had been routinely exempted from the Obama administration's enforcement priorities.[40] These developments have led some observers to speculate that the major change introduced by Trump-era enforcement priorities has to do with "who" is at risk of deportation rather than "how many" are being deported.[41]

This change in enforcement practice undermines the idea that there are such things as "protected categories" of noncitizens, creating a situation in which almost any noncitizen can imagine themselves a candidate for deportation— irrespective of whether they have broken a law or had a run-in with immigration enforcement. As De Genova (and several other immigration scholars)[42] have explained, the impact of immigration enforcement should be viewed in light of this potential to be deported, which shapes the behavior of the vast majority of noncitizens who are never brought before an immigration court. But if we accept these arguments, it becomes more apparent how the features that appear to distinguish Trump-era immigration enforcement underscore its continuity with the enforcement strategies that precede it.

It is important to keep in mind that theories of deportability and neoliberal prudentialism (among others) were developed over a decade before the election of Donald Trump, to explain an enforcement stratagem that can be traced at least as far back as the Clinton era (though as Calavita's research indicates, its germinal features were present in the Bracero era[43]). This is why the unprecedented toughness of Trump's immigration agenda can be understood as operating within a "normal" that has been cultivated by the past several decades of U.S. immigration policy. Even the intensification of immigration enforcement under the Trump administration can be understood as a "normal" feature of a linear escalation that has unfolded from the 1990s onward, whereby the enforcement actions of each new administration outpace those of its predecessors.

But ironically, deportation rates have been sluggish under the first few months of the Trump administration, despite its record high arrest rates. The Trump administration has actually deported 12 percent fewer noncitizens in its first one hundred days than were deported by the same time in 2016.[44] This is partly because the deportation case load of the immigration court system is very backlogged, a collateral effect of its massively expanded size.[45] The inability of the Trump administration to accelerate deportation rates has also been compounded by its failure to get many of its immigration priorities funded in the May 2017 federal budget (including construction of the border wall, expansion of detention beds, and a hiring increase for immigration enforcement and border patrol agents).[46] But it is even more telling that Trump administration officials have played down the scale of their enforcement agenda by insisting that they are not carrying out a mass deportation program[47]—which begs the question of how exactly one distinguishes a mass deportation program from a major increase in immigration enforcement actions (also considering that the annual rate of enforcement actions that we take as "normal" today exceeds the scale of "mass deportation" programs, like Operation Wetback, which Trump touted on the campaign trail[48]). These statements illustrate how the Trump administration is simultaneously attempting to position itself as tougher on immigration than the Obama administration, and also operating within the normal rule of law.

But as we explained above, this is not only rhetoric. The Trump administration has been able to channel its get-tough enforcement agenda through programs, policy levers, and executive powers crafted by prior administrations because there are real continuities in the way immigration enforcement has been used by all of these administrations. For example, although one of Trump's executive orders terminated the Priority Enforcement Program (PEP) that was initiated by the Obama administration, it replaced PEP with the more aggressive Secure Communities enforcement program that had been initiated by the George W. Bush administration (and was active through most of Obama's tenure as president).[49] The Trump administration has also created incentives for local police to enforce federal immigration laws by reviving the 287(g) program, authorized by the 1996 Illegal Immigration Reform and Immigrant Responsibility Act (IIRIRA) that was enacted under the Clinton administration.[50]

Trump's maneuvers on Obama-era protections for undocumented migrant youth offer more insights into the balance his administration is trying to strike between "continuity" and "change." In a surprising departure from his campaign trail rhetoric, President Trump initially decided not to terminate the Deferred Action Childhood Arrivals program created by President Obama, which grants qualified undocumented migrant youth an indefinite reprieve from deportation.[51] At the same time, the Trump administration underscored its enforcement priorities by escalating the deportation of DACA recipients facing criminal allegations (increasing DACA revocations for criminal reasons by 25 percent during the first few months of 2017).[52]

In September 2017, Trump made a radical about-face, and announced his intentions to terminate the DACA program—appearing to have returned to his campaign trail stance on the program.[53] But days after this announcement, he began holding meetings with Democrats to explore legislative possibilities for granting DACA recipients a permanent status contingent on immigration enforcement targets being met.[54] At the time of this writing, it is unclear whether a deal has been reached, and it seems likely that there will be more surprise developments in store for DACA recipients in the months ahead.

The Trump administration's position on H-1B work visa holders has been characterized by a similar fluidity. H-1B is another program that Trump promised to eliminate on the campaign trail.[55] Thus far, the administration has decided to let the program stand, but it has used discretionary authority to end the expedited review of H-1B visa applications—a decision that effectively reduces H-1B admissions—and has drawn criticism from the business community accordingly.[56]

The willingness of the Trump administration to frustrate employer demands for guest workers may lend more credibility to its economic nationalism, which has been amplified by an April 2017 executive order titled "Buy America and Hire American."[57] However, the executive order does not create any new programs or procedures for vetting work visa applicants. It only affirms the Trump administration's commitment to protecting U.S. jobs, using existing legal channels, and has been assessed by many analysts as being little more than a symbolic politics, comparable to Trump's use of the bully pulpit to shame multinationals into bringing jobs back to the United States.[58] But a few weeks after issuing this Executive Order, the Trump administration managed to get Indian-owned infotech corporations to commit to hiring more U.S. workers, after accelerating its investigations into abuses of the work visa system.[59] These developments seem to confirm the predictions of earlier reports, which speculated that Trump-era restrictions on the H-1B labor supply would mainly impact foreign-owned corporations rather than U.S. firms.[60] The end result for H-1B visa recipients, however, is similar to that for DACA recipients.

In both cases, noncitizens are being reminded of their precarious legal status while being given the impression that they still have a shot at gaining a secure status. The possibility of removal (or visa nonrenewal), conditioned by the right combination of incentives, sets the stage for an extralegal mode of power that encourages the subject to let go of an expectation of guaranteed rights and adapt to the prerogatives of a sovereign decision maker (which could be an immigration officer, an employer, or any person with the authority to set in motion a process that leads the subject to be charged with a deportable violation). This exercise of power has arguably always been a feature of U.S. immigration law and can be traced to the plenary power principle, which was first clarified in the late nineteenth century.[61]

Neoliberal governing priorities, which are distrustful of binding legal agreements, give this mode of power more room to operate. This may also be why temporary legal status has become the new normal for migrants today. Noncitizens today often spend ten years or more living under a probationary status (as quasi-stateless people) before their application for permanent status is accepted, and a great many have adjusted to a life that is permanently defined by legal precarity. Meanwhile, the neoliberal push to marketize almost every aspect of social life has produced a similar weakening of social, political, and civil rights for citizens.[62] The Trump administration may be exercising this mode of power in a more freewheeling way than have prior administrations, but it is also exploiting a discretionary authority that has been cultivated and expanded by these same governing administrations. The chapters in this book provide many examples of how Obama-era policies fostered the same kind of legal precarity and vulnerability previously described.

ORGANIZATION OF THE BOOK

The prior discussion mapped the policy and political context for the book's contents, using the analysis of neoliberalism as a connecting thread. All of the book's contributors problematize the current age of punishment in a way that is broadly consistent with this analysis. But it would be misleading to suggest that the arguments of all the contributors can be assimilated into a single theoretical framework.

The diversity of arguments presented by the contributors highlights another goal of the book: to introduce the reader to a burgeoning academic literature. The mere existence of these differences speaks to the maturation of the field of critical immigration-enforcement studies. Since *Keeping Out the Other* was published, several immigration-enforcement texts have been published, each providing an important perspective into the workings of the deportation-detention apparatus—and some of which have been edited by contributors to this volume.[63] Over the past decade, critical research on immigration enforcement has also made inroads into the academic mainstream, and once again, the books and journal articles produced by the contributors to this volume have played a role in this process.[64] So it is important to note that the chapters in this book do not just cover different policy topic areas; they also present the reader with an argument and a treatment of theory that is more or less unique to the research history, intellectual influences, and (inter)disciplinary orientation of each contributor.

The book is organized into two sections. The first section provides a broad overview of the issues defining immigration enforcement and immigration policy across several national contexts. The second section takes a more focused look at the destructive effects of deportation on migrant communities through case studies that deploy an ethnographic research methodology.

MACRO PERSPECTIVES ON IMMIGRATION
ENFORCEMENT AND BORDER CONTROL

The chapters in the first section of the book engage several issues that are defining the policy debate over immigration enforcement today, including mass deportations, border control, securitization strategies, the local enforcement of immigration laws, and the detention system. These chapters also offer a transnational account of Obama-era immigration policy.

In addition to the United States, the chapters in this section examine the policy context of the United Kingdom, Canada, and Australia, and present an analysis of the global detention industry (which is dominated by U.S. multinational corporations). As noted earlier, this analysis is U.S.-centric. The United States gets the most attention, and U.S. policy also crops up as a theme in the treatment of other national contexts. But this chapter selection could just as easily be described as Anglo-centric because it includes a discussion of the United Kingdom and three of the world's leading immigrant-receiving nations (the United States, Canada, and Australia), whose relationship to the United Kingdom—and to each other—is rooted in the history of the British colonial project. This colonial history explains why the United States, Canada, and Australia are the only advanced industrialized nations that can claim to be created from the ground up by immigration (inventing the idea of the immigration nation in the process). It also bears emphasizing that UK and U.S. elites played a leading role in shaping the contemporary paradigm of economic globalization and neoliberal governance.[65] So although these chapters are not broadly representative of the world's migrant-receiving nations, they discuss national policy contexts that share a very specific genealogy and have played an important role in crafting the architecture of the global migration regime.

In chapter 2, Tanya Golash-Boza begins the analysis with a discussion of recent trends in U.S. immigration policy and enforcement, focusing on deportation and border enforcement actions carried out during the two terms of Barack Obama's presidency. This chapter can also be read as a prehistory of the enforcement practices that are defining the era of "nationalist-neoliberalism" under the Trump administration.[66] The chapter's title, "Obama's Legacy as 'Deporter in Chief,'" communicates its core argument, which is that the Obama administration presided over an unprecedented intensification of immigration enforcement practices. Golash-Boza marshals U.S. government statistics to show that the Obama administration deported more noncitizens during its two terms in office than any prior U.S. administration.

This argument carries a new significance in the early years of the Trump era, as there are pundits who have begun to take issue with Obama's get-tough record on enforcement. David Frum, for example, has argued that enforcement actions under Obama were artificially inflated because much of the increase in deportations in the Obama era was due to increases in border removals, not interior removals.[67] Because interior removals typically apprehend noncitizens who have been living in the United States for a number of years, they are viewed as being more disruptive than border removals, which target unlawful entrants who recently crossed the border. Hence, Frum's argument implies that most of the deportations carried out by the Obama administration were a form of "catch and release," a turn of phrase referring to ineffective enforcement practices that do little to inhibit reentry. In contrast, Golash-Boza shows that Obama presided over record numbers of border *and* interior removals (while also noting that there was a decline in interior removals during his second term).

The Obama administration also introduced a new practice, under Operation Streamline, of prosecuting unlawful border crossers in the federal courts, imprisoning these people, and then deporting them.[68] The majority of border patrol apprehensions conducted in the final years of the Obama administration were processed this way. The practical effect of Operation Streamline, similar to the intentions behind the Trump administration's efforts to expand the detention system,[69] was to end catch and release. It subjected unlawful entrants to a more intensive set of sanctions, which ensured that they would spend months, possibly years, in federal prison and immigration detention before being "returned home." Although this practice could be interpreted as inflating deportation statistics, it also reflects the decision of the Obama administration to criminalize hundreds of thousands of migrants for a violation that had formerly been treated as a civil offense.

Golash-Boza uses the outcomes of Operation Streamline and other Obama-era enforcement practices to expose the tension between the administration's public statements on deportations (which were described as targeting persons with serious criminal convictions) and the kinds of violators who were typically deported. She also raises some prescient concerns about the Obama administration's reliance on executive power, which has set a precedent that will likely be continued by the Trump administration.

In chapter 3, Deirdre Conlon expands on Golash-Boza's argument with a comparative look at immigration policy trends under UK prime minister David Cameron and U.S. president Barack Obama. Conlon shows that despite their different rhetoric on immigration—Cameron being assertively for immigration control and Obama adopting the position of a pro-immigration centrist—their policy record is very similar. Of course, there is a much stronger continuity between the immigration rhetoric of Cameron's conservative party (headed by Prime Minister May at the time of this writing) and that of President Trump. But this is also why Conlon's analysis of the Cameron-Obama relationship is insightful: because it draws attention to shared priorities that cannot be deduced from the public statements of elected officials. As a result, Conlon's analysis of the continuities of Cameron's and Obama's immigration policies also hints at the continuities that traverse the Obama and Trump eras.

Conlon introduces the concept of countertopography to frame her analysis, explaining how it can be used to both analyze and decenter dominant narratives. Conlon uses her countertopography to articulate her critical policy review with research findings based on interviews with migrant rights and migrant support organizations in the United States and the UK. She uses concepts developed by activist scholars to explain what is most distinct about the current strategies of migrant rights groups, which have become focused on nurturing network capacities. This can also be described as a mobilization strategy that absorbs and "re-wires" neoliberal tropes (of resilience and connection) rather than subjecting them to a conventional, oppositional politics.

In chapter 4, Graham Hudson explains how the punitive trends documented in chapters 2 and 3 have played out in Canada. His review of Canadian law and enforcement practices teases out the relationships between deportation practices, border control, and securitization strategies. Hudson also introduces readers to the crimmigration thesis, originated by Juliet Stumpf.[70]

Crimmigration describes the process whereby criminal law becomes a framework for rationalizing and framing immigration policies (*Governing Immigration Through Crime* has further developed this thesis as it pertains to the United States).[71] Corollary developments include the use of public prisons to house immigrant detainees, immigration offenses being used as a pretext for criminal incarceration, and policies that escalate the immigration consequences (culminating in deportation) for criminal convictions. This interdependent relationship between criminal and immigration enforcement has been examined by many researchers—including many of the contributors to this book—and is a common thread for much of the critical immigration-enforcement research being conducted today. The crimmigration thesis has also been used to explain policy trends in many national contexts (a few examples include the Netherlands, Italy, and Slovenia); as such, it offers a good example of continuities spanning the Obama and Trump eras in the United States, which are also reflected in transnational policy trends. Hudson, for example, illustrates how the crimmigration paradigm took hold in Canada during the same time that it was emerging in the United States.[72]

But Hudson also raises concerns about using the criminological concept of punishment as a framework for challenging deportations. Although many migrants would agree (as demonstrated by many of our chapters) that they are indeed living in an "age of punishment," Hudson cautions that, as a legal strategy, the argument that deportation is punishment can be counterproductive—

especially because national governments regard deportation as an administrative action that operates outside of the legal definition of punishment. Hence, for a deportation to be regarded as "unjust punishment," it is necessary to show how it deviates from the "normal" administration of a deportation order. Hudson goes on to explain how these kinds of distinctions fail to account for the full-scope human rights consequences of deportation practices.

On the one hand, Hudson offers practical advice to migrant rights advocates about how to craft legal arguments (and what to avoid). On the other hand, he raises questions of political philosophy concerning the relationship between sovereign power and the law. Can legal principles be used to challenge the sovereign right of the state to exclude and remove nonmembers considering that sovereignty is typically understood as an authority that precedes and exceeds the law? And if this is not possible, then of what use is it to define deportation as "unjust punishment"? With this argument, Hudson challenges legal and immigration scholars to develop new ways of problematizing deportation.

Chapter 5 shifts gears, moving from courts of law to the framing of immigration policy in the public sphere. In this chapter, Greg Martin and Claudia Tazreiter explain how Australian policy has been shaped by anxieties over asylum seekers and national security (also a prominent theme of the public debate over immigration in Canada and the UK). This chapter is also distinguished by the way it refocuses the recent history of immigration policy in Australia around movement activism, engaging these policies from the vantage point of the collective action frames and interventions of migrant rights and human rights organizations.

Martin and Tazreiter use social movement theory to conceptualize the political theater in which these actions play out and highlight the importance of emotions as a mode of governance and civil disobedience. One implication of this analysis is that emotional affect—when properly mobilized—can be converted into political capital. This is how collective outrage over the punitive effects of immigration policy can be leveraged to change policy—even if this emotional reality is at odds with the jurisprudence governing immigration law (i.e., insisting that deportation is not punishment). But Martin and Tazreiter also explain how state power governs through emotions. Moreover, as the Trump-Brexit phenomena illustrates, one of the great strengths of anti-immigrant movements is their emotional resonance. There is also a relationship between the emotional power of these movements and the exertion of a sovereign will that supersedes the law. Keeping this in mind, Martin and Tazreiter's political sociology of emotions seems to offer a different vantage point on the same dilemma that Hudson grapples with in chapter 4, concerning the scope and limits of sovereign power. This dilemma is also a defining feature of chapters 6 and 7.

NEOLIBERALISM AND SOVEREIGN POWER: CONNECTING THE DOTS

Chapter 6 problematizes sovereign power from yet another perspective. In this chapter, Matthew B. Flynn and Michael Flynn advance a critical theory of the interlocking networks of private-public sector actors and institutions that compose the global detention system. They use Gideon Sjoberg's theory of bureaucratic capitalism to discuss the organization and operating imperatives of this system. A central theme of Flynn and Flynn's argument is that the cruelty and scale of the detention system is propelled by self-interested actors and is ultimately shaped by a transnational, bureaucratically organized process of capital accumulation. Throughout the chapter, they use Sjoberg's theory to criticize the blind spots of Giorgio Agamben's theory of sovereign power (and, to a lesser extent, Michel Foucault's theory of biopolitics).

Flynn and Flynn focus their attention on how scholars have interpreted Agamben's theory of sovereign power, which is typically used to argue that immigration enforcement effects an exclusion on the grounds of social membership, which is sought as an end in itself. This Agambenian argument rests on the premise that the nation-state is a political community that can only sustain itself through acts of exclusion. In contrast, Flynn and Flynn insist that this "sovereign desire" to exclude is not an essential feature of national law, that the global detention system is not organized around a paradigm of national-sovereign power at any rate, and that it is possible to use an actor/interest-driven political action theory informed by an organizational theory of modern bureaucracies both to explain the detention system and to strategize how to best reform it. They also argue that Juliet Stumpf's crimmigration thesis, which is informed by a theory of sovereign power, can be incorporated into their theory of immigration enforcement qua bureaucratic capitalism.

Flynn and Flynn challenge immigration enforcement researchers to consider whether the critique of neoliberalism that informs so much of our work is well served by an Agambenian theory of sovereign power or by any theory that treats immigration enforcement as being teleologically derived from the imperatives of sovereign power. Their critique also carries important implications for our continuity argument about the Obama and Trump eras.

The overtly nativist and racist rhetoric of the Trump campaign made a strong case for Agamben's view of sovereignty and social exclusion. Trump's election created a situation in which a far right identity politics—defined by inherited culture, race, nativity, and religion—is now in direct communication with the presidential cabinet. Consistent with Agamben's theory, this vision for social membership seeks to exclude "undesirables" as an end in itself—a politics that clearly distinguishes the Trump and Obama presidencies. On the other hand, Flynn and Flynn's argument about bureaucratic capitalism and the global detention industry offers a better explanation of the continuities that span the Obama and Trump eras.

For example, the Trump and Obama administrations have taken very different positions on the involvement of private contractors in the federal prison industry; but this is also a relative difference that can be measured in degrees. The Obama administration embarked on a plan to phase out the use of private contractors (which includes contracts for federal detention services) in the last year of its second term.[73] The Trump administration, in contrast, rescinded these plans within months of taking office, and punctuated its commitment by issuing a multi-million-dollar contract to the GEO Group to build a new detention center in Texas.[74] Although these maneuvers fly in the face of the growing consensus around prison reform, they reaffirm a set of priorities that has guided the expansion of the private prison industry from the 1980s onward (with the approval of Democratic and Republican administrations).[75] The stubborn resilience of the private prison industry also corroborates Flynn and Flynn's argument that profit motives and the allure of organizational efficiency (supplied by the private-sector bureaucracy) offer a better explanation of the expansion of immigrant detention than the sovereign desire to exclude.

In chapter 7, Philip Kretsedemas offers another vantage point for thinking about these issues. This chapter examines the U.S. federal jurisprudence that has been used to rule on local and state immigration laws seeking to restrict noncitizen rights. The contemporary expansion of these local laws began in the early 2000s and accelerated further after the failure of comprehensive immigration reform under George W. Bush in 2007.[76] The Trump presidency may spell the end of this expansion, since the interests driving these restrictive local laws— which had been in opposition to the federal government—now have an ally in the White House. Kretsedemas also speculates that the principle of federal supremacy, used by federal courts under the Obama administration to restrict the law-making powers of local governments, will likely be used by the Trump administration to support its immigration policy.

Kretsedemas focuses his analysis on two hundred years of U.S. Supreme Court opinions, which shows that the court has consistently used the principle of federal supremacy to resolve disputes between federal and local governments concerning immigration law-making powers. He explains that these federal-local struggles have more to do with defining the terms of sovereign power than with defending migrant rights. He also finds that the Supreme Court's discourse on sovereignty makes for a good fit with neoliberal governance.

In this case, the sovereign prerogative of the federal government is concerned with fostering international commerce for the purpose of increasing the wealth of the nation, with this process necessitating a political arrangement that is beholden to the will of a "final decider." As a result, sovereign power can be articulated in alliance with national or globalized projects of capital accumulation. This kind of sovereign prerogative is conducive to the theory of bureaucratic capitalism—advanced by Flynn and Flynn—but nonetheless remains a mode of sovereign power. It is also more consistent with Michel Foucault's theory of disciplinary power (which Foucault contrasts against the sovereign power of the feudal and ancient state) than it is with Agamben's theory of sovereignty and bare life—though it does not preclude the possibility that sovereign power can be used in the way discussed by Agamben.[77] It can be described as a "modernized" sovereign prerogative that operates through a field of privatized coercive mechanisms, rather than through public acts of exclusion, and that safeguards a public good ultimately defined by an interest in growth and security that "necessitates" a unilateral structure of decision-making authority.

ETHNOGRAPHIES OF DEPORTATION AND DEPORTABILITY

The second section of the book examines immigration enforcement from the bottom up—as it has been experienced by migrants. These chapters offer another vantage point for engaging the issues that were explored in part 1 of the book, concerning the policing of social membership and the neoliberal priorities that operate through immigration enforcement.

In chapter 8, David C. Brotherton and Sarah Tosh explain how the policing of social membership plays out in courtroom proceedings that seem predestined to end in decisions that result in the deportation of black and brown youth from poor urban neighborhoods. Brotherton and Tosh use a theoretical framework that focuses on the relationship between emotional affect and social structure. They explain that vindictiveness is the reigning emotion in the day-to-day operation of deportation proceedings in the immigration courts. They also take care not to reduce vindictiveness to an individual personality trait of system workers, although they offer several accounts of the racist sensibility that guides the decisions of courtroom lawyers. Instead, they observe how vindictiveness is encoded within the law itself rather than being "enacted" or "improvised" by courtroom judges.

This analysis of how emotions operate through the law offers some insight into the relationship between sovereign and legal authority. Brotherton and Tosh document a social reality that does not allow for neat distinctions between an Agambenian view of sovereign power and the clinical rationality of Sjoberg's bureaucratic capitalism. The courtroom proceedings they describe are inherently bureaucratic. Brotherton and Tosh also explain how the vindictiveness of the law is typically transmitted by courtroom judges in a disinterested or even reluctant manner, giving the impression that they are merely "following orders." But their research also documents a legal process in which courtroom deliberations seem to be decided in advance by an ascribed social membership that predetermines the application of the law. If this is the case, then it is not possible to describe these deportation proceedings simply as an effect of punitive laws.

Brotherton and Tosh are also describing a process in which the vindictiveness of the law affirms a racialized paradigm of social membership that is not explicitly defined by the law. This situation recalls Hudson's argument about the difficulty of using legal definitions of punishment to problematize deportation. The concept of punishment presumes a logical relationship between behavior and sanction, which can form the basis for a judgment on the reasonableness of the punishment administered. In contrast, exclusion based on social membership appeals to a sovereign imperative that does not have to be justified by the law, even though it can be put in communication with the law. Hannah Arendt offers a complementary analysis of how the inegalitarian aims of racist ideologies were well served by the hierarchical and formalistic procedures of bureaucratic organizations—and how this race-bureaucracy nexus was used to undermine the egalitarian aspirations of the modern nation-state (particularly the principle of equality before the law).[78] Brotherton and Tosh shed some light on the relevance of Arendt's analysis for an ethnography of immigration court proceedings in the present day.

In chapter 9, Carolina Sanchez Boe explores a similar relationship—that between racial exclusion and legal-bureaucratic discourse. Her research examines the social experience of deportability and illegalization for undocumented African migrants living in France. She explains how the punitive direction that French immigration law has taken from the 1990s onward has only created more "illegality"—by imposing restrictions on the rights and legal status options that led many migrants who entered France with legal status to be retroactively "illegalized." Boe's ethnography documents the survival strategies of African migrants caught in this situation who belong to a population she describes as the "undeported." She uses her field notes to explain how this condition creates "spaces of legal non-existence" that are ostensibly located within the nation but also play an important role in defining its borders.

In chapter 10, Shirley Leyro offers another perspective on the experience of deportability, focusing on a diverse cross section of Latin American migrants living in New York City. Leyro's research documents the stories of both authorized and unauthorized migrants, many of whom live in mixed-status families. She uses her interview data to show how the threat of deportation affects migrants' perceptions of national social membership and their prospects for integration. Similar to the migrants in Boe's study, most of Leyro's interviewees felt alienated and identified as nonmembers of the United States—even if they had been living and working in the country for a decade or more (and have well-developed U.S.-resident networks of family and friends). Even more significant, this sense of alienation spanned all of Leyro's interviewees, regardless of legal status. Her closing discussion uses the concept of legal violence to illustrate how the vindictiveness discussed by Brotherton and Tosh shapes the identities and emotional worlds of Latino migrants.

The next chapter in this section focuses on the postdeportation survival strategies of noncitizens (overwhelmingly male) who have been returned "home." Migration scholars are sometimes faulted for overusing the term *diaspora*.[79] Deportees, however, constitute a genuine diaspora, which describes a community that has been forced out of a homeland and dispersed across many nations. In chapter 9, Boe references the concept of the "deportspora" (coined by another researcher) to describe this phenomenon; and in chapter 11, María Dolores París Pombo and Gabriel Pérez Duperou reference Daniel Kanstroom's discussion of the U.S. deportation diaspora to frame their analysis.

París Pombo and Pérez Duperou focus on the experience of men who were deported to Mexico. They explain how these men, who are now compelled to remain on one side of the U.S.-Mexico border, maintain fragile transborder relationships with family members (including wives and children) who are still living in the United States. The support networks of church organizations—particularly the Catholic Church—figure prominently in this ethnography. These faith-based networks play a critically important role in reorienting the postdeportation subjectivities of these men. París Pombo and Pérez Duperou describe how the rejuvenation of these men's faith-based commitments allows them to cultivate socioemotional orientations that support their reintegration into Mexican society (and which primarily involve distancing themselves from what they see as a shallow and materialistic U.S. lifestyle). They caution, however, that the social networks of these church organizations are fragile and insular, and that the socioemotional reorientation that is enabled by church membership does not necessarily lay the foundations for a successful socioeconomic integration into mainstream Mexican society.

The final chapters of the book explore emerging topics in deportation studies, most of which have not been treated in any prior immigration-enforcement reader. Each chapter provides a unique insight into deportation dilemmas from the Obama era that will extend into the Trump era.

In chapter 12, Lisa Sun-Hee Park examines the growing trend of medical deportations—a process in which hospitals take the initiative to arrange the deportation of patients without legal status (typically low-income persons who do not have health insurance or who do not have the private funds to cover their share of their health expenses). Park explains that the first documented medical deportation occurred in 2001 and that they have since become a growing trend.

Park uses an ethnographic case study to illustrate the way that medical deportations are carried out through negotiations between federal law enforcement and local hospital administrators (sidestepping local police). She shows that although federal enforcement agents can be very aggressive in pushing for deportation, hospital administrators have considerable discretionary authority in determining how or whether to bring cases to the attention of the Department of Homeland Security.

This analysis draws attention to a deportation process that could be explained by Flynn and Flynn's analysis of bureaucratic capitalism or by a Foucauldian theory of disciplinary biopower (the analysis of neoliberalism being the connecting thread that allows these perspectives to communicate). In this case, the policing of social membership is informed by deliberations over fiscal costs, legal status, and the ethics of humanitarian care that are carried out by hospital administrators who are also in dialogue with federal agents. Medical deportations can be understood as a process in which the deliberations of hospital bureaucracies are blurring and converging with those of the federal immigration system. This development may be a harbinger of similar processes occurring within other public and private sector institutions. The next two chapters in this section offer a complementary analysis, drawing attention to deportation processes guided by rational-bureaucratic imperatives that are primarily concerned with maximizing the discipline and utility of noncitizen bodies.

In chapter 13, Sofya Aptekar discusses the experiences of deported U.S. veterans and explains how the U.S. government tries to reconcile the patriotic symbolism of veteran status with the reality of veteran deportability. She explains that although the presence of undocumented immigrants in the military rank and file is not unheard of, the vast majority of deported veterans are noncitizens who had a legal status that was subsequently revoked due to criminal convictions.

Aptekar's research demonstrates that the tiered system of legal statuses that characterizes neoliberal immigration policy (defined by degrees of precarity and permanence) also permeates the U.S. military. Although the military is a powerful symbol of the national political community and one of the principle means through which its sovereignty is secured, the policing of social membership—as described by the crimmigration thesis—extends into the ranks of the military itself. In this case, social membership is not overdetermined by an ascribed racial category. Rather, the terms of social membership are informed by a means-end rationality whereby nonwhite bodies are separated into more or less disciplined, prudent, and productive types. Hence, the key distinction is not between white and nonwhite but between the law-abiding, nonwhite, foreign-born veteran who is deemed a good candidate for naturalization and the nonwhite, foreign-born veteran who is deported for a minor criminal violation. The tragedy here is that even veterans are not spared from the vindictiveness that has been generated by racialized moral panics over immigration—not that they are racially categorized in the same way as the Dominican youth discussed by Brotherton and Tosh in chapter 8.

In chapter 14, Payal Banerjee explains how a similar racialized, disciplinary regimen is experienced by South Asian guest workers, most of whom are H-1B visa holders. Several researchers have used the critique of neoliberalism as a framework for examining the coercive workings of the H-1B visa system in particular and guest-worker schemes more generally.[80] Banerjee's research is significant because it offers one of the few critical ethnographies of the H-1B guest worker program.

Banerjee does not tell the stories of South Asian guest workers who were actually deported, since this is an unusual occurrence. However, her research offers an important insight into the mechanics of deportability. As Banerjee explains, the prospect of deportation constantly hovers over the relationship between guest workers and their sponsoring employers, influencing the way these workers make decisions about their lives, even though the threat of deportation is rarely actualized. Banerjee's research documents the stress that this situation produced for these workers, even before the onset of the Trump era. She also shows that although guest workers have a critical consciousness about their precarious legal status, this awareness in and of itself does not mitigate its coercive effects. Through these insights, Banerjee's research provides an important look into how deportability conditions the subjectivity and workplace behavior of high-skilled migrants.

In chapter 15, Yolanda Martín examines a relatively new horizon for antideportation advocacy. Martin focuses on the use of the UN Convention Against Torture (CAT) as a legal strategy to defend noncitizens in deportation proceedings. She explains that CAT is a provision included in a 1996 human rights convention ratified by the United States, which specifically protects noncitizens from being deported to nations where they would be tortured. Martín admits that deportation relief based on CAT is rare, but it is part of a movement toward using human rights law as a basis for strengthening migrant rights.

One of the principle features of a human rights defense is the idea that all people are deserving of baseline rights and protections regardless of legal status. Martín uses Linda Bosniak's concept of the alien citizen to establish this premise—describing a person who is not a citizen under national law but who is nevertheless allowed to exercise the same rights as a citizen. In the rest of the chapter, she explains how she has used this paradigm of legal rights to protect people who could be described as "citizen aliens"—deportees who have formal citizenship in the nations to which they have been returned but who are unable to exercise these rights due to the social stigma of their deportee status.

Martín's ethnography—which focuses on Dominicans—shifts between the arbitrary circumstances that lead her subjects to be criminalized and brought before U.S. immigration courts, and the conditions these deportees experience once "returned" to the Dominican Republic. She uses her research to document the physical brutality and social and structural violence that define the experience of Dominican deportees, and explains how the cumulative effect of this violence meets the definition of torture outlined in the CAT.

Of all the activist and advocacy perspectives presented in this book, Martín's may be the most farsighted. Human rights focus our attention on an ethical and normative framework that is not limited by the constraints of national membership, even if—as some scholars have argued—these rights still have to be worked out in dialogue with the legal and political institutions of the nation-state.[81] Of course, human rights are also a contested body of ideas that come with their own set of hazards and antagonisms, as demonstrated by criticism of how human rights discourse has been used to justify military interventions and reinforce Eurocentric valuations of non-Western cultures.[82] It is also likely that many branches of the U.S. government—especially the immigration courts and the Department of Homeland Security, which fall under the direct oversight of the executive office—will be less receptive to human rights arguments in the Trump era. The same observation could be made about the United Kingdom. Yet this could also mean that the legal systems of other nations will become more significant—as a terrain for establishing human rights precedents.

Researchers have also documented a kind of human rights discourse that is being used by noncitizens—and their advocates—to challenge and reconfigure the normative framework that is often used to define noncitizen rights.[83] In this case, human rights can become part of a bottom-up democratic conversation—and mobilization—that takes issue with the moral blind spots of a migration system that sustains itself through the production of disposable people. In this way, human rights could offer a new vantage point for reframing conventional questions of migrant integration, political equality, and legalization by focusing our attention more squarely on the myopic assemblage of discipline-productivity-disposability that has taken shape under neoliberalism. And instead of using human rights discourse to advocate a transcendent ideal that sidesteps the problem of racism—and other aspects of social difference—it can be used to directly engage these problems by examining the relationship between disposability/exclusion and the policing of social membership. These sorts of concerns also make it possible for migrant rights discourse to connect with other bodies of rights discourse that speak to the concerns of marginalized citizen populations. The challenge of undoing crimmigration, for example, requires an advocacy model that is able to speak to both criminal justice reform and immigration reform, as well as support efforts to strengthen legal-procedural transparency, which pertains to many other policy and social justice issues.

Even so, it bears emphasizing that these directions for migrant rights activism and advocacy—and their potential intersections with human rights discourse—are only suggested by the book's contents. These are the ethical and political horizons that the book points toward, but it does so by focusing our attention on critical examinations of immigration policy and enforcement. Thus, we should end this opening chapter by reiterating the core aim of the book, which is to problematize the age of punishment that currently defines immigration policy. We hope the book will prove useful for questioning souls of all varieties—students, researchers, community workers, activists, and policy makers—who are not only looking for an introduction to the key issues defining immigration policy and immigration enforcement today but also prepared to think beyond their limits.

NOTES TO CHAPTER 1

1. Department of Homeland Security, "Table 39. Aliens Removed or Returned: Fiscal Years 1892 to 2014," 2014 *Yearbook of Immigration Statistics,* last modified November 1, 2016, https://www.dhs.gov/immigration-statistics/yearbook/2014/table39.

2. Ibid.

3. The annual rate of border enforcement actions is more erratic than the steady increase in deportations/removals, but in the 2000s and earlier, they accounted for most (and as much as 80 percent) of all enforcement actions. With the onset of the recession in 2008, border enforcement actions dropped precipitously, due in large part to the reduced flow of unauthorized entrants. In the latter years of the Obama administration, border apprehensions for unlawful entrance rose again, but these were not reflected in the rate of "returns" by border enforcement, because most of these unlawful entrants were formally prosecuted and issued deportation orders. The end result is that the removal of these migrants was counted under the tally of formal deportations/removals (carried out by Immigration and Customs Enforcement) rather than the "returns" carried out by the border patrol. This change in enforcement tactics has contributed to the process whereby deportations and interior enforcement actions have steadily eclipsed border enforcement actions; see enforcement data for 2014. Department of Homeland Security, "Table 35. Aliens Apprehended by Program and Border Patrol Sector, Investigations Special Agent in Charge (Sac) Jurisdiction, and Area of Responsibility: Fiscal Years 2012 to 2014," 2014 *Yearbook of Immigration Statistics,* last

modified November 18, 2016, https://www.dhs.gov/immigration-statistics/yearbook/2014/table35; Department of Homeland Security, "Table 39. Aliens Removed or Returned: Fiscal Years 1892 to 2014."

4. As of 2012, immigration-related convictions counted for 30 percent of all federal convictions, whereas drug convictions accounted for 33 percent. Michael T. Light, Mark Hugo Lopez, and Ana Gonzalez-Barrera, "The Rise of Federal Immigration Crimes: Unlawful Reentry Drives Growth," Pew Research Center: Hispanic Trends, March 18, 2014, http://www.pewhispanic.org/2014/03/18/the-rise-of-federal-immigration-crimes/. But in prior years (2005–2009), immigration-related convictions had been steadily exceeding drug convictions. See Philip Kretsedemas, *Migrants and Race in the US: Territorial Racism and the Alien/Outside* (New York: Routledge, 2014), 15–16.

5. For a statistical overview of the years in which the Latino federal prison population first began to eclipse the black, non-Latino federal prison population (1998–2009), see Kretsedemas, *Migrants and Race*, 16–18.

6. This is discussed in more detail in chapter 7 of this book. See also Monica Varsanyi, ed., *Taking Local Control: Immigration Policy Activism in U.S. Cities and States* (Stanford: Stanford University Press, 2010).

7. See Ana Kralj, "Controlling Otherness: Media and Parliamentary Discourse on Immigration in Slovenia," in *Migrant Marginality: A Transnational Perspective*, ed. Philip Kretsedemas, Jorge Capetillo-Ponce, and Glenn Jacobs (New York: Routledge, 2013), 85–103; Georgios Karyotis and Stratos Patrikios, "Religion, Securitization and Anti-immigration Attitudes: The Case of Greece," *Journal of Peace Research* 47, no. 1 (2010): 43–57; Alice Bloch, "The Right to Rights? Undocumented Migrants from Zimbabwe Living in South Africa," *Sociology* 44, no. 2 (2010): 233–250; Jon E. Fox, Laura Moroşanu, and Eszter Szilassy, "The Racialization of the New European Migration to the UK," *Sociology* 46, no. 4 (2012): 680–695.

8. Peggy Levitt, *The Transnational Villagers* (Berkeley: University of California Press, 2001); Nina Glick Schiller, Linda Basch, and Cristina Szanton Blanc, "From Immigrant to Transmigrant: Theorizing Transnational Migration," *Anthropological Quarterly* 68, no. 1 (1995): 48–63.

9. Saskia Sassen, "Regulating Immigration in a Global Age: A New Policy Landscape," *Annals of the American Academy of Political and Social Science* 570 (2000): 65–77; Nina Glick Schiller, "A Global Perspective on Migration and Development," *Social Analysis: The International Journal of Social and Cultural Practice* 53, no. 3 (2009): 14–37.

10. Guillermina Jasso, Vivek Wadhwa, Gary Gereffi, Ben Rissing, and Richard Freeman, "How Many Highly Skilled Foreign-Born Are Waiting in Line for U.S. Legal Permanent Residence?," *International Migration Review* 44, no. 2 (2010): 477–498; Philip Kretsedemas, *The Immigration Crucible* (New York: Columbia University Press, 2012), 13–46.

11. Timothy Hatton and Jeffrey Williamson, *Global Migration and the World Economy: Two Centuries of Policy and Performance* (Cambridge: MIT Press, 2008), 307–311, 377–391.

12. This is epitomized by a recommendation for Swedish migration policy, which could be regarded as an ideal-type rendition of priorities that are currently shaping the immigration policies of most industrialized nations. Hatton and Williamson, *Global Migration*, 373–378.

13. David Harvey, *A Brief History of Neoliberalism* (Oxford: Oxford University Press, 2007).

14. Jamie Peck, *Workfare States* (New York: Guilford, 2001); Alejandra Marchevsky and Jeanne Theoharis, *Not Working: Latina Immigrants, Low-Wage Jobs, and the Failure of Welfare Reform* (New York: NYU Press, 2006).

15. Harald Bauder, *The Immigration Dialectic: Imagining Community, Economy, and Nation* (Toronto: University of Toronto Press, 2011), 116–134; Philip Kretsedemas, "Reconsidering Immigrant Welfare Restrictions: A Critical Review of Post-Keynesian Welfare Policy," *Stanford Law and Policy Review* 16 (2005): 463–485.

16. Doris Meissner, Donald M. Kerwin, Muzaffar Chishti, and Claire Bergeron, "Immigration Enforcement in the United States: The Rise of a Formidable Machinery," Migration Policy Institute, June 2013, http://www.migrationpolicy.org/research /immigration-enforcement-united-states-rise-formidable-machinery; Leila Østerbø, "The Cost of Fortress Europe," Migrant Report, June 18, 2015, http://migrantreport .org/the-money-trails/.

17. Harvey, *Brief History of Neoliberalism*.

18. William Connolly, *The Fragility of Things: Self-Organizing Processes, Neoliberal Fantasies and Democratic Activism* (Durham: Duke University Press, 2013), 52–80; Harvey, *Brief History of Neoliberalism*, 64–86; Tomas Undurraga, "Neoliberalism in Argentina and Chile: Common Antecedents, Divergent Paths," *Revista de Sociologia e Politica* 23, no. 55 (2015): 11–34.

19. Kitty Calavita, *Inside the State: The Bracero Program, Immigration, and the I.N.S.* (New Orleans: Quid Pro, 2010).

20. Katharine Donato and Douglas Massey, "Effect of the Immigration Reform and Control Act on the Wages of Mexican Migrants," *Social Science Quarterly* 74, no. 3 (1993): 523–541. See also Katharine Donato, Jorge Durand, and Douglas Massey, "Stemming the Tide? Assessing the Deterrent Effects of the Immigration Reform and Control Act," *Demography* 29, no. 2 (1992): 139–157; Julie Phillips and Douglas Massey, "The New Labor Market: Immigrants and Wages After IRCA," *Demography* 36, no. 2 (1999): 233–246.

21. See Ryan King, Michael Massoglia, and Christopher Uggen, "Employment and Exile: U.S. Criminal Deportations, 1908–2005," *American Journal of Sociology* 117, no. 6 (2012): 1786–1825. For further discussion, see Dario Melossi, *Crime, Punishment and Migration* (New York: Sage, 2015).

22. Nicholas De Genova, "Migrant 'Illegality' and Deportability in Everyday Life," *Annual Review of Anthropology* 31 (2002): 419–447.

23. David Kirk, Andrew Papachristos, Jeffrey Fagan, and Tom Tyler, "The Paradox of Law Enforcement in Immigrant Communities: Does Tough Immigration Enforcement Undermine Public Safety?," *Annals of the American Academy of Political and Social Science* 641 (2012): 79–98; Irum Shiekh, "Racializing, Criminalizing and Silencing

9/11 Deportees," in *Keeping Out the Other: A Critical Introduction to Immigration Enforcement Today*, ed. David C. Brotherton and Philip Kretsedemas (New York: Columbia University Press, 2008), 81–107.

24. Jonathan Xavier Inda, *Targeting Immigrants: Government, Technology, and Ethics* (New York: Wiley-Blackwell, 2008). For a complementary analysis, see Alfonso Gonzales, *Reform Without Justice: Latino Migrant Politics and the Homeland Security State* (Oxford: Oxford University Press, 2013).

25. Michael Welch, *Detained: Immigration Laws and the Expanding I.N.S. Jail Complex* (Philadelphia: Temple University Press, 2002), 9–34.

26. David C. Brotherton and Luis Barrios, *Banished to the Homeland: Dominican Deportees and Their Stories of Exile* (New York: Columbia University Press, 2011).

27. This is discussed in chapter 2 of this volume. See also Tanya Golash-Boza, *Deported: Immigrant Policing, Disposable Labor and Global Capitalism* (New York: NYU Press, 2015).

28. Robert Chang, *Disoriented: Asian Americans, Law, and the Nation-State* (New York: NYU Press, 2000); Leo Chavez, *The Latino Threat: Constructing Immigrants, Citizens, and the Nation*, 2nd ed. (Stanford: Stanford University Press, 2013).

29. See also Juan Perea, ed., *Immigrants Out! The New Nativism and the Anti-Immigrant Impulse in the United States* (New York: NYU Press, 1996).

30. For more on Waldinger's explanation of racial-ethnic job queues that are constructed by both employers and workers, see Roger Waldinger, "Black Immigrant Competition Re-Assessed: New Evidence from Los Angeles," *Sociological Perspectives* 40, no. 3 (1997): 365–386; Roger Waldinger, *Still the Promised City? African-Americans and New Immigrants in Postindustrial New York* (Cambridge: Harvard University Press, 1996). See also Lisa Catanzarite, "Brown-Collar Jobs: Occupational Segregation and Earnings of Recent-Immigrant Latinos," *Sociological Perspectives* 43, no. 1 (2000): 45–75.

31. David C. Brotherton and Philip Kretsedemas, eds., *Keeping Out the Other: A Critical Introduction to Immigration Enforcement Today* (New York: Columbia University Press, 2008).

32. The Illegal Immigration Reform and Immigrant Responsibility Act (IIRIRA) and the Antiterrorism and Effective Death Penalty Act (AEDPA) being the two principle acts of federal legislation. The Personal Responsibility and Work Opportunity Reconciliation Act (PRWORA; popularly known as the "welfare reform act") can also be included among the 1996 immigration reform laws due to the unprecedented restrictions it imposed on immigrant eligibility for federal means-tested services.

33. But with the caveat that the United States has been the dominant partner in the U.S.-UK relationship. See Saskia Sassen, *Territory, Authority, Rights* (Princeton: Princeton University Press, 2006), 141–222. David Harvey also notes that while late twentieth-century neoliberalism is the brainchild of U.S. intellectuals and policy makers, the emergence of neoliberalism as a transnational governing paradigm cannot be explained simply by the might of the United States. See Harvey, *Brief History of Neoliberalism*, 5–38. It also follows that the new defensive posture of the United States and the United Kingdom does not necessarily signal the end of economic globalization, only a shift in the balance of powers that is driving it forward.

34. See Sasha Breger Bush, "Trump and National Neoliberalism," *Dollars and Sense,* January/February 2017, http://dollarsandsense.org/archives/2016/1216bregerbush.html.

35. BBC World News, "Donald Trump Protests Attract Millions Across US and World," January 21, 2017, http://www.bbc.com/news/world-us-canada-38705586.

36. Authorized by the widely criticized Executive Order 13769: Protecting the Nation from Foreign Terrorist Entry into the United States, issued January 27, 2017, and later revised and reissued on March 6, 2017.

37. Immigration and Customs Enforcement, "ICE ERO Arrests Climb Nearly 40 Percent," May 17, 2017, https://www.ice.gov/features/100-days.

38. Transactional Records Access Clearinghouse (TRAC), *ICE Targeting: Odds Noncitizens Ordered Deported by Immigration Judge Through May 2017,* http://trac.syr.edu/phptools/immigration/court_backlog/apprep_outcome_leave.php.

39. Including Executive Order 13768: Enhancing Public Safety in the Interior of the United States, issued January 25, 2017, https://www.whitehouse.gov/the-press-office/2017/01/25/presidential-executive-order-enhancing-public-safety-interior-united; Executive Order 13767: Border Security and Immigration Enforcement Improvements, issued January 25, 2017; and Executive Order 13769: Protecting the Nation from Foreign Terrorist Entry into the United States, issued January 27, 2017.

40. Executive Order 13768.

41. Aria Bendix, "Immigrant Arrests Are Up, but Deportation Is Down," *The Atlantic,* May 17, 2017, https://www.theatlantic.com/news/archive/2017/05/under-trump-immigrants-arrests-are-up-but-deportation-is-down/527103/; Anna O. Law, "This Is How Trump's Deportations Differ from Obama's," *Washington Post,* https://www.washingtonpost.com/news/monkey-cage/wp/2017/05/03/this-is-how-trumps-deportations-differ-from-obamas/?utm_term=.95b0c59897f1.

42. Brotherton and Barrios, *Banished to the Homeland*; De Genova, "Migrant 'Illegality'"; Inda, *Targeting Immigrants.*

43. Calavita, *Inside the State.*

44. Law, "This Is How Trump's Deportations Differ from Obama's." As a point of comparison, Barack Obama ended his first year in office by escalating deportations 8 percent above the final year of the George W. Bush administration (which was also the peak year for formal deportations under the 2001–2008 Bush administration). See removal statistics for 2009 and 2008 in Department of Homeland Security, "Table 39. Aliens Removed or Returned: Fiscal Years 1892 to 2015," Yearbook of Immigration Statistics, 2015, https://www.dhs.gov/immigration-statistics/yearbook/2015/table39.

45. Law, "This Is How Trump's Deportations Differ from Obama's"; Zoe Tillman, "Immigration Court Backlog Could Pose Problems for Trump's Enforcement Plans," BuzzFeed News, February 23, 2017, https://www.buzzfeed.com/zoetillman/backlogged-immigration-courts-pose-problems-for-trumps-plans?utm_term=.khVMXLLYw#.cxmz9WWN5.

46. Ron Nixon, "Trump's Immigration Proposals 'Conspicuously Absent' from Spending Bill," *New York Times,* May 3, 2017, https://www.nytimes.com/2017/05/03/us/politics/trump-immigration-spending-bill.html.

47. Jessie Hellmann, "Trump Shifts Immigration Plan: No 'Mass Deportations,'" *The Hill*, June 25, 2017, http://thehill.com/blogs/ballot-box/presidential-races/284910 -trump-shifts-tone-no-mass-deportations; Andrew Rafferty, "DHS Chief Kelly Pledges 'No Mass Deportations' During Talks with Mexico's Leaders," *NBC News*, February 23, 2017, http://www.nbcnews.com/politics/politics-news/rex-tillerson-tasked-helping-soothe -tensions-mexico-n724366.

48. Operation Wetback has been embraced by immigration control activists as a hallmark example of a mass deportation program, and it was referenced approvingly by Trump during the 2016 presidential campaign, as an example of the kind of enforcement agenda he would adopt if elected. See "An Arizona Reader Remembers the Original Operation Wetback," VDare.com, August 5, 2011, http://www.vdare.com/letters/an -arizona-reader-remembers-the-original-operation-wetback; Philip Bump, "Donald Trump Endorsed 'Operation Wetback'—But Not by Name," *Washington Post*, November 11, 2016, https://www.washingtonpost.com/news/the-fix/wp/2015/11/11/donald-trump -endorsed-operation-wetback-but-not-by-name/?utm_term=.9c344bbf083c. For its day, the operation was an unprecedented effort which deported over 1 million Mexican migrant workers between 1954 and 1955—effectively capping the peak years of the Bracero labor program (Calavita, *Inside the State*). However, the total annual number of border enforcement actions carried out during the time frame of Operation Wetback (reaching approximately 1.1 million—counting both removals and returns) are on par with the typical annual rate of removals and returns in recent years (which equaled or exceeded the 1.1-million mark between 1991 and 2008). See Department of Homeland Security, "Table 39. Aliens Removed or Returned: Fiscal Years 1892 to 2015." These peak levels have declined from 2009 onward due to a significant decline in border enforcement actions, which has been attributed to a decline in unauthorized entrants (mainly due to the sluggish economy, but also, more recently, from fear of the Trump administration immigration agenda). American Immigration Council, "Immigration Enforcement in a Time of Recession," September 9, 2010, https://www .americanimmigrationcouncil.org/research/explaining-recent-decline-unauthorized -migration; David Frum, "How Trump Is Upending the Conventional Wisdom on Illegal Immigration," *The Atlantic*, April 24, 2017, https://www.theatlantic.com/politics /archive/2017/04/how-trump-is-upending-the-conventional-wisdom-on-illegal -immigration/524058/. But the decline in border enforcement actions has had no effect on formal removals, which continue to escalate and, from 2007 onward, have been holding at a rate that is more than ten times the size of 1954 removal statistics. See Department of Homeland Security, "Table 39. Aliens Removed or Returned: Fiscal Years 1892 to 2015."

49. Executive Order 13768.

50. Authorized by Executive Order 13768. See also Josh Saul, "Doubling as Immigration Officers, Sheriffs Applaud Trump Order," *Newsweek*, February 12, 2017, http:// www.newsweek.com/texas-sheriffs-welcome-trump-order-deport-undocumented -immigrants-555476. Some policy analysts have also observed that the Obama administration's decision to replace Secure Communities with the Priority Enforcement

Program in 2012 is best understood as a reform but not a dismantling of Secure Communities. See Miriam Valverde, "Trump Says Secure Communities, 287(g) Immigration Programs Worked," *Politifact*, September 6, 2016, http://www.politifact.com /truth-o-meter/statements/2016/sep/06/donald-trump/trump-says-secure-communities -287g-immigration-pro/.

51. Kaitlan Collins, "Candidate Trump Promised to Terminate DACA. President Trump Says DREAMers Should 'Rest Easy,'" Daily Caller, April 21, 2017, http:// dailycaller.com/2017/04/21/candidate-trump-promised-to-terminate-daca-president -trump-says-dreamers-should-rest-easy/. DACA created a renewable two-year period deferral from deportation for qualitied undocumented migrants, which also allows them to acquire a work permit and, for those who qualify, the right to travel internationally and re-enter the United States. Although DACA was created by the discretionary authority that the Executive Office wields over immigration policy, it was not issued as an executive order. See U.S. Citizenship and Information Services, "Consideration of Deferred Action for Childhood Arrivals (DACA)," https://www.uscis.gov/humanitarian /consideration-deferred-action-childhood-arrivals-daca.

52. Keegan Hamilton, "Trump Told Dreamers to 'Rest Easy,' but Here's Proof They Shouldn't," Vice News, May 3, 2017, https://news.vice.com/story/trump-told-dreamers -to-rest-easy-but-heres-proof-they-shouldnt; Leeron Hoory, "Organizations Stand Up to Homeland Security Over DACA Detentions," March 8, 2017, http://www.vocativ.com /409272/organizations-homeland-security-daca-dreamer-detentions/.

53. Michael Shear and Julie Hirschfield Davis, "Trump Moves to End DACA and Calls on Congress to Act," *New York Times*, September 5, 2017, https://www.nytimes .com/2017/09/05/us/politics/trump-daca-dreamers-immigration.html?mcubz=0.

54. Ed O'Keefe and David Nakamura, "Trump, Top Democrats Agree to Work on Deal to Save 'Dreamers' from Deportation," *Washington Post*, September 14, 2017, https://www.washingtonpost.com/news/powerpost/wp/2017/09/13/trump-top-democrats -agree-to-work-on-deal-to-save-daca/?utm_term=.aebf3867b733. The DREAM Act (Development, Relief and Education for Alien Minors Act) is a piece of legislation, aimed at legalizing young adult undocumented migrants. President Obama introduced DACA, in large part, due to the inability of the Congress to pass the DREAM Act. See Marisa Bono, "When a Rose Is Not a Rose: DACA, the DREAM Act and the Need for More Comprehensive Immigration Reform," *Thurgood Marshall Law Review* 40 (2015): 193–222.

55. Kaitlan Collins, "Why Hasn't Trump Followed Through on His Promise to Get Rid of the H1B Visa and DACA Programs?," *Daily Caller*, March 8, 2017, http://dailycaller.com/2017/03/08/why-hasnt-trump-followed-through-on-his-promise-to - get-rid-of-the-h1b-visa-and-daca-programs/.

56. "U.S. Suspends Fast Processing of High-Tech Visa Applications," Reuters, March 4, 2017, http://fortune.com/2017/03/04/us-high-tech-visa-applications/.

57. Executive Order 13788: Presidential Executive Order on Buy American and Hire American, issued April 18, 2017.

58. Muzaffar Chishti and Jessica Bolter, "Despite Political Resistance, Use of Temporary Worker Visas Rises as U.S. Labor Market Tightens," Migration Policy Institute,

June 20, 2017, http://www.migrationpolicy.org/article/despite-political-resistance-use
-temporary-worker-visas-rises-us-labor-market-tightens; Adam Davidson, "The Empti-
ness of Trump's 'Buy American' Executive Order," *New Yorker*, April 20, 2017, http://
www.newyorker.com/business/adam-davidson/the-emptiness-of-trumps-buy-american
-executive-order; David Shepardson and Ginger Gibson, "Trump Again Vows to Bring
Back U.S. Jobs, but Offers Few Details," Reuters, February 23, 2017, http://www.reuters
.com/article/us-usa-trump-ceos-idUSKBN162209.

59. Kenneth Rapoza, "Trump Has Already Beat India on H-1B Visa Issue," *Forbes*,
June 26, 2017, https://www.forbes.com/sites/kenrapoza/2017/06/26/trump-has-already
-beat-india-on-h1-b-visa-issue/#754f8dec1f62. The criticism levied against these corporations, which focused on abuses of B1 business visas, has also been documented by
research conducted by advocates of the rights of work visa holders. See Payal Banerjee,
"Indian Information Technology Workers in the United States: The H-1B Visa, Flexible
Production, and the Racialization of Labor," *Critical Sociology* 32, no. 2-3 (2006): 425–
445 (also see chapter 14 in this volume).

60. Kenneth Rapoza, "Silicon Valley Has Very Little to Complain About on H1-B
Immigrant Visas," *Forbes*, April 5, 2017, https://www.forbes.com/sites/kenrapoza/2017
/04/05/silicon-valley-has-very-little-to-complain-about-on-h1-b-immigrant-visas
/#64f27e373ac1.

61. Hiroshi Motomura, "Immigration Law After a Century of Plenary Power: Phan-
tom Constitutional Norms and Statutory Interpretation," *Yale Law Journal* 100, no. 3
(1990): 545–613.

62. Connolly, *Fragility of Things*, 52–80; Harvey, *Brief History of Neoliberalism*, 5–38;
Jamie Peck and Andrew Tickell, "Neoliberalizing Space," *Antipode* 34, no. 3 (2002):
380–404.

63. See Deirdre Conlon and Nancy Hiemstra, *Intimate Economies of Immigration
Detention: Critical Perspectives* (London: Routledge, 2016); Nicholas De Genova and
Nathalie Peutz, eds., *The Deportation Regime: Sovereignty, Space, and the Freedom of
Movement* (Durham: Duke University Press, 2010); Julie A. Dowling and Jonathan
Xavier Inda, eds., *Governing Immigration Through Crime: A Reader* (Stanford: Stanford
University Press, 2013); Michael J. Flynn and Matthew B. Flynn, eds. *Challenging Im-
migration Detention Academics, Activists and Policy-Makers* (Cheltenham: Edward
Elgar, forthcoming); Nick Gill, Deirdre Conlon, and Dominique Moran, eds., *Car-
ceral Spaces: Mobility and Agency in Imprisonment and Migrant Detention* (Farnham:
Ashgate, 2013); Tanya Golash-Boza, ed., *Forced Out and Fenced In: Immigration Tales
from the Field* (Oxford: Oxford University Press, forthcoming).

64. For a few recent examples of this vast literature, see Susan Bibler Coutin, *Ex-
iled Home: Salvadoran Transnational Youth in the Aftermath of Violence* (Durham: Duke
University Press, 2016); Garth Davies and Jeffrey Fagan, "Crime and Enforcement in
Immigrant Neighborhoods: Evidence from New York City," *Annals of the American
Academy of Political and Social Science* 641, no. 1 (2012): 99–124; Heike Drotbohm and
Ines Hasselberg Deportation, eds., "Anxiety, Justice: New Ethnographic Perspectives,"
special issue, *Journal of Ethnic and Migration Studies* 41, no. 4 (2015); Nancy Foner and
Patrick Simon eds., *Fear, Anxiety and National Identity: Immigration and Belonging in*

North America and Europe (New York: Russell Sage, 2015); Tanya Golash-Boza, *Deported: Immigrant Policing, Disposable Labor and Global Capitalism* (New York: NYU Press, 2015); King, Massoglia, and Uggen, "Employment and Exile"; David Alan Sklansky, "Crime, Immigration, and Ad Hoc Instrumentalism," *New Criminal Law Review: An International and Interdisciplinary Journal* 15, no. 2 (2012): 157–223; Lisa Sun-Hee Park and David Pellow, *The Slums of Aspen: Immigrants vs. the Environment in America's Eden* (New York: NYU Press, 2013).

65. See note 3.

66. This term was coined by Sasha Breger Bush. See Sasha Breger Bush, "Trump and National Neoliberalism: And Why the World Is About to Get Much More Dangerous," *Common Dreams*, December 24, 2016, http://www.commondreams.org/views /2016/12/24/trump-and-national-neoliberalism.

67. See the exchange conveyed in David Frum and Conor Friedersdorf, "Debating Immigration Policy at a Populist Moment," *Atlantic Monthly*, March 9, 2017, https:// www.theatlantic.com/politics/archive/2017/03/debating-immigration-policy-at-a -populist-moment/518916/.

68. This is discussed in chapter 2. See also note 3 (this chapter) for an account of the statistics and change in prosecutorial practice that took place under the auspices of Operation Streamline.

69. But these efforts to significantly expand detention beds (by as much as 500 percent) have been thwarted by the May 2017 federal budget agreement. See note 46. Also see Chris Hayes and Brian Montopoli, "Exclusive: Trump Admin. Plans Expanded Immigrant Detention," *MSNBC*, March 3, 2017, http://www.msnbc.com/all-in/exclusive -trump-admin-plans-expanded-immigrant-detention.

70. Juliet Stumpf, "The Crimmigration Thesis: Immigrants, Crime and Sovereign Power," *American University Law Review* 56, no. 2 (2006): 368–419.

71. Dowling and Inda, *Governing Immigration Through Crime*.

72. Barbara Faedda, " 'We Are Not Racists, but We Do Not Want Immigrants': How Italy Uses Immigration Law to Marginalize Immigrants and Create a (New) National Identity," in *Migrant Marginality: A Transnational Perspective*, ed. Philip Kretsedemas, Jorge Capetillo-Ponce, and Glenn Jacobs (New York: Routledge, 2013); Ana Kralj, "Constructing Otherness: Media and Parliamentary Discourse on Immigration in Slovenia," in Kretsedemas, Capetillo-Ponce, and Jacobs, *Migrant Marginality*; Maartje van der Woude et al., "Crimmigration in the Netherlands," *Law and Social Inquiry* 39, no. 3 (2014): 560–579.

73. Carrie Johnson, "Justice Department Will Phase Out Its Use of Private Prisons," NPR, August 18, 2016, http://www.npr.org/sections/thetwo-way/2016/08/18/490498158 /justice-department-will-phase-out-its-use-of-private-prisons.

74. Christopher Dean Hopkins, "Private Prisons Back in Mix for Federal Inmates as Sessions Rescinds Order," NPR, February 23, 2017, http://www.npr.org/sections/thetwo -way/2017/02/23/516916688/private-prisons-back-in-mix-for-federal-inmates-as-sessions -rescinds-order; Julian Aguilar, "Trump Signed Off on a New Private-Prison Immigration Detention Center in Texas," *Business Insider*, April 14, 2017, http://www.busines- sinsider.com/trump-private-prison-immigration-detention-center-texas-2017-4.

75. Madison Pauly, "A Brief History of America's Private Prison Industry," *Mother Jones,* July/August 2016, http://www.motherjones.com/politics/2016/06/history-of -americas-private-prison-industry-timeline/.

76. This is discussed at the beginning of chapter 7. See also Philip Kretsedemas, *The Immigration Crucible: Race, Nation and the Limits of the Law* (New York: Columbia University Press, 2012), 170n6.

77. Foucault's theory of biopolitics, which we do not treat in depth in this book, offers a connecting thread between disciplinary power and Agamben's theory of sovereign power—though it is still possible to read Foucault in a way that avoids the blindsights for which Agamben has been criticized. See Giorgio Agamben, *State of Exception* (Chicago: University of Chicago, 2005); *Sovereign Power and Bare Life* (Stanford: Stanford University Press, 1998); Michel Foucault, *Security, Territory, Population: Lectures at the Collège de France, 1977–78* (Houndmills, Basingstoke: Palgrave MacMillan, 2007); *Discipline and Punish: The Birth of the Prison* (New York: Random House, 1975).

78. Hannah Arendt, *The Origins of Totalitarianism* (New York: Harcourt, Brace, Jovanovich, 1973), 185–221.

79. See Stefan Helmreich, "Kinship, Nation, and Paul Gilroy's Concept of Diaspora," *Diaspora: A Journal of Transnational Studies* 2, no. 2 (1992): 243–249.

80. Philip Kretsedemas, "The Limits of Control: Neoliberal Policy Priorities and the US Non-immigrant Flow," *International Migration* 50 (2012): e1–e18; Olivia Ruiz, "Migration and Borders: Present and Future Challenges," *Latin American Perspectives* 33, no. 2 (2006): 46–55; Stuart Tannock, "White-Collar Imperialisms: The H-1B Debate in America," *Social Semiotics* 19, no. 3 (2009): 311–327.

81. Most famously, there is Hannah Arendt's argument that all human rights are derived first from the civil rights of the national political sphere; Hannah Arendt, *The Origins of Totalitarianism* (New York: Meridian, 1951), 227–303. See also Etienne Balibar, "(De)Constructing the Human as Human Institution: A Reflection on the Coherence of Hannah Arendt's Practical Philosophy," *Social Research* 74, no. 3 (2007): 727–738. For a contemporary discussion, see Stefan Heuser, "Is There a Right to Have Rights? The Case of the Right of Asylum," *Ethical Theory and Moral Practice* 11, no. 1 (2008): 3–13.

82. Mark Duffield, *Global Governance and the New Wars* (London: Zed Books, 2014), 75–107; Dorothea Hilhorst and Bram J. Jansen, "Constructing Rights and Wrongs in Humanitarian Action: Contributions from a Sociology of Praxis," *Sociology* 46, no. 5 (2012): 891–905.

83. Benjamin Gregg, *The Human Rights State: Justice Within and Beyond Sovereign Nations* (Philadelphia: University of Pennsylvania Press, 2016), 42–60; Alexandre Lefebvre, *Human Rights as a Way of Life: On Bergson's Political Philosophy* (Stanford: Stanford University Press, 2013); William O'Neill, "Rights of Passage: The Ethics of Forced Displacement," *Journal of the Society of Christian Ethics* 27, no. 1 (2007): 113–135.

PART I

Controlling Borders and Migrant Populations

2. PRESIDENT OBAMA'S LEGACY
AS "DEPORTER IN CHIEF"

TANYA GOLASH-BOZA, UNIVERSITY OF CALIFORNIA, MERCED

On April 5, 2014, activists around the United States organized more than eighty protests in a national day of action against deportations. This day was chosen because it marked the day the two millionth person would be deported under the Obama administration. The number two million was significant for two reasons: (1) it marked the number of people deported during the eight-year Bush administration, and (2) it was more than the sum total of deportations carried out in the first one hundred years of U.S. deportations (1892 to 1992).

The number of deportations today is far higher than it has been historically. In 1892, 2,801 immigrants were removed from the United States. The number of removals ebbed and flowed for the next century, never surpassing 40,000 removals a year. The average number of removals between 1900 and 1990 was 18,275 per year. In the 1990s, however, that number began to escalate. Between 1990 and 1999, there were a total of 788,078 removals, an average of 78,000 per year. By 2013, annual deportations were five times that amount, at an average of 1,200 people per day.[1] Removal is "the compulsory and confirmed movement of an inadmissible or deportable alien out of the United States based on an order of removal" and is commonly understood as deportation.[2] This unprecedented number of removals happened when President Obama was in office, and removals increased every year during his first five years as president.

FIGURE 2.1 Removals, 1892–2014

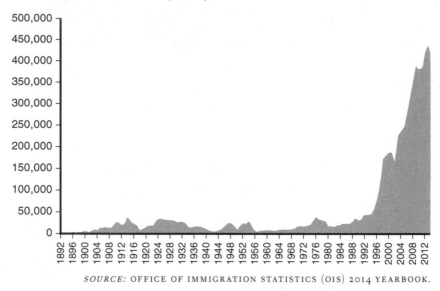

SOURCE: OFFICE OF IMMIGRATION STATISTICS (OIS) 2014 YEARBOOK.

The major reason for the escalation in removals during the 1990s was the passage of restrictive laws in 1996. In 1997, the first year these laws were in effect, there were 114,432 removals. This number went up to 174,813 the following year. President Bill Clinton signed these bills into law at the beginning of his second term. During the entire term of his presidency (1993–2000), there had been 869,646 removals. President Bush surpassed this figure, with approximately two million removals during his two terms in office.[3] By the time President Obama finished his sixth year in office, he had more than surpassed two million removals (see figure 2.1).

Many people find it ironic that President Obama, the son of a Kenyan immigrant, may go down in history as the president who deported the largest number of people. This chapter explores how and why President Obama has emerged at the "deporter in chief" as well as how he changed course during his last two years in office.

A LOOK AT THE NUMBERS

How many deportations took place during the Obama administration? The answer to this question requires a bit of estimation and addition, as we do not yet have complete data for his time in office. President Obama took office on Janu-

Table 2.1

Obama's Removal Record, OIS Data	
2009	272,330
2010	381,738
2011	386,020
2012	416,324
2013	434,015
2014	407,075
2015	333,341
2016	333,341[a]
2017	101,372[b]
TOTAL	3,065,556

Source: Data from Department of Homeland Security, "Table 39. Aliens Removed or Returned: Fiscal Years 1892–2015," *Yearbook of Immigration Statistics* 2015, https://www.dhs.gov/immigration-statistics/yearbook/2015/table39.
[a] Annual estimate based on 2015 annual data.
[b] Removals for 111 days of fiscal year 2017 based on a proportionate estimate of 2016 annual data.

ary 20, 2009. This is partway through fiscal year 2009, which ended on September 30, 2009. That means Obama was in office for 254 of the 365 days in FY 2009. In that year, there were 391,341 deportations—a daily average of 1,072. As Obama was in office for 254 days, we can estimate that he oversaw 272,330 deportations during that fiscal year. Fiscal years 2010 to 2015 are the most straightforward, as Obama was in office for the entire time, and we have data from the Office of Immigration Statistics (OIS) for those years, meaning we can add on those years without any caveats.

As of this writing, the OIS has not released data for fiscal years 2016; thus, we have to estimate for President Obama's second term by plugging in the numbers from 2015. Obama left office on January 29, 2017, which is partway through FY 2017. As of that date, he would have been president for 111 days of the fiscal year, giving us an estimate of 101,372 removals. When we add these numbers up, as shown in table 2.1, we reach a figure of 3,065,556 removals during his eight-year term.

When we use the more recent numbers from Immigration and Customs Enforcement (ICE), they show a slightly different trend, with deportations peaking in 2012 (see table 2.2). The ICE numbers add up to 2.7 million—not quite 3 million removals but still far more than any previous administration.

Based on the numbers (somewhere between 2.7 and 3 million), it seems legitimate to argue that President Obama has overseen a massive deportation

Table 2.2

Obama's Removal Record, Using ICE Data	
2009	271,281
2010	392,862
2011	396,906
2012	409,849
2013	368,644
2014	315,943
2015	235,413
2016	240,255
2017	73,064[a]
TOTAL	2,704,217

Source: U.S. Immigration and Customs Enforcement, "FY 2015 ICE Immigration Removals," https://www
.ice.gov/removal-statistics.
[a] Removals for 111 days of fiscal year 2017 based on a proportionate estimate of 2016 annual data.

program. Readers familiar with Mexican American history may question the contention that the current moment is unique, as two notorious moments of mass deportation have occurred that parallel the present. In the next section, I take a look at these moments to see how they compare to present conditions.

MASS REPATRIATION OF THE 1930s
AND OPERATION WETBACK

On February 26, 1931, about four hundred Mexicans were enjoying the afternoon in La Placita, a public park in Los Angeles, when armed immigration agents arrived, closed off the entrances, and ordered everyone present to line up and produce documentation of legal entry and residency or U.S. citizenship. The next week, the first official repatriation train left Los Angeles for Mexico with over four hundred people on board.[4] Balderrama and Rodríguez estimate that the United States returned as many as one million Mexicans and their children to Mexico in the 1930s. This massive project of coercion involved local sheriffs, schools, social workers, and the Mexican consulates as well as U.S. federal agents.[5] In relative terms, the scale of this operation was much larger than that of today because in 1930, about 1.5 million Mexicans and Mexican Americans lived in the United States (as compared to nearly 30 million today), and hundreds of thousands of Mexicans as well as Mexican Americans were repatriated. These repatriations, however, went largely unrecorded, making it difficult to make direct comparisons.

In 1950, the border patrol began massive roundups of Mexicans in a series of operations that would come to be known as Operation Wetback. One example of an Operation Wetback raid happened on July 30, 1952. At dawn, about one hundred border patrol agents began arresting Mexicans by the hundreds in an area near Brownsville, Texas. By the end of the day, they had arrested five thousand people and transported all of them to the bridge that led back to Mexico. These sorts of roundups continued through 1954, when the border patrol announced it had deported more than one million Mexican immigrants during this operation. These mass arrests created fear and tension among immigrant communities, as Mexicans were forced to leave their loved ones, their belongings, and their lives in the United States and return to Mexico.[6] Although undeniably massive in scale, Operation Wetback focused on returning Mexicans who were attempting to enter the United States and thus differs from the current form of enforcement, which focuses on removing people who are living in the United States.

Now that we have established that the current moment of mass deportation can be considered unique, let us explore how and why this came to be. Deportations are the removal of surplus labor from a country. Ruth Wilson Gilmore has characterized mass incarceration as a "prison fix," made possible because of a surplus not only of labor but also of capital, land, and state capacity.[7] In her more recent work, Gilmore brings deportations into this analysis, arguing that they are part of the expansion of the coercive arm of the state.[8] Similar to mass incarceration, mass deportation requires a tremendous amount of state investment and state capacity.

Mass deportation does not just happen—it has to be orchestrated, and state officials have to consciously decide to enhance the state capacity for repression in order to remove noncitizens. Insofar as the president is at the head of the executive branch of the government and is thus at the helm of responsibility for immigration law enforcement, it is critical to analyze the president's position and tactics in order to understand how and why a policy of mass deportation was implemented in the United States.

When President Obama took office, his immigration enforcement policy was identical to that of George W. Bush and thus can be characterized as a right-wing policy. After his first term, and as antideportation protests escalated, President Obama's position shifted a bit, and his immigration enforcement policy became more centrist. By the end of his term, deportation numbers had gone back down but were still far higher than they have been historically. Obama also offered some relief to a small sector of undocumented immigrants, but that relief was only temporary. It may seem surprising to characterize a Democrat's policies as right wing, or even centrist, but this has been a critical trend in the Democratic Party in the United States. As we will see in the next section, the legislative basis for the current deportation program was made possible due to two bills signed into law by Democratic president Bill Clinton in 1996.

1996 LAWS

The slow and steady rise from less than 100,000 to over 400,000 removals a year is largely due to two bills President William Jefferson Clinton signed into law in 1996: the Antiterrorism and Effective Death Penalty Act (AEDPA), and the Illegal Immigration Reform and Immigrant Responsibility Act (IIRIRA). AEDPA and IIRIRA expanded the grounds on which people could be deported. They also narrowed the grounds on which people could appeal a deportation, thereby making large numbers of immigrants deportable.

AEDPA and IIRIRA eliminated judicial review of some deportation orders, required mandatory detention for some noncitizens, and introduced the potential for the use of secret evidence in certain cases. Six years prior, the Immigration Act of 1990 expanded the definition of who could be deported for engaging in criminal activity and made many immigrants deportable for having committed "aggravated felonies."[9] The 1996 laws further expanded the definition of an aggravated felony and made deportation mandatory. Under IIRIRA, aggravated felonies include any felony or misdemeanor in which the person is sentenced to at least one year in prison, regardless of whether the sentence is served or suspended. These crimes can be relatively minor, such as shoplifting or the combination of two minor illegal drug possessions. These cases do not require judicial review, meaning that a person does not have the right for a judge to take into account the specifics of the case or the ties the person has to the United States. In addition, Congress appropriated more funds to immigration law enforcement, thereby ensuring that the laws would be enforced. As a consequence, deportations nearly quadrupled, from 50,024 in 1995 to 188,467 in 2000. The second substantial rise in deportations is connected to the creation of the Department of Homeland Security in 2002, discussed in the next section.

FOLLOW THE MONEY

Deportations have continued to escalate, and the number of deportations that take place each year is directly related to the amount of money invested in immigration law enforcement. Each year, the Department of Homeland Security (DHS) requests billions of dollars from Congress to enforce immigration laws.

The FY 2011 budget for DHS was $56 billion. To put this in perspective, the FY 2011 budgets for the Department of Education and Department of Justice were $77.8 billion and $29.2 billion, respectively. The rise in deportations over the past decade primarily stems from executive branch decisions to expand immigration law enforcement as part of the broader project of the War on Terror.

A recent report by the Migration Policy Institute—a global think tank based in Washington, D.C., that studies the movement of people—found that the U.S. government spends more on federal immigration enforcement than on all other principal federal criminal law enforcement agencies combined.[10] My calculations confirm this: immigration enforcement spending heavily outweighs domestic law enforcement spending. In FY 2011, the U.S. government spent $27 billion on ICE, U.S. Customs and Border Protection, and the U.S. Coast Guard. In contrast, the U.S. government spent a total of $13.7 billion on domestic law enforcement, including the Federal Bureau of Investigation, the Drug Enforcement Administration, the Secret Service, the U.S. Marshals Service, and the Bureau of Alcohol, Tobacco, Firearms and Explosives. These budgetary details are important because, as president, Barack Obama was in charge of the executive branch's budget. Moreover, President Obama appointed Janet Napolitano to head the DHS, knowing that immigration policy enforcement had long been one of her priorities. Notably, the DHS is charged with keeping the nation safe from terrorism, making it far from obvious why the department dedicates half its budget to immigration law enforcement.

Deportations have escalated each year because the DHS has requested money from Congress to achieve a higher number of deportations, and Congress has honored these budget requests. Alongside the increase in deportations, we have seen a significant rise in detentions. Immigrant detention increased from a daily average of 5,532 in 1994 to 34,000 in 2011.[11] The number of detainees has remained steady since 2011, in part due to what is known as the "detention bed mandate."

In 2009, then senator Robert Byrd added a line to the DHS appropriations bill stating that the department is required to "maintain a level of not less than 34,000 detention beds." This "detention bed mandate" requires immigration detention facilities to fill thirty-four thousand beds each day with noncitizens who are either awaiting deportation or awaiting an immigration hearing. Not only has this mandate played a significant role in the continued escalation of deportations, but it also has been included in the annual appropriations bill ever since. In 2015, the appropriations bill stated: "Funding made available under this heading shall maintain a level of not less than 34,000 detention beds through September 30, 2015."[12] This mandate has been profitable for private corporations, particularly Corrections Corporation of America (now operating under the name CoreCivic) and the GEO Group. In 2015, 62 percent of ICE immigration detention beds were in for-profit facilities, up from 49 percent in 2009.[13]

BORDER VS. INTERIOR REMOVALS

Obama has been called "deporter-in-chief" for overseeing the most expansive removal program in history. But who is counted among the two million deportees is the subject of widespread debate.[14] Conservative pundits claim that ICE is counting *border removals* toward the annual 400,000 deportations quota to show that Obama has been tough on deportation. On the other hand, immigrant rights activists claim that the administration is enhancing *interior removals*, tearing immigrant families and communities apart.[15]

The distinction is important. For example, catching migrants at the border and returning them to their home countries (as is typical of border removals) is different from arresting long-term U.S. residents in their home, in front of their children, and sending them back to countries they left long ago (as is typical of interior removals). Nevertheless, the distinctions between these types of removals are imprecise; 7 percent of border removals between 2004 and 2013 involved people who had lived in the United States for more than one year, and 11 percent of interior removals during that period involved people who had been in the United States for less than two weeks.[16] Even so, when an undocumented immigrant living in the United States is removed, this generally counts as an interior removal. A border removal, in contrast, typically involves a person who crossed the border less than two weeks before being apprehended.

A report by the Migration Policy Institute offers detailed data on interior and border removals.[17] At the time of its writing, the 2014 report revealed that Obama was not only on track to carry out far more removals than any of his predecessors but was also poised to oversee more interior removals than any U.S. president.

For context, before 1995, there were never more than 50,000 overall removals (border plus interior) in any given year. The first year that we have data that separates interior from border removals is 2003, in which there were 30,000 annual interior removals. By 2008, Bush's last year in office, this number rose to 140,000 interior removals per year. It is clear that Bush initiated an immigration enforcement policy targeting interior removals. The Obama administration continued Bush's legacy by further enhancing the focus on interior enforcement. Moreover, interior removals reached a peak (188,000 annual deportations) in 2011—two years *after* Obama took office.[18]

In 2012, perhaps in response to widespread criticism from Latinos, Obama reversed course. As a result, interior removals fell to 131,000 in 2013, a sharp drop but still far higher than any year under the Bush administration except for 2008. Overall, during Obama's first term alone, there were nearly three-quarters of a million interior removals—far more than Bush's record-setting numbers.[19]

Beyond the evidence on interior versus border removals, we also know the number of years deportees lived in the United States before being apprehended.

From 2003 to 2013, there were 1.3 million interior removals. Nearly half of them (47 percent) had lived in the United States for at least three years; one in six (216,000) for at least ten years.[20] The deportations of long-term U.S. residents are often the most harmful to families and communities, as they are the most likely to lead to family separation

The two million deportations during Obama's first five years of office do not necessarily mean that two million families were separated; nevertheless, his program of mass deportation resulted in at least 216,000 people who had lived in this country for more than ten years being torn from their homes over the past decade. That amounts to the city of Rochester, New York, being slowly depleted of its population over the course of ten years. Or, perhaps more accurately, imagine every father in San Francisco being removed from this country.

FELONS, NOT FAMILIES?

President Obama claimed, "If we're going to go after folks who are here illegally, we should do it smartly, and go after folks who are criminals, gangbangers, people who are hurting the community—not after students. Not after folks who are here just because they're trying to figure out how to feed their families."[21] His policies, however, tell a different story.

The American Civil Liberties Union uncovered documents that revealed that ICE agents targeted undocumented immigrants convicted of minor traffic crimes to meet their criminal deportation quotas.[22] Because of policies like these under Obama, we have seen a rise not only in deportations generally but in deportations involving immigrants who have lived in the United States for long periods of time. These deportations have happened primarily through cooperation between local law enforcement and immigration enforcement agents. President Obama supported this cooperation and pushed for immigration law enforcement to focus on criminal aliens.

The Obama administration insisted that the focus on interior enforcement was making our communities safer. However, the numbers belie Obama's claim that he was focused on deporting criminals.[23] To be sure, the percentage of criminal removals under the Obama administration (46 percent) *was* higher than that under the Bush administration (36 percent). By 2013, fully 87 percent of interior removals involved people with criminal convictions. However, the data reveal that people with fairly minor convictions account for the majority of criminal removals in 2013. About 28,000 people were deported for traffic crimes, 14,000 for drug possession, and nearly 5,000 for "nuisance offenses" such as trespassing and vandalism.[24]

On April 6, 2014, the *New York Times* reported that nearly two-thirds of the two million deportations since Obama took office involved either people with no criminal records or those convicted of minor crimes.[25] Just two days later, TRAC Immigration issued an even more detailed—and more damning—report.[26] The report, which looks at deportations carried out by ICE, found that although 57 percent of deportations in 2013 were of people who had criminal convictions, most of those convictions were minor:

> ICE currently uses an exceedingly broad definition of criminal behavior: even very minor infractions are included. For example, anyone with a traffic ticket for exceeding the speed limit on the Baltimore-Washington Parkway who sends in their check to pay their fine has just entered ICE's "convicted criminal" category. If the same definitions were applied to every citizen . . . evidence suggests that the majority of U.S. citizens would be considered convicted criminals.

In other words, not only did nearly half of all deportations involve people with no criminal record, but large numbers of "criminal" deportations involved people charged with traffic offenses. According to the TRAC report, each year of the Obama administration, the percentage of deportations involving a criminal conviction increased, although most of those convictions were minor.[27] For example, about a quarter of the criminal convictions involved the immigration crime of "illegal entry." The difference between a person deported on noncriminal grounds for being undocumented and one deported on criminal grounds for illegal entry is almost entirely a question of prosecutorial decisions. In other words, the 47,000 people deported for illegal entry were converted into criminals for reporting purposes. The next largest category is traffic offenses—the majority driving under the influence or speeding—which account for nearly another quarter of all criminal deportations. Although safe driving is valued in this country, in common parlance in the United States, we do not generally refer to people with traffic convictions as "criminals." The third largest category is drug offenses. Notably, the most common offense in this category was marijuana possession, which has been decriminalized in Washington, Colorado, and other locations.

The TRAC data render it clear that the increase in the number of noncitizens who were deported on criminal grounds under the Obama administration was mostly a consequence of an increase in the deportation of noncitizens with immigration and traffic violations—convictions considered criminal using only a very broad definition of the term. In fact, based on ICE's own definition of a serious or "Level 1" offense, only 12 percent of all deportations in 2013 were of people convicted of such offenses.

Although President Obama claims to have focused immigration law enforcement priorities on criminals, the TRAC report reveals that this is simply not true. Instead, the evidence is conclusive that the administration's deportation policy deported hundreds of thousands of parents of U.S. citizens, put thousands of kids in foster care, and created a massive "Latino problem" for the Democratic Party.[28]

DHS policy under Obama aimed to focus on criminal aliens, achieve a quota of at least 400,000 deportations a year, and strengthen the U.S.-Mexico border. Because fewer people are trying to cross the U.S.-Mexico border, these policies translated into increasing numbers of deportations of people who have lived in this country for years and who have children who are U.S. citizens. Between July 1, 2010, and September 30, 2012, nearly a quarter of all deportations—or 204,810 deportations—involved parents with U.S.-citizen children.[29] This is remarkable, considering that in the ten years spanning 1997 and 2006, the DHS deported about 100,000 people with U.S.-citizen children.[30]

Focusing on criminals sounds like a smart plan. However, few people deported on criminal grounds are serious criminals. In 2011, 86,000 people were prosecuted by the Department of Justice for immigration crimes—nearly all for illegal entry or illegal reentry.[31] As noted earlier, the difference between a person who is deported on noncriminal grounds and one who is deported on criminal grounds for illegal entry is nominal. About a quarter of people deported on criminal grounds are deported for immigration crimes, and another 50 percent are deported for drug or traffic crimes. Again, these are crimes only if you prosecute them. An undocumented immigrant can be processed civilly for entry without inspection or criminally for illegal entry, although the action—crossing the border—is the same. A person found with marijuana can be prosecuted criminally for a drug offense, fined, or simply let go. When your goal is to enhance the number of criminal deportees, it makes sense to prosecute these offenses criminally and claim you are deporting criminals. These federal prosecutions are decisions made by the Department of Justice, part of the executive branch.

OBAMA'S LEGACY OF MASS DEPORTATION

Any discussion of this legacy of mass deportation must contend with the racial implications of these enforcement measures. As it turns out, President Obama's program of mass deportation was on par with other racially tainted tragedies in our history—Indian boarding schools that kept Native American children from their parents; internment camps where Japanese citizens and Japanese Americans were forced to live during World War II; and Jim Crow laws, which denied equal opportunities to African Americans.

As much as many Americans would like to think we have buried racially discriminatory episodes deep in our history, contemporary mass deportation proves otherwise. Mass deportation primarily affects nonwhite people, is carried out without due process, and separates millions of children from their parents.

Under Jim Crow laws, African Americans were denied access to schools, housing, and the ballot box. When long-term residents of the United States are deported for such crimes as marijuana possession or tax evasion, some face a life of exile from the only country they have ever known. Like Jim Crow laws, deportation laws primarily affect one group of people: more than 97 percent of people deported last year were Caribbean or Latin American immigrants, even though they account for only 60 percent of noncitizens.[32]

Many of these deportees were deported to countries they barely know. I recently interviewed 150 deportees in Jamaica, the Dominican Republic, Guatemala, and Brazil, who recounted horror stories of police brutality, gang violence, homelessness, and a life of poverty and isolation. The deportation of legal permanent residents has hit black immigrants particularly hard; using data from the DHS and the U.S. Census Bureau, I calculated that one of every twelve male Jamaican and Dominican legal permanent residents has been deported since 1996.[33] Similar to Jim Crow laws, deportation laws are draconian and target particular groups.

The United States currently detains upwards of 30,000 immigrants per day, much as it imprisoned more than 120,000 people of Japanese origin during World War II without trials or other court processes. The DHS has broad discretion to arrest and detain any person it suspects does not have the legal right to be in the United States. People held by the DHS do not have the same rights and safeguards as criminal suspects. They do not have the right to a speedy hearing before a judge, nor do they have the right to appointed counsel.

Native American children were taken from their parents in the early twentieth century, and the same thing is happening to immigrants today. One Guatemalan deportee I interviewed had a custody hearing for her daughter in California, which she was unable to attend. Her absence led to a termination of her parental rights.

When immigrants face deportation on criminal grounds, judges are often unable to take their family ties into account before ordering a deportation. Current immigration laws barely distinguish between a long-term legal permanent resident with U.S.-citizen children convicted of writing a bad check and a visa overstayer convicted of murder. Both of these crimes can be considered aggravated felonies and can lead to deportation with no due process.

In 2012, more than 400,000 people were deported. Nearly 100,000 of them were parents of U.S. citizens. Tens of thousands of these children will grow up in the United States knowing that the U.S. government took away their right to grow up with one or both of their parents.

OBAMA'S CHANGE IN COURSE

Nevertheless, these criticisms of the Obama administration must also account for the change in course in the last years of his administration. In late 2016, OIS issued a report that indicated that deportations reached a peak of 434,015 in 2013, then declined to 407,075 in 2014 and 333,341 in 2015.[34] The latest data indicate that deportations may have gone down significantly in 2014 and 2015. ICE issued its own report that indicates that removals decreased from 368,644 in FY 2013 to 315,943 in FY 2014, and then down again to 235,413 removals in FY 2015 (see figure 2.2).[35]

These numbers from ICE do not align perfectly with OIS data. However, they do provide new information on interior removals. The Migration Policy Institute report shows that interior removals went from 30,000 in 2003 to a peak of 188,000 in 2011. ICE data show interior removals at 223,755 in 2011, followed by a marked decline. Notably, interior removals were less than 70,000 in 2015; of course, 70,000 is still far higher than 30,000. Nevertheless, it appears there was a decline in interior removals since 2012. Why would President Obama change course?

In order to answer this question, let us look at three decisions he made that seem to have affected removal rates. One is the appointment of Jeh Johnson as secretary of the Department of Homeland Security, who was sworn in on December 23, 2013. Whereas Janet Napolitano had a background in immigration enforcement from her home state of Arizona, Jeh Johnson is from the Pentagon and thus may have been more focused on antiterrorist policies than

FIGURE 2.2 ICE Removals, Fiscal Year 2008–2015

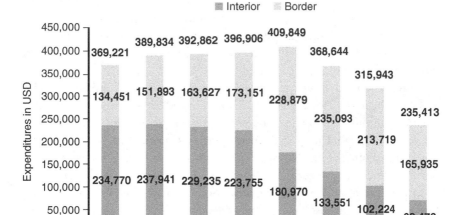

SOURCE: U.S. IMMIGRATION AND CUSTOMS ENFORCEMENT, "FY 2015 ICE IMMIGRATION REMOVALS," HTTPS://WWW.ICE.GOV/REMOVAL-STATISTICS.

on anti-immigrant policies. President Obama may have realized that the up-swing in deportations was related to the appointment of a pro-enforcement sec-retary and may have consciously appointed someone with a different profile. The second key factor is the ending of the Secure Communities program and the replacement of that program with the Priority Enforcement Program (PEP), which was fully implemented in July 2015. But since both of these decisions were implemented after interior removals began to decline in 2012 (see fig-ure 2.2), they do not suffice as a comprehensive explanation. The final impor-tant factor, which dates to 2012, is the executive action Deferred Action for Childhood Arrivals (DACA, created on June 2012).

The appointment of Jeh Johnson, the replacement of Secure Communities with PEP, and the signing of DACA and DAPA can be attributed to two main causes: grassroots pressure and political calculus. The appointment of Johnson was likely a result of Obama's political calculus, as there was not much grass-roots pressure to appoint Johnson (who happens to be the grandson of notable sociologist Charles S. Johnson). When Johnson was appointed to lead the DHS, the agency was the subject of extensive criticism, even ridicule. When Janet Napolitano stepped down, Bloomberg published an article calling for the bloated, wasteful, and ineffective DHS to be shut down.[36]

Once appointed, Johnson advocated for more sensible immigration policy en-forcement. In a speech in October 2015, Johnson argued, "Notwithstanding the political rhetoric, we are not going to deport eleven million people." He then went on to explain the problems embedded in the Secure Communities pro-gram as well as ICE detainers.[37] Presumably, Obama anticipated Johnson's posi-tion on immigration policy before his appointment to the position. One final way that political calculus played a role is that once Obama's second term was safely in place, he may have decided that mass deportation was no longer worth any political capital he gained from it.

This brings us to the end of the controversial Secure Communities program and its replacement with PEP. The DHS announced on November 20, 2014, that Secure Communities would be discontinued and replaced with the Priority En-forcement Program. Under PEP, when a person is arrested and booked by a law enforcement officer for a criminal violation, his or her biometric data is sent to ICE to determine whether the individual is a priority for removal. ICE priori-tizes the deportation of people who have committed certain crimes, gang mem-bers, and those who pose a danger to national security.[38] Although there are few concrete differences between the two programs, data show that there have been fewer interior removals under PEP. In addition, it is likely that the end of the controversial Secure Communities program was due to a groundswell of grass-roots pressure to end it.

In addition to this downswing in removal, in 2012, President Obama created DACA, which granted work permits and temporary relief from deportation for undocumented immigrants who came to the United States as minors.[39] In November 2014, Obama signed an executive action that established deportation priorities and sought to expand DACA to the parents of children brought to the United States as minors: Deferred Action for the Parents of Americans and Lawful Permanent Residents (DAPA).[40] However, this action has faced stiff resistance. In 2015, a federal court issued a temporary injunction on DAPA,[41] and in mid-2016, a Supreme Court decision made it clear that DAPA would not go forward. More recently, in September 2017, the DACA program was terminated by the Trump administration.

Despite the pending and likely termination of both programs, it is still important to understand how they work. There are two parts to DACA and DAPA: the deferred action on deportation, and the issuance of temporary work permits. The deferred action on deportation gave DACA recipients a temporary protection from deportation. The issuance of temporary work permits allowed recipients in some cases to secure better employment. But the vast majority continue to work in the same jobs they worked in as undocumented people.

Similar to the end of Secure Communities, the implementation of DACA and the proposal of DAPA can be attributed to grassroots movements. Immigrant rights groups have been pushing Congress to propose and pass a bill called the Development, Relief, and Education for Alien Minors (DREAM) Act since 2001 yet have been unsuccessful in getting a bill passed. These efforts have nevertheless led to a national movement that fights for the rights of DREAMers—youth who are undocumented yet have grown up in the United States and completed most of their schooling in this country. During the first decade of the twenty-first century, these youths created various organizations—including United We Dream, the National Day Laborer Organizing Network, and the Immigrant Youth Justice League—that have pushed for the passage of the DREAM Act as well as comprehensive immigration reform. When President Obama announced DACA, he began by expressing concern for the plight of DREAMers and then went on to explain that the implementation of DACA was necessary given the "absence of any immigration action from Congress to fix our broken immigration system."[42]

As Jeh Johnson pointed out, it is not feasible to deport eleven million people. It thus makes sense to implement programs that economize immigration enforcement spending by focusing on enforcement priorities. Both PEP and DACA do this. The strategy behind PEP is to focus energies on immigrants who have committed crimes, and the strategy behind DACA is to provide relief to those immigrants who are most integrated into this country due to their arrival at a young age. Both of these programs are also part of Obama's legacy. Unfortunately, both of them are also easily undone. In contrast, the deportation of three million people cannot be undone so easily. These three million deportations have torn apart hundreds of thousands of families and created an unfortunate legacy for our first black president.

Unfortunately, the legacy of our current president, Donald J. Trump, could be even more detrimental to immigrants than Obama's. Through his rhetoric and practice, Trump has used fear and intimidation to push immigrants back into the shadows. While campaigning, Trump promised to repeal DACA. Fears were heightened among "DACAmented" youth when, on February 14, 2017, a young DACA recipient, Daniel Ramirez, was detained during an ICE home raid.[43] Although it is not clear whether this was a lawful detention, his arrest sent a strong message to DACAmented youth that they are not safe during a Trump presidency, and these fears have been realized by the Trump administration's decision to terminate DACA.

On the campaign trail, Trump criticized Obama for not deporting enough criminals—even though 92 percent of all interior removals in 2016 were of people with criminal convictions. Nevertheless, on January 25, 2017, Trump issued an executive order called Enhancing Public Safety in the Interior of the United States, which includes a new priority system. Whereas Obama prioritized immigrants who had been convicted of crimes, Trump's order includes immigrants who have been charged with a criminal offense or who may have committed a crime but have not been charged—giving immigration enforcement officers broad leeway to deport people like Daniel Ramirez, who have no criminal record. Now, any immigrant with so much as a traffic ticket must worry that they will make it to the top of the priority list and find ICE agents literally knocking at their door. These fears were exacerbated in mid-February 2017 when ICE agents conducted home raids in cities across the country and apprehended about six hundred undocumented immigrants.[44]

These home raids served as a signal of what a "deportation force" might look like under Trump. Nevertheless, it is becoming increasingly clear that the point is not to deport all eleven million undocumented immigrants but to strike fear in their hearts—as well as the hearts of their millions of family members. Despite the existence of these fear tactics, we can expect immigrants and immigrant rights activists to continue to organize and demand justice for immigrants in the United States. The passage of DACA and the proposal of DAPA were due in large part to pressure from grassroots organizers, which will continue to fight for immigrant rights.

United We Dream, the National Day Laborer Organizing Network, the Immigrant Youth Justice League, and other immigrant rights organizations are demanding not only a stop to all deportations but also legalization for all undocumented immigrants. Legalization for all would improve wages and working conditions for everyone, as unscrupulous employers would not be able to take advantage of the undocumented status of migrants. Legalization for all would make the United States safer by allowing all undocumented migrants to come out of the shadows and obtain proper documentation to work, drive vehicles, and participate in U.S. society. Legalization for all would allow U.S. citizens to remain with their families and not feel threatened by the possibility of deportation of their immigrant family members. Legalization for all would take us a long way toward fulfilling the human rights of immigrants in the United States. Legalization for all—not weak protections from deportation—would have a lasting effect on immigrants and their families. So long as migrants in the United States remain vulnerable to deportation, they continue to be vulnerable to exploitation.

NOTES TO CHAPTER 2

1. All data on removals in this paragraph is derived from the Department of Homeland Security, "Table 39. Aliens Removed or Returned: Fiscal Years 1892 to 2015," *Yearbook of Immigration Statistics 2015* (Washington, D.C.: DHS 2015), https://www.dhs.gov/immigration-statistics/yearbook/2015.

2. John Simanski, *Immigration Enforcement Actions: 2013* (Washington, D.C.: DHS, 2014), https://www.dhs.gov/sites/default/files/publications/ois_enforcement_ar_2013.pdf.

3. The exact count of all removals conducted during the George W. Bush presidency (2001–2008) is 2,012,539. This count, and all other data on removals in this paragraph, is derived from Department of Homeland Security, "Table 39. Aliens Removed or Returned: Fiscal Years 1892 to 2015."

4. Francisco Balderrama and Raymond Rodríguez, *Decade of Betrayal: Mexican Repatriation in the 1930s* (Albuquerque: University of New Mexico Press, 2006); Antonio Olivo, "Pilsen Store Has Designs on History," *Chicago Tribune*, November 26, 2011, http://articles.chicagotribune.com/2011-11-26/news/ct-met-latino-museum-20111126_1_pilsen-color-barrier-mexican-american.

5. Abraham Hoffman, *Unwanted Mexican Americans in the Great Depression: Repatriation Pressures, 1929–1939* (Tucson: University of Arizona Press, 1974).

6. Kelly Lytle Hernandez, *Migra: A History of the U.S. Border Patrol* (Berkeley: University of California Press, 2010).

7. Ruth Wilson Gilmore, *Golden Gulag: Prisons, Surplus, Crisis, and Opposition in Globalizing California* (Berkeley: University of California Press, 2006).

8. Ruth Wilson Gilmore, "Mass Incarceration, Deportation, Stop and Frisk: The Urban Ecology of the Prison-Industrial Complex" (presentation, Third Annual Robert Fitch Memorial Lecture, Long Island City, N.Y., May 6, 2014).

9. Austin Fragomen and Steven Bell, *Immigration Fundamentals: A Guide to Law and Practice* (New York: Practicing Law Institute, 2007).

10. Migration Policy Institute, *U.S. Spends More on Immigration Enforcement than on FBI, DEA, Secret Service and All Other Federal Criminal Law Enforcement Agencies Combined*, January 7, 2013, http://www.migrationpolicy.org/news/us-spends-more -immigration-enforcement-fbi-dea-secret-service-all-other-federal-criminal-law.

11. Tanya Golash-Boza, *Immigration Nation: Raids, Detentions and Deportations in Post-911 America* (Boulder: Paradigm, 2012).

12. Department of Homeland Security Appropriations Act, 2015, H.R. 240, 114th Cong. (2015), https://www.congress.gov/bill/114th-congress/house-bill/240/text.

13. Sharita Gruberg, "How For-Profit Companies Are Driving Immigration Detention Policies," Center for American Progress, December 18, 2015, https://www.american-progress.org/issues/immigration/report/2015/12/18/127769/how-for-profit-companies -are-driving-immigration-detention-policies/.

14. Suzanne Gamboa, "Conflicting Views on Approaching 2 Million Deportations," *NBC Latino*, October 16, 2013, http://nbclatino.com/2013/10/16/conflicting-views-on -approaching-2-million-deportations/.

15. Mickey Kaus, "Amnesty Backers Gettin' Frazzled?," *Daily Caller*, March 31, 2014, http://dailycaller.com/2014/03/31/amnesty-backers-gettin-frazzled/.

16. Mark Rosenblum and Kristen McCabe, *Deportation and Discretion: Reviewing the Record and Options for Change* (Washington, D.C.: Migration Policy Institute, 2014).

17. Ibid.

18. Ibid., Figure 2, p. 19

19. Ibid.

20. Rosenblum and McCabe, *Deportation and Discretion*, Tables 5 and 6, pp. 23–24.

21. Elizabeth Llorente, "Presidential Debate: On Immigration, Romney and Obama Affirmed Their Stances," *Fox News*, October 17, 2012, http://www.foxnews.com/politics /2012/10/17/presidential-debate-on-immigration-romney-and-obama-affirmed-their -stances.html#ixzz2LMjywkEN.

22. Andrew O'Reilly, "Immigration Agency Under Fire for Alleged Deportation Quotas," *Fox News*, February 15, 2013, http://www.foxnews.com/politics/2013/02/15 /immigration-agency-under-fire-for-alleged-deportation-quotas.html.

23. Stephen Dinan, "95 Percent of Deported Illegals Were Criminals," *Washington Times*, October 16, 2014, http://www.washingtontimes.com/news/2014/oct/16/obamas -deportation-policy-leaves-most-illegal-immi/.

24. Transactional Records Access Clearinghouse, "Changes in Criminal Enforcement of Immigration Laws," TRAC's Immigration Project, May 13, 2014, http://trac .syr.edu/immigration/reports/354/.

25. Ginger Thompson and Sarah Cohen. "More Deportations Follow Minor Crimes, Records Show," *New York Times*, April 6, 2014, http://www.nytimes.com/2014/04/07/us /more-deportations-follow-minor-crimes-data-shows.html.

26. Transactional Records Access Clearinghouse, "Secure Communities and ICE Deportation: A Failed Program?," *TRAC's Immigration Project*, April 8, 2014, http://trac .syr.edu/immigration/reports/349/.

27. Ibid.

28. Seth Wessler, "Thousands of Kids Lost from Parents in U.S. Deportation System," *Colorlines*, November 2, 2011, http://www.colorlines.com/archives/2011/11/thousands_of_kids_lost_in_foster_homes_after_parents_deportation.html; Seth Wessler, "U.S. Deports 46K Parents with Citizen Kids in Just Six Months," *Colorlines*, November 3, 2011, http://www.colorlines.com/articles/us-deports-46k-parents-citizen-kids-just-six-months.

29. Seth Wessler, "Nearly 205K Deportations of Parents of U.S. Citizens in Just Over Two Years," *Colorlines*, December 17, 2012, http://www.colorlines.com/articles/nearly-205k-deportations-parents-us-citizens-just-over-two-years.

30. Jonathan Baum, Rosha Jones, and Catherine Barry, "In the Child's Best Interest? The Consequences of Losing a Lawful Immigrant Parent to Deportation," Chief Justice Earl Warren Institute on Race, Ethnicity and Diversity, March 2010, http://eric.ed.gov/?id=ED536693.

31. Transactional Records Access Clearinghouse, "Decline in Federal Criminal Immigration Prosecutions," *TRAC's Immigration Project*, June 12, 2012, http://trac.syr.edu/immigration/reports/283/.

32. Tanya Golash-Boza and Pierrette Hondagneu-Sotelo, "Latino Immigrant Men and the Deportation Crisis: A Gendered Racial Removal Program," *Latino Studies* 11, no. 3 (2013): 271–292.

33. Tanya Golash-Boza, *Deported: Immigrant Policing, Disposable Labor, and Global Capitalism* (New York: NYU Press, 2015).

34. Department of Homeland Security, "Table 39. Aliens Removed or Returned: Fiscal Years 1892 to 2015."

35. U.S. Customs and Immigration Enforcement, "FY 2015 ICE Immigration Removals," https://www.ice.gov/removal-statistics.

36. Charles Kenny, "The Case for Abolishing the DHS," *Bloomberg.com*, June 16, 2013, http://www.bloomberg.com/news/articles/2013-07-15/the-case-for-abolishing-the-dhs.

37. U.S. Department of Homeland Security, "Remarks by Secretary of Homeland Security Jeh C. Johnson at Congressional Hispanic Caucus Institute 2015 Public Policy Conference—as Delivered," October 7, 2015, https://www.dhs.gov/news/2015/10/07/remarks-secretary-homeland-security-jeh-c-johnson-congressional-hispanic-caucus.

38. U.S. Immigration and Customs Enforcement, "Priority Enforcement Program," November 20, 2014, https://www.ice.gov/pep.

39. U.S. Department of Homeland Security, "Deferred Action for Childhood Arrivals," July 17, 2015, http://www.dhs.gov/deferred-action-childhood-arrivals.

40. U.S. Citizenship and Immigration Services, "2014 Executive Actions on Immigration," April 15, 2015, https://www.uscis.gov/immigrationaction.

41. Center for Migration Studies, "Federal Court Halts DAPA and Expanded DACA Programs," February 16, 2015, http://cmsny.org/federal-court-halts-dapa-and-expanded-daca-programs/.

42. The White House, "Remarks by the President on Immigration," news release, June 15, 2012, https://www.whitehouse.gov/the-press-office/2012/06/15/remarks-president-immigration.

43. Daniel Ramirez Medina, "Daniel Ramirez Medina: I'm a 'Dreamer,' but Immigration Agents Detained Me Anyway," *Washington Post*, March 13, 2017, https://www.washingtonpost.com/posteverything/wp/2017/03/13/im-a-dreamer-immigration-agents-detained-me-anyway/?utm_term=.854b0c58c0b5.

44. Lisa Rein, Abigail Hauslohner and Sandhya Somashekhar, "Federal Agents Conduct Immigration Enforcement Raids in at Least Six States," *Washington Post*, February 11, 2017, https://www.washingtonpost.com/national/federal-agents-conduct-sweeping-immigration-enforcement-raids-in-at-least-6-states/2017/02/10/4b9f443a-efc8-11e6-b4ff-ac2cf509efe5_story.html?utm_term=.3ffe98a7c745.

3. IMMIGRATION POLICY AND MIGRANT SUPPORT ORGANIZATIONS IN AN ERA OF AUSTERITY AND HOPE

DEIRDRE CONLON, UNIVERSITY OF LEEDS

Topography—derived from the Greek words *topos*, meaning "place," and *graphia*, meaning "writing"—involves both detailed description and an account of the features of a site or locale.[1] It is both a methodological tool and a mode of engaging with and understanding a specific place. Topography is commonly used in physical geography as well as in military planning and, according to Carroli, is considered "essential for planning any . . . major public works or reclamation project."[2] Its use in these settings hints at the potential significance of topography within the context of a discussion of immigration policy in the age of punishment. In many countries, immigration policies increasingly cast migrants as "enemies" that threaten the economy, national security, and culture of the society. With this, military-like responses—involving security forces and use of technologies of war in the interests of the state—are rationalized and materialized without question. Securitization as immigration policy also aligns with neoliberal capitalism with an increasing array of profit-focused private sector actors that have roles and stakes in expanding immigration enforcement, producing a system that scholars term the "immigration industrial complex."[3] As a contrast to topography's deployment in military operations and its allegiance with capitalism's exploits, countertopography employs the same tools but in a critical manner in an effort to envision and activate alternative responses to problematic programs and policies. Cindi Katz describes countertopography as the "non-innocent, thick description of particular sites that detail the ways in which processes [such as immigration policy] affect particular places and/or groups."[4]

In this chapter, I present a topography and countertopography of support, advocacy, and activist groups that work with migrants in different ways, at different scales, and in the distinct social and political contexts of the United States and the United Kingdom. The chapter draws on an empirical study conducted between 2010 and 2012 that examined the challenges faced and strategies developed by migrant support organizations in the United States and the United Kingdom in an era marked by distinct political rhetoric—"hope" in the United States and "austerity" in the United Kingdom—yet that saw the expansion of increasingly harsh immigration policies in both contexts. Drawing on work by Cindi Katz, among others, I offer a topography of immigration policies in the United States and the United Kingdom under the respective leaderships of Barack Obama and David Cameron.[5] In keeping with a topographical approach, which emphasizes the specificities of a particular place, I call attention to the distinctive rhetoric of Obama and Cameron as candidates, then outline a number of developments in immigration policies that were instituted under each leader's government. With this, I develop a detailed descriptive account—a topography—of two distinct settings where, despite different rhetoric, we see a convergence of increasingly punitive immigration policies.

Following this, I turn to some of the effects and responses to these policies that have been developed by migrant support organizations working in the United States and United Kingdom. By emphasizing responses that connect groups as they grapple with the difficult circumstances in which they find themselves, I want to highlight the contour lines of counterresponses to the effects of contemporary immigration policy and practice. In Katz's schema, contour lines "simultaneously retain the distinctiveness of a particular place, marking not elevation but rather a relation to a process," and enable us to imagine and perhaps materialize "a potential terrain of translocal politics."[6] Thus, the second half of the chapter develops a countertopography that points to some of the ways migrant support organizations have had to respond to harsh rhetoric and policies, and identifies emergent practices and possibilities for advocacy and activism amid illusory hope and actual austerity within immigration and migrant support arenas. The chapter concludes with a brief consideration of the significance of countertopography for critical understanding and action around immigration in the age of punishment. Before turning attention to the political campaign rhetoric of Obama and Cameron, the next section presents a brief overview of countertopography as a key concept that frames the approach and analysis presented in this chapter.

COUNTERTOPOGRAPHY: AN OVERVIEW

Critical geographer Cindi Katz's project on countertopography invites scholars to develop detailed analyses of particular places and social relations in order to apprehend, connect, and facilitate strategic responses to global processes—such as capitalism—across different locations and groups. The concept draws on Marxist and feminist analyses and critically engages knowledge production and tools in geography, most notably topography, which, Katz observes, has been deployed in deeply detrimental ways to facilitate the exploits of global capitalism.[7]

The figurative, conceptual, and political appeal of countertopography resonates broadly. As a result, the project has been taken up in various disciplines, including literature, feminist studies, and critical social science.[8] It has also been used within a range of research settings, such as discussions of gender and transnationalism, explorations of social movements in South America, and the development of critical methodologies for examining the intersections between research and activism in geography.[9]

The task of developing a countertopography involves using research and strategy-building tools in "non-innocent" ways in a manner that might work toward unsettling the exploitative practices to which topographical analyses have been put.[10] As such, contour lines are not simply invoked as metaphor; instead, according to Katz, they offer a way to connect distinct sites and groups to overlapping processes without erasing the "situatedness" of a given place or position. Tracing connections as well as differences becomes a way to identify the "contours of com mon struggles" and thus to develop effective responses to the detrimental effects of processes and practices, such as increasingly punitive immigration policies.[11]

A TOPOGRAPHY OF IMMIGRATION POLICY UNDER BARACK OBAMA AND DAVID CAMERON

This section focuses on the rhetoric on immigration from political leaders Barack Obama and David Cameron between 2010 and 2012—a period that overlapped the aforementioned research project on which this chapter draws. This period coincides with Obama's reelection campaign for U.S. president (and subsequent win in 2012) and Cameron's election as UK prime minister with a coalition government in 2010. I then provide a brief account of immigration initiatives introduced and implemented under both leaders in an effort to present a topography of their respective immigration policies and to highlight their characters.

At the time of writing this chapter, both political leaders had stepped down— Obama's term ended in 2016, and Cameron resigned in the wake of the outcome of the UK referendum on European Union (EU) membership—in the midst of increasingly open hostility toward immigrants and an implementation of policies not only explicitly exclusionary but also punitive. Both the newly installed Trump administration in the United States and the United Kingdom's conservative government under Prime Minister Theresa May have made it clear that their approaches to immigration will be equally, if not more, unforgiving. Since their inauguration as political leaders, Trump and May have instituted immigration control measures that elicit anxiety and fear within migrant communities. Immigrant exclusion, excision, and banishment are promulgated as necessary for a productive economy and secure society and couched in claims about "making America great again" or "taking back control."[12] Current events are not the primary focus here; nonetheless, given this chapter's attention to topography and countertopography and to contour lines that may extend *temporally* as well as spatially, the ensuing discussion may prove useful for identifying continuities between the period of austerity and fear considered in this chapter and the calamitous and increasingly hostile social and political climate for immigrants that is presently unfolding.

At first glance, Barack Obama and David Cameron might appear to be odd bedfellows. This is partly because as a Democrat, Obama's political views, at least ideologically, were distinct from those of David Cameron. As leader of the conservative Tory Party, Cameron was a champion of small government, tax cuts, and "the Big Society" in ways that more closely align his ideology with that of the Republican Party in the United States.

As candidates for election—Obama in 2008 and again in 2012, and Cameron in 2010—their stances on immigration also appeared to be quite distinct. Ostensibly aligning his sympathies with immigrants in 2008, Obama gave immigrants and those who advocate on their behalf hope by pronouncing, "The system isn't working when . . . communities are terrorized by ICE [Immigration and Customs Enforcement] immigration raids—when nursing mothers are torn from their babies, when children come home from school to find their parents missing, when people are detained without access to legal counsel. . . . [And] when the system isn't working, people who love this country can come together to change it."[13]

As part of his first-term election platform, Obama promised to make immigration reform a top priority. But as described in the pages that follow, his accomplishments in this area were quite abysmal. Thus, on the campaign trail in 2012, Obama once again promised comprehensive immigration reform. A week after being sworn in as president of the United States for a second term, Obama observed, "A call for action can now be heard coming from all across the country. [And so] the time has come for commonsense comprehensive immigration reform."[14] Before outlining his four-point framework for immigration reform, he proclaimed, "The time is now, now's the time," repeating "now's the time" again and again—indeed, four times over—presumably to assert and reassure those for whom this had been a jaded promise that he would deliver immigration reform during his second term in office.[15]

In contrast to this, in the United Kingdom, with the run-up to his election in 2010, David Cameron demonstrated little empathy for immigrants. Instead, laying out the Conservative Party's election manifesto in April 2010, Cameron made the matter-of-fact observation: "Immigration [in the United Kingdom] today is too high and needs to be reduced. We don't need to attract people to do jobs that could be carried out by British citizens, given the right training and support."[16] This scathing, unsympathetic tone continued once Cameron was elected prime minister and in the face of the largest wave of net migration the country had ever seen.[17] In his 2011 immigration speech, Cameron reiterated that "for too long, immigration has been too high."[18] He went on to say, "I remember when immigration wasn't a central political issue in our country—and I want that to be the case again."[19] In general, then, from his election in 2010 onward, Cameron's stance on immigration consistently emphasized crackdowns and cutbacks in keeping with the conservative mantra of lean(er) government, apparent efficiency, and austerity.

Despite the fact that the tone of their rhetoric differed, as elected officials, both Obama and Cameron orchestrated and presided over greatly expanded and increasingly harsh immigration enforcement policies. Like his Republican predecessor, during his first term in office President Obama's administration instituted striking increases in immigration enforcement expenditures. The 2011 immigration enforcement budget was over $17 billion; this represented a figure (adjusted for inflation) fifteen times greater than 1986 spending on immigration enforcement and 24 percent higher than spending allocated to all other federal criminal law enforcement agencies.[20] Obama also oversaw massive expansion of border patrol personnel, with 2012 staffing levels increasing roughly 40 percent over 2007 levels to 21,370 personnel, such that by its own admission, the border patrol became "better staffed than at any time in its history."[21] Giving the lie to Obama's message of hope, his first-term legacy also included the highest annual rate of immigration detention on record, with over 400,000 individuals detained in 2011 alone and 1.5 million people deported between 2009 and 2011.[22] The implementation of programs such as Secure Communities as well as the replacement of workplace raids with what have been described as "stealth, 'silent' audits of employer documents" made it clear—thanks in good measure to the Obama administration—that by 2012, the United States had "built a formidable immigration enforcement machinery."[23]

There were a number of more forceful moves toward immigration reform during Obama's second term; nonetheless, the president's legacy on immigration is perhaps best characterized as one mired in aspiration and hope rather than the actual realization of promises. For instance, in the wake of several failed efforts to pass legislation under the DREAM Act, Obama introduced Deferred Action for Childhood Arrivals (DACA) as an executive order in June 2012.[24] While this program has given a substantial number of younger undocumented immigrants reprieve from the possibility of deportation, it does not provide a pathway to citizenship, and whatever hope DACA offered was dashed by the Trump administration's decision to terminate the program in September 2017. After attempts to pass a bipartisan-crafted immigration reform bill failed in the House of Representatives (after succeeding in the Senate), Obama issued another executive order—Deferred Action for Parents of Americans and Lawful Permanent Residents (DAPA)—in November 2014.[25] This program would have granted work authorization and temporary protections against deportation to parents with a child who was a U.S. citizen or legal resident.[26] However, the initiative was immediately challenged by a number of states and subsequently taken up by the Supreme Court. A June 2016 split decision by the judges on the court meant that the promise of security for undocumented immigrants was stymied yet again, and any further positive action for immigrants while Obama was in office became untenable.[27]

To be clear, the lack of progress on immigration issues was, in large measure, the work of conservatives, including the Supreme Court, with the broader conservative community's embrace of Donald Trump's immigration agenda as further testament to this approach. During his presidency, Obama repeatedly tried to actualize reforms that might benefit immigrants—at least in the short term. Yet many of the reforms Obama proposed would not have offered a panacea for undocumented immigrants in the United States. Neither DACA nor DAPA conferred any additional rights beyond temporary protection from deportation to noncitizens, and neither program offers a pathway to citizenship.[28] Immigration and Customs Enforcement (ICE) officials emboldened by the new administration are also detaining record numbers of young people with DACA status.[29] As an additional indication of Obama's ambivalence on immigration, his proposals for immigration reform prioritized and strengthened border control and workplace enforcement measures, and promised to make attainment of legal immigration status easier for only the "best and the brightest around the world," while undocumented residents would be expected to "go to the back of the line behind all those who apply legally."[30] In effect, then, reforms proposed and instituted during Obama's presidency were far from radical and, indeed, quite closely resembled the initiatives instituted by the United Kingdom's Conservative Party leader, David Cameron.

Consistent with his preelection promises, David Cameron's record is marked by extensions of punitive policy and enforcement that resound President Obama's, albeit on a smaller scale. While the number of people deported from the United Kingdom declined between 2010 and 2012 (60,244 in 2010; 53,961 in 2012), the number of individuals detained in the United Kingdom increased by almost 11 percent, with an annual detention rate of 28,905 people. By 2013, the annual detention rate had increased 16 percent over 2010 figures to 30,423 people.[31] Perhaps more telling than these numbers are the changes to immigration rules enacted by law while David Cameron was in power. Cameron's goal of making immigration a political nonissue focused on curtailing the number of migrants entering the United Kingdom until that number reaches pre-1990 levels. Before the uncertainty and open hostility toward EU migrants unleashed by the United Kingdom's Brexit referendum in June 2016, a series of policies as well as two immigration bills were passed in Parliament that instituted significant limitations on certain migrants' rights and severe penalties for "unlawful" presence in the United Kingdom.

For instance, since April 2012, migrants entering the country on domestic worker visas are no longer eligible to apply for permanent residency, which, in effect, rules out permanent settlement for an entire category of migrants. Like Obama's immigration reform proposals, Cameron's policies tended to prioritize immigration by "high value" migrants, such as "graduate entrepreneurs" and "exceptionally talented" individuals. However, even before the aforementioned referendum on EU membership, the number of skilled workers permitted entry into the United Kingdom had become increasingly constrained. The Immigration Act 2014 introduced restrictions on accessing health care, made it illegal for private landlords to rent property to tenants who cannot produce proof of their legal right to reside in Britain, and introduced the "deprivation of UK citizenship" for migrants with leave to remain, where the possibility of third country settlement exists.[32] More recently, Immigration Act 2016 was enacted.[33] This set of laws further extends draconian enforcement measures by allowing authorities to freeze bank accounts for individuals without a documented right to reside in the country. Though recently ruled unlawful by the UK's Supreme Court, the law also eliminated the possibility for migrants to appeal a decision related to their immigration status by implementing a "deport first, appeal later" policy for migrants whose applications to remain have been judged unsuccessful in immigration court.[34] In the end, Cameron did not achieve his goal of reducing immigration to the United Kingdom to "tens of thousands rather than hundreds of thousands," with net migration increasing annually since 2012.[35] Nonetheless, the impact of the Brexit vote remains to be seen, and Cameron's legacy is one that includes making day-to-day survival for migrants as well as those who advocate for them increasingly austere.[36]

On closer inspection, or through a brief topography of the rhetoric and policies enacted and presided over under Obama's Democratic administration and Cameron's Conservative government, it is clear that Obama and Cameron shared common ground in advancing immigration policies imbued with punitive ideology and practice. Furthermore, in keeping with topography's traditional use, the initiatives instituted by each leader's government illuminate a carefully planned and securitized approach to immigration policy intended to deter, marginalize, and excise migrants in exacting and comprehensive ways that almost resemble military operations.

A STUDY OF MIGRANT SUPPORT ORGANIZATION RESPONSES

Having presented an account that indicates some of the ways U.S. and UK immigration policies resonate, the remainder of the chapter examines how migrant support organizations in both settings responded to the resulting climate, which might be characterized as deferred (if not defunct) hope as well as ever-increasing austerity and castigation of migrants. The discussion that follows draws on evidence from a cross-national empirical study that posed the overarching question: How do migrant support organizations that seek to counter or oppose the effects of harsh immigration policies grapple with the punitive political, economic, and social climate they confront?[37] While there is a good deal of media and scholarly attention given to migrants' experiences, much less is known about the impact of ongoing economic and sociopolitical forces for migrant support organizations; given the paucity of research in this area, a countertopography of organizational responses is significant.

The research, which was conducted between 2010 and 2012, does not encompass the entirety of President Obama's or Prime Minister Cameron's periods of office, nor was the project explicitly focused on how migrant support groups responded to their policies specifically. Instead, with an interest in and concerns about possibilities for countering the carceral climate that imbues immigration in both the United States and the United Kingdom of late, the project sought to examine whether and how such practices develop in light of a generally unfavorable climate toward migrants as well as the impact of these challenging times for migrant support organizations' work.[38]

Methodologically, the project involved participation by migrant support organizations in the United States and the United Kingdom, with groups involved in various forms of support, such as welfare and social support and legal assistance, as well as volunteer-run detention visitor programs and advocacy groups geared toward specific populations, such as children and women. An initial focus on organizations that support asylum seekers quickly broadened to include groups that work with destitute asylum seekers who have exhausted all legal channels associated with the right to remain in the United Kingdom, as well as undocumented, irregular, and detained migrants who are variously classified in both the United States and the United Kingdom. As such, the sample was inclusive and reflects a countertopographical approach with its emphasis on continuities despite differences. Groups also varied in terms of size, motivation for their work, and scale of operations. Interestingly, few organizations had either formal or informal ties with migrant support groups in other countries; this further hints at the potential value of an analysis such as this, which attempts to identify points of commonality in cross-national settings.

A total of fifty-four organizations completed an online survey that included a series of open-ended questions inviting respondents to give an outline of (1) organizational successes, (2) challenges faced by the group, (3) the organization's resource and knowledge needs, and (4) how restrictive immigration policy and legislative changes were impacting the group's work.[39] This was followed by an in-depth interview with representatives from thirty-five organizations that had completed the survey, as well as three focus groups with members of a range of support groups, some of whom had not completed the initial survey. Responses to the questions related to challenges faced and impacts of policy changes are the focus of discussion in the following section.

RESPONSES TO HOPE AND AUSTERITY: A COUNTERTOPOGRAPHY

A countertopography provides an account of processes and policies while considering their effects. Thus, this section identifies some of the points of connection—or contour lines—that link differently situated organizations in relation to the impact of and responses to the processes of austerity and migrant marginalization associated with the governments overseen by Cameron and Obama. The section outlines two of the most commonly identified and interrelated challenges that migrant support groups reported, then highlights some of the ways they responded. In this process, and also consistent with countertopography, the discussion attempts to indicate the specificity of responses while emphasizing continuities and resonances across distinct organizations and in UK-U.S. contexts.

The top two challenges respondents identified were a lack of funding and disconnectedness across the migrant support sector. A lack of funds is, of course, not unique to migrant support organizations, nor is it a surprise during periods of austerity. Indeed, there is little new about this observation, as indicated in the responses of several U.S.-based groups. Some participants noted that "funding challenges in the midst of the economic downturn" had worsened, and one legal service provider elaborated:[40]

Honest to God it's gotten worse. I don't know what to say. I mean, I started this office with my own money. I worked without a salary for two years, and we've been able to keep it going because I've been doing a lot of the litigation and I'm the director and I do all the bookkeeping and finances and fund raising and not very well. And . . . I'm 67 years old, I can't keep doing it at this rate and it's harder now than when I started.[41]

Other participants took the situation as a given, noting, "There is always such little funding available for immigration work."[42] While it was also the top challenge for organizations in the United Kingdom, funding losses were more recent there and thus were possibly felt to be more pressing than for U.S.-based groups. As one UK group noted, "The economic climate—public sector cuts will impact on government funding and subsequently us; [it has the] potential to harden people's attitudes and make them less supportive, including financially."[43] This can also be explained, in part, by the United Kingdom's history of state support for welfare and social programs, which has been slowly but certainly dismantled over a generation, as indicated in another UK-based group's response: "A significant proportion of our funding comes from government sources[,] and the operational side is about to be severely cut back with huge implications for our clients."[44]

This challenge affected support groups in a variety of ways. Some groups had to reduce services or institute staff cutbacks—responses that some felt had further damaging effects for migrants. For others, funding cuts meant an increasing reliance on volunteers. The experiences and challenges that disconnectedness engenders are similarly common to a broad range of nonprofit organizations, with many groups noting a sense of isolation from other groups doing similar work. Where connections did exist, they tended to be time limited or "issue specific"; in addition, connections with other groups tended to be at the regional or national level, with much more limited interaction at the local level or among different scales. Groups reported that being disconnected affected timely access to information and resources as well as the ability to provide services, among other things. Of particular significance vis-à-vis this finding was how groups responded to funding cuts, with many groups forging alliances with other organizations in an effort to rally against the impact of limited funding.

Common responses to lack of funding included paring down the organization's core mission and eliminating services that were not consistent with it. Another response involved becoming more entrepreneurial—for instance, by engaging in microenterprises that draw on the skills and resources of migrants who access support-organization services. These responses might be understood as having neoliberal effects in the sense that they shrink or roll back services and responsibilize those who are in need in troubling ways.

Yet another response involved turning inward, or becoming more self-reflective, and in this process, organizations also found ways to address their second challenge: the issue of being disconnected. Thus, when groups "faced themselves" and their funding situation, a strategic and practical response was to interact more with other migrant organizations in order to plug gaps and to help each other stay afloat. Examples included partnering with other groups on funding bids, looking to other organizations for services they can no longer afford to provide, and forming alliances with law schools to increase pro bono legal assistance. Walter Nicholls describes such alliances as "inter-activist" strategies that permit migrant support organizations to amplify their work.[45] Nicholls notes that when "activists combine resources derived from different networks [they] create potentially powerful synergies. [They] also develop creativity and know-how in stitching together networks and resources to maximize their amplification effects."[46]

Consistent with this, several interview participants tended to characterize the challenges and networking responses their organization had developed as opportunities rather than a sign of defeat. In other words, if punitive policies and harsh times have molded migrant support groups into self-aware and self-responsible actors, they also appear to have augmented support organizations' capacity to act by forcing them to "inter-act" and forge alliances.

Another finding highlights how inter-activism functions to support oppositional politics among migrant advocacy groups, the character of which has changed in the contemporary era. This was particularly notable in the United States in response to a question that asked whether (and if so, how) changes to immigration law and policies affected organizations' work.[47] First, participants' responses made it very clear that enforcement-focused policies have had a very damaging effect on immigrants. For instance, one respondent observed that "programs like Secure Communities have had a chilling effect, people are really scared,"[48] and others indicated "more reports of discrimination. There is increased fear and distrust of authorities."[49]

In their work, too, groups noted that already limited resources were being diverted to defensive advocacy and organizing instead of to developing proactive advocacy positions, which were deemed to be more feasible when attitudes toward migrants were more positive. As one group noted, "It sets us back, meaning we have to advocate for more basic rights and look for ways to overcome additional obstacles. . . . The attitudes of funders and partners have been diverted as a result."[50] This was echoed in another response: "We have had to shift from an affirmative mode of advocacy to a defensive mode. Rather than having the luxury of focusing on the passage of good legislative changes, we have to posture ourselves defensively."[51]

At the same time, however, as organizations have reacted by adopting protective and defensive advocacy stances, the current climate has served to galvanize the responses of increasingly aligned yet distinct groups in noteworthy ways. This can be illustrated by examining groups' responses to a survey question asking about "views about government." Without doubt this question oversimplifies the complexity of relationships between migrant support organizations and political power, as some respondents pointed out. Nonetheless, in the context of this chapter, the responses are significant for revealing a connection between inter-activism as a practical response and countertopography as a political project and thus may be relevant to understanding possibilities for social and political change in the current climate.

While groups in the United Kingdom were more likely than those in the United States to articulate an explicitly oppositional stance, the majority of re-spondents in both settings generally aligned themselves with the state, noting that they sought out opportunities to cooperate or reform government rather than resist or oppose those in positions of power. This finding may seem surprising, es-pecially in light of the harsh rhetoric, punitive climate, and policies that demand defensive advocacy. Indeed, it might be tempting to suggest that the migrant sup-port sector as a whole has been defeated by austerity and false hope. Yet on closer inspection, these views of government are consistent with an inter-activist position, in which working together or in alignment with others can serve to amplify efforts toward social and political change. In fact, a number of groups noted the impor-tance of this approach to achieving goals, including policy change; for example, one group explained:

> It's hard for our organization to see what it looks like on the ground. But we also have much more of an inside voice and recognition with the federal government, and so we're able to advocate. Then the local organizations . . . have such great information and experience because they're working closely with . . . the impacted population. [We] recognize where I sit versus where the people on the ground sit and recognize the strengths and barriers to both these positions.[52]

Thus, working with one another *and* with those in political power—even in a harsh social and political climate—was understood to be conducive, and perhaps necessary, to success.

As a framework for understanding contemporary political possibilities, coun-tertopography is instructive here also. As previously noted, in addition to detailed description, a countertopography is intended as a means of facilitating and ad-vancing effective responses to egregious processes and their effects. In her ana-lysis, Katz urges caution against seeing or celebrating every "autonomous act [as] an instance of resistance."[53] In place of this, Katz provides a nuanced typol-ogy that delineates different shades of practices that respond to or counter the damaging effects of punitive policies and processes. These include resilience, reworking, and resistance. While Katz reserves resistance for responses by indi-viduals or groups that actively redress imbalances of power or resources, resil-ience describes "material and spiritual survival [as well as the] recuperation of dignity," and reworking refers to "pragmatic responses" in the face of inequity that may involve "recalibrat[ing] power relations or . . . redirecting and in some cases reconstituting available resources."[54]

Within this framework, the inter-activist responses to harsh immigration policies that migrant support organizations describe can be understood as acts of resilience and reworking. Working together is a pragmatic act of resilience that enables migrant support groups to survive in these austere times, while working with government rather than in opposition to those in power can serve to "undermine inequities on the very grounds on which they are cast."[55] In doing so, groups can amplify one another's work while "retooling themselves as political subjects and social actors."[56] With this, it is possible to see that migrant support organizations are not defeated or doomed in the face of increasingly harsh conditions. Instead, what has emerged as a necessary and effective counterresponse to the current climate are inter-activist approaches that—while perhaps more muted than the prevailing rhetoric and discourse on migration—are savvy, reflexive, and "non-innocent."

This chapter has provided an account—a topography—that compared and contrasted the rhetoric and policies on immigration associated with governments overseen by President Obama in the United States and Prime Minister Cameron in the United Kingdom. In addition to highlighting distinctive preelection positions, the chapter has described commonalities between the United States and the United Kingdom in implementing harsh and increasingly punitive immigration policies that have had disturbing impacts for immigrants as well as migrant support organizations in both settings. Using countertopography as a framework for identifying both distinctive and common responses to these immigration policies, the chapter has identified the importance of inter-activism as a strategic and political response to said policies. A vital element of countertopography involves identifying connections in an effort to imagine potential collective responses that materialize political alternatives and realize social change.

At the time of writing the first draft of this chapter, 52 percent of voters in England had just recently chosen to end that country's membership in the European Union after more than forty years and a project that in theory had held the promise of recognition if not unity among differently situated groups in European society.[57] The aftermath and consequences of this vote are still being debated, and much remains unclear. It has, however, unleashed waves of open hostility, with reports of racist attacks on ethnic minorities who are assumed to be migrants spiking in the weeks after the referendum, and hate crimes now reported to occur regularly.[58] Meanwhile, in the United States, Donald Trump became the Republican candidate in the 2016 election for president and is now installed in that role on the back of a campaign that promised to "build a wall" to stop migrants—particularly Mexicans—from entering the United States and that plans to "ban Muslims" from the country, among other vitriolic, anti-immigrant proposals.[59] Trump's first months in office demonstrate that he hopes to realize this agenda, as he implements a seemingly hapless yet strategic program of immigration enforcement that could aptly be characterized as warfare against immigrants. With these developments, the United States and the United Kingdom appear to be on a common trajectory, where already unforgiving policies are becoming ever more punishing. The snapshot empirical study of migrant support organizations discussed in this chapter indicates that immigration policy in recent years has produced distinctive and disturbing effects. Coinciding with these punitive immigration policies, migrant support organizations have formed strategic inter-activist alliances both within the sector and defensively in relation to the state. Even more recently, in response to Donald Trump's executive orders and Theresa May's equivocations on the future status of EU migrants in England, there are a growing number of alliances among distal and disparate groups. This is evidenced, for example, by the recent surge in contributions to organizations such as the American Civil Liberties Union, as well as by national and international solidarity marches and activism, such as One Day Without Us.[60] With this, migrant support organizations and allies have begun to identify contour lines that are "the terrain of a trans-local [and trans-institutional] politics."[61] As the age of punitive immigration policy deepens in the United States and the UK, facilitating and materializing a countertopographic response is increasingly urgent. Perhaps, then, former president Obama's 2012 campaign message has renewed meaning and prescience; for migrant support groups and the possibility that a countertopography of austerity and hope engenders, "the time is, indeed, now."[62]

NOTES TO CHAPTER 3

The author wishes to acknowledge research participants, as well as colleagues Nick Gill, Imogen Tyler, and Ceri Oeppen, who were collaborators on an ESRC-funded project from which this chapter draws, "Making Asylum Seekers Legible and Visible: An Analysis of the Dilemmas and Mitigating Strategies of Asylum Advocacy in the UK and US" (RES-000-22-3928-A). Thanks also to Philip Kretsedemas and David Brotherton for their patience and editorial guidance on this chapter.

1. Linda Carroli, "Fieldworking: Defining Terms," *Placeblog*, October 14, 2012, https://placing.wordpress.com/2012/10/14/fieldworking-defining-terms/.

2. Ibid.

3. See Deirdre Conlon and Nancy Hiemstra, "Examining the Everyday Micro-Economies of Migrant Detention in the United States," *Geographica Helvetica* 69

(2014): 335–344; Roxanne Doty and Elizabeth Wheatley, "Private Detention and the Immigration Industrial Complex," *International Political Sociology* 7 (2013): 426–443; Tanya Golash-Boza, "The Immigration Industrial Complex: Why We Enforce Immigration Policies Destined to Fail," *Sociology Compass* 3, no. 2 (2009): 295–309.

4. Cindi Katz, "On the Grounds of Globalization: A Topography of Feminist Political Engagement," *Signs: Journal of Women in Culture and Society* 26, no. 4 (2001): 1213–1234.

5. Ibid.; see also Cindi Katz, "Vagabond Capitalism and the Necessity of Social Reproduction," *Antipode* 33, no. 4 (2001): 708–727; Geraldine Pratt and Brenda Yeoh, "Transnational (Counter)topographies," *Gender, Place and Culture* 10, no. 2 (2003): 159–166; Deirdre Conlon, "A Countertopography of Migrant Experience in Ireland and Beyond," in *Migrations: Ireland in a Global World*, ed. Mary Gilmartin and Allen White (Manchester: Manchester University Press, 2013), 183–198.

6. Katz, "Vagabond Capitalism," 722.

7. Katz, "On the Grounds of Globalization."

8. Pratt and Yeoh, "Transnational (Counter)topographies"; Conlon, "Countertopography of Migrant Experience."

9. See Sara Koopman, "Cutting Through Topologies: Crossing Lines at the School of the Americas," *Antipode* 40, no. 5 (2008): 825–847; Melissa Wright, "Gender and Geography: Knowledge and Activism Across the Intimately Global," *Progress in Human Geography* 33, no. 3 (2008): 379–386.

10. Katz, "On the Grounds of Globalization," 1215.

11. Katz, "Vagabond Capitalism," 722.

12. Donald Trump, https://www.donaldjtrump.com/; Boris Johnson, "The Only Way to Take Back Control of Immigration Is to Vote Leave on 23 June," Statement on Immigration Statistics, May 26, 2016, http://www.voteleavetakecontrol.org/boris_johnson_the_only_way_to_take_back_control_of_immigration_is_to_vote_leave_on_23_june.html.

13. Barack Obama, "Remarks at the 2008 National Council of La Raza Annual Meeting," The American Presidency Project, July 13, 2008, http://www.presidency.ucsb.edu/ws/?pid=77652.

14. Barack Obama, "Remarks at Del Sol High School," The American Presidency Project, January 29, 2013, http://www.presidency.ucsb.edu/ws/index.php?pid=103194&st=&st1.

15. Ibid.

16. David Cameron, *Invitation to Join the Government of Britain: The Conservative Manifesto 2010*, April 2010, http://conservativehome.blogs.com/files/conservative-manifesto-2010.pdf, 21.

17. For the period between 1997 and 2009, net migration in the United Kingdom was 2.2 million people.

18. BBC News, "In Full: David Cameron Immigration Speech," April 14, 2011, http://www.bbc.co.uk/news/uk-politics-13083781.

19. Ibid.

20. Doris Meissner, Donald Kerwin, Muzaffar Chisti, and Claire Berger, *Immigration Enforcement in the United States: The Rise of a Formidable Machinery* (Washington,

D.C.: Migration Policy Institute, 2013). The federal agencies concerned are the FBI, DEA, Secret Service, U.S. Marshals Service, and ATF.

21. U.S. Department of Homeland Security, "FY 2011 Budget in Brief," https://www .dhs.gov/publication/dhs-budget, 9.

22. The number of individuals detained in 2011 was 429,247, and the average daily population of immigration detainees was 33,330. See Meissner et al., *Immigration Enforcement in the United States.* The United States deported 396,906 people in 2011 and 410,000 in 2012; this represented the largest number of deportations in U.S. history. See Corey Dade, "Obama's Deportation Policies Have Failed, Immigrant Advocates Say," NPR, June 11, 2012, http://www.npr.org/sections/itsallpolitics/2012/06/11/154782404 /immigrant-advocates-obamas-deportation-policy-a-failure. See also Meissner et al., *Immigration Enforcement in the United States.*

23. Secure Communities was implemented from 2008 to 2015 and involved sharing information related to an individual's criminal history and immigration status between different levels of law enforcement agencies. The program was subject to significant criticism in association with its negative impact on police-community relations, and several states refused to participate in it. In 2015, Secure Communities was scrapped in favor of a program with an apparently more targeted focus on high-level "priority" offenses as a basis for detention and deportation. See Wendy Feliz, "DHS Faces Challenges as It Rolls Out the Priority Enforcement Program," Immigration Impact, August 4, 2015, http://immigrationimpact.com/2015/08/05/priority-enforcement -program-launch/; Bonnie Stern Wasser, "ICE to Establish I-9 Center and Increase Employer Audits," *Seattle Immigration Lawyer Blog*, January 20, 2011, http://www.seat tleimmigrationlawyerblog.com/2011/01/ice-to-establish-i-9-center-an.html. See also Miriam Jordan, "Crackdown on Illegal Workers Grows," *Wall Street Journal*, January 20, 2011, https://www.wsj.com/articles/SB10001424052748703951704576092381196958362; Meissner et al., *Immigration Enforcement in the United States*, 12.

24. Development, Relief, and Education for Alien Minors (DREAM Act), S. 1291, 107th Cong. (2001), www.dreamact2009.org; Department of Homeland Security, USCIS, "Consideration of Deferred Action for Childhood Arrivals (DACA), June 15, 2012, https://www.uscis.gov/humanitarian/consideration-deferred-action-childhood -arrivals-daca.

25. Kathleen Hennessey, "Obama Legacy: Immigration Stands as Most Glaring Failure," Associated Press, June 30, 2016, http://bigstory.ap.org/article/db6bf66811a540569 47ff3cd92690faa/obama-legacy-immigration.

26. Randy Capps, Heather Koball, James D. Bachmeier, Ariel G. Ruiz Soto, Jie Zong, and Julia Gelatt, "Deferred Action for Unauthorized Immigrant Parents: Analysis of DAPA's Potential Effects on Families and Children," Migration Policy Institute, February 2016, www.migrationpolicy.org/research/deferred-action-unauthorized-immigrant -parents-analysis-dapas-potential-effects-families.

27. See Sylvia Longmire, "What the Supreme Court's Split Decision on DAPA/ DACA Means for Immigrants," Homeland Security, June 28, 2016, www.inhomelandse curity.com/what-the-supreme-courts-split-decision-on-dapadaca-means-for-immigrants/.

28. Hannah Fordyce, "DACA and DAPA: The Downsides," *Journal of Gender, Race and Justice* 18 (2015), https://jgrj.law.uiowa.edu/article/daca-and-dapa-downsides.

29. Oliver Laughland, "Dreamer Detained by Ice Agents While in Process of DACA Status Renewal," *The Guardian*, March 1, 2017, https://www.theguardian.com/us-news/2017/mar/01/dreamer-detained-ice-agents-daca-immigration-status.

30. Barack Obama, "Remarks at the 2008 National Council of La Raza Annual Meeting."

31. United Kingdom Home Office, *Home Office Immigration Statistics—Users Guide*, May 23, 2013, https://www.gov.uk/government/publications/user-guide-to-home-office-immigration-statistics—9; Jerome Phelps et al., "The State of Detention: Immigration Detention in the UK in 2014," Detention Action, October 2014, http://detentionaction.org.uk/wordpress/wp-content/uploads/2014/10/The.State_.of_.Detention.pdf.

32. See Immigration Act 2014, www.legislation.gov.uk/ukpga/2014/22/enacted; Ruth Grove-White, "What You Need to Know About the Immigration Bill," Migrant Rights Network, May 14, 2014, www.migrantrights.org.uk.

33. See Immigration Act 2016, http://www.legislation.gov.uk/ukpga/2016/19/contents/enacted.

34. Sian Lea, "The Immigration Act 2016 in Plain English," *Human Rights News, Views, and Info*, May 31, 2016, http://rightsinfo.org/immigration-act-2016-plain-english.

35. BBC News, "In Full: David Cameron Immigration Speech."

36. These measures augment already punitive initiatives in which migration activists are increasingly subject to prosecution for providing support. See Liz Fekete, "Europe: Crimes of Solidarity," *Race and Class* 50, no. 4 (2009): 83–97.

37. Nick Gill, Imogen Tyler, and Deirdre Conlon, "Making Asylum Seekers Legible and Visible: An Analysis of the Dilemmas and Mitigating Strategies of Asylum Advocacy in the UK and US," May 2012, ESRC reference number: RES-000-22-3928-A.

38. See Nick Gill, Deirdre Conlon, Dominique Moran, and Andrew Burridge, "Carceral Circuitry: New Directions in Carceral Geography," *Progress in Human Geography* (forthcoming), 1–22, doi:10.1177/0309132516671823.

39. Fifty-three percent of respondents were based in the United States, 47 percent in the United Kingdom. For a more detailed account of the study, see Nick Gill, Deirdre Conlon, Ceri Oeppen, and Imogen Tyler, *Networks of Asylum Support in the UK and USA: A Handbook of Ideas, Strategies and Best Practice for Asylum Support Groups in a Challenging Social and Economic Climate*, 2012, https://steedee.files.wordpress.com/2012/03/networks-of-asylum-support-print2.pdf. See also Nick Gill, Deirdre Conlon, Imogen Tyler, and Ceri Oeppen, "The Tactics of Asylum and Irregular Migrant Support Groups: Disrupting Bodily, Technological, and Neoliberal Strategies of Control," *Annals of the Association of American Geographers* 104, no. 2 (2014): 373–381.

40. 71US (survey response). To protect anonymity, responses were coded: numbers refer to unique respondents and letters to a respondent's geographic location (i.e., United States or United Kingdom).

41. 5US (interview June 1, 2011).

42. 10US (interview June 27, 2011).

43. 10UK (interview June 28, 2011).

44. 1UK (interview June 14, 2011).

45. Walter Nicholls, "Policing Immigrants as Politicizing Immigration: The Paradox of Border Enforcement," *ACME: An International E-Journal for Critical Geographies* 14, no. 2 (2015): 512–521.

46. Ibid., 517.

47. In the United States, state-level policies include SB-1070, which was instituted in Arizona. Federal policies include 287(g) agreements (initiated with the Immigration and Nationality Act in 1996 but implemented on a comparatively small scale until after September 11, 2001), and Secure Communities, which was in place from 2008 to 2015. In response to intense criticism and refusals to participate, Secure Communities was replaced with the Priority Enforcement Program. For discussion, see Feliz, "DHS Faces Challenges." In the United Kingdom, indicative examples include those discussed on page 6 of Feliz's report.

48. 1US (survey response).

49. 10US.

50. 40US (interview June 22, 2011).

51. 118US (interview July 28, 2011).

52. 40US, see note 60.

53. Cindi Katz, *Growing Up Global: Economic Restructuring and Children's Everyday Lives,* (Minneapolis: University of Minnesota Press, 2004), 241.

54. Ibid., 246, 247.

55. Ibid.

56. Ibid.

57. "EU Referendum: Full Results and Analysis," *The Guardian,* June 23, 2016, http://www.theguardian.com/politics/ng-interactive/2016/jun/23/eu-referendum-live -results-and-analysis.

58. Kate Lyons, "Racist Incidents Feared to Be Linked to Brexit Result," *The Guardian,* June 26, 2016, http://www.theguardian.com/politics/2016/jun/26/racist-incidents -feared-to-be-linked-to-brexit-result-reported-in-england-and-wales; Tom Batchelor, "Brexit: Hate Crimes Could Soar Once Article 50 Is Triggered, Police and Community Groups Warn," *Independent,* February 11, 2017, http://www.independent.co.uk/news /uk/crime/brexit-latest-article-50-hate-crimes-police-eu-negotiations-a7574591.html.

59. Associated Press, "What Did Trump Say About Immigrants?" *Boston Globe,* June 29, 2015, https://www.bostonglobe.com/arts/television/2015/06/29/what-did-donald -trump-say-about-immigrants/ForaqpQHjwgeKRdVUdYrdM/story.html.

60. Liam Stack, "Donations to A.C.L.U. and Other Organizations Surge After Trump's Order," *New York Times,* January 30, 2017, https://www.nytimes.com/2017/01 /30/us/aclu-fund-raising-trump-travel-ban.html; http://www.1daywithoutus.org/.

61. Katz, "On the Grounds of Globalization."

62. Obama, "Remarks at Del Sol High School."

4. ORDINARY INJUSTICES

Persecution, Punishment, and the Criminalization of Asylum in Canada

GRAHAM HUDSON, RYERSON UNIVERSITY

In 2009 and 2010, approximately six hundred Sri Lankan Tamils arrived off the western coast of Canada aboard the MVs *Ocean Lady* and *Sun Sea*. Without permission to enter Canadian territory, the ships were interdicted and boarded by the Royal Canadian Mounted Police, who detained the passengers and later transferred them into the custody of the Canadian Border Services Agency (CBSA). Although the passengers were seeking asylum, the government characterized the arrivals as a serious security issue, stating that at least one-third of the passengers aboard the *Sun Sea* were "suspected human smugglers and terrorists" working to reconstitute the LTTE's "base of operations overseas in order to renew resistance to the Government of Sri Lanka."[1] These statements reflect the Canadian government's long-standing attempt to associate irregular migration with insecurity and criminality.[2]

As has happened in the past, Parliament responded to the unauthorized boat arrivals with a range of preventive and deterrent measures.[3] Between 2010 and 2013, it amended the Immigration and Refugee Protection Act (IRPA) three times, cumulatively expediting the removal of persons deemed to be inadmissible to Canada on the grounds of security and serious or organized criminality.[4] Because persons deemed inadmissible on these grounds do not have a right to claim refugee status, they may be deported to face the well-founded fear of persecution; the government need not even inquire into the existence of such a risk. In

2013, Parliament removed the right of persons declared inadmissible on grounds of security and organized crime to apply for stays of removal based on humanitarian and compassionate (H&C) grounds. H&C considerations allow persons to secure status notwithstanding formal ineligibility. They function to ensure some degree of proportionality between the conduct that disqualifies one from status and the gravity of the immigration consequences (e.g., breakup of family units).

State responses to the MVs *Ocean Lady* and *Sun Sea* are a good starting point for understanding the securitization of migration in Canada. Some of the measures truly were new to the Canadian landscape and at least conceptually related to perceived national security risks associated with irregular migration—as baseless as those perceptions often are in fact. But many of the measures, policies, and practices added to an already firm foundation that previous governments had laid down since 9/11—and even before. But despite historical trends, securitization masked a second (possibly even the primary) objective of the measures: to relieve pressure from an overburdened refugee determination system by restricting the ability of "undesirable" migrants to access justice.[5] By 2009—the year the *Ocean Lady* arrived—there was a backlog of 62,000 refugee claims. Between 2010 and 2012, the system took 21 months to produce a decision to recognize refugee status, and an average of 4.5 years to finally reject the claims of what the government started calling "bogus refugees."[6] The language of security and the timing of the irregular arrivals provided a convenient opportunity to limit access to justice to persons stigmatized, ex ante, as deceitful, dishonest, and undeserving of refugee status.

The purpose of this chapter is twofold. First, I wish to convey the extent to which Canada has deprived deserving people of the right to (claim) refugee status and protection. It has engineered a system in which scant evidence of a risk to security or of engagement in genuinely serious or organized criminality authorizes deportation to face persecution and other serious harms. In addition, the removal of H&C considerations for such persons eliminates the need to assess whether deportation may be unjust under the circumstances. In both cases, our system may be faster and cheaper, but it is fundamentally unfair. Second, I reflect on how this practice has been normalized and what place the notion of "punishment" can hold in legal and theoretical resistance to sovereign power.

Using Juliet Stumpf's notion of crimmigration as a frame of reference, I question the value of describing immigration measures and consequences as punitive. While perhaps useful in bolstering procedural protections in cases of "extreme sanction," the notion of punishment and its analogues may have the counterproductive effect of diminishing the perceived seriousness of "ordinary" immigration consequences—that is, sanctions that do not qualify as "extreme" or "grave." I present Canada's validation of deportation-to-persecution as evidence of this problem.

The chapter begins with an overview of the securitization of irregular migration in Canada, including general policies and institutional frameworks. Next, I explore the processes through which determinations of inadmissibility and the removal of alleged security risks occur. Third, I explore how the concept of punishment and its analogues inform constitutional challenges to criminalized immigration law. Here I argue that invoking protective principles germane to criminal law risks granting greater legitimacy to the faulty premise that access to constitutional rights depends on there being an ordinary immigration consequence "plus" some punitive quality—that is, extreme, grave, or irreparable harm. Coming full circle, I end with a review of how the refugee claims of passengers aboard the *Ocean Lady* and *Sun Sea* have been handled in the context of administrative law.

(IRREGULAR) MIGRATION AND SECURITY IN CANADA

Irregular migration is a nontechnical term that describes the cross-border movement of persons in the absence of authorization from originating, transit, or receiving states.[7] From the perspective of a receiving state, an irregular migrant is one who enters, remains, or engages in activity within a state without authorization. In Canada, irregular migrants include those who enter the country without prior authorization, overstay visas, engage in activities not mandated by valid permits (e.g., unauthorized work), or remain in Canada after a claim for refugee protection has been denied.[8] Related terminology includes *illegal migrant, illegalized migrant, non-status migrant, undocumented migrant,* and *refugee/migrant with precarious status.*[9]

Strictly speaking, asylum seekers fall within the above definition of irregular migration insofar as they tend to apply for refugee status after arriving in Canada without authorization. While Canada officially abides by the international rule that asylum seekers are entitled to claim refugee status, it has found ways to restrict access to fair proceedings. In 2013, the auditor general of Canada stated:

> Preventing illegal entry has been a policy priority for the Government of Canada, especially since the 11 September 2001 terrorist attacks in the United States. In 2004, the National Security Policy identified defending against illegal entry as part of Canada's core national security interests.[10]

In fact, the Canadian government considers migrant smuggling to be "a profit-driven organized crime that exploits vulnerable people, funds terrorist activities, undermines the integrity of Canada's borders and immigration system, and threatens the national security of Canada and its partners."[11] We see here a range of goals, including protecting national and international security, disrupting terrorist financing and organized crime, and solidifying state sovereignty. What is not stated here is a range of economic goals related to the efficient maintenance of the refugee status determination (RSD) system.[12] Indeed, under former prime minster Stephen Harper, the government framed discourses about asylum seekers around the language of deceit, dishonesty, and fraud in an effort to cast doubt about the veracity of many asylum claims. Parliament used this language to remove important procedures through what it called the Protecting Canada's Immigration System Act:

> Bill C-31, Protecting Canada's Immigration System Act, is part of our plan to restore integrity to our asylum system and restore Canadian's confidence in our immigration system. The bill would make Canada's refugee determination process faster and fairer and would result in faster protection for those who legitimately need refugee protection. It would also, and this is the important aspect of it, ensure faster removal of those whose claims are withdrawn, those claims that are bogus and those claims that have been rejected. Bill C-31, the protecting Canada's immigration system act, is part of our plan to restore integrity to our asylum system.[13]

This rationale stigmatizes an indefinite but sizable portion of asylum seekers as "queue jumpers" and "bogus" refugee claimants who try to bypass the system to advance their own economic interests. The twin discourses of security and fraud frame asylum seekers as persons who engage in either harmful or wrongful behavior and are therefore undeserving of the benefits of our fair system.

We should not view legislative provisions in the abstract. These changes reflect deeper shifts in policy and practice within the executive branch. A defining feature of the gradual process of criminalization and securitization of irregular migration is the division of responsibility over the border between two separate entities. Immigration, Refugees and Citizenship Canada (IRCC) is responsible for attracting migrants, processing claims, and managing settlement. Partly because irregular migrants are not formally recognized within IRPA, the IRCC does not have a prominent role in contending with irregular migration, save for a recent initiative in combating fraud and misrepresentation by intervening in hearings before the Immigration and Refugee Board of Canada (IRB).[14] Ever since 2003, border control has rested with the CBSA, which is housed within Public Safety Canada—a department that also oversees the Royal Canadian Mounted Police, Corrections Canada, and the Canadian Security Intelligence Service. The CBSA is mandated to enforce a wide range of federal statutes, including those related to border control, customs and excises, criminal law, and national security. Toward this end, it engages in a wide range of operations, including security checks, investigations, detention, and some intelligence work. The CBSA is also party to a number of domestic and international joint force networks, working closely with foreign agencies as well as local, regional, and federal police forces.

These operations are ostensibly meant to assist in the capacity of the IRCC and the IRB to make sound determinations about whether migrants and refugees are admissible to Canada. For example, front-end security screenings assist the IRB in determining whether one is eligible to claim refugee status; reasons for denial of eligibility include whether there are good reasons to believe that the claimant poses a security risk, has violated international or human rights, or is involved in serious or organized criminality.[15] A claimant's refugee determination hearing cannot proceed until the security-screening process is complete.

THRESHOLDS FOR DENIAL OF REFUGEE STATUS AND PROTECTION: SECURITY AND "SERIOUS" OR "ORGANIZED" CRIMINALITY

Canada has carefully constructed an exclusionary legal and policy framework that (1) deters persons from arriving to Canada in the first place, and (2) makes it harder to apply for and acquire refugee status from within Canada. The result has been the systematic dismantling of the right to protection from persecution, in flagrant contravention of the UN Convention Relating to the Status of Refugees (aka Convention on Refugees); there is also compelling evidence to conclude that Canada is free to deport persons to face the de facto risk of torture or similar abuse, in violation of the UN Convention Against Torture.[16] These processes unfold through a series of administrative and discretionary decisions that connect in such a way as to label persons both inadmissible to Canada and ineligible to apply for refugee status or protection.

Sections 97 and 101 of IRPA establish eligibility to claim protection as a refugee (i.e., from a well-founded fear of persecution) or as a protected person (i.e., from the substantial risk of death, torture, or cruel and unusual treatment or punishment). Normally, a successful claim under both grounds leads to the acquisition of permanent residence status and then citizenship. However, a person is ineligible to apply for refugee status if he or she has been deemed inadmissible on the grounds of security (sec. 34), violating human or international rights (sec. 35), serious criminality (sec. 36), or organized criminality (sec. 37).

Most often, determinations of inadmissibility are made by the Immigration Division of the IRB, which is an independent administrative tribunal. Inadmissibility hearings are adversarial but include relatively informal rules of evidence and procedure. Standards of proof are very low. In cases concerning security, violation of human or international rights, and organized criminality, the state need only show that there are "reasonable grounds to believe" one is inadmissible. However, the standard is a balance of probabilities when the allegation relates to serious criminality committed abroad and there is no record of conviction for the alleged offense. Section 173 of IRPA states that the IRB is not bound by any rule of evidence and may base its decision on any evidence it "considers credible or trustworthy in the circumstances." In cases concerning security, the IRB may base its decision on secret evidence submitted in the absence of the affected person and his or her lawyer if it is of the view that disclosure *could* be injurious to national security or endanger the safety of any person. Affected persons and their lawyers never see this evidence, receiving only summaries.[17]

Persons who have been found inadmissible on grounds of security, violating human or international rights, serious criminality, or organized criminality do not have a right to appeal this determination to the Immigration Appeal Division.[18] Many are also subject to indefinite detention pending final determination of their cases. The precise number of asylum seekers who are detained in Canada (as well as for how long and on what grounds) is unclear. What *is* clear is that it is happening more often, and that persons subject to admissibility hearings on the grounds of security and criminality are typically detained in federal and provincial prisons.[19] Detention in geographically remote and highly securitized institutions interferes with the right to legal counsel, as lawyers must travel to and then acquire clearance to visit their clients; strict rules on outbound phone calls from federal correctional institutions also limit solicitor-client communication. Finally, detention cuts claimants off from family, support networks, the Internet, and important documents. It is also possible that the optics of treating migrants as though they were criminals leads to negative bias among decision makers.

Once one has been found inadmissible on the grounds of security or serious or organized criminality, he or she is subject to removal. Ordinarily, persons subject to removal are entitled to a pre-removal risk assessment (PRRA), in which an immigration officer assesses whether a person is at risk of persecution (i.e., a Convention refugee) or grave human rights abuses, including torture (i.e., a person in need of protection). However, persons deemed inadmissible on the mentioned grounds may ask for a PRRA only to screen for a substantial risk of death, torture, or cruel and unusual treatment or punishment; they are not entitled to protection from persecution. Even then, persons whose PRRAs have been refused do not have a right to appeal. Although they do have a right to apply for judicial review of a negative decision, it does not have the effect of staying their removal.

To make matters worse, there are procedures in place that allow the government to knowingly deport to torture. In 2002, the Supreme Court of Canada ruled in *Suresh v. Canada* that Canada is "generally" prohibited from the practice, but it may deport persons to face torture under "exceptional" circumstances. This is to say that there is a presumption against deportation to torture, which the government may rebut if it demonstrates evidence of a "serious threat to national security."[20] The court specified that

> a person constitutes a "danger to the security of Canada" if he or she poses a serious threat to the security of Canada, whether direct or indirect, and bearing in mind the fact that the security of one country is often dependent on the security of other nations. The threat must be "serious," in the sense that it must be grounded on objectively reasonable suspicion based on evidence and in the sense that the threatened harm must be substantial rather than negligible.[21]

Section 115(2) of IRPA and associated regulations provide the framework for deportation to torture, which is triggered when the minister has grounds to believe that a person constitutes a danger to the public of Canada or to the security of Canada. The process involves a few steps. First, an immigration officer assesses a risk of torture. Due to long-standing doctrine, the risk of torture must be personalized—it does not count if the risk one faces is no greater than that faced by the average person living in a given jurisdiction. Some claimants have been returned to high-risk jurisdictions, such as Somalia and Sri Lanka, precisely on this basis.[22] The example of Somalia is apt. Tellingly, Canadian regulations prohibit the CBSA from personally delivering deportees to Somalia due to the risk to employees of the state. Instead, they drop deportees off in neighboring countries, such as Kenya, and pay a private contractor to fly the person the rest of the way.[23]

If the immigration officer determines that there is a risk of persecution or torture, the minister or ministerial delegate is free to either accept this report or reject it. If the minister or delegate accepts the report, he or she may either issue a danger opinion (meaning the person is deemed to be a danger to the public) or accept that the person cannot be removed. During this stage, affected parties are not entitled to an oral hearing. All that is required is that the affected person receive disclosure of any nonsensitive or nonprivileged evidence relied on by the minister; be able to submit written challenges to the relevance, reliability, and sufficiency of the disclosed evidence; and be able to submit evidence and make arguments about the risk of persecution or torture as well as (the extent of) the risk he or she poses to the security of Canada. Finally, the minister is obligated to provide the affected person with the reasons behind the ultimate decision.[24] The decision to issue a danger opinion may then be judicially reviewed by the Federal Court. I am aware of only one instance in which the Federal Court allowed the government to deport a person to face torture.[25] In all others, the courts have not allowed it.

The real problem lies in the capacity of the immigration officer or the minister to deny the existence of a risk of torture despite compelling evidence to the contrary. This has happened in a number of cases concerned with deportation to torture. The most well known of these cases are *Sogi v. Canada (Minister of Citizenship and Immigration), Dadar v. Canada (Minister of Citizenship and Immigration),* and the case of Jama Warsame.[26] In *Sogi,* the government initially recognized a risk of torture and tried to invoke the *Suresh* exception. After the Federal Court invalidated the danger opinion on other grounds, the government conducted a second PRRA, this time mysteriously finding that there was no risk of torture. It proceeded to deport Mr. Sogi, who was subject to extrajudicial physical and mental punishment.[27] In each of these cases, the UN Committee Against Torture assessed the evidence and found that there was a risk of torture. As previously noted, applying for judicial review of negative decisions or filing claims before treaty-monitoring bodies does not stay decisions of removal.

The Supreme Court has instructed courts to intervene only if a danger opinion is "unreasonable," meaning that it was made "arbitrarily or in bad faith, it cannot be supported on the evidence, or the Minister failed to consider the appropriate factors."[28] As long as a decision is reasonable, it does not matter that it was wrong. This is hardly a high bar. In this way, de facto torture does not "exist" in the realm of law if there is at least some material basis for ignoring it. I have argued elsewhere that Canada should employ a far more rigorous system for making decisions about deportation in the contexts of security and torture, perhaps using an independent administrative tribunal.[29] At the very least, it should provide a right to an appeal and stays of removal during appeals or judicial reviews.

International law governing deportation to persecution/torture is sourced in the Convention on Refugees and the Convention Against Torture. The Convention Against Torture imposes a categorical ban on deportation to torture; I take it as self-evident that the exception to torture carved out in IRPA and validated by Canada's Supreme Court is contrary to international law. And what of deportation to persecution? Article 1(F) of the Convention on Refugees denies refugee status to anyone who has participated in international crime, has committed serious nonpolitical crimes before arriving in the country of refuge, or is guilty of acts contrary to the purposes and principles of the UN Charter.[30] Article 33(2) allows states to deport a refugee if there are reasonable grounds for believing he or she is a "danger to the security of the country in which he is, or who, having been convicted by a final judgment of a particularly serious crime, constitutes a danger to the community of that country."[31] States may also remove recognized refugees for a limited set of "exceptional" reasons, including national security.

Compliance with international law hinges on the process through which determinations of inadmissibility and exclusion are made. Leaving aside the procedural problems previously noted, there are a host of substantive problems with the criteria used to designate persons as security risks or as serious or organized criminals. For example, section 34(1)(b) of IRPA states that a person is inadmissible to Canada if he or she engaged in or instigated subversion by force of "any government," which includes an authoritarian government. This provision catches persons who engage in, or are associated with, armed struggles against violent and oppressive regimes—hardly a class of persons who should be ipso facto excluded from refugee protection under international law. More egregiously, section 34(1)(f) deems one inadmissible if he or she was a member of an organization for which there are reasonable grounds for believing was, is, or will engage in subversion, espionage, or terrorism. Courts have interpreted this provision to apply even if the person was a member before or after the organization engaged in the proscribed activities. Thus, one is inadmissible on security grounds for belonging to an organization in which one ceased being a member. These sorts of security designations are arbitrary, are overly broad, and do not advance the principles and purposes of the exceptions to refugee status and protection outlined under international law.

Similar issues affect every category of inadmissibility previously mentioned. The definition of "serious" criminality, for example, includes having been convicted (1) in Canada of an offense for which the maximum punishment is ten years, and (2) outside of Canada of an offense that would be punishable by a maximum of ten years if committed in Canada. These provisions are problematic because they do not require the person to have actually been sentenced for ten years, only that the maximum punishment for the offense is ten years. Many such offenses in Canada are hybrid offenses, meaning that they may be prosecuted as summary convictions (typically carrying no more than six months' imprisonment) or as indictable offenses (ten-year maximum). Examples include theft over $5,000, possession of stolen property valued over $5,000, possession of restricted weapons with ammunition, and dangerous driving leading to injury. If the crown prosecutes an offense summarily, and the offender is convicted to six months, the immigration system codes the offense as "serious."

Obviously, the choice of a prosecutor to proceed summarily indicates that the offense is not considered serious within the criminal justice system. The seriousness of the offense should be assessed through the lens of the sentencing judgment, which rests on a number of critical principles—including that a sentence must be proportionate to the gravity of the offense and the degree of responsibility of the offender. Judges will consider a range of aggravating and mitigating factors. To label all offenses "serious" because they carry the possibility of ten years' imprisonment ignores the practical reality that such a sentence falls outside the normal sentencing range, as delimited by the principle of proportionality and prosecutorial discretion over whether to proceed summarily.

Finally, until recently, the government had the option of prosecuting asylum seekers with human smuggling offenses. Section 37 of IRPA renders a person inadmissible on the grounds of organized criminality, while section 117 imposes criminal consequences, including the possibility of life imprisonment. After the arrival of the MVs *Ocean Lady* and *Sun Sea*, the government took the astounding position that these offenses also apply to asylum seekers who provided mutual assistance to other asylum seekers or performed menial tasks aboard vessels. In several cases, members of the IRB decided that passengers were inadmissible on the grounds of organized criminality because they cooked and cleaned aboard the MV *Sun Sea* or monitored and repaired equipment to ensure the vessel stayed afloat after the crew that organized the voyage abandoned ship.[32]

In *Bo10 v. Canada* and *R. v. Appulonappa*, the issue arose as to whether provisions of IRPA that prohibit human smuggling should apply to persons who facilitate the entry into Canada of asylum seekers for reasons unrelated to financial gain, such as mutual assistance and humanitarian work.[33] The government took a hard line that human smuggling provisions should be applied to "all organizing or assisting of unlawful entry of others into Canada, including assistance to close family members and humanitarian assistance."[34] The Supreme Court of Canada rejected this argument, limiting the application of human smuggling provisions to persons who profit financially or materially from human smuggling.

NOTHING OUT OF THE ORDINARY: CONSTITUTIONAL LAW AND THE NORMALIZATION OF INJUSTICE

The concept of crimmigration is a useful lens with which to interpret the deeper history and normative implications of the securitization of irregular migration in Canada. As a neologism coined by Juliet Stumpf, crimmigration is still in the process of being fully defined.[35] On most accounts, the term seems primarily descriptive, giving an account of the imbrication, blurring, or even fusion of the functional, normative, and discursive barriers between criminal law and immigration law. Stumpf sees in this process an ironic interplay of legal form and function, such that each form of law serves as a means of both implementing and rationalizing sovereign power consistently with exclusionary conceptions of social membership. In particular, criminal law and immigration law each rationalize authoritative "choices about who should be members of society: individuals whose characteristics or actions make them worthy of inclusion in the national community."[36] Both criminals and migrants are pushed to the margins of society, if not physically removed from social space.

Stumpf sees in this process the overarching influence of punishment, which she defines as both the power "to exact extreme sanctions and the power to express society's moral condemnation."[37] In this sense, punishment is closely related to sovereign power. But reference to expressions of moral condemnation conveys a paradoxical process of justification that suggests a political or possibly legal limit on sovereign power. While always imperfect, justifications—at least those that rely on law—hinge on the goals (conscious and unconscious) of punishment, whether and how these goals can be actualized, whether punishment is necessary to achieve these goals, and whether there are adequate constraints on the capacity of the state to punish arbitrarily.[38] And it is here that the stubborn distinctiveness of legal form rises up to the surface of Stumpf's conception of crimmigration—and with it, the promise of some semblance of legal substance.

In criminal law, punishment is justified by reference to formal (sentencing) goals or purposes, including retribution, deterrence, rehabilitation, and incapacitation, as well as to the deontological and consequentialist theories that underpin them. It is also justified by reference to procedures that ensure a strong link between attributions of criminal responsibility and demonstration of moral fault or blameworthiness. Of course, we know that these justifications obscure a wide range of extraneous and extralegal motives, structures, and social processes and, ultimately, the instrumental if not vindictive targeting of particular individuals and groups. But still, the process of justification provides an opportunity to hold the executive branch to account for ideals it has set for itself and remains a vital field of contestation.

Immigration law lacks justification for punishment precisely because officials do not generally consider detentions, deportations, and exclusion to be punitive. This begs the question of what is served by us insisting that there is "truly" something punitive about criminalized measures. The answer seems to be our ambivalent orientation to the role of law as an antidote for sovereign power, which we glimpse (imperfectly) in the criminal context. I suspect the notion of crimmigration is less a descriptive term about whether there is, in fact, a punitive quality to select immigration laws and practices than a rhetorical starting point for arguing that the constraints and principles found in criminal law ought to be applied to criminalized immigration settings. Crimmigration helps us analogize the impacts of executive power in criminal and immigration settings, so that we may better argue that immigration consequences and criminal consequences are not different in kind with respect to the rights of affected persons. From this starting point, we infer that the rights that formally exist in criminal law ought to be applied to immigration law.

This process of analogical reasoning is evident in American constitutional litigation—and for good reason. In the United States, core constitutional norms relating to procedural fairness are restricted to criminal proceedings, applying only to immigration proceedings or practices that are "punitive" in character.[39]

Over the years, the Supreme Court of the United States has had mixed views on the punitive qualities of deportation in the context of criminality.[40] In the 1889 case of *Chae Chan Ping v. United States*, a majority held that deportation proceedings are "civil" and not criminal in nature.[41] But in the 2010 case of *Padilla v. Kentucky*, the Supreme Court seemed to revise this position when reviewing the constitutionality of allowing deportations in the absence of adequate legal advice about the immigration consequences of a guilty plea.[42] Deciding the case on another ground, the court stated in obiter dictum that it is "most difficult to divorce the penalty from the conviction in the deportation context."[43] In *Fong Haw Tan v. Phelan*, decided in 1948, the court went so far as to say that "deportation is a drastic measure and at times the equivalent of banishment or exile."[44] Judges, albeit often in dissent, have compared deportation and banishment as early as 1893.[45]

By contrast, the Supreme Court of Canada has consistently stated that "deportation is not imposed as a punishment" and is "not concerned with the penal consequences of the acts of individuals."[46] The nature of Canada's constitution is part of the official basis for this position. With the exception of a few rights, the application of the Canadian Charter of Rights and Freedoms does not depend on citizenship or immigration status. What is more, the applicability of constitutional norms is rarely exclusive to a particular field of law. Section 7 of the Charter, for example, protects an individual's right to life, liberty, and security, and the right not to be deprived thereof except in accordance with principles of fundamental justice.[47] The court's position has regularly been that the threshold for the applicability of a Charter right relates to the "interest at stake" and not the formal nature of the proceeding that threatens that interest.[48]

A cardinal principle in section 7 jurisprudence is that as the risk of a deprivation of life, liberty, or security increases, so too must the quality and fairness of procedural protections. This means that such elements of a fair trial as knowing the case against you, being able to respond to that case, and having decisions made based on the facts and the law move in lockstep with the substantive impact of a decision. In *Singh v. Canada (Minister of Citizenship and Immigration)*, the court decided that refugee claimants are entitled to at least an oral hearing when issues of credibility arise, precisely because getting decisions wrong can lead to deportation to face persecution. In *Suresh*, the court analogized deportation to torture with extradition to capital punishment, the latter of which arose in the case of *United States v. Burns*. The court reasoned that just as extradition is normally acceptable, so too is deportation. But in *Burns*, the court held that section 7 prohibits extradition to face capital punishment. In kind, it ruled in *Suresh* that section 7 is fully engaged in the context of deportation when there is some sort of irreparable harm at play, including the risk of torture.

And here we see the crack in the court's overall logic about the strength of constitutional protections: immigration decisions only attract constitutional scrutiny if a claimant can demonstrate some sort of "irreparable harm" over and above the removal; the constitution does not recognize immigration consequences simpliciter. Over time, courts have expanded the definition of what counts as "ordinary" consequences, excluding all but the gravest human rights abuses from constitutional consideration. Despite issuing a favorable judgment in *B010 v. Canada*, the court decided that section 7 is "not engaged at the stage of determining admissibility to Canada" and that the benefit of the Charter "is typically engaged" only during the actual removal stage.[49] In *Febles v. Canada*, the court expressly denied the applicability of the Charter to decisions about whether a person should be excluded from refugee status under Articles 1(E) and 1(F) of the Convention on Refugees.[50]

The court reasoned that persons denied the right to a fair admissibility hearing or the right to claim refugee status can choose to apply for a PRRA and "a stay of removal to a place if he would face death, torture or cruel and unusual treatment or punishment if removed to that place."[51] But notice that this list of human rights abuses is incomplete, excluding as it does persecution. In the baffling case of *Peter v. Canada*, the Federal Court found section 7 of the Charter to be inapplicable to legislation that removes the right to claim protection from persecution. In the view of Justice Annis, removal to persecution "does not expose the applicant to irreparable harm, in the sense that if the decision of the removals officer is overturned, the applicant is prevented from being readmitted to Canada."[52] In other words, since the claimant will not be killed, maimed, or disfigured, the consequences of removal are not that serious. No consideration was given to the fact that protection from persecution is an international right, perhaps because Justice Annis was unduly confident in the quality of inadmissibility and exclusion determinations. The Federal Court of Appeal overruled this decision on the grounds that it was premised on an insufficient factual foundation.[53] But it also declined to pronounce on the substantive issues, meaning that the constitutionality of this portion of the removal process remains unsettled.

And so while section 7 of the Charter is formally applicable to immigration proceedings, the notion of "irreparable harm" ensures that it is unavailable to all but those who face the gravest of human rights abuses. And when the Charter does apply, it is only at the final moment before the person will be removed from the country. Practically speaking, persons will have been removed before their rights can be vindicated in a court. In many ways, this deportation-plus-irreparable-harm standard resembles the formal immigration–criminal proceeding distinction found in the American context.

I see the appeal of using the language of punishment when challenging immigration law, but it is not clear whether it is a sound strategy of resistance. My concern is with the unintended negative effects of approaching punishment as "extreme sanction" or, less directly, of having to show some similarity between immigration consequences and criminal consequences as a threshold for rights recognition. This approach risks granting greater legitimacy to the faulty premise that access to constitutional rights depends on there being deportation plus some extreme, grave, or irreparable harm. Most harmful immigration measures do not lead to grave human rights abuses, but they still contravene international law and any responsible interpretation of constitutional rights. Take the case of Deepan Budlakoti as an example. Deepan is a Canadian-born man who, due to a variety of factors, never acquired Canadian citizenship. In 2010, he was convicted of weapons trafficking, possession of an illegal firearm, and drug trafficking and sentenced to three years' imprisonment. The government of Canada has since been trying to deport him to India—a country he has never visited, lived in, or been a citizen of.[54] Even in this overtly criminalized context, where deportation is triggered by a criminal conviction, used as a substitute for incarceration, and imposed on someone who has never lived anywhere else, courts convince themselves that it is neither punitive nor irreparably harmful.

WITHOUT CRIMINAL LAW: REFUGEE CLAIMS AND ADMINISTRATIVE LAW

I will end by reviewing how the refugee claims of most passengers of the *Ocean Lady* and *Sun Sea* were handled. My concern here relates to the whittling away of rights and the rule of law, even when one is permitted to file a claim for refugee status. My review of all available decisions before the Refugee Protection Division (RPD) of the IRB relating to the MVs *Ocean Lady* and *Sun Sea* indicate an appalling level of inconsistency in decisional output. In addition to some of the structural, access-to-justice issues previously noted, this variation is related to the absence of an internal system for the hierarchical settlement of questions about the content, scope, and application of (ambiguous) law. There are a few cases in which it is doubtful the adjudicator based his or her decision on the facts and the law.

We should begin by recalling that refugee status is conferred on one who demonstrates a well-founded fear of persecution on the basis of race, religion, nationality, membership in a particular social group, or political opinion. The majority of passengers aboard the MVs *Ocean Lady* and *Sun Sea* initially claimed that they were at risk of persecution due to their perceived associations with the LTTE. Two personal characteristics were relevant here: (1) being Tamil (certainly a social group), and (2) being aboard the vessels (possibly a social group). This position seems straightforward: the boat arrivals were high profile, the government of Canada and Sri Lankan authorities both vociferously asserted that those aboard the vessels were associated with the LTTE, and Sri Lanka has a well-known record of committing international crimes against the Tamil population. So, membership in a social group is clearly relevant, and political opinion may be relevant if the Sri Lankan government perceives passengers to be associated with, and have information about, the LTTE.

The problem with initial claims was that in many cases the passengers were not refugees when they left Sri Lanka; a good number of claimants came to Canada for economic or familial reasons, not to flee persecution. The risk of persecution materialized only when they were identified as being passengers aboard the vessels. Those who become refugees only after arriving in a country of asylum are known as "sur place refugees."[55]

In the first round of cases, some RPD members accepted these sur place claims, while others did not. Those that accepted the claims decided that being both Tamil and a passenger exposed the claimant to persecution based on social group and political opinion. For example, one RPD member concluded that the passengers were "Tamils suspected of being LTTE members," "Tamils suspected of having information on LTTE members," or classifiable as an "LTTE associate or supporter in the diaspora working to reinvigorate the LTTE."[56] Members who rejected the claims did so on the grounds that there was insufficient evidence of persecution or, more common, that the persecution related to categories not recognized in the Convention on Refugees—that is, that being passengers aboard a vessel does not qualify one as being a member of a social group or having a political opinion. For these members, persecution must be motivated entirely by membership in a social group, political opinion, or another expressly recognized ground. If persecution is motivated by other, extrinsic grounds, Canada is not obligated to intervene.

There is some support for this position. In Canada, there are three categories of social groups: (1) those defined by possession of an innate, unchangeable characteristic; (2) voluntary associations founded on or fundamental to human dignity; and (3) former voluntary associations that have achieved an unalterable, historical permanence.[57] Being a passenger aboard a vessel falls into none of these categories. Similarly, few of the passengers could adduce evidence that they held dangerous political opinions, as they were not members or conspicuous supporters of the LTTE. In other words, while the passengers were at risk of persecution, it was for legally irrelevant reasons.

But certainly being Tamil was a relevant factor, as was perceived political opinion. A good number of RPD members thought so. How can we explain a situation in which receipt of refugee status depends less on factual and legal similarities and more on which RPD member one was (un)lucky enough to get?

Some studies have suggested that variations in decisional output within the RPD relate to the personal characteristics of individual adjudicators rather than the factual or legal issues involved.[58] Not wanting to go that far, I would say that variability is attributable in good part to the fact that the RPD has a sharply limited authority to create or even develop general law. Its role is to apply law that is given to it by statute (Parliament) and case law (the Federal Court, the Federal Court of Appeal, and the Supreme Court of Canada). The decisions made by a particular RPD member have no precedential weight and thus are not binding on other members. What is more, the Refugee Appeal Division (RAD) can only overturn the decisions of individual cases; it cannot impose new rules or principles of general application on members whose decisions are not being appealed. The relationship between RAD and the RPD is not like that between trial courts and appellate courts. With limited power to definitively settle questions of law, there is bound to be inconsistency in decisional output.

Escalating disorder did not escape the attention of the Federal Court of Canada. Reviewing the terrain, Justice Harrington made the following comments:

> All I can say is that we have come to a very sad state of affairs. Depending on the member of the RPD who decides the case, a passenger may or may not be found to be a refugee *sur place*. . . . In my view, it is a great injustice that passengers on these two ships should be treated so differently. There is no sound basis for predicting who will be welcomed here as a refugee and who will be thrown out.[59]

In Canada, judges may review all administrative and discretionary decisions exercised pursuant to IRPA to ensure that they are correct or, at the least, simply reasonable.[60] In most cases of concern to us, judges intervene only if a decision is unreasonable, meaning that it does not fall within the range of outcomes permitted by IRPA, does not take into account relevant factors, takes into account irrelevant factors, or rests on the elusive concept of "bad faith."

Using this power, the Federal Court quickly moved to clarify how sur place claims should be handled. One thing was been made clear: the RPD may not confer refugee status simply because an individual was a passenger aboard the vessels; some evidentiary link between persecution and membership in a particular social group or to political opinion has to present.[61] However, reviewing judges have consistently held that refugee status may be granted if persecution arises due to a combination of factors, only some of which are officially recognized in the Convention on Refugees.[62] This is part of a long-standing "mixed-motive" doctrine, which recognizes that those who persecute often do so for a variety of reasons, including economic incentives, opportunism, and self-promotion.[63] As long as one of the motives for persecution relate to the prohibited grounds of persecution itemized in the Convention on Refugees, claimants need not prove it was the sole or even the primary motive.

There was some controversy here. According to the government, Federal Court judges used the mixed-motive doctrine to effectively rewrite the decisions of the RPD, so as to ensure the granting of status.[64] In some cases, judges found that it is reasonable (but legally incorrect) to decide that simply being aboard the vessels makes the passengers members of a social group.[65] In other cases, judges found this decision unreasonable, referred the cases back for reconsideration, but strongly suggested refugee status could be validly conferred if reference were made to the mixed-motive doctrine.[66] In still other decisions, judges upheld status-conferring decisions by inferring that the RPD member implicitly relied on requisite doctrine.[67]

This variability underscores the novel, complex nature of the factual and legal issues at play. However, case law seems to have been settled. Judges found, rightly, that being a passenger aboard the vessels is on its own insufficient to ground a claim. They then informed members about the availability of the mixed-motive doctrine, which predated the first RPD decisions at issue by precisely twenty years. Upon reexamining a file, RPD members still had to find a reasonable possibility of persecution or a likelihood of torture linked to Convention on Refugees grounds. If a decision to grant status pursuant to this doctrine were unsupportable on the evidentiary record, a decision to confer status would be unreasonable.

It turns out that the facts of most files supported a finding of refugee status, which has since been upheld upon judicial review. Still, some RPD members have refused to confer status, even though other factually similar claims have been accepted. This variability is a necessary function of a deferential standard of review in which at least two reasonable conclusions may be drawn from the same basic evidentiary record.[68] However, there are other, deeply concerning factors at play. Some RPD members have ignored relevant evidence or relied on weak evidence when denying protection. In *B381 v. Canada (Citizenship and Immigration)*, an RPD member denied the risk of persecution because he or she refused to consider the reports of international human rights bodies and took at face value the promise of the Sri Lankan High Commission that it would treat deportees fairly. This also occurred in *S.K. v. Canada (Citizenship and Immigration)*. The Federal Court found these decisions to be unreasonable.[69]

Canada is known as "a nation of immigrants."[70] We take pride in being the first country to make multiculturalism official state policy, fancy ourselves leaders in human rights, and proclaim to have "the fairest immigration and refugee system in the world."[71] But these symbols of our national identity belie a dark history of racism, xenophobia, and exploitation. Our government's reaction to the irregular arrivals of Tamil asylum seekers attests to this history. It exploited popular fears about crime and security to prevent and deter people from seeking asylum in Canada; it has used the language of security, fairness, and efficiency to abdicate its moral and legal responsibilities to asylum seekers.

The strategy is simple: kettle "undesirable" migrants into a process that refuses to even review the risk of deportation to persecution and human rights abuses. By labeling individuals security risks and serious or organized criminals on the basis of thin evidentiary records and overly broad criteria, we may remain willfully blind to the human rights consequences of deportation. This strategy is most visible in the context of inadmissibility and exclusion determinations. It is true that the early stages of this process occur within the context of administrative proceedings. However, these hearings are heavily weighted in favor of the state, which has extremely low standards of proof; informal laws of evidence; the option of having secret hearings; and overly broad criteria of inadmissibility, which fall well below international standards governing when refugee status or protection may be denied.

The impacts of these measures are exacerbated by what can only be described as a Charter vacuum. Courts have denied the applicability of the Charter to every stage of the removal process except the final act of removal. But even here, persons labeled security or criminal risks are not entitled to a stay of removal while their claims are heard, nor are they entitled to refugee status or protection. The basis of this position has been that only the gravest of human rights abuses constitute "irreparable harm." On the other end of the spectrum, the ordinary immigration consequences of deportation are not sufficiently serious to warrant enhanced procedural protections, yet somehow the courts have found a way to push deportation to persecution toward the "ordinary consequences" side of the spectrum. As an analogue of punishment, the notion of irreparable harm reserves constitutional protection only to "extreme" or extraordinary sanction. It would seem that the courts have been lulled by—or have themselves exploited—shoddy criteria of inadmissibility and exclusion as a show of compliance with international law.

I am greatly concerned that the language of punishment has had a counter-productive influence, expanding what counts as an ordinary immigration consequence and banishing this set of injustices from the constitutional terrain. I find some hope in the decisions of some Federal Court judges to intervene in highly politicized decisions by the RPD. These decisions rested not on criminal or even constitutional law but on sound readings of administrative law, international law, and long-standing provisions of IRPA. But the executive branch has effectively dismantled access to justice, disentitling deserving claimants from the RPD. Parliament has abdicated its democratic role as a legal institution responsible for constraining rather than unfettering executive power. Judges have had to clean up the mess, in rare cases using the inherent constitutional power of judicial review, which Parliament cannot jettison. But unless they elect to use the Charter, this power is too limited to subject the executive branch to the rule of law.

NOTES TO CHAPTER 4

1. "Terrorists or Civilians? MV *Sun Sea* Passengers Face Scrutiny in Days Ahead," *Canadian Record*, August 13, 2010, http://www.therecord.com/sports-story/2565119 -terrorists-or-civilians-mv-sun-sea-passengers-face-scrutiny-in-days-ahead/.

2. W. G. Robinson, Special Advisor to the Minister of Employment and Immigration, *Illegal Migrants in Canada* (Ottawa: Supply Services Canada, 1983).

3. Parliament made changes to security-based immigration and refugee law proceedings following the irregular arrival of 174 Sikh asylum seekers in 1987; see Graham Hudson, "As Good as It Gets? Security, Asylum, and the Rule of Law After the Certificate Trilogy," *Osgoode Hall Law Journal* 52, no. 3 (2016): 905–950; Jo Anne Colson, "Canadian Refugee Policy: The Politics of the Frame" (PhD diss., Trent University, 2013).

4. Immigration and Refugee Protection Act, S.C. 2001, c. 27 [IRPA]; Faster Removal of Foreign Criminals Act, S.C. 2013, c. 16 [FRFCA]; Protecting Canada's Immigration System Act, S.C. 2012, c. 17 [PCISA]; Balanced Refugee Reform Act, S.C. 2010, c. 8 [BRRA].

5. See Idil Atak, Graham Hudson, and Delphine Nakache, "Making Canada's Refugee System Faster and Fairer: A Preliminary Analysis of the Stated Goals and Unintended Consequences of the 2012 Refugee Reform," in the Canadian Association for Refugee and Forced Migration Studies Working Paper Series (forthcoming).

6. These statistics were provided by the Immigration and Refugee Board and are on file with the author; see also Government of Canada, "Speaking Notes for the Honourable Jason Kenney, P.C., M.P. Minister of Citizenship, Immigration and Multiculturalism," February, 16, 2012, http://www.cic.gc.ca/english/department/media/speeches /2012/2012-02-16.asp.

7. For a good overview of the meaning and (empirical) study of irregular migration, see Sergio Carrera and Elspeth Guild, eds., *Irregular Migration, Trafficking and Smuggling of Human Beings: Policy Dilemmas in the EU* (Brussels: Centre for European Policy Studies, 2016).

8. Emma Newcombe, "Irregular Migration: Research, Policy and Practice," COMPAS, Annual International Conference, July 7–8, 2005, *International Migration Review* 39, no. 4 (2005): 962–964.

9. Harald Bauder, "Why We Should Use the Term Illegalized Immigrant," RCIS Research Brief No. 2013/1, http://ffm-online.org/wp-content/uploads/2013/08/RCIS_RB _Bauder_No_2013_1.pdf; Erika Khandor, Jean McDonald, Peter Nyers, and Cynthia

Wright, *The Regularization of Non-Status Immigrants in Canada: 1960–2004* (Toronto: Ontario Coalition of Agencies Serving Immigrants, 2004), http://accessalliance.ca/wp -content/uploads/2015/03/Regularization-Report.pdf; Cécile Rousseau, S. ter Kuile, M. Munoz, L. Nadeau, M. J. Ouimet, L. Kirmayer, and F. Crépeau, "Health Care Access for Refugees and Immigrants with Precarious Status: Public Health and Human Right Challenges," *Canadian Journal of Public Health* 99, no. 4 (2008): 290.

10. Office of the Auditor General of Canada, "2013 Fall Report of the Auditor General of Canada," chap. 5, sec. 5.2, http://www.oag-bvg.gc.ca/internet/English/parl_oag _201311_05_e_38799.html#hd3b.

11. Government of Canada, "Continuing the Fight Against Human Smuggling," June 8, 2015, https://www.canada.ca/en/news/archive/2015/06/continuing-fight-against -human-smuggling.html.

12. For the purposes of this chapter, I will use the term "RSD system" to refer only to claims made from within Canada.

13. Rick Dykstra (Parliamentary Secretary to the Minister of Citizenship and Immigration, CPC), House of Commons: Bill C-31 2nd Reading.

14. Government of Canada. *Evaluation of the Reviews and Interventions Pilot Project*, July 9, 2015, http://www.cic.gc.ca/english/resources/evaluation/ripp/2015/index.asp.

15. Royal Canadian Mounted Police, *Evaluation of the RCMP Enhanced Security Screening Pilot Project*, September 29, 2015, http://www.rcmp-grc.gc.ca/en/evaluation -rcmp-enhanced-security-screening-pilot-project.

16. Hudson "As Good as It Gets?"

17. IRPA, s. 86; Hudson, "As Good as It Gets?"

18. IRPA, s. 64.

19. Delphine Nakache, "The Human and Financial Cost of Detention of Asylum-Seekers in Canada," United Nations High Commissioner for Refugees, December 2011, www.unhcr.ca/beta/wp-content/uploads/2014/10/RPT-2011-12-detention_assylum _seekers-e.pdf.

20. Suresh v. Canada, [2002] 1 S.C.R. 3 at par. 89.

21. Ibid. at par. 90.

22. For just one of many examples, see Mohamed v. Canada (Citizenship and Immigration), [2011] F.C.J. No. 1869 (QL).

23. Anna Maria Tremonti, "To No Man's Land: The Story of Saeed Jama's Deportation to Somalia," *The Current*, CBC Radio, November 4, 2014, http://www.cbc.ca/radio /thecurrent/a-story-of-deportation-to-somalia-and-canada-s-voice-at-war-1.2907289/to -no-man-s-land-the-story-of-saeed-jama-s-deportation-to-somalia-1.2907291.

24. Suresh v. Canada, [2002] 1 S.C.R. 3 at pars. 122–123.

25. Nlandu-Nsoki v. Canada (Minister of Citizenship and Immigration) [2005], F.C. 17 at par. 22.

26. Sogi v. Canada (Minister of Citizenship and Immigration), [2005] 3 F.C.R. 517; Dadar v. Canada (Minister of Citizenship and Immigration), [2004] F.C. 1381; UN Human Rights Committee, "Views Concerning Communication No. 1959/2010," 102d Sess, Annex, September 1, 2011, www.un.org/en/ga/search/view_doc.asp?symbol=CCPR /C/102/D/1959/2010.

27. Amnesty International Canada, *Matching International Commitments with National Action: A Human Rights Agenda for Canada* (Ottawa: Amnesty International, 2012), 20.

28. Suresh v. Canada, [2002] 1 S.C.R. 3 at par. 41; Nagalingam v. Canada (Minister of Citizenship and Immigration), [2008] 1 F.C.R. 87 at par. 18.

29. Hudson, "As Good as It Gets?"

30. Convention on Refugees, Art. 1 (F).

31. Convention on Refugees, 189 U.N.T.S. 150, Art. 33(2).

32. X (Re), 2013 CanLII 101047 (CA IRB); X (Re), 2013 CanLII 99463 (CA IRB); B010 v. Canada (Citizenship and Immigration), [2015] 3 S.C.R. 704 at par. 12.

33. *B010*; R. v. Appulonappa, [2015] S.C.C. 59, [2015] 3 S.C.R. 754.

34. *Appulonappa* at par. 13.

35. Juliet Stumpf, "The Crimmigration Crisis: Immigrants, Crime, and Sovereign Power," *American University Law Review* 56, no. 2 (2006): 367.

36. Ibid., 397.

37. Ibid., 410.

38. Hugo Adam Bedau and Erin Kelly, "Punishment," in *Stanford Encyclopedia of Philosophy*, Fall 2015 ed., July 31, 2015, http://plato.stanford.edu/archives/fall2015/entries/punishment/.

39. For a small selection of commentaries, see Christopher N. Lasch, "'Crimmigration' and the Right to Counsel at the Border Between Civil and Criminal Proceedings," *Iowa Law Review* 99 (2014): 2131–2160; *University of Denver Legal Studies Research Paper*, no. 14–42 (2014), http://ssrn.com/abstract=2442124; Peter L. Markowitz, "Deportation Is Different," *University of Pennsylvania Journal of Constitutional Law* 13, no. 5 (2011): 1299–1136, http://scholarship.law.upenn.edu/cgi/viewcontent.cgi?article=1099&context=jcl.

40. For a detailed historical analysis of this issue, see Peter L. Markowitz, "Straddling the Civil-Criminal Divide: A Bifurcated Approach to Understanding the Nature of Immigration Removal Proceedings," *Harvard Civil Rights–Civil Liberties Law Review* 43, no. 2 (2008): 289–351, http://ssrn.com/abstract=1015322.

41. Chae Chan Ping v. United States, 130 U.S. 581 (1889).

42. Padilla v. Kentucky, 559 U.S. 356 (2010).

43. Ibid. at 1481.

44. Fong Haw Tan v. Phelan, 333 U.S. (1948) at par. 4.

45. Fong Yue Ting v. United States, 149 U.S. 698 (1893).

46. Canada (Minister of Employment and Immigration) v. Chiarelli, [1992] 1 S.C.R. 711, http://scc-csc.lexum.com/scc-csc/scc-csc/en/item/855/index.do; Reference as to the Effect of the Exercise of the Royal Prerogative of Mercy upon Deportation Proceedings, [1933] S.C.R. 269 at 278, https://scc-csc.lexum.com/scc-csc/scc-csc/en/item/8755/index.do.

47. Re B.C. Motor Vehicle Act, [1985] 2 S.C.R. 486 at par. 30.

48. Ibid. at par. 18.

49. *B010* at par. 75.

50. Febles v. Canada, [2014] 3 S.C.R. 431.

51. Ibid. at par. 67.

52. Peter v. Canada (Public Safety and Emergency Preparedness), [2014] F.C.J. No. 1132 (QL) at par. 296.

53. Savunthararasa v. Canada (Public Safety and Emergency Preparedness), [2016] F.C.J. No. 173 (QL).

54. Information on Deepan's case may be found at http://www.justicefordeepan.org /background/about-us/.

55. See UNHCR, "Handbook on Procedures and Criteria for Determining Refugee Status," Geneva, September 1979, pars. 94–96, http://www.unhcr.org/4d93528a9.pdf. Paragraph 94 provides the following definition: "A person who was not a refugee when he left his country, but who becomes a refugee at a later date, is called a refugee *"sur place."*

56. Canada (Citizenship and Immigration) v. B272, [2013] F.C. 870 at par. 74.

57. Canada (Attorney General) v. Ward, [1993] 2 S.C.R. 689 at 739, par. 70.

58. Sean Rehaag, "2014 Refugee Claim Data and IRB Member Recognition Rates," Canadian Council for Refugees, May 8, 2015, ccrweb.ca/en/2014-refugee-claim-data.

59. Canada (Citizenship and Immigration) v. A011, [2013] F.C.J. No. 685 (QL) at par. 10.

60. Dunsmuir v. New Brunswick, [2008] 1 S.C.R. 190, [2008] S.C.C. 9.

61. Canada (Citizenship and Immigration) v. B380, [2012] F.C.J. No. 1657 (QL) at pars. 23–27; Canada (Citizenship and Immigration) v. B399, [2013] F.C.J. No. 263 (QL) at pars. 16–18; Canada (Citizenship and Immigration) v. B420, [2013] F.C.J. No. 396 (QL) at par. 17; B272, at par. 75.

62. Key cases include Canada (Citizenship and Immigration) v. B451, [2013] F.C.J. No. 561 (QL); Canada (Citizenship and Immigration) v. B344, [2013] F.C.J. No. 547 (QL); Canada (Citizenship and Immigration) v. A068, [2013] F.C.J. No. 1287 (QL) [A068].

63. *Ward.*

64. A011 at par. 18.

65. Ibid., at par. 43; Canada (Citizenship and Immigration) v. B472, [2013] F.C. 151 at pars. 26–28; S.K. v. Canada (Citizenship and Immigration), [2013] F.C. 78 at par. 25; P.M. v. Canada (Citizenship and Immigration), [2013] F.C. 77 at par. 17.

66. A011 at par. 52; B451.

67. B272; B420; B399; Canada (Citizenship and Immigration) v. A032, [2013] F.C. 322.

68. Canada (Citizenship and Immigration) v. A037, [2014] F.C. 754 at par. 5.

69. S.K.; B381 v. Canada (Citizenship and Immigration), [2014] F.C. 608.

70. Franca Iacovetta, ed., with Paula Draper and Robert Ventresca, A *Nation of Immigrants: Women, Workers, and Communities in Canadian History, 1840s–1960s* (Toronto: University of Toronto Press, 1998).

71. Fransisco Rico Martinez, "Exclusionary Changes in the Conservative Immigration, Refugee and Citizenship Policies: The Beginning of the End," *Refugee Update* 82 (Summer 2015): 1, http://www.fcjrefugeecentre.org/wp-content/uploads/2012/12 /Refugee-Update-No-82.pdf.

5. SEEKING ASYLUM IN AUSTRALIA

The Role of Emotion and Narrative in State and Civil Society Responses

GREG MARTIN, UNIVERSITY OF SYDNEY
CLAUDIA TAZREITER, UNIVERSITY OF NEW SOUTH WALES

Seeking asylum in the Australian context has a history that is strongly tied to geography. As a large island in the Asia-Pacific and an immigrant nation, Australia has an established and proactive approach to the arrival of newcomers, enforced through the Migration Act 1958 (Cth). When it comes to the spontaneous arrival of asylum seekers wishing to engage Australia's obligations under the 1951 Convention Relating to the Status of Refugees and its 1967 Protocol (the Convention on Refugees), the Australian state has demonstrated a mostly punitive approach of deterrence, detention, and removal that appears out of step with the country's reputation as a human rights-observing liberal democracy.

This chapter explores this seeming disjunction through the lens of the interactions between the state and members of civil society organizations in building different narratives around the presence of asylum seekers. The state-instigated creation of narratives of fear and images of asylum seekers as suspect populations was the precursor to the criminalization of those involved in facilitating irregular migration. In addition to the complexity of migration categories and boundaries, recent decades have seen an increasing criminalization of migrants in all parts of the world, focused on those moving in irregular ways.[1] The targeting and scapegoating of migrants as "illegal" is a development that has been anticipated by some researchers, along with its dramatic social and political impact in terms of human insecurity. Populations of displaced persons—including refugees, asylum seekers, and those who are violently forced from their homes through human or natural disasters—as well as trafficked persons and migrant workers who live in forms of modern slavery constitute *irregular migrants*, in that their journeys in finding a new temporary or permanent home are likely to be unofficial, unauthorized, and hence labeled as "illegal."

Despite a long history of successful migrant and refugee settlement, Australia has implemented harsh, punitive approaches to asylum seekers who arrive without travel documents as well as other irregular migrants.[2] Since the introduction of mandatory and indefinite detention of all asylum seekers arriving without a valid visa in 1992, human rights advocates, lawyers, medical professionals, and asylum seekers themselves have highlighted a raft of long-term harms in Australia's approach. Activists have pursued several key issues on behalf of asylum seekers, including the harms of prolonged and indefinite detention, particularly of children; wrongful deportation; and the introduction of offshore processing and detention.

Mindful of this longer history of contentious politics and activism with regard to asylum seeker arrivals, this chapter explores contemporary developments in Australia's border protection policies and, in particular, the state's response to asylum seekers arriving by boat, whose claims to protection under international human rights law are processed in offshore detention centers. The chapter shows how, with respect to boat arrivals, the Australian state has used narratives of fear, contagion, risk, and security to create a "politics of affect," which it relies on to govern. Activists and advocacy organizations have, in turn, used counternarratives, which also draw on emotion and affect, highlighting the human tragedy associated with the treatment of asylum seekers in offshore detention. The collective action of asylum seeker civil society groups and activists in Australia is situated in the field of social movement studies—examined briefly in the next section—and stresses issues of emotion, affect, narratives, and storytelling, which scholars increasingly became interested in as their focus turned to the cultural dimensions of collective action.

Though this chapter is focused on Australia, recent global developments in relation to migration are an important context to keep in mind. In many parts of the world, migration has been characterized as a "crisis," whipping up resentments in local populations and misplacing the root cause of multiple issues— such as workplace insecurity and job loss, cuts to social welfare, and social change—more generally on immigration rather than on the less visible process of neoliberal globalization. Immigration was a key issue leading to the Brexit vote, with the United Kingdom withdrawing from the European Union, and was also a key feature in the political rhetoric leading to the election of Donald Trump in the United States. By comparison, Australia arguably has the most comprehensive legal and administrative measures in place both to externalize its borders and to deter and detain asylum seekers in offshore locations with no hope of ever being released or granted permission to visit family in Australia.

SOCIAL MOVEMENTS, PASSIONATE POLITICS, AND PROTEST NARRATIVES

The realm of social movement literature has become quite vast, so we have chosen to review a portion of the scholarly work that has a bearing on our discussion of campaigning and advocacy around asylum seekers in Australia. Of particular significance are those theories and approaches that have been influenced by the "cultural turn" in social movement studies.[3] In contrast to traditional approaches that have tended to focus on the political strategies collective actors use in attempting to get their demands and grievances incorporated into the polity, European thinkers in the latter half of the twentieth century observed the emergence of movements that were not focused solely on political action. These "new social movements" seemed less concerned with material redistribution, emancipation, and political inclusion than with cultural recognition, collective identity formation, and lifestyle or quality-of-life issues.

In this context, social movement scholar Alberto Melucci argues previous theories of social movements suffer from *political reductionism* because they tend to focus exclusively on the political dimension of movements without acknowledging their important cultural aspects. Moreover, given movement culture tends to be hidden in communities or submerged networks, scholars also suffer a "myopia of the visible," equating social movements with large-scale mobilizations, mass demonstrations, and public protest events.[4] Conceiving of power as existing beyond the state, Melucci considers significant what he calls the "pre-political" dimension of collective action: the cultural face of movements that resides in everyday life, social networks, and civil society.

In this theory of new movements, a premium is placed on *autonomy*—that is, independence from the state and established political actors. Indeed, Melucci argues the demands of contemporary social movements "exist beyond political mediation and independently of its results."[5] Moreover, what he calls the "democratization of everyday life" is signaled by the recognition and acceptance of *difference*, which occurs through the establishment of autonomous movements:

A new political space is designed beyond the traditional distinction between state and "civil society": an intermediate *public space*, whose function is not to institutionalize the movements nor to transform them into parties, but to make society hear their messages and translate these messages into political decision making, while the movements maintain their autonomy.[6]

Interest in the cultural features of protest and collective action has gradually developed beyond new social movement theory to include the role of narrative and storytelling, performance, festival, music, art, and ritual. Underpinning many of these topics has been a recognition of "the value of 'bringing emotions back into' social movement research."[7] Previously, when emotion and affect were studied, they were largely seen as negative and associated with the dangers of mass hysteria, crowd behavior, and fascism.[8] And that is why theories of collective action have tended to focus on rationality and cognition as key motivating factors for people getting involved in social protest.

However, scholars influenced by the sociology of emotions have become interested in "passionate politics," whereby collective action is seen as instigated by "moral shocks," which generate "such a sense of outrage in a person that she becomes inclined towards political action."[9] It is emotions, then, that enable people to be optimistic and believe with confidence in opportunities for effective change. Doug McAdam intimates as much with his conception of "cognitive liberation," which refers to circumstances whereby people mobilize "on the basis of some optimistic assessment of the prospects for successful insurgency weighted against the risks involved in each action."[10] However, critics argue that even here, cognitive liberation is essentially a rational-instrumental concept, devoid of emotional impetus. As Goodwin, Jasper, and Polletta say, "'Liberation' implies heady emotions that 'cognitive' then denies."[11]

Accordingly, scholars concerned with the role of emotions in collective action have attempted to go beyond what they see as the false dichotomies of past analyses, which have juxtaposed rationality and emotion, instrumentality and expression. They argue that ostensibly instrumental movements have emotional and expressive elements, and therefore emotions and cognition can coexist.[12] Sometimes a social movement is more emotionally driven, while at other times it will be more instrumentally focused. Nevertheless, argue Polletta and Amenta, emotions frequently *precede* collective action: "People are often motivated by anger, indignation, fear, compassion, or a sense of obligation, not optimism about the possibilities of securing political concessions through extra-institutional protest."[13]

Another key aspect of the cultural turn in social movement studies has been an appreciation for the role of narrative and storytelling, which is itself part of a wider "narrative turn" that has occurred in numerous fields of human inquiry.[14] Indeed, narrative and stories are often seen as an important feature of not only the cultural life of social movements but also the emotional lives of movements and activists.[15] To the extent that most movements exist in some form of antagonistic relationship to larger structures and to prevailing norms and values, which they seek to change, they do so partly by means of counternarratives, which are oppositional or alternative stories "at odds with or precluded by pre-existing and dominant social narratives."[16] And this is why, for many, storytelling performs a crucial function in social protest and collective action.

Moreover, as they contain rhetorical devices and story lines that link a particular experience or occurrence to others, narratives can orchestrate and amplify both the emotional experience and the meaning of collective protest events.[17] Some theorists have developed taxonomies that also link narrative, storytelling, and emotion. For example, Fine conceives of social movements as "bundles of narratives," identifying three classes: (1) horror stories; (2) war stories; and (3) happy endings, each of which "plays upon the emotions of participants."[18] To Fine, narrative is a technique functioning to cement social bonds within a movement, and strengthen members' commitment to shared organizational goals and a collective identity.[19] Indeed, when considering the question of why activists tell stories, Polletta responds, "They probably do so to sustain and strengthen members' commitment."[20]

However, as well as performing an internal function, storytelling also has external effects. For instance, Meyer shows how "stories of influence" can be considered a social movement outcome in the same way a specific change in policy or legislation can.[21] Accordingly, stories of influence constitute a "spillover effect" of movement activity.[22] An example of the wider influence of movements beyond particular policy outcomes is provided by the dramatic transformation in cultural values and attitudes about the role of women in politics and the workforce in the United States during the 1970s, despite the defeat of the Equal Rights Amendment during that period.[23] In the next section, we explore some of the ways immigration has figured in narratives of nation building in Australia's recent past.

THE CONTEXT OF IRREGULAR MIGRANTS IN AUSTRALIA: STATE NARRATIVES OF FEAR AND A POLITICS OF AFFECT

As a country of immigration with a long history of accepting large numbers of migrants, including refugees, Australia has a robust, highly formalized migration system, which has a large bureaucracy, underpinned by the Migration Act 1958 (Cth). Within this immigrant society and highly regulated immigration system, the reception of irregular migrants such as asylum seekers—particularly those arriving by boat on Australia's northern coastline—is one at stark contrast to the welcome extended to other categories of migrants. Hence, over more than three decades, Australia has implemented policies that punish asylum seekers, including children, due to the irregular and unauthorized mode of their arrival, with the rationale of deterring future asylum seekers—especially those attempting to arrive by boat. This approach has continued since the introduction of mandatory detention in 1992, though recent years have seen a harsher approach, with the removal of asylum seekers to offshore detention facilities. The Australian state has drawn on feelings of fear and risk among Australians to produce an "emotionally charged narrative of boat arrivals [that] is generative of affect in the ripples and reverberations flowing through the spaces of national imagining."[24]

Accordingly, the state can be regarded as emotional. Indeed, nation-states rely on feeling, emotion, and affect to rule. And this is no less so in the field of immigration, in which the demonization of asylum seekers, primarily due to their mode of arrival by boat, is a particular form of "statecraft" whereby, in the case of Australia, successive governments have persuaded the Australian public via a "politics of affect" that asylum seekers pose a significant threat to security and to the "Australian way of life."[25] So, on the one hand, we seek here to explore the official (i.e., state) narratives of fear, contagion, and protection of the nation (national security). On the other hand, we examine what social movement scholars call "counternarratives," which, in the case of seeking asylum in Australia, have consisted of cycles of contending narratives about protecting vulnerable people and safeguarding human rights, as articulated by various activists and civil society organizations.

The election in September 2013 of the conservative government of Tony Abbott further confirmed and entrenched the long-standing politics of affect that has existed in Australia in relation to asylum seekers.[26] In this context too state narratives of fear and the criminalization of asylum seekers and associated human smuggling intensified. As if to signal its intentions and make them clearer, the Australian government rebranded the previously named Department of Immigration and Citizenship as the Department of Immigration and Border Protection (DIBP). Furthermore, asylum seekers who had been labeled "irregular maritime arrivals" became "illegal maritime arrivals" (IMAs). While both labels have the effect of dehumanizing and distancing individual asylum seekers, as well as their stories and histories in seeking protection, the overt criminalization associated with being called "illegal"—and, for those in immigration detention, being labeled a "detainee"—constituted an escalation of an administrative art in creating a category of migrant to be feared, hated, and scapegoated.

The DIBP's most recent report on asylum trends is revealing in this regard, dividing the report strictly between IMA and non-IMA arrivals, where the latter are people arriving in Australia by plane with a valid visa (e.g., student, visitor or working holiday maker, or work visa), and who subsequently lodge an application for protection.[27] While migration specialists (DIBP officers, lawyers, and academics) understand these distinctions as arbitrary and not necessarily having any bearing on the voracity of an individual's claim for protection, the general public consume the emotive and inflammatory news headlines about "boat people" and more easily form a view of asylum seekers arriving by boat as undeserving because they are believed to be exploiting an orderly migration system and conspiring with criminal elements, such as human smugglers.[28] In this sense, then, although certain dilemmas with respect to irregular migrant arrivals are of a wholly practical nature—such as their numbers, their mode of entry, and the claims they make to remain—overall, the dilemmas are moral in nature:

> The state draws on and indeed builds an emotional register enacted about irregular arrivals through moral codes that trace lines through layers of social fabric like a tailor's tacking thread, holding that which is real (the suit fabric/the person asking for asylum) to that which is tentative or imagined (the suit pattern tissue paper/imagined threats and contagions and strategies to "disappear" the unwanted).[29]

It is notable that upon being elected, the new government of Prime Minister Abbott quickly put Operation Sovereign Borders into effect, with a military commander charged explicitly with stopping boats at all costs. As part of this operation, Australian Customs purchased an unspecified number of "disposable lifeboats" for $2.5 million; bright orange in color, these high-tech vessels are launched from large naval vessels and, once filled with asylum seekers picked up in Australian waters, are towed back to Indonesian waters, then cut adrift.[30] To draw on social movement terminology, the class of narrative being used here is clearly that of a "war story," as described by Fine.[31] However, in this instance, the story—or "lifeboat narrative," as it has been described—is being told by the state, not activists, albeit the narrative functions similarly to play on the emotions and galvanize public opinion about asylum seekers.[32] And in the post-9/11 context, this technique is not unusual among Western nation-states, which have tended to conflate what might be called the "war on asylum" and the "war on terror," just as asylum seekers and terrorists are frequently seen as synonymous.[33] These state narratives were integral to Operation Sovereign Borders, which, in combination with the rebranding of the DIBP and its militarization, left much of the Australian public in no doubt as to the imminent threat posed by asylum seekers arriving in boats.[34]

A suite of policies was announced quickly under the banner of Operation Sovereign Borders, with the issue of asylum seekers arriving by boat as key.[35] Included in this drive for border enforcement and security, which targeted the arrival of asylum seekers in small vessels on Australia's northwestern shoreline, was the reintroduction of offshore processing and detention. Offshore processing had its first incarnation in 2001, under the conservative Howard government, and its second incarnation under the social democratic government of Julia Gillard. Under Operation Sovereign Borders, agreements were negotiated with the governments of Nauru (a small Pacific island nation) and Papua New Guinea (PNG). Asylum seekers attempting to arrive in Australia by boat and engage

Australia's protection obligations under the Convention on Refugees were sub-sequently sent to detention and processing facilities on Nauru and Manus Island, PNG. As part of this policy, the Australian government negotiated a multibillion dollar contract with the private company Transfield Services—renamed Broad-spectrum in late 2015, although we will continue to refer to the original name here—to manage the operations of the DIBP on Nauru and Manus Island. The contract was renewed in August 2015 for AUD 2.2 billion. As of December 31, 2016, 380 people were in immigration detention on Nauru, of which 45 were children, and 866 adults were in detention on Manus Island, PNG.[36]

Early in its tenure as manager of the detention centers, Transfield faced criticism regarding the conditions of detention and the high levels of sexual, emotional, and physical abuse occurring in the centers, including self-harm. However, the Australian government has attempted to cover up these abuses by introducing federal legislation that restricts press freedoms. Infringements on press free-doms have been introduced via amendments made in 2014 to the Australian Security Intelligence Organisation Act 1979 (Cth), which, among other things, prohibit media reporting of "special intelligence operations" and anything that "relates to" them. It has been argued the effect of this particular provision is to criminalize reporting that may be in the public interest, since it could reveal incompetence or wrongdoing on the part of the authorities.[37]

Freedom of the press has been limited further by the enactment of the Tele-communications (Interception and Access) Amendment (Data Retention) Act 2015 (Cth), which provides the executive branch with new powers to apply for "journalist information warrants," which can compel telecommunications companies to surrender the metadata of journalists that may reveal a source. Concerns this would stifle investigative journalism in Australia were soon real-ized after documents obtained under Australia's Freedom of Information Act re-vealed that "eight stories on Australia's immigration policy last year [2014] were referred to the Australian Federal Police for the purpose of 'identification, and if appropriate, prosecution' of the persons responsible for leaking the informa-tion."[38] Federal legislation has also criminalized whistleblowing, such that under the Border Force Act 2015 (Cth), a prison sentence of up to two years can be imposed on detention center workers who blow the whistle on center conditions. It has been said this amounts to a deliberate attempt by the Australian govern-ment to keep atrocious conditions in offshore detention centers—including sexual abuse and self-harm—a secret.[39]

Notwithstanding the official culture of silence and secrecy that surrounds the daily circumstances of offshore detention on Nauru and Manus Island, infor-mation has slowly filtered out to the Australian public, and what amount to "hor-ror stories" about conditions in offshore detention centers have helped instigate new waves of activism and dissent over government actions.[40] The following three short vignettes provide some context for considering activism on the asylum issue in the period since offshore processing was reintroduced in 2012:

> Evidence that sexual assaults, child abuse, and other human rights violations inside the Australian government's offshore asylum seeker processing centres are being covered up has led one of the country's biggest superannuation funds to dump contractor Transfield Services.[41]

> As an Australian citizen I'm ashamed at what these vulnerable people have to go through to then be tortured in a detention centre. . . . I'd like to leave you with these questions. Is it OK for this company to profit from the abuse of vulnerable men, women and children in mandatory detention centres? And my second question is, do you think reputable organizations like hospitals, and universities, and indeed other companies will continue to do business with this company if it continues to do business in abuse? Thank you.[42]

> Sydney will host its 19th biennale from March 21. It's one of the most significant international art events on the local calendar. But questions have arisen over its connection to Australia's policy of interning asylum seekers who arrive by boat without a visa. The Biennale of Sydney's major sponsor is Transfield, a company which is also a major contractor involved in running detention centres on Nauru and Manus Island. It recently announced plans to take on more work at these centres.

> My own awareness of this connection occurred in the context of my work as a Sydney-based academic and tertiary design educator.

> After receiving marketing from the Biennale and a suggestion to take my students to the event I was faced with a clear choice: could I support an event funded by profits of mandatory detention, a policy slammed by the UNHCR as inhumane and non-compliant with international law? My answer: emphatically, no.[43]

The history of dissent and protest aimed at Australia's policies on asylum seekers has a long trajectory, since mandatory detention was introduced by Paul Keating's Labor (social democratic) government in 1992.[44] However, aside from a few notable exceptions, dissenting voices have been in the minority, with seemingly little impact on policy. What is less clear-cut is the societal impact of dissenting action. One exception to the apparently widespread consent of the Australian public to punitive policies toward asylum seekers has been public attitudes on children in detention. Organizations such as ChilOut and GetUp have been able to harness this groundswell of public opinion and effect some policy change—even if temporary. These changes resulted from evidence of the harms befalling children of immigration detention, including widespread psychological distress and mental disorders stemming from, among other things, observing adult asylum seekers self-harming and attempting suicide in the face of intractable, indefinite detention and the attendant loss of hope. In the next section, we explore recent examples of dissent and activism garnered in opposition to the Australian government's policies and practices toward asylum seekers, some of which draw on emotion and affect in presenting counternarratives.

OFFSHORE DETENTION AND PROCESSING OF ASYLUM SEEKERS: OUT OF SIGHT BUT NOT OUT OF MIND

Although this chapter's focus is on the more recent period, beginning with the implementation of Operation Sovereign Borders, it is important to recognize the context within which dissent and activism emerges, as well as the ways it develops and erupts at particular points over time. Indeed, cycles of protest and contention with respect to the Australian government's treatment of asylum seekers have a long history, with social movements and campaign organizations engaged in advocacy stretching back over twenty-five years, since the beginning of the immigration detention program that targeted, in particular, asylum seekers arriving in an "irregular" manner.[45]

For example, the advocacy group GetUp is one of a number of civil society organizations that has been engaged in public information and advocacy campaigns on a range of issues since 2005. From its inception, the issue of the treatment of asylum seekers in Australia, including mandatory detention, has been a key focus of the organization; however, GetUp now works on a range of human rights and social justice issues, including indigenous rights, poverty and inequality, environmental justice, and animal rights. Like many contemporary social movements, GetUp's tactics are intended to deliberately eschew political party affiliation, relying instead on citizen participation and activism.

Two recent examples of activism highlighting the problems associated with Australia's offshore detention program have both been directed at Transfield and its operation of offshore detention centers. First we explore the No Business in Abuse (NBIA) campaign, which focuses on shareholders in the company; next we look at the split that occurred between many prominent Australian artists and Transfield—the major funder-sponsor of the Sydney Biennale art festival in 2014.

In April 2015, under pressure to disclose conditions in its two offshore detention centers on Nauru and Manus Island, Transfield appeared before an Australian Senate committee and, under questioning, disclosed the harms asylum seekers suffer while in offshore detention, including sexual assault. From September 2012 to April 2015, the company reported 253 incidents of "actual self-harm," 10 of which were "critical" cases. The company also reported 211 assaults in the period between September 2012 and April 2015—an average of one reported assault every five days. In addition, thirteen incidents of "use of force" and nine sexual assaults were reported in relation to the Nauru facility.[46] This news report went on to quote Shen Narayanasamy, a Melbourne-based lawyer and the executive director of NBIA, who is also an executive director of human rights campaigns at GetUp: "Transfield is being paid $60 million a month to run camps in which people are trying to kill themselves every four days and sexual assaults occur every four months—that Transfield is prepared to report."[47]

With its founding in early 2015, the NBIA articulated a core mandate of communicating with companies, investors, and the Australian public regarding investment in organizations that are in breach of guidelines on respecting human rights. In November 2015, the NBIA published a report on Transfield's immigration detention operations, detailing the company's core aims and motivations. Notably, the report drew strongly on universal human rights principles and jurisprudence, such as the United Nations Guiding Principles on Business and Human Rights.[48]

In a short time, NBIA used campaigning and networking with other like-minded organizations, such as GetUp, to further its goal of informing shareholders and the public about where their superannuation savings were being invested. By mid-2015, these targeted campaigns had an impact in the form of divestment from Transfield; for instance, the superannuation fund HESTA sold its stake in Transfield services in August, citing evidence of human rights violations in offshore detention centers as the trigger. The $32 billion fund was reported as saying that the risks attached to Transfield were too high, with HESTA's chief executive, Debby Blakey, stating, "A substantial body of evidence is available pointing to the negative impacts of prolonged mandatory detention of asylum seekers[;] both the United Nations and the Australian Human Rights Commission are among respected authorities that have said it is a breach of human rights law."[49]

At the same time, a number of other superannuation funds divested from Transfield, while others considered their position. In a Machiavellian turn of events, it was the confidentiality agreements required by government contracts in detention arrangements that led to HESTA's eventual decision to divest from Transfield. These confidentiality clauses were cited as the reason Transfield was not able to divulge full or detailed answers to questions that investors required in order to feel confident about the company's operations.

Secrecy surrounding offshore detention practices, the use of confidentiality clauses, and claims about safeguarding the privacy of asylum seekers by the DIBP have long been criticized by civil society and advocacy organizations as a smoke screen to deny the Australian public full information about the policies and actions carried out in its name. Although it has had little impact to date, many nongovernmental organizations, activists, lawyers, artists, writers, and filmmakers have continued to use various modes of communication to help reveal the human face of Australia's asylum seeker policies. Asylum seekers too have attempted to counter the Australian state's deployment of emotion and affect to cultivate their own emotional connection and a sympathetic ear, communicating directly with the Australian public, such as in the case of the following excerpt from a publicly released letter signed by numerous asylum seekers held in detention on the Australian mainland:

> Please imagine what we feel, what we fear after this leakage of our personal informa-tion by people who promised to protect us guaranteeing our safety and privacy. Please imagine the anxiety and stress building inside us. Please imagine the fear we feel for our families in our home countries. And this is all that we have to experience on top of struggles we already are going through.[50]

More recently, a group of artists threatened to withdraw from the Sydney Bien-nale in March 2014, protesting Transfield's sponsorship of the event and voicing similar concerns to those of NBIA regarding the company's complicity in the abuse of asylum seekers via its operation of offshore detention centers on Nauru and Manus Island. The artists' threatened boycott received widespread media and public attention, which eventually led to Transfield withdrawing its sponsorship from—and all involvement with—the Sydney Biennale.

Like the NBIA and Sydney Biennale examples, a wide range of groups, organ-izations, and campaigns have emerged or reemerged in opposition to asylum seeker policy and its increasingly harsh, punitive, and secretive manifestation off-shore. For instance, a large number of organizations, groups, and social move-ment activists came together throughout 2015 and into 2016 under the umbrella #LetThemStay. This campaign focused on 267 asylum seekers detained on the Australian mainland and under threat of being removed to Nauru. Many of the 267 were babies and young children born in Australia, and most had previously been held in detention before being brought to Australia to receive medical attention that could not be provided on Nauru or Manus Island.

It is notable that a number of the groups and alliances that have emerged in response to this situation appear to defy the expected membership of protest and dissent. Two of these groups are Grandmothers Against Detention of Refugee Children, and Academics for Refugees. Groups of doctors and health profession-als have been a new and particularly active presence in protesting and speaking out about the treatment and possible deportation of babies and children in their care. However, as previously discussed, the Border Force Act 2015 (Cth) prevents doctors and other health-care professionals from speaking out publicly about what they witness in offshore detention facilities. If they do blow the whistle on de-tention conditions, they may be subject to a period of two years' imprisonment. In defiance of the silencing provisions of the Border Force Act 2015 (Cth), David Isaacs—a consultant pediatrician at a university teaching hospital in Sydney, where he also runs a refugee clinic—wrote a powerful opinion piece for a major broadsheet newspaper in early 2016, proposing that Nauru and Manus Island are Australia's Guantanamo Bay:

> Arguably, there are four things that make Guantanamo so bad: lack of due process for imprisoning people there, lack of accountability (limited information, no transparency), indefinite imprisonment without due process (seemingly arbitrary legal processing, lack of clear end-point to imprisonment) and severe physical and mental maltreatment.
>
> Nauru and Manus share the first three characteristics with Guantanamo. Nauru and Manus, like Guantanamo, are "black sites," out of sight and mind of the public, shrouded in secrecy, with severe restrictions on reporters. The Australian Border Force Act means employees including doctors, lawyers, teachers and guards who report the truth face two years [of] imprisonment. Yet, for an Australian offshore detention policy to be successful in deterring people-smuggling—the stated intention—none of these four things are necessary. Therefore, even if you accept the government's justification for the Australian asylum seeker policy, the current treatment is unethical.[51]

The divestment campaigning of NBIA and GetUp is reminiscent of other cases of anticorporate activism, including historical calls for responsible investment, such as refusal to invest in enterprises benefiting the slave trade.[52] More recent campaigns include the pressure put on American universities in the 1970s and 1980s to divest in South African-related companies in protest of apartheid. Sarah Soule argues that these protests were helped greatly by the fact that the American public was appalled by what was happening in South Africa, and by prodivestment pressures emanating from the U.S. Congress, which passed several pieces of anti-apartheid legislation in the mid-1980s.[53]

Central to anti-apartheid student activism during this era was the formation of shantytowns: "makeshift shacks constructed of miscellaneous building materials (e.g., wood, plastic, cardboard, tar paper, and metal), which were built to encourage administrators to divest of their South African-related securities."[54] Shantytowns were a source of great embarrassment to American universities at the time and a visible reminder of their association with companies and banks having ties to South Africa; as a result, universities frequently repressed shantytowns, with the help of campus police. Similarly, superannuation funds such as HESTA have deemed it too risky to their reputations to be associated with Transfield's controversial activities in offshore detention centers and thus have divested from the company.

While American students were involved in other acts of civil disobedience, such as sit-ins, blockades, hunger strikes, rallies, and marches, Soule notes it is the boycott that "is perhaps the quintessential tactic used by those outsiders who are displeased by the actions of a given corporation."[55] We see this clearly in the collective action of artists who threatened to boycott the 2014 Sydney Biennale because Transfield was the sponsor. And, like the prodivestment campaigns of American students in the 1970s and 1980s, Transfield's withdrawal from this event was in no small part due to the widespread media and public attention the threatened boycott received. However, unlike the U.S. prodivestment movement, the history of government antagonism toward asylum seekers in Australia indicates we are unlikely to see anything resembling positive legal and humanitarian reform in this area anytime soon.

Regardless of the difficulty of predicting the impact of the dissenting collective action examined in this chapter, civil society activism on behalf of noncitizens nevertheless has the potential to put states and corporations on notice. Here, advocacy for an extension of human rights to nonmembers of a polity encompasses nongovernmental organizations and social movements, as well as the wider citizenry who demonstrate a "rooted" cosmopolitanism through solidarity with outsiders. Moreover, like the movements studied by Melucci (discussed previously), these cycles of contentious politics operate both below and beyond the sphere of state politics—that is, at the local grassroots level and through transnational networks.

Notwithstanding that, it is important to recognize the role of global cosmopolitanism in establishing universal human rights; the role of states as guarantors of international human rights; and the role of domestic courts, which interpret international human rights law in national settings.[56] Adopting this approach, Kate Nash takes issue with not only global cosmopolitanism but also the multiplicity of movements that demand human rights "from below," arguing that human rights law is state centric "in that it is virtually exclusively through states that international human rights law is made and enforced."[57] Importantly, acts of civil disobedience and dissent are also material manifestations of public will, not only signaling the need for a response from the state but also asserting the fundamental role of dissent embodied in the very event.[58] Indeed, Judith Butler affirms the power of the materiality created through such a "politics of the street" when she states the following:

> So when we think about what it means to assemble in a crowd, a growing crowd, and what it means to move through public space in a way that contests the distinction between public and private, we see some way that bodies in their plurality lay claim to the public, find and produce the public through seizing and reconfiguring the matter of material environments; at the same time, those material environments are part of the action, and they themselves act when they become the support for action.[59]

To be sure, the cases explored in this chapter are only some of the most recent examples of a long and growing repertoire of activism and redress sought through the courts on the treatment of asylum seekers by the Australian state. In a very recent case, the Supreme Court of Papua New Guinea held that the detention of asylum seekers on Manus Island—many of whom had been assessed as refugees and were therefore entitled to protection under the Convention on Refugees— breached their right to personal liberty under the PNG Constitution, as well as their fundamental human rights, as guaranteed by international human rights law and conventions.[60] Although Australian government officials responded by resolving not to alter border protection policies and stating that no detainees will be resettled in Australia, the decision of the PNG Supreme Court is significant for confirming asylum seekers' rights and establishing the Australian state's breach of its international human rights obligations.

While the High Court of Australian has been less sympathetic to refugee rights, in 2011 it did decide the "Malaysian solution" of the Gillard Labor government was invalid because Malaysia was not a party to the Convention on Refugees, and hence was not legally bound to provide protections and access to effective procedures for asylum seekers as required under the Migration Act 1958 (Cth).[61] Accordingly, the High Court made permanent injunctions preventing the removal to Malaysia of eight hundred asylum seekers who had arrived in Australia by boat.

With the issue of immigration detention, the retraumatization that detention causes to asylum seekers has become the focus of research and advocacy. And many detention cases end up in the courts. By late 2011, the Australian government had paid $18 million in compensation to asylum seekers for wrongful detention, and $5 million to former detainees for negligence.[62] As the NBIA has argued in its recent report on offshore detention, the harms inflicted by immigration detention in Nauru and Manus Island are yet to be fully documented and understood.[63]

Finally, in this chapter we have presented a view of the state as emotional and reliant on a "politics of affect" to govern, which it does at least partly by generating certain narratives around nationhood, which include, in the case of immigration and asylum seekers, stories about who is and who is not included, and on what bases inclusion and exclusion occurs. This idea of the state as emotional is by no means novel; however, in the area of immigration, it does appear contrary to the highly bureaucratic and increasingly militarized image of the Australian state's DIBP, wherein immigration officials make hard-nosed decisions based on legal-rational norms.[64]

In contrast, Reilly and La Forgia have argued that rather than seeing immigration officers simply as bureaucrats we should treat them as moral human beings on whom we are placing the very heavy burden of making decisions about whether to return people to countries where they may be in grave danger.[65] Their point is that asking immigration officials to make these decisions as part of an informal and secretive screening process that has been used in Australia since 2012 is contrary to notions of democratic deliberation, which requires issues—especially contentious issues, such as the treatment of asylum seekers—be discussed publicly to ensure "our mutual interaction and influence over each other."[66] Instead, by effectively outsourcing our democratic angst to immigration officers, Reilly and La Forgia contend we are asking those individuals "to bear our democratic responsibility for the making of difficult judgments."[67] However, as we have shown in this chapter, not all Australian citizens are content to stand by and watch while the state displays its disregard for international human rights law, under which asylum seekers have numerous protections. For those Australians, state narratives intended to instill feelings of fear, contagion, invasion, and so forth, are countered with stories about the human consequences of the inhumane treatment of asylum seekers in offshore detention centers. As with the state narratives, activist counternarratives are emotional and involve a politics of affect.

NOTES TO CHAPTER 5

1. Nichols Papastergiadis, "Wars of Mobility," *European Journal of Social Theory* 13, no. 3 (2010): 343–361; Sharon Pickering, Marie Segrave, Claudia Tazreiter, and Leanne Weber, "Migration Control and Human Security," in *Research Companion to Migration Theory and Policy Research*, ed. Juss Satvinder (Aldershot: Ashgate, 2013).

2. Klaus Neumann, *Across the Seas: Australia's Response to Refugees: A History* (Collingwood: BlackInc., 2015).

3. Hank Johnston and Bert Klandermans, "The Cultural Analysis of Social Movements," in *Social Movements and Culture*, ed. Hank Johnston and Bert Klandermans (London: UCL Press, 1995), vii.

4. Alberto Melucci, *Nomads of the Present: Social Movements and Individual Needs in Contemporary Society* (London: Hutchinson Radius, 1989), 44.

5. Alberto Melucci, *Challenging Codes: Collective Action in the Information Age* (Cambridge: Cambridge University Press, 1996), 216.

6. Alberto Melucci, "The Symbolic Challenge of Contemporary Movements," *Social Research* 52, no. 4 (1985): 815, original emphasis.

7. Jeff Goodwin and Steven Pfaff, "Emotion Work in High-Risk Social Movements: Managing Fear in the U.S. and East German Civil Rights Movements," in *Passionate Politics: Emotions and Social Movements*, ed. Jeff Goodwin, James M. Jasper, and Francesca Polletta (Chicago: University of Chicago Press, 2001), 301.

8. Greg Martin, *Understanding Social Movements* (London: Routledge, 2015), 99.

9. James M. Jasper, *The Art of Moral Protest: Culture, Biography, and Creativity in Social Movements* (Chicago: University of Chicago Press, 1997), 106.

10. Doug McAdam, *Political Process and the Development of Black Insurgency, 1930–1970* (Chicago: University of Chicago Press, 1982), 34.

11. Jeff Goodwin, James M. Jasper, and Francesca Polletta, "Introduction: Why Emotions Matter," in *Passionate Politics: Emotions and Social Movements*, ed. Jeff Goodwin, James M. Jasper, and Francesca Polletta (Chicago: University of Chicago Press, 2001), 7.

12. Ibid., 15.

13. Francesca Polletta and Edwin Amenta, "Conclusion: Second That Emotion? Lessons from Once-Novel Concepts on Social Movement Research," in *Passionate Politics: Emotions and Social Movements*, ed. Jeff Goodwin, James M. Jasper, and Francesca Polletta (Chicago: University of Chicago Press, 2001), 305.

14. Joseph E. Davis, "Narrative and Social Movements: The Power of Stories," in *Stories of Change: Narrative and Social Movements*, ed. Joseph E. Davis (Albany: State University of New York Press, 2002), 3.

15. Jeff Goodwin, James M. Jasper, and Francesca Polletta, "The Return of the Repressed: The Fall and Rise of Emotions in Social Movement Theory," *Mobilization* 5, no. 1 (2000): 76.

16. Davis, "Narrative and Social Movements," 25.

17. Ron Eyerman, "How Social Movements Move: Emotions and Social Movements," in *Emotions and Social Movements*, ed. Helena Flam and Debra King (London: Routledge, 2005), 46.

18. Gary Alan Fine, "Public Narration and Group Culture: Discerning Discourse in Social Movements," in *Social Movements and Culture*, ed. Hank Johnston and Bert Klandermans (London: UCL Press, 1995), 135.

19. Ibid., 128.

20. Francesca Polletta, "Plotting Protest: Mobilizing Stories in the 1960 Sit-Ins," in *Stories of Change: Narrative and Social Movements*, ed. Joseph E. Davis (Albany: State University of New York Press, 2002), 48.

21. David S. Meyer, "Claiming Credit: Stories of Movement Influence as Outcomes," in *Culture, Social Movements and Protest*, ed. Hank Johnston (Farnham: Ashgate, 2009), 55–75.

22. David S. Meyer and Nancy Whittier, "Social Movement Spillover," *Social Problems* 41 (1994): 277–298.

23. Meyer, "Claiming Credit," 59.

24. Claudia Tazreiter, "Lifeboat Politics in the Pacific: Affect and the Ripples and Shimmers of a Migrant Saturated Future," *Emotion, Space and Society* 16 (2015): 103.

25. Greg Martin, "Stop the Boats! Moral Panic in Australia Over Asylum Seekers," *Continuum* 29, no. 3 (2015): 304–322.

26. Tazreiter, "Lifeboat Politics in the Pacific," 105.

27. Australian Government, *Asylum Trends Australia, 2012–13 Annual Publication*, Department of Immigration and Border Protection, 2013, https://www.border.gov.au/ReportsandPublications/Documents/statistics/asylum-trends-aus-2012–13.pdf.

28. Martin, "Stop the Boats!"

29. Tazreiter, "Lifeboat Politics in the Pacific," 99.

30. Jennifer Rajca, "Australian Lifeboats Used to Send Asylum Seekers Back to Indonesia Cost $2.5 Million," *News Limited*, February 24, 2014, http://www.news.com.au/national/australian-lifeboats-used-to-send-asylum-seekers-back-to-indonesia-cost-25-million/story-fncynjr2-1226836532115; George Roberts, "Asylum Seekers Give Details on Operation Sovereign Borders Lifeboat Turn-Back," ABC News, March 18, 2014, http://www.abc.net.au/news/2014-03-17/asylum-seekers-give-details-on-operation-sovereign-borders/5326546.

31. Fine, "Public Narration and Group Culture," 135.

32. Tazreiter, "Lifeboat Politics in the Pacific."

33. Martin, "Stop the Boats!"; Tazreiter, "Lifeboat Politics in the Pacific," 104.

34. Madeline Gleeson, *Offshore: Behind the Wire on Manus and Nauru* (Sydney: NewSouth, 2016).

35. Claudia Tazreiter, "'Stop the Boats'! Externalising the Borders of Australia and Imaginary Pathologies of Contagion," *Journal of Immigration, Nationality and Asylum Law* 29, no. 2 (2015): 141–157.

36. Australian Government, "Immigration Detention Statistics," Department of Immigration and Border Protection, 2016, https://www.border.gov.au/ReportsandPublications/Documents/statistics/immigration-detention-statistics-31-dec-2016.pdf.

37. George Williams, "The Legal Assault in Australian Democracy," Sir Richard Blackburn Lecture, ACT Law Society, May 12, 2015, https://www.actlawsociety.asn.au/documents/item/1304.

38. Ibid.

39. Editorial Board, "Australia's Brutal Treatment of Migrants," *New York Times*, September 3, 2015, http://www.nytimes.com/2015/09/03/opinion/australias-brutal-treatment-of-migrants.html?smid=fb-share&_r=1.

40. Fine, "Public Narration and Group Culture," 135.

41. Sally Rose, "HESTA Dumps Transfield Citing Detention Centres Abuses," *Sydney Morning Herald*, August 18, 2015, http://www.smh.com.au/business/banking-and-finance/hesta-dumps-transfield-citing-detention-centre-abuses-20150818-gj218u.html.

42. Former asylum seeker, Mohammad Ali Baqiri, addressing Transfield Annual General Meeting; quoted in Chloe Hooper, "Burning the Stakeholders: Shen Narayanasamy Takes on Transfield," *The Monthly*, December 2015, https://www.themonthly.com.au/issue/2015/december/1448888400/chloe-hooper/burning-stakeholders.

43. Matthew Kiem, "Should Artists Boycott the Sydney Biennale Over Transfield Links?," *The Conversation*, February 12, 2014, https://theconversation.com/should-artists-boycott-the-sydney-biennale-over-transfield-links-23067.

44. Claudia Tazreiter, *Asylum Seekers and the State: The Politics of Protection in a Security-Conscious World* (Aldershot: Ashgate, 2004). See also Tazreiter, "Lifeboat Politics in the Pacific."

45. Tazreiter, *Asylum Seekers and the State*.

46. Sally Rose, "People in Detention on Nauru Try to Harm Themselves Every Four Days: Transfield Response to Senate," *Sydney Morning Herald*, September 25, 2015, http://www.smh.com.au/business/people-in-detention-on-nauru-try-harm-themselves-every-four-days-transfield-response-to-senate-20150924-gju7gq.html.

47. Ibid.

48. Shen Narayanasamy, Rachel Ball, Katie Hepworth, Brynn O'Brien, and Claire Parfitt, *Business in Abuse: Transfield's Complicity in Gross Human Rights Abuses Within Australia's Offshore Detention Regime* (Melbourne: No Business in Abuse, 2015), https://d68ej2dhhub09.cloudfront.net/1321-NBIA_Report-20Nov2015b.pdf.

49. Rose, "HESTA Dumps Transfield."

50. Asylum seekers quoted in Tazreiter, "Lifeboat Politics in the Pacific," 106.

51. David Isaacs, "Nauru and Manus Island Are Australia's Guantanamo Bay," *The Age,* March 7, 2016, http://www.theage.com.au/comment/nauru-and-manus-island-are-australias-guantanamo-gay-20160228-gn5qtg.html.

52. Sarah Soule, *Contention and Corporate Social Responsibility* (Cambridge: Cambridge University Press, 2009), 12.

53. Ibid., 91.

54. Ibid., 88.

55. Ibid., 12–13.

56. Martin, *Understanding Social Movements,* 243–244.

57. Kate Nash, "Human Rights, Movements and Law: On Not Researching Legitimacy," *Sociology* 46, no. 5 (2012): 808.

58. Costas Douzinas, "The 'Right to the Event': The Legality and Morality of Revolution and Resistance," *Metodo: International Studies in Phenomenology and Philosophy* 2, no. 1 (2014): 151–167.

59. Judith Butler, "Bodies in Alliance and the Politics of the Street," *Transversal Texts,* September 2011, http://transversal.at/transversal/1011/butler/en.

60. Eric Tlozek and Stephanie Anderson, "PNG's Supreme Court Rules Detention of Asylum Seekers on Manus Island Is Illegal," *ABC News,* April 27, 2016, http://www.abc.net.au/news/2016-04-26/png-court-rules-asylum-seeker-detention-manus-island-illegal/7360078.

61. Martin, "Stop the Boats!" 306.

62. Debra Jopson and Catherine Armitage, "Government Faces 'Mass Action' to Compensate Refugees Held at Detention Centres," *Sydney Morning Herald,* July 14, 2012, http://www.smh.com.au/federal-politics/political-news/government-faces-mass-action-to-compensate-refugees-held-at-detention-centres-20120713-2219u.html.

63. Narayanasamy et al., *Business in Abuse.*

64. Tazreiter, "Lifeboat Politics in the Pacific," 100–101.

65. Alexander Reilly and Rebecca La Forgia, "Secret 'Enhanced Screening' of Asylum Seekers: A Democratic Analysis Centering on the Humanity of the Commonwealth Officer," *Alternative Law Journal* 38, no. 3 (2013): 143–146.

66. Ibid., 144.

67. Ibid., 145.

6. CRITIQUING ZONES OF EXCEPTION

Actor-Oriented Approaches Explaining the Rise of Immigration Detention

MATTHEW B. FLYNN, GEORGIA SOUTHERN UNIVERSITY
MICHAEL FLYNN, GLOBAL DETENTION PROJECT

Until the end of the Cold War, immigration detention was used infrequently in most countries, increasing in prominence during periods of perceived crisis and diminishing as conditions changed.[1] However, over the course of the last two to three decades, new immigrant detention laws have been adopted, specialized institutions have been created to tend to detainee populations, and more countries have begun implementing such measures.[2] In part because of its novelty, the concept of immigration detention remains widely contested, and there is lack of clarity about the forces that have led to its expansion. Complicating matters is the fact that the formative years of the growth of immigration detention in many countries—for example, the 1990s in many European Union countries— appear to coincide with a decline or stabilization of migratory pressures.[3]

Immigration detention thus shares a similar puzzle to that of many national prison systems: expansions occur at times that do not always correspond with a growth in potential detainee populations. In many countries, when the prison population began expanding, crime rates were not going up; similarly, immigration detention does not necessarily correspond with increases in asylum seekers or irregular migrants.[4] Likewise, there is little evidence that detention stems the growth of cross-border flows.[5] According to the United Nations High Commissioner for Refugees (UNHCR), "There is no empirical evidence that the prospect of being detained deters irregular migration, or discourages persons from seeking asylum."[6] Statistical tests of restrictive immigration practices in major migrant-receiving countries reveal that more deportation and detention does not result in less immigration.[7] Furthermore, some studies have shown that when destination countries implement "alternatives to detention," such as reporting procedures or conditional release, most people comply with immigration procedures and do not abscond.[8]

So why have countries, especially in the Global North, been turning toward this practice? Such a movement toward increasing state control of people's cross-border movements appears paradoxical given the recent deregulation of international trade and finance. A prominent answer to this puzzle in the academic literature is one advanced by some poststructuralist scholars, who claim that detention represents a symbolic act of national sovereignty to demarcate those within the fold of nation-state protections by excluding those who are not, which becomes more pressing because of the disruptive impacts of globalization. Such an argument begs the question of why states frequently attempt to conceal their detention practices instead of broadcasting them.[9] Another question also not addressed by poststructuralist scholarship concerns the interests and motivations of the actors involved in what is effectively the commodification of "the other" through state-backed detention efforts. If the concern lies in the exercise of state power over human beings, how do societal forces affect the increasing criminalization of immigrant flows? Lastly, immigration detention results in significant human rights abuses, even as relevant international treaty regimes have appeared to gain prominence in shaping global norms. What analysis best informs our understanding of these human rights abuses and the proper ways to challenge the use of detention?

We argue that insights from the sociology of organizations offer better responses to these questions and indicate political efforts that could better address problems associated with immigration detention than poststructuralist accounts. In particular, the work of Gideon Sjoberg and his analytic framework of "bureaucratic capitalism" provide sensitizing concepts that are general enough to be applied to the diverse detention regimes we observe across the world while also drawing attention to the key actors and processes involved in detention.[10] In other words, we analyze immigration detention as a complex organization that has a bureaucratic structure, secures resources to sustain operations, and operates in an evolving field occupied by the social control industry.

This chapter reviews poststructuralist literature on immigration detention and its apparent theoretical and empirical shortcomings. It then analyzes the concept of immigration detention from the standpoint of Sjoberg's "bureaucratic capitalism," highlighting human agency, the state-corporate nexus, rationalization processes, hierarchical structures, and secrecy systems. We conclude with a discussion of the differing policy implications between poststructuralist theories and actor-oriented approaches to this phenomenon.

FROM ZONES OF EXCEPTION TO
WEBS OF CONTROL

Many scholars working on immigration detention have sought to apply a post-structuralist conceptual framework that analyzes the role of narratives, discourses, and disciplines that compete for hegemony and legitimize action for the control of populations.[11] Michel Foucault termed this "biopolitics." Building on this tradition, political philosopher Giorgio Agamben developed two concepts that have influenced work on immigration detention.[12] First is *homo sacer,* or "bare life," a term from Roman law referring to a banned or an accursed person, which Agamben borrows to denote depoliticized life, or a life in contrast to that of the citizen. The second is "zones of exception," which Agamben borrows from the German legal scholar Carl Schmitt, referring to areas where the sovereign power of the state operates without constraints, as typified by his use of the term in regard to refugee camps.

To understand the development of states, Agamben argues that politics revolves around determining in-groups—denoted as citizens, or those who receive state protections and rights—and out-groups—those who lack all rights and are reduced to bare life. Sovereignty is thus exercised by inclusive exclusion, acting on itself by defining what it is not through the creation of zones of exemption, which is viewed as a necessary part of the creation of state power and sovereignty. But there are important distinctions between Agamben's thought and that of his predecessors.[13] In comparison to Schmitt, he considers that zones of exception have become the rule of politics and not just what it is based on. And whereas Foucault distinguishes between sovereign power—the right to take life, which characterizes premodern societies—and more covert forms of disciplinary power employed by modern societies for social control, Agamben reduces these biopolitical practices to a stark form of sovereign power.

Poststructuralist scholars argue that the political situation of migrants demonstrates the normalizing of Agamben's ideas about bare life and zones of exception.[14] Rajaram and Grundy-Warr argue that detention practices in Australia, Malaysia, and Thailand demonstrate that "the refugee becomes a controllable figure that can be held in discursive stasis—the meaning and identity of the refugee may be created according to the needs and whims of sovereign law."[15] Tsoukala argues that the policing of illegal migrants at transit zones and the use of detention centers are differing forms of a technology of discipline that controls "time and space through the control of human flows rather than through immobilized human bodies."[16] Mountz points to the special role that islands play in the sovereign's promotion of security at a distance, arguing that detaining migrants on archipelagos represents—both legally and metaphorically—permanent zones of exclusion. Instead of Foucault's panopticon—through which everyone in a community is equally submitted to processes of surveillance and control—Bigo argues that a new "banopticon" has created permanent zones of exception that normalize the control of a designated group of outsiders by criminalizing illegal residence.[17]

These authors help underscore two apparently contradictory aspects of Agamben's writings: that the refugee, an ideal type of *homo sacer*, is nevertheless also an integral part of the nation-state system, which for Agamben involves discursive efforts to delimit the meaning of being human. The efforts of the member states of the European Union in 2015–2016 to discursively redefine refugees from Syria's civil war as migrants subject to detention and deportation, and thereby demonstrate the "protection" of their borders and citizens, comes to mind.

Despite the compelling characterizations of contemporary immigration control measures that many of these poststructuralist arguments make, they are arguably hampered by important theoretical and empirical complications. First is the circular logic in which detention becomes the normal operation of sovereign power. Tsoukala writes that "exclusion underlies sovereignty; freedom of movement becomes the new criterion for exclusion; and the exception is the necessary condition for the establishment of new zones that will further confirm sovereignty."[18] If this type of argumentation were explanatory, then logically we should also expect to see corollary results—namely, that when states fail to create explicit zones of exception, their sovereign systems somehow weaken or fail. But in fact there does not appear to be any inherent necessity for the state to deny rights to "the other" in order to be able to uphold the rights of its members, which is demonstrated in part by the lack of immigration detention regimes in certain parts of the world, most notably in South America, where the norm is not to detain migrants or asylum seekers.[19]

By not specifying actors in the process of legal discourse or merely presenting them as unreflective actors expressing the underlying logic of state power, poststructuralist scholars tend to posit a functionalist argument susceptible to teleological thinking.[20] In other words, the outcomes they seek to explain are transformed into social causes. Agamben takes this to the extreme. For him, refugee camps, detention centers, and so on, become equated with sovereign power in which there are no social actors exercising their will on others; rather, the camp merely depicts the true, naked reality of sovereign power. As Genel states, "The transformation of the analysis of the camp into a figure of political space appears to result in a rather reductive paradigm."[21] In contrast, Foucault emphasizes the instrumentalist logic of biopower as a means to an end as opposed to just an end; that is, detention and related practices embody the modern impulse to separate and control populations. Still, without a concept of agency included in the theoretical framework, detention appears as necessary and overdetermined as opposed to contingent and reversible.

A second issue is the conflation of citizenship rights with human rights. While these critical perspectives highlight the contradictions faced by liberal democracies when they violate the same rights they claim to uphold, citizenship rights are analytically distinct from human rights.[22] Citizenship rights, referring to the relationship of rights and obligations between states and citizens deriving from membership in a political community, result in the creation of in-groups versus out-groups. But human rights are claims to human dignity with universal application regardless of one's nationality or citizenship status. Globalization, while potentially weakening the nation-state system in key ways and sharpening citizenship claims for protection, does not necessarily result in the creation of zones of exemption where human rights are weakening and where the "refugee is outside the law," as Rajaram and Grundy-Warr claim.[23] The problem is that differential citizenship status—not the lack of rights per se—can enable human rights abuses of detained migrants, especially when due process guarantees do not apply in "administrative" detention situations.

On the other hand, countries with strong constitutional safeguards, providing equal protection for citizens and noncitizens in judicial proceedings, have in some cases developed immigration detention systems that contrast sharply with those of other countries. Thus, for instance, although European Union law provides that member states can keep a person in immigration detention for up to eighteen months, France—known for its strong constitutional guarantees—continues to limit detention to much shorter periods (less than forty-five days) and requires stronger judicial oversight of immigration decisions than do many of its EU neighbors.[24] Regions with even fewer rights protections, such as the Gulf States, where the conditions of migrants have been described as a modern form of slavery, appear closer to Agamben's depiction of bare life.[25]

The larger point is that analyzing relevant legal norms can require carefully identifying the particularities of a given detention situation, which often does not factor prominently in the work of poststructuralist scholars. As one critic writes, with its "breathtaking historical sweep, the biopolitical paradigm displays a marked loss of specificity in its analyses of contemporary biopolitical phenomena."[26] Poststructuralist writers who find equivalence between contemporary migrant detention systems and World War II–era extermination camps can deeply mischaracterize today's detention practices (and do a disservice to the terrible legacy of the Nazi camps).[27]

Third, scholarly use of loose metaphors to denote extreme events decontextualizes the complex role of race, class, and political economy associated with the evolution of sovereignty and detention. Even Duffield, channeling Foucault's biopolitics but also employing Agamben's language, places the sociocultural categories of race central to the sovereign division between the protected, benefiting "mass society" of the developed world and the increasingly mobile, albeit underdeserving, underdeveloped world.[28] The response to today's refugee crisis underscores the importance of race and the religious other in efforts to interdict and detain asylum seekers. If the people fleeing conflict came not from Syria, Afghanistan, or Africa but from another European country, would the response be so harsh and categorical in its denial?

There is also an obvious class dimension, since the racialized other who pertains to the mobile elite can—as Bauman puts it—become "exterritorial," obtain privileged status as professionals in trade deals, and enjoy visa approvals while the rest are condemned to their locality.[29] The logical extension of Bauman's ideas about the prison as a *"factory of exclusion"* to the question of migration leads us to conclude that detention penalizes the impoverished masses for attempting mobility.[30]

Although Duffield and Bauman advance their arguments by emphasizing racial categories and elite prerogatives, their poststructuralist bias does not provide an adequate understanding of the materialist basis for contemporary social change. Across the developed world, and even the undeveloped word, political economies have shifted from Fordist-based economies—organized around full employment, inclusion, and stable livelihoods—to post-Fordist economies—premised on flexible labor, exclusion, and insecurity.[31] As Melossi argues, the wave of globalization that began in the 1970s led to "capitalist arrogance, increasing social inequality, deep divisions in the working class due to the new 'post-Fordist' setting, massive migration flows, soaring imprisonment rates and a new culture of penal cruelty."[32] Young adds to this causal chain by including relative deprivation and "ontological insecurity," which he argues leads to more crime and violence and the resultant reaction of society based on the scapegoating of out-groups. But as others have shown (and Young admits), there is no linear relation between crime, or in our case, visa infractions, and penalization.[33]

At base, the spread of immigration detention—as well as other forms of immigration control—represents novel state responses for governing economic transformations occurring at the global, national, and local levels. This insight applies to much of the scholarly work looking at the neoliberal bases of incarceration. For example, in the view of Wacquant, the penalization of the poor represents the heavy hand of neoliberal states engaged in the penal management of poverty amidst welfare retraction, wage compression, and economic insecurity witnessed on both sides of the Atlantic.[34] Additionally Gilmore, like Melossi, highlights the disruptive tendencies of capitalism as the root cause of the expanding prison system in California. She highlights how the state's post-Depression growth strategy broke down in the 1970s, leading to a surplus unemployed population; surplus unproductive land; surplus capital, lacking profitable investment opportunities; and surplus state capacity. The "prison fix" offered a solution to these multiple crises.[35]

Similarly, Flynn contends that economic insecurities resulting from neoliberal globalization provide the basis for xenophobic politics that channel class-based concerns into ethno-nationalist campaigns targeting ethnically and racially distinct out-groups. Lesser-educated white males in high-income countries who had enjoyed job security, pensions, and middle-class lifestyles in the Fordist economy now face levels of precarity that had previously been the reserve of women and minorities in low-status jobs.[36] The rise of right-wing parties in Europe and Donald Trump's success in mobilizing white working-class voters using anti-immigrant rhetoric—as well as calls on both sides of the Atlantic for more detention and deportation of migrants and asylum seekers—are buttressed by these economic trends.

While these authors correctly identify the rise in penalization as an exercise in neoliberal statecraft, shaped by the tendencies of capitalist reproduction and crisis, their analyses privilege sociostructural forces more than social actors. Focusing on the latter privileges an analysis of the power elite operating through organizational structures that not only push economic globalization but whose consequences also affect the changing dynamics of sovereignty as well as penal policy. The spread of new transnational organizations across borders—including private multinational corporations, official intergovernmental organizations, and nongovernmental organizations—represents a qualitative change to sovereignty.[37] This does not represent the end of the state per se but a reshaping of the role of the state.[38] An appropriate metaphor for understanding this new global reality, as employed by Holton, is as a complex web of multiple actors and interests involved in various forms of conflict and cooperation.[39] Needless to say, the lead organizations in driving global markets, including the shift to a post–Fordist-Keynesian economy, are corporations.[40] Consequently, understanding the politics behind immigration requires analysis of these new corporate-bureaucratic structures.

In sum, Agamben's approach to achieving an ontologically pure notion of sovereignty stripped to bare life through "the jargon of exception" removes a key facet of democratic politics: "the political significance of people as a multiplicity of social relations that condition politics and that are constituted by the mediations of various objectified forms and processes (for example, scientific knowledge, technologies, property relations, legal institutions . . .)," as Huysmans writes.[41] Economic globalization does not necessitate new symbolic efforts to exercise state sovereignty as much as shift economic risks faced by individuals and communities and change relationships between international organizations, states, and their citizens and noncitizens. Understanding these new arrangements and the politics of migrant detention thus requires a look into the new organizational structures of this novel social control industry.

BUREAUCRATIC CAPITALISM AND THE
WAREHOUSING OF HUMAN BODIES

In economic sociology, the central problematic of contemporary immigration detention regimes is not the inexorable impulse of sovereignty to demonstrate its power through inclusive exclusion. Rather, it begins with the premise that complex organizations are a fact of life in modern society. For good or bad, they play a central role in social reproduction through the management, production, and distribution of goods and services. Complex organizations also embody power relations and actively shape institutional fields—not only discursively, as poststructuralists emphasize, but also through the wider political economy. Disciplinary power thus takes concrete shape by looking at specific organizational arrangements for managing human populations, including migrant flows. Along this line of reasoning, Gideon Sjoberg provides a conceptual framework of "bureaucratic capitalism" that is neither deterministic nor teleological for understanding the growth, variation, and abuses associated with immigration detention.[42]

A focus on formal organizations, moreover, allows researchers to connect ongoing social inequities, embedded in class structures, to rights abuses. For poststructuralists, class position does not play a key role, despite the fact that the upper and middle classes rarely find themselves in detention. In contrast, Sjoberg emphasizes that corporate organizations, such as the social control industry, sustain privileges for some while denying rights to others. "The prison-industrial complex in the United States serves two functions. It sweeps the 'unwanted' (especially members of racial and ethnic minorities) off the streets, and it provides a stable market for producers of a rather wide range of goods and services," contends Sjoberg.[43] In other words, we can see the increased use of immigration detention centers as a means to profit from the active creation of vulnerable groups as exploitable commodities.

The flip side of profit making is Sjoberg's concept of "social triage"—harm for some to the benefit of others—which results more from human creativity and bureaucratic structures than as a functional necessity of the state. In immigration studies using this concept, Dunn argues that the lack of bureaucratic responses to the thousands of migrant lives lost in the desert between Mexico and the United States is a form of social triage, since addressing their needs would not benefit powerful elites in comparison to the billions spent on border security, walls, and so on, which have very little effect.[44]

Using Sjoberg's economic sociology, we can analyze the growth and operations of detention centers in terms of bureaucratic capitalism and social actors in a variety of contexts. In doing so, we can highlight the tendencies that lead to human rights abuses and consider alternative organizational arrangements. Specifically, our analysis of the immigration control industry will adapt the framework developed by Sjoberg to assess a variety of dimensions of immigration detention regimes, including the corporate-state nexus; human agency; rationalization processes; hierarchy, blamability, and responsibility; and secrecy systems.[45]

THE CORPORATE-STATE NEXUS

The focus on complex organizations as the drivers of modern capitalism helps highlight the increasingly blurred lines between the state and corporate sectors apparent in developed and most developing countries. "In effect, in most highly industrialized orders we find hybrid organizations that are a mix of the public and the private."[46] While in some countries the role of the private sector is greater than others, there are clear connections between the two. Still, the central problematic is the comprehensive nature of these arrangements, which is particularly evident in contemporary efforts to manage and control international migration. So, contrary to Agamben argumentation focused on the relationship between the state and biological life, the sociological perspective articulated here emphasizes the role of organizations as mediating the links between state and society.

Not surprisingly, many immigration scholars have viewed detention as part of a wider industry, business, or complex.[47] As an operational definition, Manges Douglas and Sáenz see the "immigration detention complex" as revolving around "contracts that link government, which supplies immigrant detainees to prison facilities, with the private industry responsible for building, maintaining, and administering such prisons."[48] Although they are focused on the United States' experience, a more expansive view of subcontracting must include arrangements between central authorities and local authorities, nonprofit organizations, other nonstate actors, and large corporate entities, which can be used to analyze immigration detention across countries where there is fear of foreigners, a confluence of elite power, and racialized-nationalistic discourses toward "the other."[49]

The immigration industrial complex involves many interrelated nongovernmental actors, and various levels of government will vary from place to place. In the United States, official actors include the Department of Homeland Security's Immigration and Customs Enforcement (ICE) and the Marshals Service, as well as municipal governments and local police forces. In Europe, the EU sets regional policies and offers additional funding, but member states are the primary enforcers and operators. In both cases, there are numerous opportunities for subcontractors to profit and generate resources for their organizations, be it a charitable organization or a large transnational corporation like CoreCivic (formerly the Corrections Corporation of America, or CCA), GEO, MTC, or G4S (formerly Group 4 Securicor).[50] In fact, in the United States, local jails have obtained lucrative contracts from federal authorities to detain migrants.[51]

A focus on the corporate-state nexus draws attention to the organizational arrangement of detention within and across countries to trace resource flows, interests driving policy initiatives, and delegation of responsibility.

In the United States, for-profit companies play an outsize role in detainee-management facilities in comparison to other countries. According to Detention Watch Network, private-run facilities housed 15,942 people on a daily basis in 2009, nearly half of the total detained population.[52] Data from the Global Detention Project (GDP) show that the United States detained 440,557 people in 2013 for an average of thirty-one days for those awaiting deportation and sixty-four days for asylum applicants at a daily cost of $119/per day.[53] As of 2013, government expenditures on detention had reached $1.96 billion.

Focusing on the corporate-state nexus also draws attention to the "revolving door" between the public and private sectors. Several authors have noted the close ties between the private and public sectors in the U.S. security state—especially since the 9/11 terrorist attacks—as being increasingly geared at immigration control.[54] Some writers have highlighted how corporate interests, for example, were served by the creation of the U.S. Department of Homeland Security through the Homeland Security Act of 2002. "DHS was conceived and created in a way that made it possible for private industry to become the driving force behind much of its operations," claims Fernandes.[55] The new federal agency reorganized immigration control by assuming the responsibilities of the Immigration and Naturalization Service (INS) and creating two new agencies: Immigration and Customs Enforcement and Citizenship and Immigration Services.

The web of influence across the state-corporate divide is evident at the individual level, especially in the case of CoreCivic.[56] Michael Conlon left his position as the head of the Federal Bureau of Prisons and twenty-two years of public service in 1993 to head up strategic planning for the corporation. He later served as CoreCivic 's chief operating officer and executive vice president. Kim Porter left the INS after twenty-five years to manage the company's relationships with ICE. Circulating key personnel inside and outside government provides "seamless connections between CoreCivic and its federal funders."[57] Table 6.1 uses data collected from lobby watchdog group LittleSis.org to demonstrate the revolving door between staff and leadership of CoreCivic and key organizations that influence policy related to the social control industry. More recently, GEO hired three lobbyists who were former aids of Senator Jeff Sessions, Trump's new attorney general.[58]

The role of the private sector in Europe differs from the U.S. experience in part because of the former's less centralized immigration governance structure. The Schengen Agreement, eradicating borders within the European community while strengthening external borders, took effect in 1995. The EU adopts regional directives and norms, but member states retain overall responsibility for

Table 6.1

CoreCivic, Interlocking People	
Organization	*Interlocking People*
Senate Subcommittee on Immigration, Border Security and Refugees	Donna M Alvarado, Dennis Webster Deconcini
Bill Frist	Bart Verhulst, Jeb Beasley
Federal Bureau of Prisons	Joseph Michael Quinlan, Harley G. Lappin
U.S. Marshals Service	Chuck Kupferer, Anthony Odom
Navistar International Corporation	John R. Horne, John D. Correnti
Arizona Board of Regents (ABOR)	Anne L. Mariucci, Dennis Webster Deconcini
Pulte Homes, Southwest Gas, Arizona State University	Anne L. Mariucci
Greif, First Horizon National Corp., Tennessee Student Assistance Corporation	Mark A. Emkes
U.S. Senate, Democratic Party, 1994 Group, Parry Romani Deconcini & Symms, Senate Judiciary Committee	Dennis Webster Deconcini
U.S. Department of Defense, ACTION, University System of Ohio, CSX Corporation	Donna M. Alvarado
U.S. Department of the Treasury, U.S. Department of Health and Human Services	Ben Shuster
U.S. Immigration and Customs Enforcement	Kim Porter
U.S. Postal Service, White House, Third Way, White House Olympic Task Force, Ford Foundation, Bingham McCutchen LLP, Swidler, Berlin & Strelow, Senate Judiciary Committee, Genesco	Thurgood Marshall Jr.
Central Intelligence Agency	Chuck Kupferer
Office of the Governor of Texas, ALEC Public Safety, Elections Task Force	Laurie Shanblum
Horatio Alger Association, Lamar Alexander	Charles L. Overby
Arizona House of Representatives	Brad Regens
Nashville Chamber of Commerce	Jeb Beasley
Tennessee Department of Economic and Community Development	Kelly Durham

Source: LittleSis.org.

conducting programmatic actions related to migration matters. When analyzing the degree of privatization across European member states and in the United States, Menz connects the increasing neoliberal economic policy environment to increased privatization.[59] He argues that variation in neoliberalism (similar to variation in capitalism) accounts for extensive privatization of immigrant detention in the United Kingdom, Australia, and the United States on the one hand and the lack thereof in Germany and the Netherlands on the other. The underlying rational, according to him, is the belief in the alleged efficiency of the private sector grounded in a neoliberal ideology.

While the ideological persuasion of policy makers cannot be underestimated, the situation in Europe is more complex than an either-or dichotomy along variations of neoliberalism predicated on path-dependent models. Flynn and Cannon, reviewing the cases of Germany, Italy, and Sweden (as well as South Africa), demonstrate the various reasons and motivations for outsourcing.[60] In fact, government agencies in Portugal and France contract private, not-for-profit organizations to provide a range of services to detainees, including social, legal, and psychological counseling, while Italy outsources the management of detention facilities to the Red Cross. There are multiple bureaucratic arrangements for organizing detention practices, which depends on changing conditions, varied institutional legacies, and human creativity.

HUMAN AGENCY

While poststructuralist accounts tend to circumvent the role of actors involved in the growth of immigration or depict them as unreflective spokespersons of discourses and scripts of the new state of exception, Sjoberg emphasizes that human beings are reflective, engage in calculative rationality, create typologies, pursue part–whole logic, and undertake a diverse array of social and interpretative actions.[61] Moreover, his economic sociology views human beings as molded by organizations while also actively shaping normative constraints. Importantly, organizations cannot be understood as reducible to the individuals that comprise them, such as a methodological individualism that may seek to aggregate the individual preferences of its members. Rather, agency must be understood through the hierarchical relations within an organization, while also considering corporate units acting as collective actors. Along the corporate-state nexus, we can analyze the dual levels of human agency through strategizing and devising goals, deploying neoliberal ideologies, peddling influence to affect policies, and pushing legislation in relation to migrant detention.

Ackerman and Furman highlight three ways by which private interests influence policies related to immigrant detention in the United States.[62] First, campaign contributions seek to influence politicians. Between 1998 and 2012, private prison operators donated $900,000 to politicians at the federal level and $6 million at the state level. More donations occurred at the state level, especially in the states of California and Texas, to influence state criminal laws. CoreCivic has also used political action committees to provide resources to politicians on the

House Committee on Homeland Security.[63] GEO is reported to have donated $250,000 to a Trump-affiliated political action committee during the 2016 U.S. presidential election.[64] Second, CoreCivic, GEO, and other entities—including the sector's industry association, the Association of Private Correctional and Treatment Organizations—pay lobbyists to ensure that bills at the federal and state levels expand the use of private prisons. Between 1998 and 2015, top corporate and nonprofit entities involved in the prison and detention business paid $34.3 million to influence policies, according to data aggregated from OpenSecrets.org.[65] Figure 6.1 reveals trends in lobby expenditures between 1998 and 2015 and shows how spending jumped after the 9/11 terror attacks to a high of $4 million in 2005 from around $500,000, followed by annual disbursements between $1.5 million to close to $2.5 million thereafter.

The third strategy involves the use of policy-making networks. Private prison operators pay millions to members of the American Legislative Exchange Council (ALEC), which proposes legislation; sets up dedicated task forces; and provides a space for lobbyists, politicians, and the private sector to gather.[66] Comparable strategies and policy-making networks exist in the UK, including activities by CoreCivic's local affiliate and think tanks like the Adam Smith Institute pushing neoliberal agendas.[67]

Private operators allege that they are not attempting to influence legislation related to criminal justice, but the evidence suggests otherwise.[68] From the Illegal Immigration Reform and Immigrant Responsibility Act of 1996 to post-9/11 efforts to increasingly criminalize the undocumented, including DHS/ICE programs like "catch and return," the Secure Border Initiative, 287(g), and Secure Communities, as well as controversial state initiatives like Arizona's SB1070, the demand for beds has outstripped installed capacity. But a close examination reveals the disconnect between standard operating procedures and reality—a situation that can best be understood through creative rule making and zealous goal attainment. ICE claims that it "focuses primarily on dangerous and repetitive criminal aliens" for detention and deportation, but the agency lists the majority of "book-ins," or those taken into custody, as "non-criminals."[69] Information obtained by the GDP show that 18,690 of the 32,000 people in detention "had no criminal conviction, not even for illegal entry or low-level crimes like trespassing."[70] Part of the reason for the high rates of incarceration and deportation of foreigners convicted of minor crimes includes ICE's bed-capacity mandate. The DHS Appropriations Act of 2010 first introduced a daily bed-capacity mandate of 33,400, which remained at that level until 2015, when DHS lowered its requested mandate to roughly 31,000. Additionally, internal documents reveal that the agency specified a target of 400,000 deportations a year.[71] The Trump administration has issued new guidelines to maximize the number of deportations and detentions.[72]

FIGURE 6.1 Corporate Lobbying Expenditures by Top Private Detention/ Prison Companies in U.S. Dollars, 1998–2015

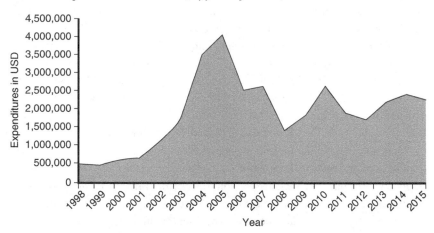

SOURCE: OPENSECRETS.ORG, INCLUDING CCA/CORECIVIC, GEO, LCS, MTC, DEVEREUX, WACKENHUT, BOYS TOWN, CATHOLIC CHARITIES, CORNELL CORRECTIONS, AND BAPTIST CHILD AND FAMILY SERVICES 2016, HTTPS://WWW.OPENSECRETS.ORG/LOBBY

RATIONALIZATION, EFFICIENCY, AND DIVISION OF LABOR

While outsourcing of immigration detention can be seen as increasing division of labor across the corporate-state nexus, at the operational level detention involves management, human resources, accounting, and so on—be it a private corporation like CoreCivic or a local public jail. Here, human agency using part–whole logic, rationalization efforts, and downward pressure onto custodial personnel who then pressure detainees reveals a central aspect of bureaucratic capitalism to reduce costs and increase revenues through efficient use of division of labor and compartmentalization. In these roles, human beings creatively achieve organizational goals that range from positively portraying a corporate face to the public and inventing ways to maximize rents. Private detention operators allegedly have built-in motives to provide adequate services to secure future contracts, but viewing human actors as balancing the competing goals of engaging in acceptable treatment of the human product on the one hand and taking advantage of captive labor on the other provides more nuance to varied situations.[73]

Studies on the internal economies of immigration detention centers demonstrate how they appear to save taxpayer resources by reducing costs through the overexploitation of captive consumers and labors.[74] City and county jails in the United States profit by restricting access to goods and services in order to charge inmates monopoly prices for phone calls, consumer items, and other products. Conlon and Hiemstra reveal how New Jersey's Essex County government receives a commission rate of 54 percent per call in its telephone contract with Global Tel*Link, which translates into an annual income of $925,000.[75] Also, in order to reduce overhead costs, operators employ detainees to carry out maintenance and cleaning. In fact, courts have upheld the right to pay detainees $1–$3 per day, which, according to one estimate, translates into $5–$6 million in savings for one 187-bed facility. Conlon and Hiemstra also discovered the subcontracting of detainee labor to private interests.

There are striking parallels between the United States and the United Kingdom in pursuing microeconomic rationalization processes. Burnett and Chebe uncovered similar levels of overexploitation of detainee labor for day-to-day operations.[76] Paying wages at £1–£1.25 an hour or even providing redeemable vouchers is framed as a privilege for the incarcerated. They underscore the irony that "considering the fact that, on the one hand, the government is massively increasing resources and personnel to investigate and prevent undocumented working whilst, on the other, it is sanctioning conditions in IRCs [immigration removal centers] that have many of the hallmarks of undocumented working."[77]

Clearly, rationalization processes have translated into tremendous profit gains for private contractors and for entrepreneurial public governments. According to its 2014 annual report, CCA reported average per diem revenue (or what it calls "compensated man-day") for the facilities it owns and manages at $70.55 and per diem operating costs at $47.34.[78] The $23.21 daily profit per human detained represents a per diem operating margin of 32.9 percent. Between 2012 and 2014, the company's revenue hovered around $1.7 billion, with net profits between $150 million and $300 million on an annual basis. The GEO Group—operating 106 facilities with a capacity of around 85,500 beds in the United States, the United Kingdom, Australia, and South Africa—has also experienced growing profits. Its revenues have steadily increased from $1.1 billion to $1.5 billion between 2011 and 2013, along with net income increasing from $63.5 million to $115 million during the same period.[79] Here, social triage connects with the increasing financialization of global capitalism that, according to Sassen, links up to "expulsions" of vulnerable humanity.[80] Furthermore, the changing political scenario is not lost on investors. CoreCivic's stock plummeted after the Obama administration's Justice Department announced that it would phase out contracts to private prison operators, only to bounce back after Trump's election. The new administration's attorney general, Jeff Sessions, reversed the decision on using private prisons.[81]

HIERARCHY, BLAMABILITY, AND RESPONSIBILITY

Many observers of immigration detention see the outsourcing of detention to private actors or to subnational governmental entities as a form of delegating responsibility to reduce costs and avoid legal issues.[82] Outsourcing occurs not only to achieve efficiency and flexibility but also to shift blame and legal burdens. In fact, most countries define immigration detention as an administrative action not subject to the same due process protections provided in criminal law. Nonetheless, immigration detention can involve potentially "aggressive forms of direct interaction" between detainees and staff, which has direct bearing on Sjoberg's idea of "social triage," whereby the most vulnerable are sacrificed at the expense of the privileged.[83] Along the corporate-state nexus, specific forms of hierarchy and blamability connect distant rule makers to vulnerable detainees. Elite managers and government administrators push directives downward, along with blame and responsibility, to subordinates. When problems arise, those at the lowest end of the hierarchy face the direst circumstances, including job insecurity, dismal pay, and punitive action.

Sjoberg notes that "people with the least knowledge of the system must interact with those organizational personnel who are the most constrained by the normative rules."[84] In other words, immigrants with the least knowledge of immigration laws and skills to navigate complex bureaucracies confront staff and guards who enjoy limited job prospects in their home countries. Investors, executives, and upper management thus profit by pitting these groups against one another in a bureaucratic setting and social environment overladen with ethno-nationalist rhetoric. Moreover, employees at detention centers tend to receive inadequate training, thus leading to several human rights abuses.[85]

SECRECY SYSTEMS

Finally, bureaucratic capitalism highlights attempts to shroud state-private relations, rationalization processes, and hierarchical relations from public view. "We should not underestimate the power of secrecy arrangements; they are often the basis of corporate fraud or governmental malfeasance (yes, even the violation of human rights)," contends Sjoberg.[86] If sovereign power aims to demonstrate its will over biological life, why do states often demonstrate an aversion to the release of public data about it?[87]

A focus on the differing organizational arrangements governing detention in the United States and Europe reveal important distinctions in terms of monitoring and supervision that have important consequences for upholding the rights of those incarcerated. In the EU, international organizations and supranational bodies, such as the Council of Europe's Committee for the Prevention of Torture, engage in extensive surveillance and oversight of detention operators. According to Flynn and Cannon, "Significant influence is exerted on some countries after official visits are made by such organizations, obliging them to provide detailed responses to each point of concern raised."[88] In addition, most member states of the Council of Europe are also parties to the protocol to the UN Convention Against Torture (CAT), which requires members to set up independent "national preventive mechanisms" to ensure that states properly treat all people deprived of their liberty.

The degree of independent human rights monitoring found in Europe is starkly absent in the United States, which has not ratified the CAT protocol and, indeed, according to GDP data, only ratified seven of sixteen relevant human rights conventions that provide protections to detainees. One problem is that ICE is often both contractor and supervisor. Despite a consistent string of detainee abuses occurring in facilities operated by CoreCivic and other private corporations, ICE continues to renew their contracts.[89]

The use of immigration detention and the magnitude of funding states dedicate to locking up asylum seekers and irregular migrants continue to grow, despite the lack of evidence demonstrating the efficacy of detention measures in diminishing the numbers of undocumented persons, disrupting immigration flows, or being appreciably more effective—in many contexts—than noncustodial measures at ensuring the presence of individuals at immigration hearings. Poststructuralists argue that detention efforts represent a contemporary way in which sovereignty demonstrates its power to exclude through inclusion and that as globalization disrupts traditional notions of borders, detention increases in importance as an apparatus of population control. According to this view, state power carves out legal and physical spaces to control the movement of noncitizens while abusively restricting their rights. While this approach has some merits, it also has a number of theoretical problems. Most notable are its use of teleological argumentation, conflation of citizenship and human rights, and disregard of social forces in the wider political economy.

Given their problematic analysis, poststructuralists sometimes arrive at apparently contradictory policy suggestions. Agamben argues that the concept of the refugee should be divorced from the concept of human rights, since states fail to protect such persons accordingly.[90] Rajaram and Grundy-Warr also highlight the inadequacy of nation-states to protect refugees based on the 1951 Convention on Refugees and argue in favor of a new independent tribunal to adjudicate whether irregular migrants should obtain the protections based on alternative international rights instruments such as the Universal Declaration of Human Rights and the International Convention on the Protection of the Rights of All Migrant Workers.[91] This suggestion may result in tangible improvements, especially in light of the dramatic setbacks in Europe's adherence to the global refugee regime in the wake of current refugee and asylum challenges, but their argument still leaves questions of implementation, the role of the nation-state, and the political means to achieve such an end.

In contrast, analytical frameworks that emphasize social actors, like Sjoberg's "bureaucratic capitalism," show that the key to understanding immigration detention regimes can be found by viewing them as complex social organizations. Accordingly, the state is both problem and solution, and so too are other types of organizations, including for-profit corporations as well as not-for-profit entities. More importantly, researchers can critically examine differences across detention regimes by examining the corporate-state nexus; how humans creatively act to change policies, enact rules, and reinterpret mandates; rationalization processes seeking efficiency to maximize resources for the organization; hierarchical relations for outsourcing of responsibility; and varying degrees of transparency. All these factors not only help us understand the operations of immigration detention but also offer possible solutions to redress abuse and correct human rights violations—including forms of "social triage," through which socially marginalized populations suffer to the benefit of elite groups.

If organizational arrangements are the problem, then a version of human rights that goes beyond individualistic notions of human rights must gain hold. For Sjoberg, human rights are "social claims made by individuals (or groups) upon organized power arrangements for the purpose of enhancing human dignity."[92] Such an approach seeks to make organizations morally accountable, whether they are operated by the state or by the private sector. On one level, we must consider whether some activities of the "social control industry" should even be profitable, such as immigrant detention.[93] But as we have seen, this is only part of the problem, since publicly operated jails also seek new forms of revenue generation. Arguably, there is a need for a more radical restructuring of the immigration detention complex to ensure that government agencies and their subcontractors are better held to account with respect to their efforts to uphold the rights of immigrants and asylum seekers. On the other hand, given the inherent, deep-seated nature of some of the problems associated with detention regimes, it seems more reasonable to argue that the best way forward is applying continued pressure for increased transparency of detention facilities, as well as proposing remedies that fall short of incarceration and promoting public discourse that highlights the self-defeating rationales that have given rise to this system.

NOTES TO CHAPTER 6

An earlier version of the argument presented in this chapter was published in Matthew B. Flynn, "From Bare Life to Bureaucratic Capitalism: Analyzing the Growth of the Immigration Detention Industry as a Complex Organization," *Contemporary Readings in Law and Social Justice* 8, no. 1 (2016): 70–97. The authors would like to thank Ashley Addison for her research assistance.

1. This chapter employs the definition of immigration detention developed by the Global Detention Project (GDP): "The deprivation of liberty of non-citizens for reasons related to their immigration status." See GDP, "FAQ," https://www.globaldeten tionproject.org/faq.

2. Michael Flynn, "There and Back Again: On the Diffusion of Immigration Detention," *Journal on Migration and Human Security* 2, no. 3 (2014): 165–197.

3. For detailed information about the evolution of immigration detention regimes in Europe, see the reports on the periodic country visits by the Council of Europe's Committee for the Prevention of Torture, http://www.cpt.coe.int/en/states.htm. See also the EU statistical profiles produced by the GDP, https://www.globaldetentionproject.org/regions -subregions/europe. Two key indicators of migratory pressure are the number of annual asylum claims and yearly statistics on the apprehension of undocumented foreigner nationals. Historic data on these can be found at Eurostat, http://ec.europa.eu/eurostat.

4. Norval Morris, "The Contemporary Prison," in *The Oxford History of the Prison: The Practice of Punishment in Western Society,* ed. David Rothman and Norval Morris (Oxford: Oxford University Press, 1995), 202–234.

5. Stephen Castles, "Towards a Sociology of Forced Migration and Social Transformation," *Sociology* 37, no. 1 (February 2003): 13–34; James Hollifield, Philip Martin, and Pia Orrenius, eds., *Controlling Immigration: A Global Perspective* (Stanford: Stanford University Press, 2014); J. Sampson, "Does Detention Deter?," International Detention Coalition, April 17, 2015, http://idcoalition.org/detentiondatabase/does-detention-deter/.

6. Alice Edwards, *Back to Basics: The Right to Liberty and Security of Person and "Alternatives to Detention" of Refugees, Asylum-Seekers, Stateless Persons and Other Migrants* (Geneva: United Nations High Commissioner for Refugees, 2011).

7. Tom Wong, *Rights, Deportation, and Detention in the Age of Immigration Control* (Stanford: Stanford University Press, 2015).

8. Edwards, *Back to Basics.*

9. Michael Flynn, "Sovereign Discomfort: Can Liberal Norms Lead to Increasing Immigration Detention?," in *Immigration Detention, Risk and Human Rights,* ed. Maria João Guia, Robert Koulish, and Valsamis Mitsilegas (Cham: Springer International, 2016), 13–23.

10. Gideon Sjoberg, "Observations on Bureaucratic Capitalism," in *Sociology for the Twenty-First Century: Continuities and Cutting Edges,* ed. Janet Abu-Lughod (Chicago: University of Chicago Press, 1999), 23–35.

11. Poststructuralism has become a large label to describe a diverse set of authors. Our focus is on the work of Giorgio Agamben and, to a lesser extent, Michel Foucault, as well as authors influenced by them.

12. Giorgio Agamben, *Homo Sacer* (Turin: G. Einaudi, 1995); Giorgio Agamben, *State of Exception* (Chicago: University of Chicago Press, 2005).

13. See Jef Huysmans, "The Jargon of Exception—on Schmitt, Agamben and the Absence of Political Society," *International Political Sociology* 2, no. 2 (2008): 165–183. See also Katia Genel, "The Question of Biopower: Foucault and Agamben," *Rethinking Marxism* 18, no. 1 (2006): 43–62, 187.

14. Didier Bigo, "Detention of Foreigners, States of Exception, and the Social Practices of Control of the Banopticon," in *Borderscapes: Hidden Geographies and Politics at Territory's Edge*, ed. Prem Kumar Rajaram and Carl Grundy-Warr (Minneapolis: University of Minnesota Press, 2007); Alison Mountz, "The Enforcement Archipelago: Detention, Haunting, and Asylum on Islands," *Political Geography* 30, no. 3 (2011): 118–128; Prem Kumar Rajaram and Carl Grundy-Warr, "The Irregular Migrant as Homo Sacer: Migration and Detention in Australia, Malaysia, and Thailand," *International Migration* 42, no. 1 (2004): 33–64; Anastassia Tsoukala, "The Administrative Detention of Foreigners in France: The Expanding Exclusionary Spaces," in *The Police, State, and Society: Perspectives from India and France*, ed. Ajay K. Mehra and René Lévy (New Delhi: Pearson Education, 2011), 186–196.

15. Rajaram and Grundy-Warr, "Irregular Migrant as Homo Sacer," 14.

16. Tsoukala, "Administrative Detention of Foreigners in France," 187.

17. Bigo, "Detention of Foreigners."

18. Tsoukala, "Administrative Detention of Foreigners in France," 195.

19. See Global Detention Project, "Ecuador and Argentina Profiles," https://www.globaldetentionproject.org/countries/americas/ecuador and https://www.globaldetentionproject.org/countries/americas/argentina, respectively; Pablo Ceriani, "Back to Basics? The Limited Use of Immigration Detention in South America: An Interpretation Based on International Human Rights Treaties and Principles," in *Challenging Immigration Detention: Academics, Activists and Policy-Makers*, ed. Michael J. Flynn and Matthew B. Flynn (Cheltenham: Edward Elgar, 2017).

20. See Nicos Mouzelis, *Sociological Theory: What Went Wrong? Diagnosis and Remedies* (New York: Routledge, 2003).

21. Genel, "Question of Biopower," 57.

22. See Michael Flynn, "The Hidden Costs of Human Rights: The Case of Immigration Detention" (Working Paper No. 7, Global Detention Project, 2013), https://www.globaldetentionproject.org/the-hidden-costs-of-human-rights-the-case-of-immigration-detention.

23. Rajaram and Grundy-Warr, "Irregular Migrant as Homo Sacer," 41.

24. For an assessment of the impacts of constitutional protections on immigration detention practices, see Daniel Wilsher, *Immigration Detention: Law, History, Politics* (Cambridge: Cambridge University Press, 2011).

25. Michael Flynn and Mariette Grange, *Immigration Detention in the Gulf* (Geneva: Global Detention Project, 2015), https://www.globaldetentionproject.org/wp-content/uploads/2016/06/Immigration_Detention_in_the_Gulf_GDP_Version001.pdf.

26. Sinnerbrink, quoted in Edwards, *Back to Basics*, 372.

27. Writes Levy, "Agamben and his enthusiastic followers lack any proportionality when they distastefully lump together varieties of refugee camps, Auschwitz, and even gated communities. Refugees are not cannon fodder for radical metaphysical arguments and should not be equated to (a historically inaccurate) mass of passive, half-dead inmates of Auschwitz's work camps." Carl Levy, "Refugees, Europe, Camps/State of Exception: 'Into the Zone,' the European Union and Extraterritorial Processing of Migrants, Refugees, and Asylum-Seekers (Theories and Practice)," *Refugee Survey Quarterly* 29, no. 1 (2010): 100–101.

28. Mark Duffield, "Racism, Migration and Development: The Foundations of Planetary Order," *Progress in Development Studies* 6, no. 1 (2006): 68–79.

29. Zygmunt Bauman, *Globalization: The Human Consequences* (Cambridge: Polity Press, 1998). See also Saskia Sassen, "Beyond Sovereignty: De-Facto Transnationalism in Immigration Policy," *European Journal of Migration and Law* 1, no. 2 (1999): 177.

30. Bauman writes about a prison, but the description fits migrant detention: "What *does matter* is that *they stay there.* . . . It was designed as a *factory of exclusion* and of people habituated to their status of the *excluded.* The mark of the excluded in the era of time/space compression is *immobility*" (italics in original). Bauman, *Globalization*, 113.

31. Loïc Wacquant, "'Suitable Enemies': Foreigners and Immigrants in the Prisons of Europe," *Punishment and Society* 1, no. 2 (1999): 215–222; Loïc Wacquant, "Crafting the Neoliberal State: Workfare, Prisonfare, and Social Insecurity," *Sociological Forum* 25, no. 2 (2010): 197–220; Dario Melossi, *Crime, Punishment and Migration* (London: Sage, 2015); Ruth Gilmore, *Golden Gulag: Prisons, Surplus, Crisis, and Opposition in Globalizing California* (Berkeley: University of California Press, 2007); Jock Young, *The Exclusive Society: Social Exclusion, Crime and Difference in Late Modernity* (London: Sage, 1999).

32. Melossi, *Crime, Punishment and Migration*, 27.

33. Young, *Exclusive Society*. For a critique of strain theory/relative deprivation as a model for criminality, see Ruth Kornhauser, *Social Sources of Delinquency: An Appraisal of Analytic Models* (Chicago: University of Chicago Press, 1978).

34. Wacquant, "'Suitable Enemies'"; Wacquant, "Crafting the Neoliberal State."

35. Gilmore, *Golden Gulag*.

36. This argument is further developed in Matthew B. Flynn, "Capitalism and Immigration Control: What Political Economy Reveals About the Global Spread of Detention," in *Challenging Immigration Detention: Academics, Activists, and Policy-Makers*, ed. Michael J. Flynn and Matthew B. Flynn (Cheltenham: Edward Elgar, 2017). See also Alejandro Portes and Rubén G. Rumbaut, *Immigrant America: A Portrait*, 4th ed. (Oakland: University of California Press, 2014).

37. Robert Holton, *Globalization and the Nation State*, 2nd ed. (Newbury Park: Palgrave Macmillan, 2011); Gideon Sjoberg, Elizabeth Gill, and Norma Williams, "A Sociology of Human Rights," *Social Problems* 48, no. 1 (2001): 11–47.

38. Saskia Sassen, *Expulsions: Brutality and Complexity in the Global Economy* (Cambridge: Belknap, 2014).

39. Holton, *Globalization and the Nation State*.

40. Gideon Sjoberg, "Corporations and Human Rights," in *Interpreting Human Rights: Social Science Perspectives*, ed. Rhiannon Morgan and Bryan S. Turner (Hoboken: Routledge, 2009), 157–176.

41. Huysmans, "Jargon of Exception," 177.

42. Sjoberg, "Observations on Bureaucratic Capitalism." Theoretically, Sjoberg blends insights from the power-elite approach of C. Wright Mills (*The Power Elite* [New York: Oxford University Press, 1957]) with the actor-oriented approaches of George Herbert Mead (*Mind, Self & Society from the Standpoint of a Social Behaviorist* [Chicago: University of Chicago Press, 1934]) and John Dewey (*The Later Works, 1925–1953* [Carbondale: Southern Illinois University, 1981]).

43. Sjoberg, "Observations on Bureaucratic Capitalism," 33.

44. Timothy Dunn, "Immigration Enforcement at the U.S.-Mexico Border: Where Human Rights and National Sovereignty Collide," in *Binational Human Rights: The U.S.-Mexico Experience*, ed. William Simmons and Carol Mueller (Philadelphia: University of Pennsylvania Press, 2014), 68–87.

45. Sjoberg, "Observations on Bureaucratic Capitalism."

46. Ibid., 26.

47. Thomas Gammeltoft-Hansen and Ninna Nyberg Sørensen, *The Migration Industry and the Commercialization of International Migration*, Routledge Global Institutions Series (New York: Routledge, 2012); Rubén Hernández-León, *Metropolitan Migrants: The Migration of Urban Mexicans to the United States* (Berkeley: University of California Press, 2008); Ruben Andersson, *Illegality, Inc.* (Oakland: University of California Press, 2014); Claire Rodier, *Xénophobie business: À quoi servent les contrôles migratoires?* (Paris: La Decouverte, 2012); Deepa Fernandes, *Targeted: Homeland Security and the Business of Immigration* (New York: Seven Stories, 2011).

48. Karen Manges Douglas and Rogelio Sáenz, "The Criminalization of Immigrants and the Immigration-Industrial Complex," *Daedalus* 142, no. 3 (2013): 199–227.

49. See Michael Flynn, "Detained Beyond the Sovereign: Conceptualising Non-State Actor Involvement in Immigration Detention," in *Intimate Economies of Immigration Detention: Critical Perspectives*, ed. Deirdre Conlon and Nancy Hiemstra (London: Routledge, 2016), 15–31.

50. CCA renamed itself CoreCivic in late 2016 in the wake of a U.S. Justice Department announcement on cutbacks in the use of private prisons in the United States.

51. See Deirdre Conlon and Nancy Hiemstra, "Examining the Everyday Micro-Economies of Migrant Detention in the United States," *Geographica Helvetica* 69, no. 5 (2014): 335–344; Michael Welch, *Detained: Immigration Laws and the Expanding I.N.S. Jail Complex* (Philadelphia: Temple University Press, 2002).

52. Detention Watch Network, "The Influence of the Private Prison Industry in the Immigration Detention Business," May 2011, http://www.detentionwatchnetwork.org/privateprisons.

53. Global Detention Project, "United States Immigration Detention Profile," 2016, http://www.globaldetentionproject.org/countries/americas/united-states.

54. Sabrina Alimahomed, "Homeland Security Inc.: Public Order, Private Profit," *Race and Class* 55, no. 4 (2014): 82–99; Fernandes, *Targeted*.

55. Fernandes, *Targeted*, 178.

56. Alissa Ackerman and Rich Furman, "The Criminalization of Immigration and the Privatization of the Immigration Detention: Implications for Justice," *Contemporary Justice Review* 16, no. 2 (2013): 251–263; R. Feltz and Baksh, "Business of Detention," in

Beyond Walls and Cages: Prisons, Borders, and Global Crisis, ed. Jenna Loyd, Matt Mitchelson, and Andrew Burridge (Athens: University of Georgia Press, 2013).

57. Feltz and Baksh, "Business of Detention," 147.

58. Isaac Arnsdorf, "Private Prison Company GEO Hires Three Firms," *Politico*, October 12, 2016, http://politi.co/2e6bRxj.

59. Georg Menz, "Neo-Liberalism, Privatization and the Outsourcing of Migration Management: A Five-Country Comparison," *Competition and Change* 15, no. 2 (2011): 116–135.

60. Michael Flynn and Cecilia Josephine Cannon, "The Privatization of Immigration Detention: Towards a Global View" (Working Paper No. 6, Global Detention Project, 2009), http://www.globaldetentionproject.org/publications/privatization-immigration -detention-towards-global-view.

61. Sjoberg, "Observations on Bureaucratic Capitalism."

62. Ackerman and Furman, "Criminalization of Immigration."

63. Feltz and Baksh, "Business of Detention."

64. Keegan Hamilton, "A Big Private Prison Operator May Have Illegally Funded a Trump Super PAC," VICE News, December 20, 2016, https://news.vice.com/story/geo -group-may-have-illegally-funded-a-trump-super-pac.

65. OpenSecrets.org, "Lobbying Database," 2016, https://www.opensecrets.org/lobby/.

66. Ackerman and Furman, "Criminalization of Immigration."

67. Menz, "Neo-Liberalism, Privatization and Outsourcing."

68. Ackerman and Furman, "Criminalization of Immigration"; Feltz and Baksh, "Business of Detention"; Rick Young, "Lost in Detention," *Frontline*, PBS, October 18, 2011, http://www.pbs.org/wgbh/pages/frontline/lost-in-detention/.

69. Immigration and Customs Enforcement, *Immigration Detention Overview and Recommendations* (Washington, D.C.: Department of Homeland Security, 2009), 11.

70. Global Detention Project, "United States Detention Profile."

71. Young, "Lost in Detention."

72. Michael D. Shear and Ron Nixon, "New Trump Deportation Rules Allow Far More Expulsions," *New York Times*, February 21, 2017, https://www.nytimes.com/2017 /02/21/us/politics/dhs-immigration-trump.html.

73. Douglas McDonald, "Public Imprisonment by Private Means: The Emergence of Private Prisons and Jails in the United States, the United Kingdom, and Australia," *British Journal of Criminology* 34 (1994): 28–48.

74. Jon Burnett and Fidelis Chebe, "Captive Labour: Asylum Seekers, Migrants and Employment in UK Immigration Removal Centres," *Race and Class* 51, no. 4 (2010): 95–103; Conlon and Hiemstra, "Examining the Everyday Micro-Economies of Migrant Detention."

75. Conlon and Hiemstra, "Examining the Everyday Micro-Economies of Migrant Detention."

76. Burnett and Chebe, "Captive Labour."

77. Ibid., 101.

78. CCA, "2014 Annual Report" (Nashville: Corrections Corporation of America, 2014).

79. Figures were taken from financial reporting websites, such as finance.yahoo.com and www.google.com/finance.

80. Sassen, *Expulsions*.

81. Eric Tucker, "Sessions: US to Continue Use of Privately Run Prisons," Associated Press, February 23, 2017, http://www.businessinsider.com/ap-sessions-us-to-continue-use-of-privately-run-prisons-2017-2.

82. Flynn and Cannon, "Privatization of Immigration Detention"; Gallya Lahav, "Immigration and the State: The Devolution and Privatisation of Immigration Control in the EU," *Journal of Ethnic and Migration Studies* 24, no. 4 (1998): 675–694; Menz, "Neo-Liberalism, Privatization and Outsourcing."

83. Menz, "Neo-Liberalism, Privatization and Outsourcing."

84. Sjoberg, "Observations on Bureaucratic Capitalism," 33.

85. Christine Bacon, "The Evolution of Immigration Detention in the UK: The Involvement of Private Prison Companies" (Working Paper No. 27, Refugee Studies Centre, 2005), http://www.rsc.ox.ac.uk/publications/the-evolution-of-immigration-detention-in-the-uk-the-involvement-of-private-prison-companies.

86. Sjoberg, "Observations on Bureaucratic Capitalism," 168.

87. For example, in the report "The Uncounted," the Global Detention Project and its partner Access Info Europe reported that of the thirty-three countries in Europe and North America to whom freedom of information requests were sent, nineteen failed to disclose details about where migrants and asylum seekers were detained. Global Detention Project, "The Uncounted," February 2015, http://www.globaldetention-project.org/publications/special-report/uncounted-detention-migrants-and-asylum-seekers-europe.

88. Flynn and Cannon, "Privatization of Immigration Detention."

89. Young, "Lost in Detention." However, DHS is now reviewing the use of private prison contractors, following the announcement of the U.S. Department of Justice that it will phase out prison contracts with private firms.

90. Giorgio Agamben, *Means Without End: Notes on Politics* (Minneapolis: University of Minnesota Press, 2000), 15.

91. Rajaram and Grundy-Warr, "Irregular Migrant as Homo Sacer."

92. Sjoberg, "Corporations and Human Rights," 42.

93. In August 2016, the U.S. Department of Justice decided to phase out the use of private operators in the federal prison system. Although most privately operated immigrant detention facilities are under the jurisdiction of the DHS, the decision to phase out private contractors appears to demonstrate the efficacy of political mobilization and scathing reports. Sally Q. Yates, "Phasing Out Our Use of Private Prisons," *Justice Blogs,* Department of Justice, August 18, 2016, https://www.justice.gov/opa/blog/phasing-out-our-use-private-prisons.

7. THE CONTROLLED EXPANSION OF LOCAL IMMIGRATION LAWS

An Analysis of U.S. Supreme Court Jurisprudence

PHILIP KRETSEDEMAS, UMASS BOSTON

Since the early 2000s, there has been an explosion of immigration laws enacted by local and state governments across the United States. Local immigration laws are not unique to the United States, but their scale, the size of the immigrant population they potentially effect, and the extensive history of legal debate on the subject make the United States a case deserving of special attention.[1]

In 2011 and 2012, the U.S. Supreme Court delivered a pair of decisions that clarified its position on this highly controversial field of lawmaking. In *Whiting v. Chamber of Commerce*, the Supreme Court upheld a law that allowed the state of Arizona to revoke the business licenses of employers who hired unauthorized migrants.[2] But the Supreme Court's subsequent decision in *Arizona v. United States* struck down several sections of Arizona's more highly publicized immigration law, which would have allowed local police to carry out warrantless arrests of person's suspected of being undocumented.[3]

In the latter years of the Obama era, some legal scholars interpreted these decisions as a sign that the federal courts are taking a more decisive stance on restricting local lawmaking powers, which implies a modest gain for advocates of immigrant rights.[4] In contrast, a few years earlier, scholars tracking local immigration laws were beginning to speculate about a pendulum swing toward a greater tolerance for local lawmaking powers, on par with the discretion afforded to local governments during the nineteenth century.[5] This chapter offers a narrative explaining how these seemingly divergent trends—toward both expanding and restricting local immigration laws—could have been occurring at the same time.

The argument I advance can also be applied to the immigration politics of the Trump era. As of this writing (in early 2017), the Trump administration had begun to shift the policy debate away from local laws that restrict migrant rights to local laws deemed overly protective of migrants (i.e., "sanctuary" laws).[6] "Anti-sanctuary" laws are also becoming a new trend in local lawmaking.[7] This development illustrates how the movement to enact restrictive local laws is now aligning itself with the federal government, instead of sticking to a principled defense of the "inherent authority" of local governments to enact immigration laws (which, if interpreted in a politically neutral way, would extend to so-called sanctuary laws). Meanwhile, the Trump administration has signaled its commitment to the same understanding of federal authority over immigration enforcement that characterized Obama-era policy, and has also affirmed that it will fully support local efforts to revoke "sanctuary" laws.[8]

So although the political field has changed dramatically, Trump-era policy may continue a trend that typified the Obama era, toward strengthening the principle of federal supremacy over immigration law and controlling the spread of undesirable local laws (with the terms of this undesirability being defined by a new set of federal prerogatives). In the discussion that follows, I situate these federal prerogatives within a broader historical context, explaining how the jurisprudence on federal supremacy has evolved over the past two hundred years and why it has become a more prominent feature of federal jurisprudence on local immigration laws from the 1980s onward.

THE CONTROLLED EXPANSION ARGUMENT

As previously noted, the nineteenth century is often contrasted to the present day as an era in which local governments had more leeway to enact their own immigration laws. I argue, however, that the current era is like the nineteenth century—not just because we are witnessing a proliferation of local immigration laws but also because the growth of these laws has occurred under a jurisprudence that upholds the supremacy of federal over local law. I describe this process as a controlled expansion, in which federal supremacy arguments have been used to police "unruly" tendencies in local lawmaking but without curtailing the overall expansion of local immigration laws. The contents of the chapter offer a detailed treatment of the jurisprudence that has shaped this process.

This argument has two interrelated themes. The core theme is that the Supreme Court has consistently upheld the supremacy of federal law over local law when it comes to questions of immigration policy. Practically speaking, this means there was never a golden age of local autonomy on immigration policy, at least not when it comes to the jurisprudence of the Supreme Court. The second theme is that neoliberal (and classical liberal) philosophies of government help explain the priorities guiding this jurisprudence.

Broadly defined, neoliberalism advocates a return to the free market philosophies of the eighteenth century. As it concerns immigration, neoliberal priorities include advocating for a free flow of migrant labor, creating incentives (and disincentives) that favor the migration of skilled or productive migrants, and reducing social spending that is perceived to encourage "government dependency" (counteracting migrant productivity).[9] Most scholars date the origins of the neoliberal paradigm to the early or mid-twentieth century.[10] As William Connolly has explained, neoliberalism calls on the state to actively create social conditions that are conducive to market forces, whereas earlier, laissez-faire economic philosophies sought to minimize state intervention in markets that, presumably, were able to function well enough on their own.[11] In this regard, neoliberalism can be distinguished from the earlier laissez-faire paradigm by its reliance on a strong activist state.

U.S. Supreme Court opinion on federal supremacy fits this model of state-market relations quite neatly, since it affirms the sovereign authority of the federal government. Moreover, when these supremacy arguments have been applied to the debate over local immigration laws, they have been singularly concerned with promoting the free flow of international commerce. But this jurisprudence predates neoliberalism. In fact, it can be traced to the classical era of free market philosophy that neoliberalism seeks to emulate. So rather than treating this jurisprudence as an "example" of neoliberal priorities, it is better understood as a rationale that presages and anticipates the neoliberal priorities of the current era.

These priorities are reflected in the seemingly contradictory workings of the U.S. immigration system. U.S. immigration policy is used to cultivate pliable flows of migrant laborers, which are admitted with a precarious legal status (catering to market forces). Meanwhile, the deportation-security apparatus (the strong arm of the state) removes noncitizens who have become undesirable or superfluous. Efforts to restrict noncitizen rights can be opposed if they appear to impose arbitrary restrictions on labor market demands for migrant workers, but restrictions on rights and the intensification of immigration enforcement can be tolerated if they incentivize behaviors that are conducive to productivity or seem to be responding to market demands. This is the context in which the Obama administration could oppose the restrictionist policy agenda of local nativist movements while presiding over an immigration system that was deporting noncitizens at a scale unprecedented in U.S. history.

Many immigration scholars have called for a stronger rights discourse to shift immigration policy from its current punitive orientation.[12] And it is worth noting that constitutional rights arguments have played an important role in shaping Supreme Court jurisprudence on local immigration laws. But when these rights arguments have surfaced in the debate over local immigration laws (and used to scale back restrictive local laws), they are usually accompanied by supremacy arguments. Furthermore, during the last two decades of Supreme Court decisions, supremacy arguments have increasingly dominated over rights arguments.

The rise and fall of constitutional rights arguments help illustrate the chapter's core argument about the dominance of the jurisprudence on federal supremacy. The changing relationship between supremacy and rights-based arguments also correlates with the growing influence of neoliberal priorities from the 1980s onward. The remainder of the chapter examines this history, focusing on the Supreme Court jurisprudence that has been used to strike down restrictive local laws. The analysis begins with the early jurisprudence on federal supremacy, followed by the rise of constitutional rights arguments (which complemented supremacy arguments), and concludes by discussing the contemporary neoliberal era, in which supremacy arguments have been used to weaken and limit the scope of rights arguments. The next section reviews the sample of cases examined in this chapter before moving on to an analysis of the jurisprudence itself.

THE SAMPLE AND A DESCRIPTION OF MACRO TRENDS

The sample of court cases discussed in this chapter was generated using a purposive method. Relevant cases were selected on the basis of three criteria: they had to be U.S. Supreme Court decisions, they had to involve state or local laws whose legality was held in question by the federal government, and the laws had to contain measures that were perceived (by a federal court of appeals) to singularly affect foreign nationals. The resulting sample was composed of forty-four decisions (excluding decisions remanded to lower courts), spanning 1813–2013. Table 7.1 provides a chronology of cases that describes the key issues of contention as well as outcomes.

One of the more notable trends documented by this table is the Supreme Court's track record of opposition to restrictive local laws. Most of the cases (those without notes) involve local laws that aimed to restrict noncitizen rights in some way. Of these thirty-eight cases, the court ruled against local immigration laws on twenty-two occasions (or about 58 percent of the time). Meanwhile, the court heard few cases involving local laws that sought to protect noncitizen rights (the remaining six of the forty-four), and it has never opposed any of these laws. So although the Supreme Court has not been uniformly opposed to local immigration laws, it has been primarily concerned with ruling on restrictive laws, and

Table 7.1

Supreme Court Decisions on Local Laws Concerning Noncitizen/Alien Rights

Year	Case	Issue of Contention	Upheld Local Law?
2013	Arizona v. Inter Tribal Council of Arizona	Unauthorized migrants (voter registration)	No
2012	Arizona v. U.S.	Unauthorized migrants (several measures)	No/Yes
2011	Chamber of Commerce v. Whiting	Unauthorized migrants (employer sanctions)	Yes
1982	Plyler v. Doe	Unauthorized migrants (access to public education)	No
1982	Cabell v. Chavez-Salido	Noncitizens and public sector employment	Yes
1982	Toll v. Moreno	In-state tuition for visa holders	No
1979	Ambach v. Norwick	Noncitizens and public sector employment	Yes
1978	Foley v. Connelie	Noncitizens and public sector employment	Yes
1977	Nyquist v. Mauclet	In-state tuition for resident aliens	No
1976	DeCanas v. Bica	Unauthorized migrants (employer sanctions)	Yes
1976	Examining Board v. Flores de Otero	Noncitizens and professional certification	No
1973	Sugarman v. Dougall	Noncitizens and public sector employment	No
1973	In re Griffiths	Noncitizens and professional certification	No
1971	Graham v. Richardson	Noncitizens and welfare benefits	No
1956	Pennsylvania v. Nelson	Noncitizens and seditious activity	No
1948	Takahashi v. Fish & Game Commission	Anti-Asian game licensing	No
1948	Oyama v. California	Anti-Asian land law	No
1941	Hines v. Davidowitz	Alien registration	No
1934	Morrison v. California	Anti-Asian land law	Yes
1927	Ohio ex Rel. Clark v. Deckebach	Noncitizens and business licensing	Yes
1925	Cockrill v. California	Anti-Asian land law	Yes
1924	Asakura v. Seattle	Anti-Asian employment	No
1923	Terrace v. Thompson	Anti-Asian land law	Yes
1923	Frick v. Webb	Anti-Asian land law	Yes
1923	Webb v. O'Brien	Anti-Asian land law	Yes
1923	Porterfield v. Webb	Anti-Asian land law	Yes
1915	Truax v. Raich	Noncitizens and employment (private sector)	No
1915	Crane v. New York	Noncitizens and public employment	Yes
1915	Heim v. McCall	Noncitizens and public employment	Yes

Table 7.1 *(continued)*

Year	Case	Issue of Contention	Upheld Local Law?
1914	*Patsone v. Pennsylvania*	Noncitizens and game licensing	Yes
1901	*Blythe v. Hinckley*	Alien land rights	Yes[a]
1890	*Geoffrey v. Riggs*	Alien land rights	Yes[a]
1886	*Yick Wo v. Hopkins*	Anti-Asian business licensing	No
1883	*People v. Compagnie Generale Transatlantique*	Port-of-call fees for alien passengers	No
1879	*Hauenstein v. Lynham*	Alien land rights	Yes[a]
1876	*Chy Lung v. Freeman*	Port-of-call fees for alien passengers	No
1875	*Henderson v. Mayor of City of New York*	Port-of-call fees for alien passengers	No
1849	*Passenger Cases*	Port-of-call fees for alien passengers	No
1837	*New York v. Miln*	Port-of-call fees for alien passengers	Yes
1830	*Spratt v. Spratt*	Alien land rights	n/a[b]
1826	*Governeur's Heirs v. Robertson*	Alien land rights	Yes[a]
1817	*Chirac v. Chirac*	Alien land rights	Yes[a]
1816	*Martin v. Hunter's Lessee*	Alien land rights	No
1813	Fairfax's Devisee	Alien land rights	No

[a] Decision upheld a local law that affirmed the right of aliens to acquire or sell U.S. property. All other "yes" decisions not noted upheld local laws that restricted alien rights in some way.
[b] Decision affirmed the right of an alien to acquire or sell U.S. property without passing judgment on the local law in question, which also affirmed this right.

the balance of its decisions has been prohibitive. This tendency describes the empirical basis for the controlled expansion argument—in which Supreme Court rulings tend to strike down restrictive laws, with these prohibitions operating in tandem with the proliferation of local immigration laws.

This chapter's focus is on explaining the legal rationales that have been used to strike down local immigration laws. In contrast, the proliferation of local immigration laws is taken as given, because the point of the analysis is to offer a new context for understanding the present-day expansion of these laws. Even so, it is worth noting that the relationship between Supreme Court rulings and the proliferation of local laws has fluctuated over time.

For example, the period between 1813 and 1901 seems to epitomize the controlled expansion argument. As Aristide Zolberg and Gerald Neuman have shown, locally enacted immigration laws were a pervasive and accepted part of the legal landscape of the nineteenth century.[13] But this era was also characterized by an almost unbroken string of prohibitive rulings by the Supreme Court. Throughout the entirety of the nineteenth century, the Supreme Court issued only one ruling in support of a restrictive local law (in the case of *New York v. Miln*).

In contrast, 1914–1934 was the period in which the Supreme Court was most likely to support restrictive laws (striking down these laws in two instances out of a total of twelve decisions; see table 7.1). In this era, federal interest in prohibiting restrictive local immigration laws appears to be at its weakest.

The period 1941–1976 describes an unbroken string of decisions that struck down restrictive laws (see table 7.1) at a time when anti-Asian restrictions, which had been a driving force of local immigration legislation in the early twentieth century, were on the downswing; plus, the race-based nature of these restrictions was expressly prohibited by the antidiscrimination and civil rights reforms of the late 1960s.

The period from 1976 onward (beginning with *DeCanas v. Bica*; see table 7.1) marks the emergence of a uniquely ambivalent era, in which the Supreme Court issued prohibitive decisions only 50 percent of the time (counting *Arizona v. U.S.*, on balance, as a prohibitive decision). This is also the era in which neoliberal economic priorities begin to shape immigrant recruitment, and local immigration laws undergo an unprecedented expansion (from 2004 onward). The Supreme Court decisions (2011–2013) that occur in tandem with this proliferation of local immigration laws fit the controlled expansion argument, though these rulings are not as consistently prohibitive as those of the nineteenth century.

Viewed in this light, controlled expansion describes the bookends of a legal history marked by substantial fluidity—with the mid- to late nineteenth century and early twenty-first century best exemplifying the controlled expansion argument. But there is a continuity of legal opinion running through all these eras that becomes more apparent when examining the case history in more depth. The next several sections use this case history to show how federal supremacy arguments have consistently informed Supreme Court opinion, and how these supremacy arguments have been singularly informed by concerns about international commerce. The analysis also accounts for the role that constitutional rights arguments played in striking down local laws, and explains how these arguments have been largely dominated by federal supremacy arguments.

EARLY JURISPRUDENCE ON FEDERAL SUPREMACY

The federal supremacy argument suffuses almost every Supreme Court decision on local immigration laws. It appears in thirty-eight of the forty-four decisions included in the sample (and in twenty-four of the twenty-seven decisions that strike down restrictive local laws).

Martin v. Hunter's Lessee (1816) is one of the earliest Supreme Court decisions that used a supremacy argument to strike down a local law attempting to restrict noncitizen rights (being preceded by an 1813 decision involving the same case).[14] The *Martin* decision can be credited for "inventing" the jurisprudence on federal supremacy that would be used for the next two hundred years to regulate the immigration powers of local governments—and is all the more significant because it supplies the argument that established the supremacy of the Supreme Court over state courts. In this case, the Supreme Court overturned a Virginia court's decision to uphold a Revolutionary-era state law that allowed for the confiscation of lands belonging to British Loyalists, who were deemed "alien enemies." In contrast, all the other nineteenth-century Supreme Court decisions concerning alien land rights involved local laws that affirmed the right of foreign nationals to own, sell, or will U.S. property to another party.[15] The Supreme Court upheld these laws in every case.

In these cases, the Supreme Court insisted that the property transactions in question were protected by international treaties between the United States and foreign governments. Hence, local laws that protected these transactions were affirmed—not because the Supreme Court was convinced of the inherent authority of state governments but because these local laws were in agreement with the federal government's interest in encouraging international commerce.

Although *Martin* struck down a local law, it was in agreement with these other rulings because it affirmed the right of aliens to engage in property transactions. The *Martin* decision is also important for the way that it articulates a laissez-faire orientation to international commerce with a supremacy argument that insists on the need for a strong, centralized state authority (acting as a "final decider" over the regulation of international commerce).

Between 1837 and 1883, Supreme Court jurisprudence on local immigration laws shifted to a series of disputes over port-of-call fees that were being imposed by local governments on alien passengers. These cases played an important role in clarifying court opinion on how to reconcile police powers—deemed to be a field of law not occupied by the federal government—and federal supremacy over international commerce. One of these cases was *New York v. Miln* (1837), which is the only nineteenth-century case in which the Supreme Court ruled in favor of a restrictive local law.

In *New York v. Miln*, the court insisted that alien passengers were not "commerce"—with the implication that taxation of these passengers did not interfere with federal supremacy over matters of international commerce.[16] As a result, the taxation of alien passengers was deemed to fall under the legitimate "police powers" of the states, which were interpreted broadly to include local government's interest in the public welfare of its citizenry (protecting them from being over-whelmed by aliens who were criticized for draining fiscal resources and possibly spreading disease). But the Supreme Court's next four decisions on port-of-call fees (spanning 1849–1883) ruled against local lawmakers.[17] In these cases, the court insisted that port-of-call fees did indeed interfere with the federal government's regulation of international commerce. Some of these decisions criticized the discriminatory nature of these laws, which appeared to target Chinese nationals (*Henderson v. Mayor of City of New York* and *Chy Lung v. Freeman*).[18] But their arguments rested principally on the court's interpretation of federal supremacy over matters of international commerce, and they all restricted the scope of the "police powers" affirmed by *New York v. Miln.*

EQUAL PROTECTION ARGUMENTS AND LOCAL IMMIGRATION LAWS

The origins of the constitutional rights argument (as it concerns local immigration laws) can be traced to the 1886 *Yick Wo v. Hopkins* decision, which involved a municipal ordinance regulating laundry businesses that was being implemented in a way that appeared to discriminate against Chinese foreign-born business owners.

Yick Wo referenced a treaty between the U.S. government and the emperor of China, which stipulated that Chinese migrants were entitled to the full protection of the law. This portion of the argument affirmed a right of "equal protection" that appealed to the logic of federal supremacy arguments—on the basis that the U.S. government's diplomatic agreements trump local law. However, the core argument advanced by *Yick Wo* was that Chinese nationals residing in the United States were entitled to the same constitutional protections afforded to U.S. citizens. The court insisted that "the Fourteenth Amendment to the Constitution is not confined to the protection of citizens. . . . [Its] provisions are universal in their application to all persons within the territorial jurisdiction, without regard to any differences of race, of color, or of nationality."[19]

According to this argument, Chinese nationals could claim inalienable rights based on the fact of their habitation in a territory that was subject to the sovereign law of the United States. Unlike the supremacy argument, this was not the kind of "equal protection" that could be modified at the discretion of the federal government (for example, by declining to renew an international treaty).

Yick Wo turned to prior Supreme Court rulings on port-of-call laws to establish the precedent for this rights argument. Specifically, the court cited *Chy Lung v. Freeman* and *Henderson v. Mayor of City of New York* as establishing the "principle of interpretation" guiding its decision.[20] But this is a rather creative reading.

Both of these decisions condemned anti-Asian discrimination, but this condemnation had no bearing on the legal rationale the court used to strike down the laws, which was exclusively reliant on supremacy arguments. Neither of these decisions so much as referenced the Fourteenth Amendment (or the equal protection clause), though both decisions occurred a decade or more after the adoption of the amendment. In fact, *Yick Wo v. Hopkins* is the first Supreme Court decision to use the equal protection clause as an argument against restrictive local laws.

Starting with *Yick Wo*, eleven Supreme Court decisions used constitutional rights arguments to strike down restrictive local laws (see table 7.2). All these decisions also relied on federal supremacy arguments (which is why constitutional rights arguments could be treated as a subset of the federal supremacy argument). Even so, the constitutional rights argument added an important new dimension to the supremacy argument. Whereas supremacy arguments protect noncitizen rights from being further restricted, constitutional rights arguments progressively expand noncitizen rights. One example is provided by *Truax v. Raich* (1915), which was the first Supreme Court decision to strike down a restrictive local law that cited *Yick Wo*.[21]

Truax v. Raich concerned an Australian national who was about to lose his job because of an Arizona law that established quotas for determining the maximum number of noncitizens who could be employed by private businesses. Because there was no international treaty stipulating fair treatment of Australian nations in the United States, the argument had to rely more exclusively on the idea that the Fourteenth Amendment was intended to apply to all U.S. residents, regardless of nationality or citizen status. As a result, *Truax v. Raich* clarified an argument, implicit in *Yick Wo*, that the constitutional rights argument applied to all noncitizens and not just a protected class covered by international treaties (i.e., Chinese nationals).

Notably, these constitutional rights arguments matured during the same era in which the Supreme Court was becoming more supportive of restrictive local laws. This trend begins in 1914–1915 with three Supreme Court decisions that supported local laws restricting noncitizen rights. These decisions found that the regulation of public employment and certain types of licensing fell within the legitimate scope of the local government's "special interest" ("special interest" being a derivation of the earlier "police powers" argument).[22] A string of decisions spanning 1923–1934 extended this argument to alien land ownership, upholding laws that targeted Chinese and Japanese noncitizens.[23]

Meanwhile, major shifts had occurred at the level of national policy. In 1921, the U.S. Congress enacted the Immigration Restriction Act (to be followed by the more comprehensive 1924 Immigration Act), which imposed the United States' first-ever national origin immigration quotas. These laws also established the legal

Table 7.2

Supreme Court Decisions Using Constitutional Rights Arguments to Strike Down Restrictive, Local Immigration Laws

Case	Year	Cited by Other Cases Using Constitutional Rights Arguments (listed in chronological order)
Yick Wo v. Hopkins	1886	Truax v. Raich Hines v. Davidowitz Takahashi v. Fish & Game Commission Graham v. Richardson In re Griffiths Sugarman v. Dougall Examining Board v. Flores de Otero Plyler v. Doe
Truax v. Raich	1915	Graham v. Richardson In re Griffiths Sugarman v. Dougall Examining Board v. Flores de Otero Toll v. Moreno[a] Arizona v. U.S.[a]
Hines v. Davidowitz	1941	Takahashi v. Fish & Game Commission Examining Board v. Flores de Otero Toll v. Moreno[a] Plyler v. Doe Arizona v. U.S.[a]
Oyama v. California	1941	Takahashi v. Fish & Game Commission Graham v. Richardson In re Griffiths Sugarman v. Dougall Examining Board v. Flores de Otero Plyler v. Doe
Takahashi v. Fish & Game Commission	1948	Graham v. Richardson In re Griffiths Sugarman v. Dougall Examining Board v. Flores de Otero Nyquist v. Mauclet Plyler v. Doe
Graham v. Richardson	1971	In re Griffiths Sugarman v. Dougall Examining Board v. Flores de Otero Nyquist v. Mauclet Toll v. Moreno[a] Plyler v. Doe
In re Griffiths	1973	Sugarman v. Dougall Examining Board v. Flores de Otero Nyquist v. Mauclet
Sugarman v. Dougall	1973	Examining Board v. Flores de Otero Nyquist v. Mauclet Toll v. Moreno[a]
Examining Board v. Flores de Otero	1976	Nyquist v. Mauclet Plyler v. Doe
Nyquist v. Mauclet	1977	Plyler v. Doe
Plyler v. Doe	1982	Nil

[a] Marks a transition away from the strong constitutional rights arguments exemplified by *Yick Wo*, *Graham*, and *Plyler*.

framework for a new migrant reality—that of "illegality"—which operated in tandem with a racialized public discourse targeting Asian and Mexican migrants.[24] This federal-level shift toward a restrictive and explicitly racialized immigration policy parallels the Supreme Court's support for local laws targeting Asian noncitizens in a string of six cases spanning 1923–1934.[25]

This period, in which the Supreme Court was most supportive of restrictive local laws, correlates with a restrictionist agenda that had made unprecedented inroads at the level of national legislation (exemplified by the national origin restrictions on immigration that were introduced by the Immigration Acts of 1921 and 1924, along with the 1923 Chinese Exclusion Act). Thus, the restrictive local laws of this era can be understood as expressing an interest that was in continuity with federal law, rather than asserting a local sovereignty independent of federal law.

Truax is distinguished for being the only decision of this era that used a constitutional rights argument to strike down a local immigration law.[26] Constitutional rights arguments do not resurface until the 1940s, with the cases of *Hines v. Davidowitz* (1941), *Oyama v. California* (1948), and *Takahashi v. Fish & Game Commission* (1948), and in all these cases, the constitutional rights argument is counterbalanced by a more strongly worded federal supremacy argument.[27] But the constitutional rights argument starts being asserted in a more forceful way in the early years of the post–civil rights era. The first signal of this shift in Supreme Court jurisprudence occurs with the 1971 *Graham v. Richardson* decision.[28]

Graham, which concerned the right of noncitizens to access welfare benefits, not only resuscitated equal protection arguments but also strengthened them with an argument that was just as creative as that in *Yick Wo*. Whereas *Yick Wo* applied the equal protection argument to aliens, *Graham* argued that aliens are deserving of these protections because they constitute a "discrete and insular minority." With this definition established, the court went on to argue that laws that potentially discriminate against aliens must be subject to "close judicial scrutiny" (the implication being that this should be comparable to the scrutiny applied to laws deemed to discriminate on the basis of race—considering the precedents set by landmark civil rights decisions like *Brown v. Board of Education*,[29] which were reinforced by federal legislation like the 1965 *Civil Rights Voting Act*). This standard of close judicial scrutiny did not fundamentally change the equal protection argument, but it raised the bar for what counts as equality.

Graham was cited by a sequence of decisions that struck down local laws attempting to restrict the employment and professional licensing of noncitizens (*In re Griffiths*, *Sugarman v. Dougall*, and *Examining Board v. Flores de Otero*).[30] The last of these decisions (*Examining Board*) was issued in 1976. It so happens that this was the same year the Supreme Court decided *DeCanas v. Bica*, which was the first of new string of decisions ruling in favor of restrictive local laws.

(Prior to *DeCanas*, the last decision ruling in favor of a restrictive local law was *Morrison v. California* in 1934.) The Decanas decision was also significant for being the first deliberation over a local immigration law to explicitly address the rights of unauthorized migrants—involving restrictions on the employment of unauthorized migrants.[31]

Notably, *DeCanas* gave the Supreme Court stamp of approval for a law with similar intentions as the controversial Arizona law that was mostly struck down by the court in 2012 (in *Arizona v. U.S.*). *DeCanas* has been justified on the grounds that at the time of the decision, the federal government had yet to completely occupy the field of lawmaking concerning the enforcement of laws against unauthorized migrants (which would not occur until the 1986 Immigration Reform and Control Act [IRCA]).[32] Nevertheless, in the context of its time, *DeCanas* appears to signal that the Supreme Court would not allow the precedent established by *Graham* to be extended to unauthorized migrants.

This is one reason why the 1982 *Plyler v. Doe* decision is so significant: because it used the criterion of close judicial scrutiny to strike down a Texas statute that barred unauthorized migrant children from the public school system. The fact that *Plyler* was issued four years before the federal government formally occupied the field of immigration enforcement lawmaking—with IRCA—underscores the important role that constitutional rights arguments played in justifying the decision (though federal supremacy arguments do make an appearance).

Plyler was framed in a way that treated migrant children as a "special class" that could be abstracted from the broader unauthorized migrant population. The implication here was that the Supreme Court was not making a blanket argument for extending the equal protection clause to all unauthorized migrants. Even so, the equal protection argument initiated by *Yick Wo* (which *Plyler* cites) certainly invites these kinds of "blanket arguments" because it makes territorial habitation—not legal status—the chief criterion for entitlement to constitutional protections.

It could be argued that *Yick Wo* was never intended for unauthorized migrants, since the legal-juridical framework defining migrant (il)legality does not mature until the 1920s, but this begs the question of how *Plyler* rationalized the extension of constitutional protections to unauthorized migrant children to begin with. Moreover, *Plyler* did not make an argument for how the presence of adult unauthorized migrants in U.S. territory differed from that of unauthorized migrant children. As a result, there was nothing in the legal rationale for *Plyler* that would logically prohibit it from being extended to all unauthorized migrants, especially considering that the jurisprudence established by *Graham* had been moving Supreme Court decisions toward a more rigorous interpretation of the equal protection argument.

However, *Plyler* marks the high point—and possibly the end point—of these strong constitutional rights arguments. It also marks the beginning of the Supreme Court's longest silence on the subject of local immigration laws; and when it finally broke this silence, nearly thirty years later, it was with a jurisprudence weighted heavily in favor of federal supremacy arguments.

THE TURNING POINT: *TOLL V. MORENO*

The reassertion of federal supremacy over constitutional rights arguments actually began before the great silence set in. The Supreme Court heard three cases in 1982 that pertained to local immigration laws: *Plyler v. Doe, Cabell v. Chavez-Salido,* and *Toll v. Moreno.*[33] *Cabell* was the only decision of the three that upheld a restrictive local law. It continued a jurisprudence upheld by *Ambach v. Norwick* and *Foley v. Connelie,*[34] which argued that the criterion of close scrutiny (introduced by *Graham*) did not apply to the state's interest in barring noncitizens from public sector jobs that were of special civic significance (a distant ancestor of the "police powers" argument inaugurated by *New York v Miln*).[35] But it is ironic that just months after the Supreme Court decided *Cabell,* it issued the landmark *Plyler* decision, which further expanded noncitizen rights.[36]

The *Toll v. Moreno* decision was the last of three rulings on local immigration laws that were issued in 1982 and, on these grounds, it could be considered to be the Supreme Court's "final word" on the matter.[37] The Toll decision ruled against a restrictive local law and, even more important, it presaged the arguments that would be used in the Obama era to oppose restrictive local laws. *Toll* is also significant for being the first decision on local immigration laws to address a legal and economic context that is the direct product of neoliberal priorities for U.S. immigration.

Toll was the culmination of a series of appeals (including two prior Supreme Court decisions) that concerned a challenge to the in-state tuition policy of the University of Maryland.[38] The appellants were G-4 visa holders. The G-4 is a type of visa issued to employees of international organizations and their dependents (the appellants were the dependent children of the principle visa holders). In its argument, the court referenced equal protection arguments made by lower courts. However, its primary argument was that local policies that withheld in-state tuition benefits from G-4 visa holders conflicted with the federal intentions guiding G-4 visa policy. The fact that the salaries of G-4 visa holders were not subject to federal taxation was interpreted as setting a precedent for their exemption from other forms of taxation, especially taxation schemes that singled them out because they were visa holders. Hence, the court argued,

the Federal Government has undoubtedly sought to benefit the employing international organizations by enabling them to pay salaries not encumbered by the full panoply of taxes, thereby lowering the organizations' costs. . . . By imposing on those G-4 aliens who are domiciled in Maryland higher tuition and fees than are imposed on other domiciliaries of the State, the University's policy frustrates these federal policies.[39]

The logic of this decision mirrors the court's earlier rulings on local laws that appear to conflict with international treaties. Of course, G-4 visa policy operates entirely within the framework of U.S. law, but it was interpreted as brokering a commercial relationship analogous to the sort of relationships governed by international treaties. This theme comes across strongly in *Toll*, in which visa holders are valued as conduits for international flows of trade and investment capital. But the *Toll* decision also takes for granted a paradigm of national sovereignty that has been transformed by neoliberal priorities for immigration.

The *Yick Wo* decision advanced an equal protection argument that insisted on strict correspondence between territorial habitation and constitutional rights. *Toll*, on the other hand, took place at a time when growing numbers of migrants were being recruited as temporary workers with limited political, legal, and social rights. As a result, noncitizen rights were becoming disaggregated from the social fact of territorial habitation.

In the early 1980s, the admission of visa holders underwent a dramatic increase, which has been sustained to this day, leading to a situation in which the inflow of nonimmigrants (mostly for reasons of commerce) has massively outpaced the growth of the "conventional" immigrant (or legal permanent resident) population by a ratio of thirty to one (and higher).[40] This transformation has led the "visitor" to displace the "permanent settler" as the quotidian subject of the U.S. migration system and has also led the temporary visa to become the primary vehicle by which most eventual settlers enter the United States.[41]

The *Toll* decision aligns itself with a sovereign authority that presides over this byzantine system of legal statuses. Instead of guaranteeing the inalienable rights of all U.S. denizens, the sovereign authority of the neoliberal era is more concerned with determining the scope of the constitutional rights that will pertain to different legal status categories, with the issuance of permanent legal status (and the right to enjoy the full scope of the constitutional rights afforded to native-born citizens) being viewed in light of migrant productivity.

This neoliberal common sense is reflected in the way the *Toll* decision constructed visa holders as deserving of protection on the basis of their economic contributions to the United States (an argument in line with the federal prerogatives guiding visa policy). As a result, G-4 visa holders could be exempted from restrictive measures by virtue of their belonging to a special class distinguished by its economic potential rather than on the basis of rights guaranteed to all (whether citizen or noncitizen).

The *Toll* decision also referenced legal scholarship that made a case for the preferability of supremacy arguments over equal protection arguments. One of these arguments, written by David Levi, criticized the precedent of close scrutiny established by *Graham* as a distortion of a jurisprudence that was primarily defined by supremacy arguments.[42] Levi's practical argument, however, was that no law employing citizen/alien distinctions could survive the test of close scrutiny, and that if left unchecked, the progressive application of this legal argument would undermine the very idea of national political membership. Notably, Levi's argument did not discuss U.S. visa policy (though visa policy was referenced in the *Toll* decision itself). If this policy context is brought into the picture, federal supremacy arguments can also be read as an attempt to resolve the apparent contradiction between a national-territorial paradigm of rights and a visa policy that was creating a growing population of "economic guests." The supremacy argument resolved this tension by preserving national-political membership as an exclusive island within a growing sea of temporary legal statuses.

RECONSOLIDATION OF FEDERAL SUPREMACY ARGUMENTS AFTER TOLL

The *Toll* decision set the tone for the Supreme Court's 2012 decision in *Arizona v. U.S. Toll* is the first federal court decision pertaining to local immigration laws that is cited in the majority opinion for *Arizona* and plays an important role in the court's framing of the case. This return to a jurisprudence that is defined, more exclusively, by supremacy arguments also correlates with a more ambivalent position on local immigration laws.

In 2011's *Chamber of Commerce v. Whiting*, for example, the Supreme Court let stand an employer sanctions law developed by the state of Arizona.[43] This decision approved a method of penalizing employers of unauthorized migrants that was almost identical to one used by a controversial local ordinance adopted by the city of Hazelton, Pennsylvania. As Benjamin Fleury-Steiner and Jamie Longazel explain, Hazelton's immigration laws can be understood as a populist reaction to the local contradictions of an aggressive neoliberal growth agenda.[44] This is why the Supreme Court's decision in *Chamber of Commerce v. Whiting* could be read as a nod of approval to the economic-nationalist sensibilities popularized by the immigration control movement.

But just one year later, in *Arizona v. U.S.*, the court struck down every section of Arizona's Senate Bill 1070 that attempted to penalize employers of unauthorized migrant workers or, more generally, to inhibit unauthorized labor migration. In its majority opinion, the court advanced arguments that were very similar to those used by the district court ruling that struck down the Hazelton laws.[45]

Furthermore, the Supreme Court subsequently refused to hear the City of Hazelton's appeal of the circuit and district court decisions that had struck down its ordinances. Prominent legal scholars have observed that this decision "will make it harder for similar . . . ordinances to pass judicial scrutiny."[46]

When this context is accounted for, the Supreme Court's flirtation with economic-nationalism (in *Chamber of Commerce*) appears to be an anomaly within a body of opinion that is inclined to prohibit local laws that appear to interfere with the flow and recruitment of migrant labor. The court's position on this matter is analogous to its early nineteenth-century rulings on alien land laws, in which migrant labor is appointed a status similar to "international commerce," falling under the exclusive authority of the federal government. Moreover, the court's move to restrict local lawmaking powers held little consequence for migrant rights or for constitutional rights more generally.

The one section of the Arizona law that the Supreme Court left in place allows local police to check the legal status of persons who are being questioned in the context of a normal interrogation. This decision did nothing to expand police authority to enforce immigration laws. In fact, it is consistent with a legal precedent (established by *Gonzalez v. Peoria* [1983]) that has found favor with immigrant rights constituencies.[47] However, the case the court cited in its support of this section of the law (*Muehler v. Mena* [2005]) affirmed its support for police discretion over Fourth Amendment rights.[48] In *Muehler*, the Supreme Court overturned a Court of Appeals for the Ninth Circuit Court decision, which found that the constitutional rights of Iris Mena—a naturalized U.S. citizen of Mexican heritage—had been violated by a police search of her dwelling, which resulted in her being detained at gun point for several hours on suspicion that she was connected to a crime ring composed of undocumented migrants (and that she might be undocumented herself).[49]

The Supreme Court summed up the rationale for its decision on *Muehler* by parenthetically noting that it found "no Fourth Amendment violation where questioning . . . did not prolong a stop."[50] Notably, this is the same standard of reasonableness that legal scholar David Cole has critically examined in Supreme Court decisions that have rejected Fourth Amendment arguments concerning the racial profiling of black youth.[51]

But in the Arizona decision, the court had sympathetic words for unauthorized migrants, noting that "discretion in the enforcement of immigration law embraces immediate human concerns. Unauthorized workers trying to support their families, for example, likely pose less danger than alien smugglers or aliens who commit a serious crime."[52] This statement is informed by a distinction between criminal and noncriminal immigrants that tolerates the kind of policing exemplified by the Mena case. It also extends these sympathies more broadly than does *Plyler*, beyond the "special class" of migrant youth. Even so, these sympathetic words were not accompanied by a legal argument for migrant rights, and when prior decisions that used constitutional rights arguments were referenced (most notably *Hines* and *Truax*), it was to advance a federal supremacy argument.

This two-pronged movement—curtailing restrictive local laws without affirming or strengthening migrant rights—is exemplified by the Supreme Court's 2013 decision in the case of *Arizona v. Inter Tribal Council of Arizona*.[53] In this case, the court struck down a state voter registration law that sought to screen voters for proof of legal status.

The majority opinion of the court was led by Justice Antonin Scalia, who had taken a very different position in the court's 2012 *Arizona* ruling. In that case, Scalia issued a dissent in favor of the "inherent authority" of local governments to enact immigration laws, and he defended every section of the law that the majority opinion had agreed to strike down. Scalia's dissent was very similar to the opinions communicated by an internal memo issued by officials in the 2000–2004 Bush White House on the subject of immigration law, which played a role in instigating the resurgence of restrictive local laws.[54] Nevertheless, the position Scalia took in *Arizona v. US* was still a minority opinion, and the fact that he led the majority opinion in the 2013 decision that struck down a restrictive local law would seem to offer powerful testimony of the hegemony of the federal supremacy argument.

Scalia's majority opinion in *Arizona v. Inter Tribal Council of Arizona* is also notable for its lack of citations to *any* prior Supreme Court decisions on local immigration law. Whereas the court's decisions from *Toll* onward have deemphasized constitutional rights arguments, Scalia's decision completely omits them. Scalia's opinion also testifies to a remarkable continuity in Supreme Court opinion on local immigration law, bookending a two-hundred-year jurisprudence that began (via *Martin* in 1816) with a very similar kind of argument: prohibiting restrictive local laws through exclusive reliance on a federal supremacy argument.

This chapter has traced the history of Supreme Court jurisprudence on local immigration laws and found that it has been mainly oriented toward prohibiting laws that attempt to restrict noncitizen rights. But this tendency toward curtailing local lawmaking powers often coexists with the proliferation of state and local immigration laws. The mid- to late nineteenth and early twenty-first centuries exemplify this tendency, in which migrant flows are at peak levels, there is a proliferation of local laws geared toward "controlling" migration in some way, and Supreme Court rulings are used to strike down the most controversial local laws without halting the proliferation of these laws.

This chapter used the concept of controlled expansion to describe this federal-local dynamic. The federal supremacy argument is the primary means through which this control has been imposed, and it describes a continuity that runs through the last two hundred years of Supreme Court opinion.

A core theme of the supremacy argument is the concern for regulating international commerce (including things analogous to international commerce, such as noncitizen passengers aboard international vessels, holders of work visas, and relations between employers and unauthorized migrant workers). Because international commerce involves negotiations between sovereign states, it follows that these matters must fall under the exclusive authority of the federal government and that the laws and policies the federal government uses to regulate these matters must preempt local laws. Whereas the relationship between market-led growth and state intervention was largely specific to matters of immigration and international commerce in the early nineteenth century, it has become a general template for all varieties of neoliberal growth strategies in the current era.

This transformation also sheds light on what is different about the controlled expansion of the current era. In the early and mid-nineteenth century, supremacy arguments struck down restrictive laws by appealing to a federal authority that defended a laissez-faire economic philosophy. These arguments initially lacked a rights argument (which extended constitutional protections to noncitizens), but when the rights argument was innovated in *Yick Wo v. Hopkins*, it was combined with the federal supremacy arguments that were used to curtail restrictive laws.

In contrast, the shift to a neoliberal economic platform in the 1980s correlates with the rise of a supremacy argument that is actively averse to rights arguments. In this era, supremacy arguments have been used—in a two-pronged movement—to curtail restrictionist laws and also to control rights arguments that had been evolving in the post–civil rights era. This tendency raises some important questions about the relevance of the debate over local immigration laws to broader concerns about the massive expansion of the deportation and detention system.

So long as Constitutional rights arguments remain a weak or absent feature of arguments against restrictive local laws, it seems unlikely that "progressive" outcomes (striking down restrictive laws) will set precedents that carry any relevance for improving noncitizen rights. In the Obama era, these outcomes offered noncitizens some protection from the policy agenda of local nativist movements, but not from the way that deportability conditioned their integration into local labor markets. In the Trump era, noncitizens are even more vulnerable. But instead of being threatened by an even more aggressive spate of local laws, the emerging struggle over sanctuary laws illustrates how noncitizens will be endangered by efforts to dismantle protective local laws.

The precedent set by Scalia's opinion in *Arizona v. Inter Tribal Council of Arizona* looms more significant now because it advanced a supremacy argument that was so thoroughly removed from rights arguments that it could be used to strike down any local immigration law, including so-called sanctuary laws. What is less clear, however, is whether the federal courts, and the Supreme Court in particular, would be prepared to use supremacy arguments to strike down protective local laws. As table 7.1 demonstrates, there are a number of occasions in which the Supreme Court has ruled in favor of restrictive local laws, but it has never struck down a local law that protected noncitizen rights—and it has not heard a case involving a protective local law since the alien land law disputes of the nineteenth century.[55]

It is possible, however, that the Trump-era struggle over local immigration laws will not result in a Supreme Court showdown between federal and local governments, comparable to *Arizona v. US*. In the early part of 2017, the Trump administration's opposition to protective local immigration laws played out in the federal budget debate rather than in the courts (with federal law makers refusing to authorize fiscal sanctions against local governments identified by the Trump administration as "sanctuary cities").[56] The Trump era has also inaugurated a new kind of legal fight over local immigration laws that pits local governments against each other, as evidenced by a law suit filed by the state of Texas against local Texas governments with "sanctuary laws."[57] At the time of this writing, the Trump administration has not indicated how or whether it will use the supremacy principle to influence the outcomes of these local struggles. It is also possible that the arguments advanced in these local-local struggles may completely side step the federal supremacy principle, but even if this happens it would allow federal supremacy to remain the dominant jurisprudence by default. Meanwhile, the Trump administration's reactivation of Secure Communities and the 287(g) program signals its support for federal-local enforcement partnerships that are consistent with the supremacy principle.[58]

Keeping these developments in mind, the more important question to pursue is not whether the jurisprudence on federal supremacy will survive the Trump era, but the terms under which it might survive. How will the jurisprudence on federal supremacy navigate the distance between an established neoliberal paradigm for immigration policy and the economic nationalist rhetoric of the Trump administration? Will Scalia's opinion in *Arizona v. Intertribal Council* turn out to be an anomaly, or will it establish the starting point for an entirely new genealogy of supremacy arguments?

If they were alive today, the justices who crafted the *Yick Wo* decision would undoubtedly be concerned about the erosion of basic rights for large populations of noncitizens who are living and working on U.S. soil. These justices were able to balance the federal supremacy argument with a robust commitment to the principle of equality before the law. But in the era of neoliberalism, the supremacy argument and the constitutional rights argument have been driven apart, and this rift is exposing the tensions between a paradigm of economic growth that has become increasingly reliant on unilateral decision-making structures that are removed from public oversight. We are fast approaching a time in which it will be necessary to decide which of these imperatives will define the political future of the United States: authoritarian bureaucracy or democracy? The continuing struggle over local immigration laws could be the bellwether that indicates in which direction we are headed.

NOTES TO CHAPTER 7

1. A total of 1,728 local immigration laws were enacted between 2005 and 2015, and the pace of this activity has increased over time, with state and local governments enacting almost five times as many laws from 2009 onward as they did in earlier years. See National Conference of State Legislatures, "State Laws Related to Immigration and Immigrants" (2005–2015 Year-End Reports), http://www.ncsl.org /research/immigration/state-laws-related-to-immigration-and-immigrants.aspx. But not all of these laws are restrictive. Except for laws explicitly focused on law enforcement, most categories of local immigration laws are almost evenly split between those that aim to protect and those that aim to restrict immigrant rights. For an example focusing on 2009 data, see Philip Kretsedemas, *The Immigration Crucible: Race, Nation and the Limits of the Law* (New York: Columbia University Press, 2012), 170n6.

2. Whiting v. Chamber of Commerce, 563 U.S. 582 (2011).

3. Arizona v. United States, 567 U.S. (2012).

4. JohnPaul Callan and Emily Callan, "Changes in the Political Tide—an Examination of How the Courts Adapt Federal Pre-Emption Doctrine in Response to a Shift in Political Opinion on Immigration," *Mississippi College Law Review* 33 (2015): 259; Kevin Johnson, "Immigration and Civil Rights: State and Local Efforts to Regulate Immigration," *Georgia Law Review* 46 (2012): 609.

5. Monica Varsanyi, "Immigration Policy Activism in U.S. States and Cities: Interdisciplinary Perspectives," in *Taking Local Control*, ed. M. Varsanyi (Stanford: Stanford University Press, 2010), 6–9.

6. This policy was communicated by Executive Order 13768, Enhancing Public Safety in the Interior of the United States, issued January 25, 2017. See also Alan Berube, "Sanctuary Cities and Trump's Executive Order," Brookings Institution, February 24, 2017, https://www.brookings.edu/blog/unpacked/2017/02/24/sanctuary-cities -and-trumps-executive-order/.

7. A report by the National Conference of State Legislatures has documented a surge in local laws opposing sanctuary cities in the first quarter of 2017. It notes that of the thirty-two states (including the District of Columbia) considering sanctuary-relevant laws, twenty-nine would prohibit sanctuary policies. National Conference of State Legislatures, "What's a Sanctuary Policy? FAQ on Federal, State and Local Action on Immigration Enforcement," March 30, 2017, http://www.ncsl.org/research/immigration /sanctuary-policy-faq635991795.aspx.

8. The main examples are the administration's decision to revive 287(g) federal-local enforcement arrangements and Secure Communities, which involve police in immi-

gration enforcement under the guidance of federal immigration enforcement (as opposed to encouraging local governments to enact their own immigration enforcement laws). These changes were authorized by Executive Order 13768, Enhancing Public Safety in the Interior of the United States, issued January 25, 2017. See also Josh Saul, "Doubling as Immigration Officers, Sheriffs Applaud Trump Order," *Newsweek*, February 12, 2017, http://www.newsweek.com/texas-sheriffs-welcome-trump-order-deport-undocumented-immigrants-555476; Miriam Valverde, "Trump Says Secure Communities, 287(g) Immigration Programs Worked Well," *Politifact*, September 6, 2016, http://www.politifact.com/truth-o-meter/statements/2016/sep/06/donald-trump/trump-says-secure-communities-287g-immigration-pro/. For an account of recent developments in the legal struggle over the antisanctuary laws, see Bernie Woodall, "U.S. Judge Throws out Texas Voter ID Law Supported by Trump," Reuters, August 23, 2017, https://www.reuters.com/article/us-usa-texas/u-s-judge-throws-out-texas-voter-id-law-supported-by-trump-idUSKCN1B3203.

9. Harald Bauder, "The Economic Case for Immigration: Neoliberal and Regulatory Paradigms in Canada's Press," *Studies in Political Economy* 82 (2008): 131–152; Philip Kretsedemas, "Reconsidering Immigrant Welfare Restrictions: A Critical Review of Post Keynesian Welfare Policy," *Stanford Law and Policy Review* 16, no. 2 (2005): 463–480.

10. Henry Giroux, *The Terror of Neoliberalism: Authoritarianism and the Eclipse of Democracy* (Boulder: Paradigm, 2004); David Harvey, *A Brief History of Neoliberalism* (Oxford: Oxford University Press, 2005); Wendy Larner, "Neoliberalism: Policy, Ideology, Governmentality," in *International Political Economy and Poststructural Politics*, ed. M. De Goede (London: Palgrave Macmillan, 2006), 199–218.

11. William Connolly, *The Fragility of Things: Self-Organizing Processes, Neoliberal Fantasies and Democratic Activism* (Princeton: Duke University Press, 2013), 52–80. Connolly's argument complements David Harvey's explanation of neoliberalism as "strong state capitalism" (referenced in chapter 1 of this text); Harvey, *Brief History of Neoliberalism*.

12. Bill Ong Hing, *Deporting Our Souls: Values, Morality, and Immigration Policy* (Cambridge: Cambridge University Press, 2006); Matthias Risse, "How Does the Global Order Harm the Poor?," *Philosophy and Public Affairs* 33, no. 4 (2005): 349–376; Andy Storey, "The Ethics of Immigration Controls: Issues for Development NGOs," *Development in Practice* 4, no. 3 (1994): 199–209.

13. Gerald Neuman, *Strangers to the Constitution: Immigrants, Borders and Fundamental Law* (Princeton: Princeton University Press, 1996); Aristide Zolberg, *A Nation by Design: Immigration Policy in the Fashioning of America* (Cambridge: Harvard University Press).

14. Martin v. Hunter's Lessee, 14 U.S. 304 (1816); Fairfax's Devisee v. Hunter's Lessee, 11 U.S. 603 (1813).

15. There are six Supreme Court decisions on this matter. These cases sometimes involved competing interpretations of local laws (as in *Hausenstein v. Lynham*), in which plaintiff arguments were supported by state and common law understandings of restrictions on alien land rights. In contrast, Supreme Court opinion uniformly insisted that these restrictions could be modified by state laws affirming alien land rights and circumvented by the terms of international treaties. See Doe ex dem. Governeur's Heirs

v. Robertson, 24 U.S. (11 Wheat.) 332 (1826); Chirac v. Chirac, 15 U.S. 259 (1817); Spratt v. Spratt, 29 U.S. 393 (1830); Hauenstein v. Lynham, 100 U.S. 483 (1879); Geoffrey v. Riggs, 133 U.S. 258 (1890); Blythe v. Hinckley, 180 U.S. 333 (1901).

16. New York v. Miln, 36 U.S. 102 (1837).

17. Passenger Cases, 48 U.S. 283 (1849); Henderson v. Mayor of City of New York, 92 U.S. 259 (1875); Chy Lung v. Freeman, 92 U.S. 275 (1876); and People v. Compagnie Generale Transatlantique, 107 U.S. 59 (1883).

18. This antidiscriminatory language played a decisive role in the legal precedent for the equal protection argument constructed by the *Yick Wo v. Hopkins* decision. See notes 19 and 20 and accompanying discussion in the body of the chapter.

19. Yick Wo v. Hopkins 118 U.S. 356, 369 (1886).

20. *Chy Lung*, 92 U.S. 275; *Henderson*, 92 U.S. 259.

21. Truax v. Raich, 239 U.S. 33 (1915).

22. Crane v. New York, 239 U.S. 195 (1915); Heim v. McCall, 239 U.S. 175 (1915); Patsone v. Pennsylvania, 232 U.S. 138 (1914).

23. Porterfield v. Webb, 263 U.S. 225 (1923); Webb v. O'Brien, 263 U.S. 313 (1923); Frick v. Webb, 263 U.S. 326 (1923); Terrace v. Thompson, 263 U.S. 197 (1923); Cockrill v. California, 268 U.S. 258 (1925); Morrison v. California, 291 U.S. 82 (1934).

24. Mae Ngai, "The Strange Career of the Illegal Alien: Immigration Restriction and Deportation Policy in the United States, 1921–1965," *Law and History Review* 21, no. 1 (2003): 69–108.

25. See note 24.

26. The one exception to this trend is *Asakura v. Seattle* (265 U.S. 332 [1924]), which was the only other Supreme Court decision in the 1914–1934 period besides *Truax* that was successful in striking down a restrictive law. But *Asakura* did so through exclusive reliance on a supremacy argument. In this regard, *Asakura* could be regarded as a "remnant" of the supremacy arguments that dominated the prohibitive rulings of the mid-nineteenth century, and also as a precursor of the direction that legal arguments against restrictive laws would take from 1982 onward.

27. Hines v. Davidowitz, 312 U.S. 52 (1941); Takahashi v. Fish & Game Commission, 334 U.S. 410 (1948); Oyama v. California, 332 U.S. 633 (1948).

28. Graham v. Richardson, 403 U.S. 365 (1971).

29. Brown v. Board of Education of Topeka, 347 U.S. 483 (1954).

30. In re Griffiths, 413 U.S. 717 (1973); Sugarman v. Dougall, 413 U.S. 634 (1973); Examining Board v. Flores de Otero, 426 U.S. 572 (1976).

31. DeCanas v. Bica, 424 U.S. 351 (1976).

32. This interpretation of *DeCanas* was advanced in the majority opinion for Arizona v. U.S., 567 U.S. 24 (2012).

33. Cabell v. Chavez-Saildo, 454 U.S. 432 (1982); Plyler v. Doe, 457 U.S. 202 (1982); Toll v. Moreno, 458 U.S. 1 (1982).

34. Ambach v. Norwick, 441 U.S. 68 (1979); Foley v. Connelie, 435 U.S. 291 (1978).

35. See note 17 and accompanying discussion in body of the chapter (for *Miln*). This argument was actually more closely related to the "special interest" language used to

uphold restrictive immigration laws in the early 1900s (see note 24), because it was not as heavily reliant on concerns about the well being of a citizen population as was the "police powers" argument (which was more directly concerned with public safety/security, fiscal matters, and public health). The "special interest," in this case, had more to do with the preservation of a civic culture—but the common denominator across all of these arguments is the idea that the interest in question can only be effectively secured by state and local governments.

36. Cabell was decided on January 12, 1982, and Plyler on June 15, 1982.

37. Toll was decided almost two weeks after Plyler—on June 28, 1982.

38. Elkins v. Moreno, 435 U.S. 647 (1978); Toll v. Moreno, 441 U.S. 458 (1978).

39. Toll v. Moreno, 458 U.S. 1, 15 (1982).

40. Kretsedemas, *Immigration Crucible*, 13–46.

41. Ibid.; Leah Vosko, Valerie Preston, and Robert Latham, eds., *Liberating Temporariness? Migration, Work and Citizenship in an Age of Insecurity* (Montreal: McGill-Queen's University Press, 2014).

42. David Levi, "The Equal Treatment of Aliens: Preemption or Equal Protection?," *Stanford Law Review* 31, no. 6 (1979): 1069–1091.

43. See note 2 and accompanying discussion in the body of the chapter.

44. Benjamin Fleury-Steiner and Jamie Longazel, "Neoliberalism, Community Development and Anti-Immigrant Backlash in Hazleton, Pennsylvania," in *Taking Local Control*, ed. M. Varsanyi (Stanford: Stanford University Press, 2010), 137–172.

45. Lozano v. City of Hazleton, 620 F.3d 170 (3rd Cir. 2010); Arizona v. United States, 567 U.S. (2012).

46. Muzaffar Chishti and Claire Bergeron, "Hazleton Immigration Ordinance That Began with a Bang Goes Out with a Whimper," Migration Policy Institute, March 28, 2014, http://www.migrationpolicy.org/article/hazleton-immigration-ordinance-began-bang-goes-out-whimper.

47. Gonzalez v. Peoria, 722 F.2d 468 (1983).

48. Muehler v. Mena, 544 U.S. 93 (2005).

49. Mena v. Simi Valley, 332 F. 3d (2003).

50. Arizona v. U.S., 567 U.S. 30 (2012).

51. David Cole, *No Equal Justice: Race and Class in the American Criminal Justice System* (New York: New Press, 1999), 16–62.

52. *Arizona*, 567 U.S. 20.

53. Arizona v. Inter Tribal Council of Arizona, 570 U.S. ___ (2013).

54. Kretsedemas, *Immigration Crucible*, 70. This was the Memorandum for the Attorney General (archived by the U.S. Department of Justice Office of Legal Counsel), issued April 3, 2002, from the Office of the Assistant Attorney General. For a redacted copy of the memo, see ACLU, "ACLU Releases Secret Memo Justifying Controversial Policy Change," news release, September 7, 2005, https://www.aclu.org/news/secret-immigration-enforcement-memo-exposed.

55. The last of these cases was actually decided in the early twentieth century. Blythe v. Hinckley, 180 U.S. 333 (1901).

56. Ron Nixon, "Trump's Immigration Proposals 'Conspicuously Absent' from Spending Bill," *New York Times*, May 3, 2017, https://www.nytimes.com/2017/05/03/us/politics/trump-immigration-spending-bill.html.

57. Jenny Jarvie, "Texas Announces Lawsuit Against Local Officials Considered Hostile Toward 'Sanctuary Cities' Ban," *Los Angeles Times*, May 8, 2017, http://www.latimes.com/nation/nationnow/la-na-texas-sanctuary-cities-20170508-story.html.

58. See note 8.

PART II

Producing Deportable Subjects

8. THE SOCIOLOGY OF VINDICTIVENESS AND THE DEPORTABLE ALIEN

DAVID C. BROTHERTON, JOHN JAY COLLEGE, CUNY
SARAH TOSH, THE GRADUATE CENTER, CUNY

In this chapter, we approach the experience and structured setting of deportation through the lens of what critical sociologist and criminologist Jock Young called "a sociology of vindictiveness."[1] By this, Young was referring to the tendencies in capitalist late modernity for punishments meted out to various others ("bad" immigrants, stigmatized members of minority populations) to be more irrational than rational and more motivated by resentment and perverse pleasure than instrumental. We also see such vindictiveness as an implicit characteristic of the culture of cruelty frequently on display by governments adopting neoliberal credos in their practices of social control and population management.[2]

This interpretation of the punishment process and its effects and affects is important, as it sheds light on a range of disturbing actions and policies of the state (and its various direct and indirect agents) in which the social exclusion of noncitizen denizens of the United States is happening at an unprecedented pace. In 2014, the National Council of La Raza chided and named President Obama "deporter in chief" for presiding over the deportation of between 2.7 and 3.3 million people during his presidency, many of whom were of Mexican heritage.[3] This act by a normally Democratic Party ally was clearly a warning not to take the Latino vote for granted in any future elections. Further, it was not lost on many commentators that it was the son of a black Kenyan immigrant who was continuing to add to the millions now forming the new American diaspora, of whom the vast majority are people of color, repatriated to the Caribbean, Mexico, Central and South America, and Southeast Asia.[4]

This situation has only become more dire under President Trump, who was elected based on campaign promises to further ramp up immigration enforcement and deportation in order to protect the American public from the supposed threat of immigrant criminality. Sure enough, within a week of taking office, President Trump signed three executive orders related to immigration. Among other things, these orders increase immigration enforcement, both at the border and throughout the country, expand the use of detention, limit access to asylum, and speed up deportation through the broader use of expedited removal.[5] They authorize the hiring of an additional ten thousand Immigration and Customs Enforcement (ICE) agents and greatly expand the pool of immigrants that fall in the agency's crosshairs, with the removal of Obama-era rules that forced agents to concentrate on the deportation of "violent and serious criminals."[6] While the most extreme of these proposed measures, including the hiring of ten thousand additional ICE agents, were "conspicuously absent" from the recent spending bill passed by Congress,[7] increased ICE authority has already led to a rise in brazen arrests and raids, many in unprecedented locations, stoking intense and widespread fear among immigrant communities.[8]

Our focus on vindictiveness in the practices of the deportation regime is based on the ethnographic observations and reflexive experiences of the first author, David Brotherton, who has participated as an expert witness in over sixty immigration removal hearings since 2007, primarily involving subjects born in the Dominican Republic.[9] Thus, any first-person recollections or personal observations in the chapter are his. These data are supplemented by open-ended interviews with immigration lawyers and former detainees on their experiences of detention and deportation proceedings, as well as archival materials related to the functions of state deportation apparatuses. Our interpretation of these data and their relationship to sociological-criminological theory will be addressed in three sections: (1) socially creating a vindictive environment, (2) immigration hearings as plays of vindictiveness, and (3) spaces of vindictiveness.

SOCIALLY CREATING A VINDICTIVE ENVIRONMENT

Although we argue that vindictiveness is embedded in the relationship between deportable aliens and the apparatuses of deportation—that is, through the structural and institutional determinants of racist and class-based immigration laws and their practices, disproportionate punishments, and the vast differences in cultural capital between the regimes and enforcers of the criminal justice–immigration system and deportable subjects—these environments have to be built and socially created and re-created on a daily basis through human interactions. In the courts, such interactions are observable on many levels as immigration lawyers struggle to provide a modicum of representation and defense for their clients. This is particularly so given the determining capacity of the legal category "aggravated felony," meaning that once a previously adjudicated crime of the subject is accorded this status (stemming from the 1988 Anti-Drug Abuse Act passed in the midst of the moral panic over crack cocaine use, what Reinarman and Levine refer to as the "crack attack"), no waivers are permissible according to the subsequent 1996 immigration laws.[10]

In this section, we describe and analyze two sites of interaction: first, when judges interact with deportable subjects, and second, when government lawyers do the same. In each case, the immigration lawyer plays a significant role but is unable to counter the built in imbalance in legal and social power despite his or her best efforts to maintain a semblance of due process. The two primary cases highlighted are intended to show how this environment is constituted in a sociocultural moment. Even under the relatively optimum conditions of New York City, the only jurisdiction in the nation that guarantees detained immigrants legal representation, the hearing still functions as a fundamental socio-legal hub and mechanism of the deportation regime—a virtual conveyor belt for social exile.[11] In almost all hearings I have attended, the presiding judge has been either a former prosecutor or a former attorney employed by the government's immigration service. This overarching pattern is confirmed by legal scholar and immigration lawyer Elizabeth Keyes, who explains that most immigration judges are former INS and DHS prosecutors and have therefore made a career out of poking holes in the cases and credibility of immigrants attempting to avoid deportation.[12] Generally, immigration lawyers do not view judges as sympathetic to the current conditions of the deportable subject or to their past social circumstances, even though an acknowledgment of the context in which the deportable subject finds him- or herself would be viewed by most people as worthy of consideration.

In fact, most immigration lawyers would agree that before the passage of the Illegal Immigration Reform and Immigrant Responsibility Act (IIRIRA) in 1996, many if not most of their clients would likely have been granted relief from deportation without much difficulty. Before 1996, the "suspension of deportation" law allowed judges to assess the burden of removal on the immigrant and his or her family even in cases with a previous criminal conviction. IIRIRA replaced this form of relief with "cancellation of removal," which is available to subjects convicted of aggravated felonies only if it can be demonstrated that the receiving country's government agents are likely to subject the deportee to torture.[13] Thus, judges come into the hearings knowing that within the confines and stipulations of the present law, there are few who can avoid falling into the pitfalls of the aggravated felony categorization—a critical master status in such proceedings—or who qualify for cancellation of removal under the Convention Against Torture provisions.

The judge is sitting in another room in another state and conducts the hearing from afar through a video screen. The deportable alien, Edwin, a dark-skinned Dominican in his late twenties, sits near his lawyer wearing his orange "prison" jumpsuit with his hands shackled. Although this is only an administrative and not a criminal court, all detainees are still handcuffed and remain in that contained condition throughout the hearing.

The judge is trying to determine the seriousness of the subject's past involvement in the drug trade. The subject was charged more than ten years ago when he was eighteen years old with delivering a bag of heroin to a dealer who then sold the merchandise to an undercover agent. The judge asks Edwin to describe his role in the drug transaction. Edwin, through a Spanish translator, says that he has put all this down in his affidavit and it is all "there in the record." The judge is not satisfied with this answer and tells Edwin to describe again his involvement in this deed. Edwin responds that he fetched the heroin from a nearby location and gave it to the customer. The judge retorts, "That means you had a much bigger role in this crime, then. Do you understand, Mr. E., what you are saying?"[1]

Edwin is visibly confused and tries to talk to his lawyer for clarification. The government lawyer interjects and tells the judge that this should be prevented and that Edwin must answer the question without any prompting from his lawyer. The judge upholds the objection. Edwin's lawyer protests and says, "I respectfully ask the court to allow me to confer with my client. Clearly he does not understand the question and the meaning and consequences of this exchange, Your Honor."

The judge rules that Edwin cannot talk to his lawyer during questioning and continues, "I am asking you again, Mr. E. I just want the truth. Tell me again your role in this drug transaction."

Mr. E. receives the Spanish translation of the judge's words and looks around the court. He obviously does not know what to do or say and is flustered. Next to me sits Edwin's mother and sister. The sister is explaining to the mother in Spanish that if the brother says that he sold the heroin he would be considered a serious drug trafficker, which is an aggravated felony, and therefore would not qualify for a waiver. The judge continues his questioning.

"Did you or did you not sell the heroin to the customer, Mr. E.?"

"Yes, that's it. That's what happened," Edwin finally utters.

Edwin's lawyer looks up at the ceiling and grimaces. The sister starts to cry, as does the mother. The government lawyer simply nods his head in obvious satisfaction at the interaction, and the judge says, "Thank you, Mr. E. That's all I wanted to know." (Field Notes, 9/3/13)

1. Judges often refer to the very broad interpretation of a "serious drug trafficker" held by former attorney general John Ashcroft, a deeply conservative and evangelical Republican politician who occupied that position under the George W. Bush administration from 2001 to 2004.

Consequently, judges enter the court highly skeptical that the deportable subject has a case and often visibly demonstrate their disdain for such claims during exchanges with immigration lawyers. The following field notes are drawn from participant observations during a hearing in New York City.

In this interaction, the power asymmetry in the courtroom is on full display. Edwin reveals his social and political impotence as he hopelessly fails to positively insert himself into this contrived social process, a process that could easily lead to his permanent exile and displacement (although he can appeal to return after ten years from outside the United States, a provision that was made three years prior to 1996). Since this is an administrative court, there is no obligation to abide by the rules of due process; and as we see, the legal and cultural norms become firmly stacked in favor of the government and its agents, both working in tandem toward the goal of socially expelling the failed, defective immigrant. As Ira Kurzban notes, the virtual certainty of this process begins with the immigration agent who chose to arrest Edwin in the first place and essentially functions as judge and jury.[14] This is due to the extraordinary concentration of power in the hands of agents of Immigration and Customs Enforcement (ICE) and its umbrella organization, the Department of Homeland Security. In this particular case, however, the subject is far removed from the image of the "criminal alien" frequently cited by President Obama as he sought to reassure the public that such threats to the United States were the primary targets of the U.S. administration.[15]

As a consequence of this statutory framework, the court's culture does not allow for any ambiguity, especially in a process where there is no longer any judicial review. Even in the small percentage of cases in which they can use discretion, extreme backlog and high levels of burnout give judges even more reason to rely on simplistic "good immigrant"–"bad immigrant" binaries, reinforced by the status of aggravated felony conviction as the primary determinant as to whether an immigrant is deserving of deportation.[16] And even if the judge were willing to put the past transgression in a more humanistic perspective or take into account, for example, the subject's state of mental health, which in this case included the early onset of depression later diagnosed as bipolar disorder, there is still the lingering prospect of being charged with "moral turpitude"— that nineteenth-century racially, class-, and gender-coded conception of moral rectitude still frequently used to judge whether an immigrant can enter or remain in the United States.

While most immigration attorneys that I have interviewed or interacted with saw this particular judge as a relative moderate, even he adopts a vindictive mien by dint of the socio-legal script from which he is obliged to read. On further inquiry into its origins, it is clear that IIRIRA was essentially imagined and constructed precisely from the standpoint of a vindictive legislature, behaving not as a judicious body creating policy for the social good but rather as an elite, unaccountable, and highly racialized political entity whose members decided to scapegoat a particular immigrant population, driven by assumptions of their impossible nature.[17]

This insight into the law's historical conjuncture is brought home in the work and observations of Ira Kurzban, a noted legal scholar and practicing immigration lawyer.[18] Kurzban asserts that such was the lack of democratic functionality of Congress during the period that IIRIRA was passed that the bulk of its members did not even have time to read this most voluminous and far-reaching legislation before endorsing it. Further underlying the layered cruelty of such a law, like a great many of the punitive legislation that gets sanctioned during the high points of moral panics, it should always be remembered that it resulted from a deeply flawed and thoroughly undemocratic political process. Moreover, as Kurzban poignantly reflects, while the law has been drastic in its consequences, it required only slight changes in the wording of the then current legislation, which itself was written to guard against the worst excesses of laws proposed during a previous moral panic: McCarthyism. In the end, both the cruelty and vindictiveness we now live with was made possible by the anti-immigrant animus of a single reactionary Texas congressman and the cowardice of a president.

The subtle changes were accomplished because Lamar Smith, who was the chairman of the House Immigration Subcommittee at the time, rewrote the immigration law by hiring lawyers from FAIR (Federation for American Immigration Reform), an anti-immigration group. He knew he could not simply eliminate all waivers, so he and his staff rewrote the waivers to make them far less useful to most people. The Republican members of Congress deferred to Smith, and the Democrats were only provided the IIRIRA legislation less than seventy-two hours before there was a vote.

As an author on immigration law, it took me several months to go through the legislation. It is unimaginable that anyone except Lamar Smith and the lawyers who worked with him had any idea of the depth and breadth of changes they proposed and rammed through Congress. President Bill Clinton was aware of the dangers of the legislation, which he noted in his signing statement. However, he did not have the political courage to veto the bill, as Harry Truman had vetoed the horrible revisions to the immigration laws under the McCarran-Walter Act of 1952.[19]

Like judges, government lawyers play an important role in the social creation of the environment met by deportable subjects.

DB: Do you see a great deal of variation among government lawyers?

Immigration Lawyer: Yes, enormously. Some of them are quite reasonable and professional. They want to get the job done, but they will listen to your motions and react with legal reason. But others are gung-ho and clearly do not like these kinds of immigrants. They believe we are getting rid of the bad apples even though frequently the weight of evidence does not support that view. They also do not see the families left behind. To them they are irrelevant. They [the deportable aliens—authors] were allowed in, and it's a privilege to live here. They should have behaved themselves. They should have had more respect for our country's laws. (Immigration lawyer #1, 5/3/16)

Here, a seasoned immigration attorney opines on the vindictive process as he observes and experiences it every day. There is no greater illustration of this process than during cross-examinations of deportable subjects by government lawyers, for it is here that the social and cultural chasm between the two is made manifest, as exchanges frequently take on the aura of the colonizer and the colonized, much like a scene from Camus's classic work *The Outsider.*[20]

In most immigration hearings, the deportable subject is usually a lower-class male of color (sometimes a female) with relatively little education, often failing to receive any schooling beyond the tenth grade. In many cases, the deportable subject, although having lived in the United States for a number of years, requests an interpreter due to poor English language skills. Meanwhile, the government lawyers betray the status and class position that befit their solid professional occupation. All possess law degrees, having spent at least five years at university, and most are white and have generally had little to do with the precarious worlds of the lower-class immigrant outside of these encounters in the courtroom. In short, they hold all the legal, social, and cultural cards needed to set about demolishing the subject and his or her claims to remain in this country. After all, that is the lawyer's job in a system that is adversarial and intricately designed to uphold the privileges of elite group power and status.

This adversarial position is further supported by an ICE-wide agency culture that views immigrants with previous convictions as criminals who should be deported, regardless of the severity of the conviction or other extenuating circumstances. Legal scholar Nina Rabin explains the origins of this culture:

> The agency's historic formation after September 11, 2001, its focus on tasks traditionally used by law enforcement in the criminal justice system, and its fixation on quantifying criminal alien removals all combine to create a culture that views all immigrants as criminal threats. This culture makes the sole fact of a conviction— without regard to its seriousness or context—a nearly irreversible determinant of the agency's approach to any given case.[21]

Therefore, despite the fact that President Obama began encouraging the use of prosecutorial discretion by ICE in 2010 in order to focus on the deportation of "aliens who pose a danger to national security or a risk to public safety," less than two percent of cases closed due to prosecutorial discretion since 2011 have involved subjects charged with criminal convictions besides immigration violations.[22]

With so few options for having the removal order canceled, on the advice of their lawyers subjects often resort to claiming that they are going to be physically threatened and tortured on their return to their country of origin, often as a result of cooperating with U.S. law enforcement after their original criminal conviction.[23] Such cooperation and its aftermath is another example of the cruelty so deeply embedded in the immigration/criminal justice system, which has been exposed to some degree through social movements such as Black Lives Matter and various private citizen lawsuits across the nation.[24] Members of law enforcement as well as prosecutors habitually offer subjects the chance to reduce their prison time in exchange for information that will contribute to the prosecution of others. However, what is rarely explained to them is that their cooperation will not translate into an opportunity to avoid deportation. Consequently, although all cooperators understand that they run the risk of being regarded as a snitch if knowledge of their complicity is not kept strictly confidential—especially if the information plays a key part in the successful prosecution of criminal associates—they do not comprehend that any claim on their part regarding the risk of revenge they face if deported will be vehemently challenged by another branch of the government during immigration hearings.

However, even during such proceedings where the deportable subject has strong claims regarding the risk of retaliation, he or she has great difficulty adequately coming to his or her own defense, especially under the intense, intimidating circumstances of a cross-examination.[25] The threats the subjects attempt to depict as social facts are often vaguely described, with the actual names of the potential perpetrators (usually drug gangs) missing or identified only through their street aliases, which when presented in court are frequently derided (however subtly) by judges and government lawyers alike. What we witness is the clash not between truth and untruth but between two worlds that might best be described as the rational, unambiguous, legalistic world of the court, which seeks clear signs of risk that can be quantified, and the opaque, transnational, often subterranean shadow world of the immigrant, who has (normally) been a bit player in the networks of the informal economy.

Thus, deportable subjects typically fail to adequately present believable scenarios in support of their claims due to (1) a lack of specific and verifiable evidence documenting the relationship between state agents and previously identified criminal gangs, (2) a lack of empirical knowledge of other deportees who have been targeted and persecuted in similar circumstances, (3) the absence of any official statistics that confirm the possibility of such claims, and (4) lack of sufficient evidence showing why security forces in the country of origin will not protect the repatriated subject (although this can be countered by the research knowledge of expert witnesses). Putting together and presenting such complex claims is made even more difficult by the fact that the subjects are usually detained throughout the pretrial period, as well as the reality that lawyers provided by the city, while dedicated, are burdened with heavy caseloads of equally complicated cases.

Consequently, in so many hearings, government lawyers react to the claims of deportable subjects with wearied skepticism, as if they have heard it all before a thousand times. Hence, many immigration lawyers choose not to put their clients on the stand, even though they might believe wholeheartedly in their client's claims and veracity. When a subject is on the stand, the government lawyer takes on the task of his or her questioning like a matador, systematically piercing the thin to nonexistent defensive armor of the deportable subject with sword after sword until the inevitable thrust of the picador brings the misery of this mismatched contest to an end. A second immigration lawyer comments on his client's performance after being put on the stand. The subject had cooperated with law enforcement and helped a government prosecutor convict his prior associates. There is every reason to believe he will face retaliation if deported, but the strength of his claims must be communicated and performed with conviction to make them credible, for his truths do not speak for themselves under conditions where "deportability" is the hegemonic truth. In this case, as in so many, it is his lack of performability that is his downfall, and he is doomed not by truth but by the setting.

> I prepped him for three or four hours yesterday. I went through everything with him, over and over again. But when I put him up there and the government attorney starts his questioning, he destroys him in a few minutes. He can't remember this, he doesn't know that, and the guy basically self-destructs. With you it's different. You stand your ground. They come for you and you stand up to them. You know the material, you know it, the country, its culture, how fucked up it is, and you don't accept this bullshit they are throwing at you. But these guys can't do that. They're hapless. No education, culturally different, live in different worlds. They're afraid, vulnerable, often don't understand what the law even says let alone what it means and the consequences. I can't stand it sometimes. Seriously, I think to myself, "What kind of job is this?" Imagine if you came from another country and you saw what goes on in these courts. You'd say, "What kind of justice is this?" (Immigration lawyer #2, 6/2/16)

IMMIGRATION HEARINGS AS PLAYS
OF VINDICTIVENESS

In a previous work, I described the deportation hearing as an exile play and likened the dramas of this process to Artaud's theater of cruelty concept.[26] In such hearings, we see all the norms and rituals expected of protocols embedded in legal codes of behavior and discourse performed by a range of players—judges, lawyers, deportable subjects, translators, correctional officers—usually before an audience of family members and friends of the deportable individual. Outwardly, the hearing appears as an example of due process, as lawyers pitch their claims for and against the deportable alien and the judge presides over the contest, using his or her best judgment and good faith to make an interpretation of the law and its limits. As we have previously noted, these laws come from another branch of the government and are supposedly indicative of the checks and balances of a functioning, healthy democracy. But as we have also noted, these laws are anything but neutral edicts affecting all equally; rather, they are an effort to restore or maintain a constructed social order in what is presumed to be an open society. Such laws, as we witness in these hearings, were designed to weed out the "bad" immigrant from the "good," the filth that despoil the sanitized nation-state, which is the ideological and historical source of their vindictiveness.[27] They are based in the "inherently performative nature of the concept of homeland security, with a focus on the constitutive role of the migrant as outsider."[28] Consequently, the hearings, since they are both legally and morally predicated on highly contradictory reasoning and antihumanistic premises, naturally become messy encounters between the aggrieved, imperiled transgressor and his or her lawyer and those state agents dedicated to upholding a certain type of social order no matter the cost. In the following, a former detainee who was recently released due to the threat of domestic violence if she is returned talks about her recent experience in a hearing. At the time of this informal interview, she was at another hearing in support of a friend who was about to be exiled.

> Judge L. at X court was so mean and difficult, he gave me such a hard time . . . shouting at me at first. "This is such a terrible thing," he said, "this involvement . . . bringing drugs into the country." That kind of thing. I agree with him; it is terrible. The same is happening with B., but what she did was ten years ago, when she was twenty-three years old, and she did probation for that. She's a changed woman. No record since and two young children. But they believe these are terrible acts done against this country. There's no sympathy for people like me and B. (Ms. D., former detainee #7, 2/12/16)

In this case, the judge is clearly performing his role as moral arbiter in the firm belief that drugs brought into the country and those who transport them are a scourge on society, as befits the theater of fear and condemnation in the long-standing war-on-drugs campaign. Ms. D. has been "othered" as the subject-object of dramatized evil, and the same is happening to her friend B., who has been held for six months in detention based on her conviction as a drug mule ten years previously.[29] During the detention period, B. lost one of her children to a former husband, who filed a complaint saying she was an "unfit" mother due to her being incarcerated; her other child was placed in the care of another family member. Ms. D. attends this hearing with another friend, both of whom were locked up for months with B. and know her story intimately, including the trials and tribulations she has already suffered due to her family life being completely upended by the deportation regime. The immigration lawyer in this case knows well the dramaturgy involved in all these cases and has pleaded repeatedly to the judge to release B. on bond so that she may return to her teen-age children, both of whom have been severely affected by the trauma of being separated from their mother. The following are field notes taken from the time we are waiting to enter the court.

We are waiting to go into immigration court for the fifth time in six months. I have written my affidavit numerous times, trying to show how the conditions for B. will be life threatening if she returns as well as the trauma that will certainly befall her children. B.'s lawyer is pacing up and down the room, visibly nervous, clutching his briefcase. He is unsure of the outcome of this hearing but has developed a close bond with B. over the last few months and will not give up on her. He wants desperately for the judge to see his client as a human being unlike the judge who dealt with Ms. D. He is convinced that this judge has a humanistic side, but in his words, "He just can't make decisions until he's absolutely certain." Still, Ms. D. did eventually get out, as it was made increasingly clear that the threats she faced were very real, which the lawyer was able to prove through court documents that the judge accepted.

The lawyer starts talking to the client's family and her friends about how best to handle the hearing, as it appears the guard is about to open the door. He's thinking about how he can get the best out of this judge in this highly charged situation. He then advises her supporters, "Listen . . . sit as close as possible to the judge, OK? Let him see you. Let him know you are there for her" (Field Notes, 2/21/16).

Remarkably in this case, the drama of the courtroom worked in B.'s favor. The pews were filled with B.'s friends and family, and the lawyer was extremely well prepared, seemingly more so than the government lawyer, who did not muster the usual objections to releasing the deportable subject on bond. B. said very little in her defense but implored the judge that she needed to get back to her children, which appeared to cause the judge some discomfort. In this particular setting, the performance of vindictiveness had its limits. The humanism of the moment finally outweighed the essentialist presumptions built into the laws and the obligations of judges to be loyal defenders of the nation's imaginary social and cultural borders. The messiness of social life finally got the upper hand in the courtroom, and the judge sided with ambiguity rather than with the binary constructions inserted by that Texas congressman and his allies more than two decades ago.

SPACES OF VINDICTIVENESS

> Ms. M.: I can't forget what went on inside there. I can't sleep at night, nothing. I gotta have some kind of psychological therapy to try to deal with things.
>
> DB: Did they have solitary in there?
>
> Ms. M.: They call it the lock. They give it to people who have a conflict with someone, with the guards or the doctors, and then they see a judge in there and he decides. Maybe twenty days or whatever. Thank God I never went there! Thank God! (Ms. M., former detainee #3, 11/5/15)

Ms. M. discusses her recent experiences in a detention facility on the East Coast, where she spent four months. It was not a private facility run by a vast global security company like CoreCivic (formerly the Corrections Corporation of America) but rather a state prison facility—paid for by and operated on behalf of taxpayers—that leases out part of its space to ICE. Ms. M. recounts her time spent there as a form of trauma, an experience so emotionally jarring and psychologically invasive that she requires ongoing therapy to recover from it. She also refers to the prevalence of solitary confinement as a form of punishment used to enforce social control in this setting. In another interview carried out within the same facility, Mr. P. concurred with Ms. M.'s experiences and sentiments, but since the interview was done in situ, his words carry feelings of dread, pain, and suffering that are more immediate.

> Mr. P.: I've never been in prison before, and now I've been here five months! It's terrible here, the treatment from the guards, the fights between the inmates. I'm so depressed right now, seriously depressed. OK, I spent one night in jail about ten years ago, and that's it. I can't sleep at night here; I just try to sleep during the day. If I fall asleep at night, I don't know what's going to happen. I might get jumped; anything can happen. We have people here who have just done a lot of time. They are real criminals, not like me. I'm a car mechanic; I've got no history of that. I just wanna get back to my family and children. This is not me.
>
> DB: Have you received any special punishment while here?
>
> Mr. P.: Yeah, I was sent to the hole for three weeks.
>
> DB: What for?
>
> Mr. P.: They said I took too long tying up my shoelaces after I'd been body searched. I know . . . as I told you, anything can happen. You can look at them [the guards—authors] the wrong way and boom . . . that's it. They don't treat us like detainees; we're inmates to them. We're all the same. I can't stand it any longer. I really can't stand it. (Mr. P., detainee #1, 10/6/15)

According to all the testimonies of the detainees, these spaces of detention are rife with vindictive practices by guards, administrators, and even lawyers, some of whom enter the facility and tell the subjects they have no way out of their removal proceedings so they had better accept their fate.[30] This is Mr. C. after being released from the same facility as Ms. M. and Mr. P.

> I gave up, I was gonna just sign out. You know, you get so down in there, thinking it's never gonna happen. I'll never get out. Every day, nothing to do. About 50 percent were signing out in there. There are no resources for the people. Some lawyer comes in once a week and basically says you have no chance. I don't know what I would have done if I didn't have these lawyers fighting for me. You know they believed in me more than I believed in myself. They visited me more than my own family. I owe them so much (subject starts to cry). (Mr. C., former detainee #5, 5/10/16)

A number of researchers and investigative journalists have written about these spaces, emphasizing the lack of oversight that continues to be the norm, the treatment of detainees as prison inmates instead of subjects in administrative limbo, and the push to extract profits in privately run facilities as corporations reduce the costs of detention and thus reduce the services and treatment offered to their charges.[31] Rather than simply serving the legal purpose of administrative confinement, the 250 or so facilities around the United States where immigrants are detained function as spaces of vindictiveness, where immigrants are punished in myriad ways for the crime of being the other. The fact that Congress has put in place a bed mandate of thirty-four thousand detainees per day speaks to the symbolic significance of immigrant detention in delineating immigrant detainees as criminals and emphasizing the government's prioritization of their punishment.[32]

The punitive function of immigration detention is further underscored by the conditions of the spaces themselves. About one-third of detainees are held in detention centers run by ICE or private companies, with the other two-thirds held in county and city jails contracted by ICE.[33] Detention standards are not mandatory, and those that do exist are based on those created for jails and prisons.[34] Furthermore, "while ICE is nominally in control, the often disparate practices of different member agencies and facilities result in a general lack of coordination in policies."[35] Detainees not only feel the punitive force of separation from their families but report physical violence and dehumanizing searches by guards, as well as insufficient and inedible food, unhygienic conditions, uncomfortable temperatures, steady disregard of routine medical care, and failure of facilities to respond to urgent medical situations.[36] It is worth noting that until now, there has not been a single ethnographic account of any of these facilities, even though they have been in existence for more than two decades.

What we see essentially in these settings is the same vindictive culture and set of practices that characterize and are symptomatic of the entire deportation regime. These spaces are the result of the penal institutional approach that the state has specifically chosen to apply to detained subjects. Therefore, we encounter similar displays of authoritarian power that are the norm in most prisons organized as total institutions. In other western European countries, such detention facilities are run on completely different premises, with more attention paid to the human rights of the subjects and to the collateral consequences for families. But in the United States, these detention spaces mimic the punitive culture that has infiltrated many other social institutions apart from prisons.

A hallmark of this culture is the dehumanization of the incarcerated subject, just as we see the pathologization of deportable subjects in immigration hearings and the fetishization of judicial rules and rituals. Based on her research in Ecuador with the families of detained migrants and previously detained deportees, human geographer Nancy Hiemstra concurs that a dehumanizing culture runs throughout the detention and deportation process, from the way that administrators refer to detainees as "bodies" to the way that authority figures treat immigrants in actual spaces of detention. She reports that these spaces are "structured in such a way that anyone with power over detainees can become a 'petty sovereign,'" with discretion to make decisions that lead to the neglect of detainees' basic needs, and that employees display negative perceptions of detainees' worth; stereotypes of migrants as immoral, dishonest, and criminal; and the perception that migrants "get what they deserve."[37]

Detainees' bodies are marked as criminal by facility uniforms, and they arrive in court wearing these uniforms and with their hands manacled. Despite their legal status as civil detainees, subjects in detention become extensions of the imprisoned multitude. What purpose does it serve to place such subjects in solitary confinement, for example? Why separate so many subjects from their families? Why are so many subjects incarcerated to begin with when they could be living with their family and friends? There is no rational necessity behind such practices, which grow out of a particular political and social order and its ideologies of containment. Such ideologies are infused with the same vindictive assumptions that have been applied historically to othered populations but that get recycled and expanded by new generations of agents of the security state. These mechanisms for internal social control among primarily nonwhite immigrant populations increasingly rely on interlocking systems of policed segregation, digital surveillance, physical terror, and eventual mass exile.[38] These practices of vindictiveness are simply other forms of legal violence that have developed extraordinary crossover possibilities, whether it be raiding homes in Long Island under the auspices of ridding society of violent gangs or the rejection of Central American children at the Texas border to show other refugees that the United States will "defend" its borders.[39]

> We try to tell them the consequences of their actions, but they don't get the seriousness of what they're facing. You remember E.? She was out of her mind, very mentally ill. That's another thing, she had been incredibly traumatized for years and years, really didn't understand where she was, and would say things all the time. Her family came to me with the case, gave me a little bit of money and said this is a slam dunk. No way can she be deported. And yet she spent eighteen months locked up, can you believe that? We had motion after motion to get her released, court date after court date . . . and still nothing. Finally, the judge let her go a few weeks ago. He finally understood this was so unjust, and yet ICE was still opposing it . . . why? They've already said she's not one of the population they're after, the bad criminals among the immigrant population who have done time, so why oppose it? So she gets out and I think, good luck to her . . . what happens now is up to her family. I've done my bit. I've done what I could, and I represented her to the best of my ability. That's how I feel. You know I hate this really. I like my job, I'm good at it, I represent my clients, but I feel so many other guys are in it for something else. You know, they're racists; you hear stuff in there you wouldn't believe—like how can you talk to someone that way? Well, you saw that today in a way. (Immigration lawyer #4, 10/3/15)

Immigration lawyer #4 sums up the deportation regime's vindictive culture and practices through recounting the experience of his latest case. The female deportable subject he is referring to is in her late thirties and was diagnosed in her early twenties with paranoid schizophrenia. She had suffered enormously from various physical and mental ailments over the last fifteen years, had been committed three times to mental health institutions, had been mostly cared for by her mother when out, and had a long history of serious drug use and physical abuse by men. Several years before, she had been gang raped and left for dead on a beach near Coney Island, thereafter spending a month in a coma after being diagnosed with post-traumatic stress disorder before being released back to her elderly mother. Almost two years ago she was picked up for "turning tricks" in South Brooklyn, and then somehow ICE intervened and she was suddenly in deportation proceedings, which she simply could not comprehend.

I attended two of her hearings, during which she cried continuously on seeing her mother, and it was clear to all in the court that this was a person in serious distress and if exiled would be dead in a very short time. Nonetheless, she was held in a detention facility for eighteen months against the very explicit advice of two social workers and a psychiatrist who examined her, all warning of a serious deterioration in her mental health. At each of the six hearings, the government lawyer opposed her receiving bond and called for her expedited removal.

This is the sociology and culture of vindictiveness in all its various aspects and dynamics. The deportable subject is dehumanized, caught in impossible legal entanglements, and moved from space to space under conditions of extreme duress, while family and friends suffer irreparable collateral damage, and for what? As we read in the works of so many authors in this book, the majority of deportees are in proceedings for minor transgressions, despite the insistence of Presidents Obama and Trump that we are targeting the "criminals" among the immigrant population—those who do not deserve the privilege of staying in the United States. This claim was particularly ironic from President Obama, who admits that the criminal justice system systematically overincarcerates, racially profiles, hands down irrational sentences, and is in need of serious reform. In this chapter, we argue fundamentally that the system of forced repatriation is irrational, is inhuman, and reproduces social practices and norms that have little to do with a functioning, open democratic society. There is really no legitimacy left to countenance the continuation of the deportation regime, which is why it relies so heavily on the culture of vindictiveness it produces to give it life while ignoring the bloody mess of so-called border control it leaves in its wake.

NOTES TO CHAPTER 8

1. Jock Young, "Merton with Energy, Katz with Structure: The Sociology of Vindictiveness and the Criminology of Transgression," *Theoretical Criminology* 7, no. 3 (2003): 389–414.

2. Henry Giroux, *Disposable Youth, Racialized Memories, and the Culture of Cruelty* (Abingdon: Routledge, 2015).

3. See Tanya Golash-Boza, chapter 2 of this book.

4. Daniel Kanstroom, *Deportation Nation: Outsiders in American History* (Cambridge: Harvard University Press, 2007); Pedro Noguera, "Exporting the Undesirable: An Analysis of the Factors Influencing the Deportation of Immigrants from the United States and an Examination of Their Impact on Caribbean and Central American Societies," *Wadabagei: A Journal of the Caribbean and Its Diaspora* 2, no. 1 (1999): 1–28.

5. Michael Shear and Ron Nixon, "New Trump Deportation Rules Allow Far More Expulsions," *New York Times*, February 21, 2017, https://www.nytimes.com/2017/02/25/us/ice-immigrant-deportations-trump.html.

6. Nicholas Kulish, Caitlin Dickerson, and Ron Nixon, "Immigration Agents Discover New Freedom to Deport Under Trump," *New York Times*, February 25, 2017, https://www.nytimes.com/2017/02/25/us/ice-immigrant-deportations-trump.html.

7. Ron Nixon, "Trump's Immigration Proposals 'Conspicuously Absent' from Spending Bill," *New York Times*, May 3, 2017, https://www.nytimes.com/2017/05/03/us/politics/trump-immigration-spending-bill.html.

8. Katie Mettler, "'This Is Really Unprecedented': ICE Detains Woman Seeking Domestic Abuse Protection at Texas Courthouse," *Washington Post*, February 16, 2017, https://www.washingtonpost.com/news/morning-mix/wp/2017/02/16/this-is-really -unprecedented-ice-detains-woman-seeking-domestic-abuse-protection-at-texas -courthouse/?utm_term=.c8ed2c9468d6; Delphine Schrank, "Trump's Season of Fear: Inside the Devastation Left by Immigrant Raids," *The Guardian*, March 13, 2017, https:// www.theguardian.com/us-news/2017/mar/13/undocumented-immigration-raids-ice -impact; Tal Kopan, "Immigration Arrests Rise in First Months of Trump administration," *CNN*, April 17, 2017, http://www.cnn.com/2017/04/17/politics/immigration-arrests -rise/index.html; Nicholas Kulish, "Torture Victim, Expecting a U.S. Handshake, Was Given Handcuffs Instead," *New York Times*, June 13, 2017, https://www.nytimes.com/2017 /06/13/us/asylum-torture-venezuela.html; Fernanda Santos, "Border Patrol Raids Humanitarian Aid Group Camp in Arizona," *New York Times*, June 16, 2017, https://www .nytimes.com/2017/06/16/us/border-patrol-immigration-no-more-deaths.html.

9. Nicholas De Genova and Natalie Peutz, *The Deportation Regime: Sovereignty, Space and the Freedom of Movement* (Durham: Duke University Press, 2010); David Brotherton, "The Theater of Cruelty and the Permanent Exile of Immigrants," in *The Criminalization of Immigration: Contexts and Consequences*, ed. Alissa Ackerman and Rich Furman (Durham: Carolina Academic, 2014), 31–49; David Brotherton and Luis Barrios, *Banished to the Homeland: Dominican Deportees and Their Stories of Exile* (New York: Columbia University Press, 2011).

10. Craig Reinarman and Harry Levine, "Crack Attack: Politics and Media in the Crack Scare," in *Crack in America: Demon Drugs and Social Justice*, ed. Craig Reinarman and Harry G. Levine (Berkeley: University of California Press, 1997), 18–51.

11. This guarantee of legal representation is due to the New York City Council's creation of the New York Immigrant Family Unity Project, first passed in 2013. In 2015, the city council provided funds to fully cover legal representation for eligible immigrants with cases before the New York City Immigration Court, as well as those New York City residents with cases before the immigration courts in Newark and Elizabeth, New Jersey. New York City is still one of the leading producers of deportable aliens in the nation. According to the Transactional Records Clearing House at Syracuse University, nearly ten thousand immigrants were repatriated from the city between January and August 2015.

12. Elizabeth Keyes, "Beyond Saints and Sinners: Discretion and the Need for New Narratives in the U.S. Immigration System," *Georgetown Immigration Law Journal* 26 (2012): 207–256.

13. Ibid.

14. Margarita Rodriguez, "Interview with Ira Kurzban," *IMTP—Magazine on Migration Issues* (Spring 2013).

15. After all, Edwin had criminally transgressed more than a decade ago, as a youth, and for his relatively minor participation in the act had received a year of probation with no prison or jail time.

16. Sharon Cohen, "Immigration Court: Troubled System, Long Waits," *Seattle Times*, April 9, 2011; Stuart Lustig, Niranjan Karnik, Kevin Delucchi, and Lakshika Tennakoon, "Inside the Judges' Chambers: Narrative Responses from the National Association of Immigration Judges Stress and Burnout Survey," *Georgetown Immigration Law Journal* 23 (2008): 57–83; Keyes, "Beyond Saints and Sinners."

17. Mae Ngai, *Impossible Subjects: Illegal Aliens and the Making of Modern America* (Princeton: Princeton University Press, 2004).

18. Rodriguez, "Interview with Ira Kurzban."

19. Ibid.

20. A seminal existentialist text on alienation experienced by both the native Algerian population and the French occupiers.

21. Nina Rabin, "Victims or Criminals? Discretion, Sorting, and Bureaucratic Culture in the U.S. Immigration System," *Southern California Review of Law and Social Justice* 23, no. 2 (2013): 200.

22. Ibid.

23. We do not know how many deportees who return to the Dominican Republic are targeted as a result of their past cooperation with U.S. authorities. However, a series of recent articles indicate that a large number of deportees are suddenly being executed by professional hit men.

24. The vast majority of criminal cases are now settled through plea deals, with many of them involving cooperating witnesses who agree to inform on their associates in exchange for lighter sentences. There is a large literature on this and the extraordinary powers that prosecutors have amassed at the expense of human rights and a fully functioning justice system based on trial by a jury of one's peers.

25. It is easy to get flustered in such settings and forget what you were going to say, as the judge is instructing you to only answer the question and the questions are coming thick and fast. Even though I have done many cross-examinations in the past, there are still moments when I cannot remember some very basic information, as is made clear in the following field notes:

Government lawyer trying to give me a hard time . . . not very inspired questions however. He is querying when I was last in the DR, how much time I have spent there, who did I talk to . . . nothing much came of it . . . then he asked me general questions . . . I suppose somewhat valid. Did I know the population of the DR? How many homicides per year? . . . I was wrong on both. . . . I just couldn't remember in the heat of the moment. . . . It should have been 10.5 million for the population and I said 7–8 million . . . and it should have been 2,000 for homicides and I said about 1,000 . . . and importantly police kill about 250–300 per year . . . a substantial amount of the total. (Field Notes 7/23/15).

26. Brotherton, "Theater of Cruelty."

27. Mary Douglas, *Purity and Danger: An Analysis of Concepts of Pollution and Taboo* (London: Routledge Classics, 1966).

28. Nancy Hiemstra, "Performing Homeland Security Within the US Immigrant Detention System," *Environment and Planning D: Society and Space* 32 (2014): 571–588.

29. Frank Tannebaum, *Crime and Community* (New York: Columbia University Press, 1938).

30. See also Susan Coutin, "Confined Within: National Territories as Zones of Confinement," *Political Geography* 29 (2010): 200–208.

31. Jennifer Chacón, "Immigration Detention: No Turning Back?" *South Atlantic Quarterly* 113, no. 3 (2014): 621–628; Roxanne Doty and Elizabeth Wheatley, "Private Detention and the Immigration Industrial Complex," *International Political Sociology* 7 (2013): 426–443; Mark Dow, *American Gulag: Inside U.S. Immigration Prisons* (Berkeley: University of California Press, 2005); Tanya Golash-Boza, "The Immigration Industrial Complex: Why We Enforce Immigration Policies Destined to Fail," *Sociology Compass* 3, no. 2 (2009): 295–309; Megan Julia and Julia Preston, "Delayed Care Faulted in Immigrants' Deaths at Detention Centers," *New York Times*, July 7, 2016, http://www.nytimes.com/2016/07/08/us/delayed-care-faulted-in-immigrants-deaths-at-detention-centers.html?_r=0; Seth Freed Wessler, "Federal Officials Ignored Years of Internal Warnings About Deaths at Private Prisons," *The Nation*, June 15, 2016, https://www.thenation.com/article/federal-officials-ignored-years-of-internal-warnings-about-deaths-at-private-prisons/.

32. Hiemstra, "Performing Homeland Security"; Michelle Chen, "The Deportation System's 'Lock-Up Quota' Is Just as Bad as It Sounds," *The Nation*, July 11, 2016, https://www.thenation.com/article/the-deportation-systems-lock-up-quota-is-just-as-bad-as-it-sounds/.

33. "About the US Detention and Deportation System," Detention Watch Network, 2013.

34. Ruthie Epstein and Eleanor Acer, *Jails and Jumpsuits: Transforming the U.S. Immigration Detention System—a Two-Year Review* (New York: Human Rights First, 2011).

35. Hiemstra, "Performing Homeland Security," 580.

36. Amnesty International, "Jailed Without Justice: Immigration Detention in the USA," Amnesty International, 2009; Coutin, "Confined Within"; Hiemstra, "Performing Homeland Security."

37. Hiemstra, "Performing Homeland Security."

38. See Kanstroom, *Deportation Nation*.

39. In 2013, a federal class-action law suit known as *Aguilar v. ICE* was settled. It was filed on behalf of twenty-two Latino men, women, and children—citizens, lawful permanent residents, and others—who in 2006 and 2007 had their homes raided by armed immigration agents in the predawn hours, without court warrants or other legal justification. The lawsuit argued that ICE's policy governing the conduct of officers during these raids was a violation of the Fourth and Fifth Amendments. The case named as defendants dozens of individual immigration agents and their supervisors—including former Department of Homeland Security secretary Michael Chertoff and former ICE director Julie Myers—as well as ICE itself.

9. BANISHED YET UNDEPORTED

The Constitution of a "Floating Population" of Deportees Within France

CAROLINA SANCHEZ BOE, SERR, AALBORG
UNIVERSITY, DENMARK

> *Friar Laurence:*
> *A gentler judgment vanish'd from his lips,*
> *Not body's death but body's banishment.*
> *Romeo:*
> *Ha, banishment! Be merciful, say "death";*
> *For exile hath more terror in his look,*
> *Much more than death: do not say "banishment."*
> SHAKESPEARE, *ROMEO AND JULIET*, ACT 3, SCENE 3

> *La prison ne peut pas manquer de fabriquer des délinquants.*
> MICHEL FOUCAULT

All foreign nationals live "on probation," as legal scholars in France and the United States have pointed out.[1] However, the latent threat of deportation, or "deportability," has increased over the past decades in France, as in many other countries, as it has become increasingly difficult to obtain legalization and to keep one's legal status.[2] Legal status greatly depends on the ability to make oneself "bureaucratically legible" by producing documentary proof of persecution and victimhood, in the case of asylum seekers, or of family, work, or other evidence upon which one's legal status depends.[3]

Increasing numbers of legal residents have lost their residency as a consequence of a criminal sentence, and along with undocumented migrants, they have been caught up in the entanglement of the criminal justice system and immigration enforcement. To many, deportation is experienced as banishment from a country where they have spent significant years of their lives to a country where their prospects for the future are often very limited[4]—a country that most 1.5 generation migrants (who emigrated to France as adolescents or children) hardly know, with many going to great lengths to avoid deportation.[5]

While the great majority of deportees are effectively deported on the grounds of their violation of immigration or criminal legislation, a small minority succeeds in staying in France, and though their precise number is unknown, evidence from pro- and anti-immigration groups suggest that they number in the tens of thousands. Many succeed in staying in France by "making themselves illegible" by destroying their identity papers, thus becoming undeportable. When they succeed in avoiding deportation, formerly legal residents live as undocumented migrants for years and decades, and many of these "undeported" are frequently arrested, incarcerated, and ordered to be deported again, but are ultimately released within France without obtaining legalization. This process contributes to the fact that 18 percent of the French prison population are foreign nationals, compared to the estimated 6–7 percent of foreign nationals that make up the general population.[6] This large percentage does not point to higher levels of criminality among foreign nationals but rather to the workings of a criminal justice system that favors incarceration of the poor, the young, and men, mainly from the marginalized neighborhoods where many immigrants live.[7] In addition, many have been convicted of misdemeanors related to being undocumented and to working in the underground economy, which requires the use of forged or doctored papers.[8]

Similar to prison researchers, migration scholars in France have paid little attention to the increasingly important role played by penal institutions in migration control. The rich and growing research on migrants' experiences of confinement in France has contributed to a greater understanding of border processes but has, so far, mainly focused on migrants' experiences of administrative detention within waiting zones and immigration detention centers, not within the criminal justice system.[9] Another rich and growing body of migration research has deployed anthropological methods to elicit the experiences of migrants caught in the "transnational corridors of expulsion" and effectively deported.[10] With their focus on migrants who were effectively deported, these studies—along with those of deportees from other countries—share the same conclusion: that the great majority of migrants who are deported will attempt to enter again in spite of having experienced detention and sometimes incarceration and in spite of the great dangers associated with reentering Europe clandestinely.[11] Though these studies of the makings of a global "deportspora" do not cover the experiences of the minority who manage to stay in Europe or the United States in spite of a deportation order, they inform us greatly of their motivations to fight against deportation, whether through legal strategies or through physical struggles.[12]

The scope of this chapter is different from that of these studies, with its emphasis on the apparent *failures* of the deportation system on the one hand and its specific focus on migrants' experiences of incarceration on the other. Drawing on ethnographic fieldwork and biographical interviews with the undeported at different stages of their path through the enforcement and criminal justice systems in France, on interviews with enforcement officers, and on my long experience working for the French nonprofit organization Cimade, this chapter analyzes the ways in which the mobility of the undeported is restricted through the processes of illegalization and deportability.[13] These processes create "domestic" border zones within the territorially defined external borders of the French nation, transforming French prisons into key sites for struggles and negotiations over inclusion and exclusion. After a short introduction to the specificities of the entanglements of criminal justice and immigration enforcement in France, the chapter analyzes how law and legal practice have created a "floating population" of foreign nationals that are subjected to a forced circular migration through prisons, detention centers, and public space.[14]

THE ENTANGLEMENTS OF CRIMINAL JUSTICE AND IMMIGRATION ENFORCEMENT IN FRANCE

Since the mid-1970s, *double peine*—"double punishment," or the deportation of foreign nationals who have been convicted of crimes and misdemeanors—has become a way for French politicians to show their firm intention to fight both crime and immigration.[15] It first became a priority at the highest level of government when Minister of the Interior Michel Poniatowski declared at the National Assembly on April 21, 1976, that he had asked all the prefects (regional police chiefs) "to deport every foreigner who had been convicted of a prison sentence."[16]

Such announcements were frequently made by both right and left governments in France, which passed increasingly restrictive laws that often appeared pursuant to debates created by the politicians themselves, as responses to the rising popularity of the extreme right-wing nationalist party, the National Front. The association between immigration and crime became a central theme of the political debate in France.[17] In 1993, in an attempt to appease extreme right-wing voters, Charles Pasqua—the Chirac administration's conservative minister of the interior—hardened the laws on legalization and naturalization.

The Pasqua laws led to a significant rise in deportations on criminal grounds, as they expanded the number of violations that could lead to a deportation order, such as the so-called *arrêtés d'expulsion*—issued by prefects and the Ministry of the Interior—and the *interdictions du territoire*—bans to reentry that, in practice, are deportation orders issued by a penal judge.[18] Bans to reentry now became the standard punishment for more than two hundred misdemeanors. The Pasqua laws made it possible to punish a foreign national who had resisted deportation with a prison sentence of six months to one year and a supplementary three- to ten-year reentry ban.[19] The laws also added a reentry ban to the prison sentences of foreign nationals who had been convicted of drug-related crimes.[20] The use of illicit drugs in France had been penalized since the passing of the law of December 31, 1970, contributing significantly to the increase in the number of foreign nationals who would be imprisoned, detained, and deported over the next four decades. The majority of those who were convicted of drug-related crimes were youths from France's disenfranchised *banlieues* (suburbs), among them many 1.5 generation migrants.[21] As the Pasqua laws on naturalization had also made it increasingly difficult for the children of immigrants to obtain French nationality, many were foreign nationals, and tens of thousands were ordered deported.

When the 1995 Paris metro bombings carried out by Algerian organization Armed Islamic Group (GIA) turned out to be the workings of Algerian-born but French-bred Khaled Kelkal, the media and leading politicians exposed him as "a youth delinquent from the suburbs" who had slid into Islamic terrorism. Kelkal's trajectory provided Pasqua with further justification for the new laws, which strongly increased the possibility of illegalizing and deporting even long-term-resident foreign nationals convicted of misdemeanors and crimes.[22] Most foreign nationals who were deported after the passing of these antiterrorist laws had in fact been convicted of minor immigration offenses or drug-related misdemeanors, and French law and border enforcement during this period can be compared to the consequences of the so-called war on drugs and of U.S. antiterrorism legislation passed in the aftermath of the 1996 Oklahoma bombings and in the years following 9/11.

In response to the rising number of immigrant youths from marginalized neighborhoods who had been incarcerated and ordered deported in the 1990s, protestant clergy and members of a coalition of nonprofit organizations, among them Cimade, organized several hunger strikes to raise awareness of their suffering. They encouraged delegalized migrants who had been ordered deported but who had avoided deportation or had been able to reenter clandestinely—the *doubles peines*—to join them, and several hunger strikes took place, especially in marginalized neighborhoods in the suburbs of Paris and Lyon, as well as in Protestant churches in some of the major cities with many immigrants.

In the early 2000s, right-wing Minister of the Interior Nicolas Sarkozy, who later became president of France, recognized that *double peine* should be abolished, both for the sake of the migrants and for the sake of public order and French society at large.[23] Though the reform of double punishment proved to be a huge disappointment, for reasons that will be explained later in the chapter, it served Sarkozy's political career. His claim to "abolish double punishment" was an important part of his political campaign, as it made him stand out as a bold politician who was not afraid of risking his popularity for the defense of an unpopular but just cause: the fate of criminal foreign nationals with a double punishment, whom the Socialist Party, which traditionally positioned itself as pro-immigrant, had been hesitant to defend. At the same time, Sarkozy did not want to be seen as being soft on immigration, and he repeatedly proclaimed his new measures to rid France of undeserving—that is, undocumented—migrants.

In 2003, Sarkozy announced that he would no longer tolerate the presence of "illegal foreigners." Inspired by New York's "zero tolerance" policies, he introduced "new management techniques" within the French administration to assess the performance of police and immigration officers. For the first time in French history, quantitative targets were set for police arrests and for deportations. Under French law, police officers already had wide discretion to carry out identity checks without any suspicion of criminal wrongdoing, including in transport hubs and in any area designated by a prosecutor. The high levels of profiling, discrimination, and violence during police identity checks of young men from marginalized neighborhoods, many of whom are French citizens whose parents or great-grandparents emigrated from France's former colonial empire, have been extensively documented. In the Paris region, many confrontations have been spurred by the violent deaths of youths in the hands of police officers, as in the widely mediated riots in France in 2005.[24]

With Sarkozy's quotas for arrests and deportations, identity controls increasingly targeted pedestrians profiled as potential undocumented migrants, leading to the arrests of undocumented migrants and of formerly legal residents who had been ordered deported as a consequence of a criminal sentence. The quota of ten thousand deportations in 2003 steadily increased each year to reach thirty thousand deportations in 2011. Several times a year between 2003 and his defeat at the presidential election in May 2012, the Sarkozy administration organized minutely orchestrated press conferences to show how the quotas announced at the beginning of the year had been reached, and even surpassed, so as to demonstrate his determination and successful performance. While targeting undocumented migrants for deportation, the Sarkozy administration also reduced the possibility of obtaining asylum. Many migrants were delegalized by the changes in legislation that have tended to restrict the ability to renew student visas, work permits, or residency based on family reunification.

Others lost their right to stay because they divorced their citizen spouse, graduated from higher education, or lost the job that had secured them a working permit, while others chose to go underground after being denied refugee status in the hope of obtaining legalization at a later stage.

The Sarkozy administration regularly branded "criminal foreigners" a threat to French society, suggesting draconian measures to neutralize them through deportation and, in the case of newly naturalized citizens, even to expand the grounds for denaturalization and subsequent deportation. Little changed with the election of President François Hollande in May 2012, despite his campaign promise to end the quota system. In January 2013, Hollande's socialist government announced that 32,912 foreign nationals had been deported in 2011, and 44,458 (+35%) were deported in 2013.[25]

The following pages will move the focus away from French politics and the criminalization of undocumented and delegalized migrants to the consequences of these laws in the everyday lives of migrants living in France.

MAKINGS AND UNMAKINGS OF BUREAUCRATIC LEGIBILITY

As it became increasingly more difficult to obtain legalization in France, the tactics and strategies deployed by migrants to avoid deportation adapted to the law, among them the use of false paperwork to make themselves bureaucratically illegible. Undocumented migrants know and pass on the information that no person can be deported without travel documents, whether a passport or a so-called laissez-passer, issued by a consulate or an embassy. Many undocumented migrants have lost, hidden, or destroyed their identity papers in the hope that doing so might slow or stop their deportation. Migrants whose fingerprints match no bureaucratic record can deliberately give a false identity when they are first arrested and sentenced in the criminal justice system.

Many undocumented migrants in prison have been sentenced for documentary fraud, as the rise in law enforcement aimed at undocumented migrants has generated "paper strategies," in which immigrants "create realities with false documents."[26] As the attention to and fight against undocumented workers has increased in France, as in other countries during the past twenty years, many undocumented immigrants have only been able to obtain employment by using fraudulent work visas and social security numbers—often with the knowledge of their French employers.[27] Similarly, the Immigration Reform and Control Act (IRCA) of 1986 included provisions to force U.S. employers to verify their workers' paperwork so that they could no longer hire as many undocumented workers as they wanted, with the option to use the threat of deportation against them.[28] These provisions, however, are easily circumvented. French anthropologist Sébastien Chauvin, who conducted fieldwork among undocumented Mexican day laborers in Chicago, has shown that employers are in the clear if they can prove that they have *verified* their workers' paperwork by taking photocopies of (what they often suspect or know to be) their workers' forged green cards and social security cards.[29]

False papers are necessary not only to work but also to circulate. As previously mentioned, police officers have wide discretion to carry out identity checks without any suspicion of criminal wrongdoing, and French law requires that all persons carry proof of their identity at all times, either a passport or a national identity card. As French citizens can apply for these two kinds of identity papers, some undocumented migrants borrow or rent a citizen's "spare" passport or identity card. This strategy requires some resemblance between the physical appearance of the real owner of the document and its holder.

Formerly legal residents who have lost their legal status and who are now undocumented may still be in possession of papers—such as green cards or *cartes de séjour* (residence permits)—with a valid expiration date that they can present to officers. Many use false identity papers that have been illegally produced and bought on the black market. With increasing illegalization, there is more money to be made from the forgery of identity papers, and in several cases, state agents have been tempted to illegally produce and sell real identity papers with the names of undocumented migrants who did not in effect hold citizenship. If a police officer discovers that a foreign national has shown them papers that were invalidated by a deportation order, whether false identity papers or those of someone else, the foreign national is not only apprehended and deported but risks receiving a prison sentence before being deported. Some, however, would rather risk multiple incarcerations than deportation.

MAKING ONESELF UNDEPORTABLE

"Gabriel," a twenty-five-year-old Congolese man, fled the Congo because he feared violence, maybe even death, as a consequence of his political engagement. He had first fled to another province of his own country, but as he feared for his safety there, he had moved on to France, where he hoped to obtain asylum. Upon his arrival in France, he sought out the advice of migrants from his Congolese network. Weighing the pros and cons of asking for asylum, Gabriel decided to stay undocumented. His friends had enough experience of asylum cases involving Congolese migrants to know that asking for asylum would be counterproductive.

His case would most likely be rejected, as he had "only" been threatened, verbally, and had no written proof of his allegations. In addition, if an undocumented migrant previously held a legal immigration status or asked for legalization, immigration authorities would likely have a file on that person and the necessary information to ask the consulate to issue travel documents. Applying for asylum, then, represented an unnecessary risk, as a police identity control in the street would mean instant deportation, because the police would know Gabriel's identity, and the Congolese authorities were bound to imprison him on his return. Gabriel decided to hide his passport, purchase false papers, find a job, and "produce documents" that could later serve as proof of presence in France, in case a change in immigration law or in his personal situation opened up an opportunity for legalization. Gabriel dreamt of becoming a designer of women's shoes, and he was actively trying to find an internship, hoping for future employment in a company that would be willing to legalize him as one of its employees.

Gabriel studied the dress codes of young French professionals and deliberately dressed "sharp," choosing the thick-rimmed glasses of the middle-class "creatives" of his partly gentrified, partly immigrant neighborhood, and he was able to avoid police controls for several years. He always paid his tickets on the Paris metro and buses, and if he had no change, he would rather walk than risk being controlled without a ticket, which, he knew, could lead to his arrest. Eventually Gabriel was subject to an identity control by police, during which he tried to say as little as possible for fear that his accent would reveal that he had grown up in Africa, not France. The policeman, however, became suspicious and double-checked Gabriel's papers, and he was sentenced to six months in prison for illegal entry and stay and using forged documents, with a reentry ban of three years.

Admission to a prison includes being rendered institutionally "legible" and easily identifiable to the prison administration. It marks the beginning of extensive record keeping in the prison's database or on preprinted forms in which information is written down by social workers or councilors and kept in paper files and computer databases. Prisoners' fingerprints now correspond to a file, which includes information about their own and their parents' date and place of birth, nationality, and contact information. Prisoners are issued an ID with their serial number, name, and photograph and are given a *carte de détenu* (detainee card), which they are to keep throughout their incarceration. Most ex-prisoners remember their six-digit prisoner number by heart, even years after their release from the criminal justice system, and describe the "dehumanizing effect," as some express it, of being summoned by a serial number rather than by their personal surname.

To most undocumented migrants, this moment is a powerful reminder of their entrapment by the state. Not only are they incarcerated, but they have also been identified for deportation.

NEGOTIATING THE BORDER

When the authorities do not possess the travel document of a person they wish to deport, deportation necessitates cooperation with the deportee's country of citizenship, which must issue a laissez-passer, an international travel document. When a foreign national is unidentified and his or her country of citizenship is unknown, the police try to determine the person's citizenship with the help of interpreters, who may be able to identify the person's accent or dialect. The authorities may also present the deportee to several different consulates or embassies in the hope that one of them will recognize the migrant. In some cases, diplomatic pressure and promises of development aid are used to motivate consulates into recognizing their citizens and issuing travel documents.[30]

Consular authorities may, however, choose to help deportees, as this example of an undocumented national from a West African country living in Paris demonstrates:

> The police agents brought me to my embassy. The employee looked at me and asked me, in our language, but with a cold tone in his voice "So, do you want to go home or not?" I quietly answered "No." The employee looked away from me at the policeman and said: "This man is clearly not one of our nationals." The policeman then took me to a few other consulates, which, of course, did not recognize me. Without a laissez-passer, they had to let me go after 32 days at the immigration detention center.[31]

Or in this case of a North African national living undocumented in France:

> My cousin works at the consulate. He got his colleague to issue a laissez-passer in my name that held a deliberate administrative mistake, making it useless at the moment of deportation. Maybe the police suspected that the consulate had done it on purpose, and that I had something to do with it, or maybe they were just pissed that day. They threatened to get me convicted of *refus d'embarquement* (refusal to embark on a flight), and transferred me to a *local de retention administrative* (an immigration detention place in a local police station). Late at night, the next day, after almost 48 hours, I was suddenly released. I was still undocumented, but at least I was free.[32]

Gabriel had also hidden his passport and given a false identity, and to his great relief, no consulate, including his own, recognized him as its citizen. After spending the maximum legal amount of days in a *centre de rétention administrative* (the French equivalent of an immigration detention center), he was released with an order to leave the French territory. Gabriel was free but not legalized, and a few months later, a random police identity control in the street led to a new arrest, a new sentence, and a new prison sentence.

In contrast to the United States, bureaucratically unidentified foreign nationals who cannot be deported from France for lack of travel documents are generally released from immigration detention centers after a maximum period of forty-five days in detention (thirty-two days before June 2011). According to estimates, around 25 percent of undocumented migrants held in detention centers are actually deported.[33] Of the remaining 75 percent who are released from French detention centers, a few are legalized, but most are released without legal status. Some, however, are brought to trial and reincarcerated after a sentence for hiding their identity papers, giving up a false identity, or having refused to embark on the flight at the moment of their deportation. Others are able to "negotiate the border" with government agents who are asked to implement these restrictive laws but who refuse to do so. Sometimes the undeported can successfully plead their case to street-level bureaucrats who act against the law or against the state.[34] Working as a paralegal lawyer, I witnessed many situations in which probation officers, police agents, or judges ignored or disrespected deportation orders that they found unfair and counterproductive to their aim, "proper" law enforcement or the reintegration of former prisoners into society. A former police officer told me that he and his colleagues were critical of Sarkozy's quotas for arrests and deportations, as "they had not joined the police to deport honest workers, but to fight real crime." One day they had been given orders to conduct identity controls in front of a shelter known to be the home of both documented and undocumented migrant workers. They systematically lowered their voices so that their superiors would not hear them and said, "This is an identity control. If you're undocumented, just show me any paper you have on you." After being shown receipts, supermarket-chain discount cards, and even a Post-it Note with a phone number on it, they proceeded to make no arrests. Undocumented migrants told me of being released from police stations and even a detention center by police officers who expressed their discontent with the current deportation practices.

Those who are released without legal status are in violation of immigration law and are exposed to police control, arrest, and another period of detention. Their fingerprints are registered and they have a criminal record, although it corresponds to a list of aliases that they have given the police at the moment of their arrest. In France, an unidentifiable migrant's name is followed by "XSD" after X se disant (X calling himself). Many XSDs manage to stay unidentified for years despite frequent encounters with the police and the criminal justice system. The list of aliases attached to their fingerprints makes them identifiable as permanent reoffenders and exposes them to being sentenced for noncompliance with previous deportation orders, which is punishable by longer prison sentences. Working as a paralegal immigration lawyer in prisons for several years, I regularly met the same unidentifiable, undocumented migrants who had made themselves illegible through the hiding or destruction of their passport and the blurring of their bureaucratic identity. I met migrants who had dozens of aliases on their criminal record, with equally as many places and dates of birth, nationalities, and names of fictitious parents.

CONSEQUENCES OF STRATEGIC UNMAKINGS OF BUREAUCRATIC LEGIBILITY

When Sarkozy's new law was unveiled in November 2003, it was a disappointment to most of the activists who had advocated for a reform of double punishment. Its provisions allowed for the amnesty of only a limited number of *doubles peines* who could prove that they had (1) arrived in France before turning thirteen years old; (2) been legal residents for ten years and were parents of an underage French citizen; (3) been legal residents for ten years and were married to a French citizen; or (4) lived in France as legal residents for more than twenty years. Many had obtained family reunification after turning thirteen and had arrived a few years too late to be considered for relief within the legal framework of the reform. As statistics show, most first-time convictions happen before a person turns thirty, so few persons had been legal residents for ten years before being sentenced to prison, and even fewer had been legal residents for twenty years. Working as a paralegal immigration lawyer during those years and meeting hundreds of deportees, the only person I defended who had lived in France for more than twenty years was a retired immigrant worker who had been sentenced to a permanent reentry ban for committing a murder. He had been living legally in France for more than forty years and was the father and grandfather of several French citizens. Luckily, he had kept all his papers, as proving that he had not left France for more than six months necessitated photocopies of three wage slips for each year he had lived in France. This was the heaviest file I ever brought to the Ministry of the Interior.

A further requirement for getting amnesty was to make a request within thirteen months after the law had passed and get the case reviewed by the interior minister, the *préfecture* (police precinct), or the penal judges who had issued the reentry ban or deportation. As Sarkozy communicated widely on the wrongful information that he had simply "abolished double punishment," many people who could have benefited from the reform never requested a review in time.

Others had lived underground for years and had meticulously avoided leaving any bureaucratic traces anywhere, as they rented flats and worked or circulated with forged paperwork or a family member's or friend's identity papers. As *doubles peines* had multiplied in their neighborhoods, many 1.5 generation youths became aware of their deportability and adopted strategies to avoid deportation, some of them taught by their elders, who had become knowledgeable of the deportation system while being incarcerated with undocumented migrants, who were unable to produce sufficient evidence of their presence in France and were not legalized. Those who did not obtain legalization remained targets for the government's deportation policies.

Fanta, for instance, had arrived from a West African country when she was in her teens and had accumulated a series of prison sentences related to drug use, prostitution, illegal stay, and the disrespecting of a deportation order. No consular authorities recognized her as their citizen, and Fanta knew from experience that she would not be deported upon her release from the women's prison where she had been incarcerated almost a dozen times. Her life was punctuated by routine immobilizations and forced movements that traversed prison, immigration detention, and life in the street. On the outside, Fanta sold sex and sometimes committed petty thefts to support herself and her addiction. Her visibility in the street made her an easy target for multiple arrests, but her bureaucratic illegibility protected her from deportation.

The floating population of unidentifiable undocumented migrants includes foreign-national drug users, who have accumulated years of forced movements and immobilizations in repressive institutions. Many of them contract life-threatening diseases, such as HIV, AIDS, and severe cases of hepatitis or diabetes. In cases in which treatment is not accessible in their country of citizenship, it is possible to ask for humanitarian legalization based on the "illness clause" of 1998.[35] Of course many of the migrants who could make such requests no longer have real identity papers and have accumulated dozens of convictions with as many different aliases. If they wish to obtain legalization, they have to prove their bureaucratic identity by producing identity documents such as passports or birth certificates, which are sometimes impossible to obtain. Like Fanta, many fear that they run a major risk if they succeed in reestablishing their identity, giving the authorities the power to decide not to grant them legalization but to deport them on the grounds of their newly acquired knowledge as to their real bureaucratic identity. Strategic unmakings of bureaucratic legibility, then, can also come with a price, when "unidentifiable" migrants are suddenly eligible for legalization due to a change of law or a change in their personal situation but are unable to produce the proper documents, sometimes with major consequences for their health.

THE CRIMINAL JUSTICE SYSTEM AND LEGALLY PRODUCED DOMESTIC BORDER ZONES

Perhaps due to the work of historians and legal scholars who study historical processes of inclusion and exclusion of minorities, or perhaps due to the ever-changing immigration laws throughout the 1990s and 2000s, anthropologists have increasingly abandoned the idea that migrants follow a linear process as they are incorporated, assimilated, or integrated into their host country. As De Genova has pointed out, many earlier studies on immigration were inspired by Robert Park's logic in "Human Migration and the Marginal Man," which distinguished between "sojourners" and "settlers" and conceptualized the condition of illegalized migrants as "liminal" as though it were a stage in a rite of passage that might eventually lead to incorporation, legal status, and citizenship. De Genova quotes Portes's critique from 1975 to argue that much scholarship on undocumented migrants, still today, is policy oriented in that it revolves around discerning whether or not immigrants will "assimilate" or not.[36] Rather than drawing on anthropology's contribution to the understanding of liminality, De Genova argues that it is more fruitful to draw on the discipline's contributions to the understanding of law and legal processes.

Echoing Foucault, who argued that "the existence of a legal prohibition creates around it a field of illegal practices," anthropologist Kitty Calavita shows how the boundaries of the law create illegal practices.[37] Legal status can be temporary or subject to disruptions, and a constant flow of migrants move in and out of legal status, sometimes several times in a lifetime. Similarly, few undocumented migrants actually entered France clandestinely; on the contrary, the great majority were initially documented but fell out of status due to changes in French legislation that suddenly saw them categorized as "illegal." Migrants can lose their legal status and become undocumented because they have overstayed their visa; their immigration status has expired; their asylum case has been rejected; or they are losing their job, getting a divorce, or being sentenced for a misdemeanor or a crime. Migrants who are undocumented at one point may later obtain legalization through collective amnesty or adjustment of status due to regulations on the labor market, by being granted refugee status, or as a consequence of a change in their personal situation.

Migrant illegalization, then, produces borders and, according to Coutin, might be understood in terms of "spaces of legal non-existence."[38] De Genova conceptualizes illegality in a similar fashion: "The spacialized condition of 'illegality' reproduces the physical borders of nation-states in the everyday lives of innumerable places throughout the interiors of the migrant-receiving states."[39]

Gabriel's trajectory also shows a continuity between the spaces of legal nonexistence within his home country and those within France, as suggested by Coutin.[40] Though Coutin's observations are based on her fieldwork among Salvadorans living in the United States, Gabriel's trajectory shows similar continuations of situations that implied legal nonexistence and high levels of insecurity, both in his home country and in the repressive institutions of the country he fled to but in which he was not able to obtain asylum. Fanta's trajectory shows how such spaces of legal nonexistence are created within the theoretical borders of the French nation-state—within different repressive institutions and in public space.

Upon release from French and U.S. prisons, foreign nationals who have served a criminal sentence may be detained in an immigration detention center. The great majority of them are detained and deported, but some are released without being legalized. The freedom of a person who is not deported but freed and not legalized is relative, as he or she can be arrested at any time and convicted and reincarcerated for being in violation of immigration law. The same applies for migrants who reenter the country clandestinely after their deportation, thus joining the ranks of undocumented migrants. Once illegalized, these foreign nationals violate immigration law by their mere presence within the borders of the country from which they are banned. Therefore, they can be arrested and sentenced for staying in or reentering the country illegally, and some of them become part of a floating population, which has been constituted by legislation and brought into forced circulation among spaces of confinement, such as police stations, immigration detention centers, and prisons.

The French case, however, demonstrates their high levels of agency and creativity as they circumvent and negotiate the border in order to avoid deportation. It also shows that the deportation regime cannot be assessed as a mere opposition between deportees and a monolithic state. Rather, street-level bureaucrats take an active part in deciding who may be allowed to stay, whether legally or illegally. Police officers, civil servants, and consulate employees sometimes act as gatekeepers of the nation and may decide to circumvent a deportation order, whether because they can gain money or recognition, or because they are opposed to the laws that they are asked to implement. They too can practice "everyday forms of resistance" when they are politically or ideologically opposed to current legal practices.[41]

Policy makers have acknowledged the situation of the undeported on several occasions. However, no reform has as yet led to a structural change in immigration laws to end these situations. Rather, small-scale reforms and arbitrary decisions from elected politicians or civil servants have contributed to solve the situations of a few, often at the expense of the majority of migrants who are concerned. In France as in other countries, one cannot help but draw the following conclusion: Not only do deportation policies not achieve the goals at which they are officially directed, but they actually take part in creating the situations that they officially aim to solve.

NOTES TO CHAPTER 9

1. Daniel Kanstroom, *Deportation Nation: Outsiders in American History* (Cambridge: Harvard University Press, 2007); Danièle Lochak, *Étrangers de quel droit?* (Paris: Presses Universitaires de France, 1980).

2. Nicholas De Genova, "Migrant Illegality and Deportability in Everyday Life," *Annual Review of Anthropology* 31 (2002): 419–447.

3. J. Scott, John Tehranian, and Jeremy Mathias, "The Production of Legal Identities Proper to States: The Case of the Permanent Family Surname," *Comparative Studies in Society and History* 44, no. 1 (2002): 4–44.

4. David Brotherton and Luis Barrios, *Banished to the Homeland: Dominican Deportees and Their Stories of Exile* (New York: Columbia University, 2011).

5. Roberto Gonzales, "Learning to Be Illegal: Undocumented Youth and Shifting Legal Contexts in the Transition to Adulthood," *American Sociological Review* 76, no. 4 (2011): 602–619.

6. Administration pénitentiaire, January 2014: 82 percent French citizens, 18 percent foreign nationals (Africa: 50 percent; Europe: 37 percent; America: 8 percent; Asia: 5 percent).

7. Laurent Mucchielli, "Délinquance et immigration: Le sociologue face au sens commun," *Hommes et migrations*, no. 1241 (January–February 2003).

8. Angélique Hazard, "Étrangers incarcérés," in *Cahiers d'études penitentiaries et criminologiques* (Paris: Direction de l'administration pénitentiaire, 2008), http://www.justice.gouv.fr/art_pix/CahEtudesPenitCrim25.pdf.

9. Nicolas Fischer, *Le territoire de l'expulsion: La rétention administrative des étrangers dans l'Etat de droit* (Lyon: Presses de l'ENS, 2016); Carolina Kobelinsky et Chowra Makaremi (eds.), *Enfermés dehors, enquête sur le confinement des étrangers* (Bellecombe-en-Bauges: Éditions du Croquant, 2009); M. Agier, *Gérer les indésirables: Des camps de réfugiés au gouvernement humanitaire* (Paris: Flammarion, 2008).

10. Peter Nyers, "Abject Cosmopolitanism: The Politics of Protection in the Anti-Deportation Movement," *Third World Quarterly* 24, no. 6 (2003): 1069–1093.

11. Maybritt Alpes, *Bushfalling: How Young Cameroonians Dare to Migrate* (Amsterdam: Universiteit van Amsterdam, 2011); David C. Brotherton and Barrios Luis, *Banished to the Homeland*; Nathalie Peutz, "'Criminal Alien' Deportees in Somaliland: An Ethnography of Removal," in *The Deportation Regime: Sovereignty, Space, and the Freedom of Movement*, ed. N. De Genova and N. Peutz, 271–309 (Durham: Duke University Press, 2010); Sine Plambech, "Between 'Victims' and 'Criminals': Rescue, Deportation, and Everyday Violence Among Nigerian Migrants," *Social Politics* 21, no. 3 (Fall 2014): 382–402; Liza Schuster and Nassim Majidi, "What Happens Post-Deportation? The Experience of Deported Afghans," *Migration Studies* 1, no. 2 (2013): 221–240; E. Zilberg, *Space of Detention: The Making of a Transnational Gang Crisis Between Los Angeles and San Salvador* (Durham: Duke University Press, 2011).

12. Nyers, "Abject Cosmopolitanism."

13. De Genova, "Migrant Illegality."

14. Michel Foucault, *Discipline and Punish: The Birth of the Prison* (New York: Random House/Vintage Books, 1979).

15. Lilian Mathieu, *La double peine: Histoire d'une lutte inachevée* (Paris: Éditions La Dispute, 2006), 98.

16. Ibid., 66.

17. Ibid., 125.

18. Mathieu, *La double peine*, 149.

19. Ibid., 141.

20. Ibid., 127.

21. Gonzalez, "Learning to Be Illegal."

22. Mathieu, *La double peine*, 195.

23. For example, Fabien Jobard, *Bavures policières? La force publique et ses usages* (Paris: La Découverte, 2002); Laurent Mucchielli and Le Gouaziou Véronique (eds.), *Quand les banlieues brulent . . . retour sur les émeutes de novembre 2005* (Paris: La Découverte, 2006); Fabien Jobard, "Police, justice et discriminations raciales?" in *Représenter la société française*, 219–223 (Paris: La Découverte, 2006).

24. Speech by Nicolas Sarkozy, Minister of Interior, at l'Assemblée nationale, July 3, 2003, http://discours.vie-publique.fr/notices/033002192.html.

25. Sylvain Mouillard, "Rétention des clandestins: la promesse manquée de Hollande," *Libération*, November 18, 2014.

26. Susan Bibler Coutin, *Legalizing Moves* (Ann Arbor: University of Michigan Press, 2003).

27. Alain Morice, "Quand la lutte contre l'emploi illégal cache les progrès de la précarité légale," in *Les lois de l'inhospitalité*, ed. Didier Fassin, Alain Morice, and Catherine Quiminal (Paris: Éditions la Découverte, 1997).

28. Kanstroom, *Deportation Nation*, 222.

29. Sébastien Chauvin, *Agencies of Precariousness: Every Day in Chicago* (Paris: The Seuil, 2010).

30. *Cette France-là*, vol. 2, 1 July 2008–30 June 2009 (Paris: La Découverte, 2010).

31. Interview, J. A. (Paris, 2007).

32. Interview, G. (Paris, 2010).

33. Fischer, *Les territoires de l'expulsion*, 216.

34. Michael Lipsky, *Street-Level Bureaucracy: Dilemmas of the Individual in Public Services* (New York: Russell Sage, 1980).

35. Miriam Ticktin, *Casualties of Care: Immigration and the Politics of Humanitarianism in France* (Berkeley: University of California Press, 2011).

36. De Genova, "Migrant Illegality," 431.

37. Foucault, *Discipline and Punish*, 280; Kitty Calavita, *Immigrants at the Margins: Law, Race and Exclusion in Southern Europe* (Cambridge: Cambridge University Press, 2005).

38. Susan Bibler Coutin, "Denationalization, Inclusion, and Exclusion: Negotiating the Boundaries of Belonging," *Indiana Journal of Global Legal Studies* 7, no. 2 (2000): 585–593.

39. De Genova, "Migrant Illegality," 439.

40. Coutin, *Legalizing Moves*.

41. James Scott, *Weapons of the Weak: Everyday Forms of Peasant Resistance* (New Haven: Yale University Press, 1985); Coutin, *Legalizing Moves*; Ticktin, *Casualties of Care*, 24.

10. FEAR OF DEPORTATION AS A BARRIER TO IMMIGRANT INTEGRATION

SHIRLEY LEYRO, CUNY

Born in Central America, Polly made the difficult decision to leave her home country for the United States to support her family financially.[1] She contacted a known smuggler, paid the fee, and in 1990 began her odyssey to the United States. She portrays her harrowing ordeal with the unemotional tone of someone describing a trip to the local market. Her narrative, however, belies the nonchalant manner in which she recounts her story.

Crossing four different countries in nineteen days, Polly made her way across the Mexican border to reach the ultimate destination of New York City. She recollects that the trip "was not terrible. . . . It was like a normal trip almost. But the problem was crossing the [Mexican] border."[2] Upon arriving in Mexico, Polly recounts being told that the next leg of the trip would have to be done by foot. Though she was told her group would walk for eight hours before stopping to rest, they actually walked for a much longer time, with barely any food and water. They trekked in the oppressive heat during the day and tried to sleep at night, despite the animal noises and cold night air. Polly ambled over hilly and mountainous terrain, climbed over large rocks and boulders, making sure not to leave any tracks behind—any trace of footprints or other markings could mean "immigration would come." And yet not long after, conditions would worsen to the point that Polly wished immigration officials would find her and end her pain and anguish.

Polly traveled with several other people, one of whom was a woman who was hurt during the trip. Polly tried to help her but eventually became fatigued and needed assistance herself. She recounts reaching a point where she told the group she could no longer continue. It was at this point that she said she was hoping to be captured, which for her would signify a rescue "because I could no longer stand it, I had reached the end." Fortunately, just as she reached her limit, the coyote told her they had arrived at a pickup point where the rest of the trip would be completed by car. Despite recounting a terrifying and harrowing tale, Polly describes her journey as a matter of simple disruption, an "inconvenience." According to her, distress and trauma were not the result of her trip to the United States but rather from her experiences after arriving: "But that has been, more than everything, not traumatic, rather just an inconvenience. To arrive in this country. . . . But afterward, more than everything else, what has affected us the most is deportation."

The "inconvenience" of Polly's trip, when juxtaposed to her struggle with living under the threat of deportation, highlights how immigration policy and enforcement can have traumatic effects. Polly's story is not unique. Oppressive U.S. immigration laws, increasingly punitive over time, have had debilitating effects on the lives of many noncitizen immigrants.[3] The threat of deportation in particular has had a significant impact, affecting not only noncitizen immigrants and their families but also the communities in which they live. Drawing on findings from my dissertation study, this chapter presents several participant vignettes to demonstrate how the vulnerability to deportation has affected the lives of immigrants in ways that also impact their integration into the United States. The personal stories and reflections of these noncitizen immigrants provide a powerful narrative about how draconian immigration policies, particularly those that result in deportation, have been inflicting anguish on their lives. Further, in this chapter I demonstrate how deportation, as a consequence of immigration enforcement, amounts to legal violence.

BACKGROUND

A prevailing assumption exists in the literature. Menjívar and Abrego frame this assumption as follows:

> When everyone living in the United States is able to fully integrate, our communities are better off. A more thorough process of immigrant integration will result in . . . a stronger sense of belonging, greater investment in the collective future of the country, and a more cohesive society.[4]

Studying the mechanisms involved in the process of how immigrants acclimate, adapt, and adjust to a host society is of premier importance, particularly when considering that the composition of American social landscape has changed dramatically as a result of a half century of large-scale migration.[5] Indeed, there is an abundance of literature in the social sciences dedicated to immigrant adaptation or lack thereof. Most research frames adaptation as integration, incorporation, acculturation, or assimilation, and explores how immigrants adapt to the communities into which they settle.[6] My study explores how fear of deportation interrupts the process by which immigrants become included in society to achieve full membership. There is not a specific theory of inclusion that will frame the study but rather a path that involves social acceptance and recognition as being part of the larger community; the ability to become involved in major institutions, such as the political system and the labor market; and the ability to access the same "life chances" of the native born.[7] This process is referred to as *integration*.

The role that fear of deportation plays in this process is not well known. I seek to contribute to the literature on the immigration experience by exploring the fear of deportation and the effects of this fear, a topic that has not been researched in depth.

The idea that immigration leads to increased crime rates has contributed to anti-immigrant rhetoric and policy.[8] Governmental efforts at ridding the United States of immigrants perceived as undesirable has led to increases in the scope and severity of immigration policies over the last twenty years. In effect, the United States has adopted a "deportation regime," with forced repatriation becoming the most prolific form of immigration control.[9] Politically, the presumption of the criminogenic nature of immigrants has been used as a rationale for immigration control, and the consequences have been immense.[10] During the five-year period between 1997 and 2012, deportations outnumber the sum total of all deportations before 1997.[11] Yet the majority of these deportations are for noncriminal violations, and most removals due to criminal violations are for minor infractions.[12] This exponential increase suggests that deportation is a real threat to the lives of all immigrants, regardless of their compliance with the law. In fact, there is no relationship between immigration and crime. The data do not support the discourse used to justify causes for removal. An increasing number of studies have refuted the immigration and crime link, and the scholarship consistently finds that immigration does not increase crime.[13] As one study concluded, "Immigrants are *less likely* to be involved in crime than are the native born."[14]

However, little is known about how living under this threat affects immigrants and the communities in which they live. In this chapter, therefore, I seek to shed light on how the fear promoted by harsh immigration policies and rhetoric, and the unprecedented rise in deportations, produces a culture of fear within

immigrant communities—which goes largely unreported and thus unaddressed—
and how this fear can have an impact on the communities in which it manifests
on multiple levels.

Both sociological and criminological research suggest that fear can have
several negative effects on the development of healthy communities. For example, fear undermines the development of social capital, cohesion, and integration,
and inhibits collective efficacy, all of which are factors that contribute to social
organization, and which sociologists have long insisted are key to safer communities.[15] In particular, the research suggests that fear operates to constantly
undermine and threaten a group's sense of solidarity. Whether documented or
undocumented, immigrants who feel a sense of vulnerability to deportation
(i.e., are conscious of their "deportability") shape their life practices in both
profound and discrete ways.[16] Building on this research, I argue that being vulnerable to deportation, and the fear associated with it, has implications on an
individual noncitizen immigrant's well-being, as well as on the communities in
which they live.

A historical entry point for immigration, New York City bears many rich opportunities to research the effects of the vulnerability to deportation. In 2012, New
York City's population reached a new peak of 8.34 million people, which included
an immigrant population of over 3 million (37 percent of the population), with
an annual average of 140,000 reaching legal permanent resident status.[17] The
most recent estimate of the undocumented population in New York City (from
2010) is 535,000 people, or about 6.54 percent of the city's population and about
16 percent of the city's immigrant population.[18]

In general, studies have framed New York as an "immigrant friendly" city
because it is easier for immigrants to integrate, particularly for the second generation.[19] Indeed, on April 25, 2012, then New York City mayor Michael Bloomberg visited the offices of a pro-citizenship organization and declared New York
City the most immigrant friendly city in the country.[20] Yet there are a significant number of deportations from the area. In 2009, 23 percent of immigrants
who exited New York City were removed by the Department of Homeland Security.[21] In addition, between 2005 and 2010, of all persons detained by Immigration and Customs Enforcement in the city, 91 percent were deported.[22] This
high proportion indicates that detention in New York City almost guarantees deportation. Meanwhile, 87 percent of persons deported have children in the United
States, highlighting the event's propensity for social devastation. In these cases,
there is indeed much to fear for the noncitizen population, particularly the undocumented if discovered. This data demonstrates that immigration enforcement
has been quite successful in New York City, thus making it an ideal location for
examining the effects of deportation on immigrants and the implications for their
communities.

Overall, New York City has taken significant measures to protect the immigrant population, such as issuing municipal IDs and providing free legal assistance to undocumented immigrants.[23] The threat of deportation, however, is ever present, and we know little about those under threat of removal—for example, how many of them are mentally ill or suffering from severe illness, or even how many children will be left abandoned by the act of permanent exile. Consequently, these positive efforts by the city have been relatively neutralized by the tenacity of competing federal and some state agencies, rendering local municipal policies basically moot. As a result, the immigrant population in this location, large in size, is living under the real threat of deportation.

This study collected data using six focus groups and thirty-three in-depth one-on-one interviews. The thirty-three interviews included a diverse sample of documented ($n=16$) and undocumented ($n=17$) immigrant adults living in New York City. Most immigrant households are of *mixed status*, meaning they include both undocumented and documented family members, therefore making it more realistic to include both authorized and unauthorized immigrants in this study.[24] The majority of participants were recruited through an affiliation at a local church. Churches are often ideal starting points for immigrants seeking a place in a new destination, especially in the absence of their ability to have formal political participation.[25]

THE IMPACT OF BEING VULNERABLE TO DEPORTATION

From the outset, all participants expressed that vulnerability to deportation made them fearful. Responses clearly showed that the possibility of deportation—and the fear associated with it—affected how participants felt they were viewed by society, including the government and fellow community members. The central themes that emerged from the data were vulnerability to deportation and the fear associated with it, which resulted in (1) participants feeling a lack of belonging; (2) participants engaging in avoidance behaviors, which affected their desire to become civically engaged; and (3) the inability of participants to form important social relationships and build social capital, all of which impede the process of integration. In addition, another theme that developed was the idea that deportation is a form of legal violence, which, along with the aforementioned themes, synergistically creates an environment that interrupts integration.

The language used by most participants indicated that they felt a lack of belonging. These feelings have a direct impact on integration, as immigrants' perception of acceptance and sense of social solidarity with the host country is related to incorporation.[26] Thus, an integral part of integration is interaction between members of the community, which allows for the formation of the trust, connectedness, and shared expectations necessary for developing social capital and social cohesion.[27] Vulnerability to deportation leads to feelings of being unwanted or unwelcome, which acts as a discourager to becoming civically and socially engaged, thus influencing the level of interaction an immigrant has with other members of the community.

Amanda, who has legal permanent resident status, was pursuing a graduate degree and had been living in the United States for fourteen years at the time of the interview. For her, the political climate and shifting sentiment toward immigration appeared to create a sense of uncertainty. This uncertainty led her to feel as if she did not belong and that the United States might never feel like home:

> For us, the fear of deportation manifests itself in the sense that this is just not our country . . . and so it gives a sense of uncertainty, and we know that uncertainty can translate into deportation in the sense that the laws can change, the government can decide to become less hospitable to immigrants, and, you know, we just don't view our presence here as permanent.

Amanda is an educated woman, gainfully employed, married with two children—both born in the United States—all factors that portray a strong sense of integration. Yet she still believes that her presence here is temporary. Amanda's perspective is based on her vulnerability to deportation and the fear associated with it, which highlights that although integration is connected to feelings of belonging, immigration policies make it clear that immigrants do not belong.[28]

Other participants shared this sentiment. For example, Stacy, also a legal permanent resident at the time of the interview, felt dubious about her treatment and vulnerability as an immigrant. When asked whether she thought her feelings of vulnerability to deportation and the accompanying fear could change, she answered as follows:

STACY: No.

INTERVIEWER: Even with citizenship?

STACY: Yeah. I ask my students—I always have this discussion. What does it mean to be American? And so they were like, Well, if you don't have an accent and stuff. And I asked, What about if I have a U.S. passport? And they were like, No. And I said, Why not? It says "American" clearly. And they were like, No, you're not.

As an immigrant, Stacy did not believe that her vulnerability would change because of her belief that American society judges citizenship with criteria other than having the appropriate paperwork.

Maria, another noncitizen immigrant with legal status, also expressed the belief that she did not belong:

> You need to belong and you need to have a home base, especially if you found a place where you wanna build something. . . . Why would you stop people from doing that? You're just disrupting their entire system and their emotional health.

Maria was born in a western European country and resides in an upper-middle-class neighborhood in New York City. She is a very proud woman who earned her PhD from an Ivy League university. Maria was keenly aware of the need to belong and expressed frustration over U.S. immigration policy and its effects. She further expressed how she felt unwelcome, stating, "I don't feel like there's a high degree of being welcome. . . . I mean, I'm so demotivated." The emotional toll of the vulnerability to deportation and the fear associated with it was evident not just in Maria's narrative but in the narratives of several other participants, who expressed similar emotional effects.

Madison, who had legal status and had been living in the United States for eleven years at the time of the interview, shared her experience:

> It just feels stressful. It just also feels like I can't actually build my life, like everything is—Like, for example, if I wanted to really put down roots and, I don't know, like get a mortgage and a house—I can't do that.

Madison spent most of her adolescence in the United States and acquired a graduate degree at an American college. Her desire is to settle in the United States, but she feels as though she cannot. Her account of the social effects of being vulnerable to deportation marks how access to common components of building a life or a home is restricted. Amanda made a similar observation: "There's definitely that effect that you just don't make roots, you don't lay down deep roots." Without access to the same things nonimmigrants have access to, participants were hampered in their ability to fully integrate into society.

Despite such hindrances, Madison exhibited a longing to have a normal, socially rich life, believing that she had earned the privilege:

> [I] created my community here, I wanna be in a place where I have spent a long time building. I became an adult in the U.S., you know? And so I feel that, because I became an adult here, because I've contributed a lot sort of socially and economically to this place, that I should have the right to stay. All of my friends are here.

Madison's feelings are understandable. That is, when someone has lived in a country for a certain amount of time, has obeyed its laws, and has even been educated in it, the person is likely to feel welcome and a sense of belonging. However, as demonstrated by participants' comments, vulnerability to deportation, and the fear associated with it, leads immigrants to feel the opposite.

Moreover, the feeling of not belonging becomes internalized and accepted as a fact of life by the noncitizen immigrant. This process of internal acceptance drives some to believe that they are not in a place they can call home. For example, Chad, who is undocumented, shared the following related sentiment about who gets deported:

CHAD: I think that one commits their own mistakes and well, sometimes, I don't know, people do not think either. That is, they feel as if they are in their own country, that they are not in a foreign country.
INTERVIEWER: And you feel you are in a foreign country?
CHAD: Well, yes, because, how do I say? Because we do not have documents. I think we are, let's say, marginalized, if you can say, because one cannot have the same rights as a citizen of this country.

Chad had been living in the United States for twenty-two years at the time of the interview and worked as a restaurant cook. He is married and has children in the United States, one of which has already begun attending college. Incredibly, he did not feel he belonged in the United States; he still felt as if he lived in a foreign country. This is a particularly impactful sentiment, as people tend to make themselves at home in places where they have been residing or situated for any length of time. Chad, however, did not feel at home, even after living in the country for over two decades.

Integration differs according to immigrants' involvement with social institutions and their sense of social solidarity with the host country.[29] Participants expressed that their feelings of not belonging also made them politically disinterested and unmotivated to become civically engaged. To exemplify this, Amanda stated the following:

Well, I mean, like being here to get involved in certain movements or political activities or certain organizations about issues that affect us, you know . . . we just don't get involved in those things because of this sense that you're not here to stay.

To Amanda, her vulnerability to deportation, and the resulting feeling of not belonging, made her feel unmotivated to participate in local institutions.

Amanda's sentiment was echoed by Polly, who had been politically active in her home country but now refrained from participating in any local community organization. She explained:

Translation: For now, I've stopped a lot . . . but now I don't want to get involved . . . in nothing that is political, in nothing . . . because I am afraid that, because I am not a citizen, they can deport me. . . . I do not want to work with organizations that work with immigrants because I am afraid that they will deport me . . . but, yes, I am interested in working with organizations once I have my citizenship.

Polly was able to acquire legal permanent resident status, which should have afforded her some sense of security. Yet, she stated, "For now, I believe not so much because, I do not know, I do not feel too secure, really, in this country." Polly's insecurity—resulting from the fear she feels from being vulnerable to deportation—makes her feel as if she is barred from becoming involved in political matters, even though they are perfectly legal. Her fear extends to her aversion of matters that might be helpful to her—in particular, those related to immigration reform.

Clearly, vulnerability to deportation can play a role in whether or not an immigrant cares to engage with local institutions and organizations. The literature indicates that such engagement is important to the formation of social capital and the process of integration. Avoiding involvement and participation with local organizations has been shown to have a negative effect in the formation of social capital.[30] In their article on how ethnicity can be a form of social capital, Min Zhou and Mingang Lin discuss how community-based organizations can serve as an effective means to counteract those forces that work in opposition to an ethnic group reaching orientation to the mainstream.[31] However, this premise is contingent on the participation and engagement of individuals with local institutions. As seen in both Amanda's and Polly's sentiments, the fear of deportation leads immigrants to avoid participation in community institutions or any other type of civic engagement. In addition, immigrant perceptions of being unwanted and not belonging, fomented by current anti-immigrant rhetoric, have been found to "create a vicious circle of distrust, perceptions of threat, alienation, and disengagement," which can also lead to the breakdown of integration and incorporation.[32]

Aside from political matters, the feeling of being unwanted and not belonging resulting from the vulnerability to deportation can lead immigrants to avoid certain social activities and physical spaces. For example, Emma, who had been in the United States for twenty-two years at the time of the interview, mentioned that she would like to visit Disney World or Miami, both in Florida. However, she realized that because she was undocumented, such a trip would carry too heavy a risk of being discovered. Traveling by plane would be impossible, and she viewed traveling by land via bus or automobile as too risky.

In general, the fear of long-distance travel was a universal concern among the undocumented participants. Emma, however, revealed another fear related to travel: "For example, I would have liked to visit city hall . . . because they say it is very pretty around there, but I do not go because those are places where there is, how do you say? Where there is much vigilance." A visit to New York City's city hall would be less than a thirty-minute subway ride away for Emma. Located in lower Manhattan, the area around city hall is visibly patrolled by law enforcement. However, because the area is also densely populated during the day by both private-sector and municipal employees, as well as tourists from all over the country (and the world), the discovery of her undocumented status would be less likely than it would be in her own neighborhood, which is less populated, making it more likely for her to be targeted and discovered should an immigration enforcement operation be sent out looking for unauthorized immigrants. Yet for Emma, her simple wish to visit city hall is untenable because of her vulnerability to deportation.

Other participants admitted that they avoided socializing. Sue, an undocumented immigrant who had been living in the United States for twenty-two years at the time of the interview, said that she avoids many social activities, "but to say that I want to go into the clubs, for example, and if immigration comes? And they take me?" Sue is a single older woman with grown children. She has an amiable personality and shared the fact that she has many friends. She does not, however, feel comfortable enough to go out and enjoy herself in social settings.

The role of trust, and the inability of participants to develop it, was a common sentiment among participants. Ellen, a woman who initially arrived in the United States from a western European country without authorization but eventually acquired legal permanent resident status, elaborated by stating, "I would say most of the residents who are here illegally, they're constantly thinking, 'I'm gonna get deported,' . . . 'then my American neighbor will say something about me.' Like things like that." Mistrust of neighbors was another common theme. Sue, the easygoing, social person, stated that she does not trust her neighbors: "What if after a while [they] get annoyed with me and call immigration on me? Because it has happened, it has happened." Meg, an undocumented immigrant who came to the United States from an eastern European country as a child, had lived in the United States for fourteen years and was attending college. She questioned whether or not her friends would betray her if they knew her secret of being undocumented: "Because . . . you never know, because someone could be an asshole and just be like, 'I don't want you here blah blah. . . .' Maybe they would, I don't know. I don't know everybody fully." This lack of trust and the avoidance patterns exhibited by participants make the formation of ties more difficult. This avoidance has been directly associated with poor integration and incorporation.[33]

Fear of deportation has led those vulnerable to it to feel they cannot trust their neighbors or even friends. Beyond being able to form social and more intimate personal relationships, trust is a key component for accepting social support from providers. Smalls explains that trust in "the intentions, the competence, and the expectations" of a provider is necessary in order to accept such services.[34] This theme brings us back to Polly. Polly's fear of being deported makes her doubt the legitimacy of the police. When asked if she would call the police in case of an emergency, she doubts she would do so: "Depends on what emergency. . . . If it is something I can resolve, maybe not. Because, the first, almost always, the first thing they do is ask—I do not give my ID to anyone." Polly's fear of being deported and the resulting distrust of the police are understandable and common among undocumented immigrants. As demonstrated in Stacy's and Amanda's reflections, the punitive nature of U.S. immigration policies does not ease a documented person's vulnerability to deportation. Thus, while Polly is a legal permanent resident, her fear of deportation is so great that for her, calling the police might expose her to a situation in which she would have to disclose that she is not a citizen. Her vulnerability to deportation and the fear resulting from it lead her to distrust the police, and this distrust extends to the point that she would think twice before calling the police in case of an emergency.

Lack of trust coupled with the above avoidance patterns can lead immigrants to isolate themselves, which results in self-segregation. A study on Latino immigrants' renegotiation of place and belongingness in a small town found that the segregated spatial negotiations of place stifled the development of a sense of belonging.[35] As previously noted, a similar negotiation of space by several of the participants was observed in this study.

It became apparent that the complexity brought on by the experience of being vulnerable to, and fearful of, deportation also influenced the nature of their social network and how they developed social ties. For example, Claire—an undocumented immigrant who had been living in the United States for twenty-one years at the time of the interview—said, "It still affected how I interacted with other people personally. Like I was always very friendly in high school, but I think there's definitely barriers that I had built in how close I would allow people to my life." For these participants, the trust necessary to form close relationships in their communities appeared inhibited, resulting in a form of compartmentalization of interactions, which led to isolation and a form of segregation. A recurring theme in participant responses is that the vulnerability to deportation and the fear associated with it lead to perceptions and behaviors that are also indications that participants are experiencing violence—in this case, *legal violence.*

Legal violence is an emerging concept and framework that builds on structural and symbolic violence and refers to the state-sanctioned harm perpetuated against immigrants via harsh immigration laws and policies. It refers to the hostile environment created and promoted when the government passes and implements laws and policies that cause physical, psychological, or emotional harm to individuals. Menjívar and Abrego found that both immigration enforcement—which they define as a broad mechanism that includes detention, deportation, raids, and traffic stops—and the fear of said immigration enforcement affect immigrants in three realms: (1) the family, (2) the workplace, and (3) schools. The fear of deportation, combined with the structural reality of legal violence, synergistically creates an environment that halts integration, not only on an individual level but also in terms of community cohesion.[36]

The term *legal violence* is not new. Robert Cover used the term to discuss how the law and its interpretation are used as a tool in the "organized social practice of violence."[37] Cover's use of the term *legal violence* refers to the direct forms of violence used by the state as a mechanism of social control by the government. Menjívar and Abrego differentiate their concept of legal violence in that "the analytical lens we use here looks beyond these more explicit and direct violent consequences of the law."[38]

This new framework of legal violence includes the notion of *structural violence*—defined by Galtung as "violence where there is no such actor . . . there may not be any person who directly harms another person in the structure."[39] Structural violence refers to an act of violence that is not attributable to one person, making the nature of the violence an indirect form. Forms of structural violence also include abuses found in the areas of policing and the situation of mass incarceration existing today in the United States.[40] In these cases, it is the state, its agents, and its policies that are the perpetrators of violence.

In addition to structural violence, the concept of legal violence is "mutually constitutive" with symbolic violence and refers to the normalization of violence, such that the targets become accustomed to their treatment and begin to accept it as standard, even justifiable.[41] The different forms of violence—inequality, racism, and other forms of class power, including those associated with structural violence—become internalized, and the targets of such abuses accept and in turn perpetuate their ill treatment, making them complicit in their domination. Pierre Bourdieu discusses the process as follows:

> When the dominated apply to what dominates them schemes that are the product of domination, or, to put it another way, when their thoughts and perceptions are structured in accordance with the very structures of the relation of domination that is imposed on them, their acts of *cognition* are, inevitably, acts of *recognition*, submission.[42]

Examples of this acceptance and internalization of violence appear in Chad's sentiments, in which he internalizes his position of not belonging. Chad believes that deportation is sometimes self-imposed because those who get caught and deported feel as though they can do as they wish, as if they were in their own country and not a foreign one. Another example was shared by Jack, an undocumented immigrant who at the time of the interview had been living in the United States for eleven years. While expressing his beliefs on why people get deported, Jack also expressed that deportations have justifiable reasons:

> Because I do not think they go and remove you for going to church or for playing sports or because you take guitar lessons. No, I think if that [deportation] happens [it is] because you are involved in a delicate situation. . . . And the other thing I have experienced or have seen is the stubbornness that exists within us to seek pleasure.

We see here Jack's belief that deportations are the result of the stubborn nature of those being removed, denoting that such removals are merited. This attitude reflects an internalization of the legal violence that deportation is deserved. The internalization of the oppression being inflicted by the state therefore becomes a form of self-harm.[43] This self-blame leads immigrants to express feelings of acceptance of their situation, after which they begin to "understand their marginalized positions as natural and can then become contributors to their own plight."[44]

Another example is when Polly agreed to plead guilty to a crime she did not commit in order to avoid deportation. This is a powerful example of legal violence being used against immigrant mothers and how such violence influences the decision-making process.[45] The fact that she was forced to make a decision that resulted in her having a criminal record demonstrates how legal violence frames the experience of immigrants and restricts their opportunities to change their legal status, putting their families in a further state of flux.

Ultimately, Menjívar and Abrego take their legal violence framework and circle back to integration: "The law can block access to society's goods and services that promote integration and success."[46] Their work seeks to "highlight especially the role of immigration laws in delimiting immigrants' short- and long-term integration experiences."[47] Thus, legal violence is another example of how the vulnerability to deportation—and the fear associated with it—is a barrier to integration.

The fear of deportation among my noncitizen immigrant subjects was prevalent, with a variety of effects stemming from this fear. One of the primary measures of successful integration is the level of social capital and other bonds that immigrants are able to form in the host country. Integral to these ties is the ability of immigrants to feel that they are welcome and belong in a host society. However, the vulnerability to deportation, and the fear associated with it, serves as a barrier to processes of integration. As a result, feelings of not belonging and not being able to take root lead immigrants to refrain from forming the trust and other social bonds that are the basis of social and civic engagement and that, in turn, lead to the formation of social capital. All the preceding examples demonstrate how deportation is a form of legal violence and a decisive barrier to integration.

However, there is another significant finding from the study: the fear and legal violence created by deportation persists across all legal statuses and cuts through time, space, and place, affecting both new- and long-term immigrants, cities with recent immigration flows, and older immigration settlement areas. As demonstrated by participant narratives, which were gathered in "immigrant-friendly" New York City, fear of deportation is not limited to new immigrants, nor to cities and regions experiencing newer waves of immigration flows. In addition, fear of deportation, legal violence, and the disruption of integration is not limited to regions with explicit anti-immigrant sentiments. Rather, said elements exist irrespective of how immigrant friendly a city might be considered.

In addition, my study looked at a variety of persons under different circumstances. Although the sample is a small fraction of the population in question, it should not be considered nonrepresentative. The fear, pain, anguish, and trauma expressed by my participants should not be minimized, as they reflect the experiences of those in the same vulnerable position among the 11.3 million undocumented immigrants and over 13 million legal permanent residents living in the United States.[48] It is clear that U.S. immigration policy is not only causing harm to individuals and their immediate families, but also causing wholesale damage to entire communities.

The relevance of the need for further research exploring the fear resulting from the vulnerability to deportation has become increasingly apparent given the recent presidential election, in which the winning candidate campaigned on charged anti-immigrant rhetoric, promises to build a wall to keep immigrants out, and vows to deport all undocumented immigrants living in the United States. Such rhetoric was hoped by many to have been experiencing a decline, with the previous administrations seeking and achieving incremental forms of immigration reform. Indeed, while this chapter discusses legal violence resulting from increasingly harsh deportation policies that led to the recent historic number of deportations, it is also true that the same administration enacted an executive action that gave relief to millions of undocumented immigrants who arrived in the United States as children. The push-pull that has previously characterized the nature of political platforms on immigration reform has now been decidedly usurped, with markedly punitive and exclusionary anti-immigration efforts.

Undoubtedly, there is a clear urgency for continued research on the impact of the vulnerability to deportation. Such studies would provide guidance to the political and private groups concerned with implementing policies that support and promote protection for the noncitizen immigrant population, and contribute to the ongoing efforts that address the continually tumultuous conditions promoted by recently enacted and proposed anti-immigration policies.

NOTES TO CHAPTER 10

1. Due to the nature of my study, all names are pseudonyms and no identifying information will be presented, including country of origin or any specific identifying elements regarding current place of residence.

2. All quotes are translated from Spanish.

3. The study this discussion is based on was not limited to the undocumented immigration population. Anyone living in the United States who is not a citizen, including legal residents, is vulnerable to deportation.

4. Cecilia Menjívar and Leisy Abrego, "Legal Violence in the Lives of Immigrants: How Immigration Enforcement Affects Families, Schools, and Workplaces," Center for American Progress, December 2012.

5. Nancy Foner and Patrick Simon, "Fear, Anxiety and National Identity: Immigration and Belonging in North America and Central Europe," in *Fear, Anxiety and National Identity*, ed. Nancy Foner and Patrick Simon (New York: Russell Sage, 2015).

6. Richard Alba and Nancy Foner, *Strangers No More* (Princeton: Princeton University Press, 2015); Richard Alba and Victor Nee, *Remaking the American Mainstream: Assimilation and Contemporary Immigration* (Cambridge: Harvard University Press, 2003); Rogers Brubaker, "The Return of Assimilation? Changing Perspectives on Immigration and Its Sequels in France, Germany and the United States," *Ethnic and Racial Studies* 24, no. 4 (2001): 531–548; Barry Edmonston and Jeffrey Passel, *Immigration and Ethnicity: The Integration of America's Arrivals* (Washington, D.C.: Urban Institute, 1994); Mark Ellis and Gunnar Almgrem, "Local Contexts of Immigrant and Second-Generation Integration in the United States," *Journal of Ethnic and Migration Studies* 35, no. 7 (2009): 1059–1076; Herbert Gans, "Toward a Reconciliation of 'Assimilation' and 'Pluralism': The Interplay of Acculturation and Ethnic Retention," *International Migration Review* 31, no. 4 (1997): 875–892; Alejandro Portes and Joszsef Borocz, "Contemporary Immigration: Theoretical Perspectives on Its Determinants and Modes of Incorporation," *International Migration Review* 23, no. 3 (1989): 606–630; Min Zhou, "Segmented Assimilation: Issues, Controversies, and Recent Research on the New Second Generation," in *The Handbook of International Migration*, ed. C. Hirschman, J. DeWind, and P. Kasinitz (New York: Russell Sage, 2001), 196–211.

7. Alba and Foner, *Strangers No More*, 5.

8. The assumed relationship between immigration and crime has been implicitly posited in criminological scholarship, most predominantly by social disorganization theory. See Clifford Shaw and Henry McKay, *Juvenile Delinquency and Urban Areas* (Chicago: University of Chicago Press, 1942). In the spirit of the Chicago school, Shaw and McKay sought to explain some of the contemporary changes found in urban spaces, specifically neighborhoods. According to social disorganization theory, community newcomers—particularly immigrants—contribute to a decreased ability of a community to exercise social control, which eventually leads to increased crime rates. There are other criminological theories that also imply a link between immigration and

crime, such as cultural deviance and social structure theories. See Robert Merton, "The Unintended Consequences of Purposive Social Action," *American Sociological Review* 6, no. 1 (1936): 894–904; Thorsten Sellin, *Culture Conflict and Crime* (New York: Social Science Research Council, 1938). Although all these theories bear relevance to the link between immigration and crime, social disorganization is still the dominant theory used to describe and explain this association.

9. Nicholas De Genova, "The Deportation Regime: Sovereignty, Space, and the Freedom of Movement," in *The Deportation Regime: Sovereignty, Space, and the Freedom of Movement,* ed. Nicholas De Genova and Nathalie Peutz (Durham: Duke University Press, 2010), 33–68.

10. Peter Brimelow, *Alien Nation: Common Sense About America's Immigration Disaster* (New York: Random House, 1995); Patrick Schnapp, "Identifying the Effect of Immigration and Homicide Rates in U.S. Cities: An Instrumental Variables Approach," *Homicide Studies* 19, no. 2 (2015): 103–122, doi:10.1177/1088767914528907.

11. Tanya Golash-Boza and Pierrette Hondagneu-Sotelo, "Latino Immigrant Men and the Deportation Crisis: A Gendered Racial Removal Program," *Latino Studies* 11, no. 3 (2009): 271–292 at 272.

12. Jacqueline Hagan, Brianna Castro, and Nestor Rodriguez, "The Effects of U.S. Deportation Policies on Immigrant Families and Communities: Cross-Border Perspectives," *North Carolina Law Review* 88 (2009): 1799–1824; Mark Hugo Lopez, Ana Gonzalez-Barrera, and Seth Motel, "As Deportations Rise to Record Levels, Most Latinos Oppose Obama's Policy," Pew Hispanic Center, December 28, 2011, http://www.pewhispanic.org/2011/12/28/as-deportations-rise-to-record-levels-most-latinos-oppose-obamas-policy/; Juan Manuel Pedroza, "Removal Roulette: Secure Communities and Immigration," in *Outside Justice: Immigration and the Criminalizing Impact of Changing Policy and Practice,* ed. David C. Brotherton, Daniel L. Stageman, and Shirley P. Leyro (New York: Springer, 2013).

13. María Vélez and Christopher Lyons, "Situating the Immigration and Neighborhood Crime Relationship Across Multiple Cities," in *Punishing Immigrants: Policy, Politics, and Injustice,* ed. Charis E. Kubrin, Marjorie S. Zatz, and Ramiro Martínez Jr. (New York: NYU Press, 2012); Matthew T. Lee and Ramiro Martínez Jr., "Immigration Reduces Crime: An Emerging Scholarly Consensus," in *Immigration, Crime and Justice,* ed. William F. McDonald (Bingley: Emerald, 2009), 3–16; Matthew Lee, Ramiro Martínez Jr., and R. Rosenfeld, "Does Immigration Increase Homicide? Negative Evidence from Three Border Cities," *Sociological Quarterly* 42 (2001): 559–580; Ramiro Martínez Jr., *Latino Homicide: Immigration, Violence and Community* (New York: Routledge, 2002); Robert Sampson, "Rethinking Crime and Immigration," *Contexts* 7 (2008): 28–33; Jacob Stowell, Steven Messner, Kelly McGeever, and Lawrence Raffalovich, "Immigration and the Recent Crime Drop in the U.S.: A Pooled, Cross-Sectional Time-Series Analysis of Metropolitan Areas," *Criminology* 47 (2009): 889–928.

14. Jacqueline Hagan, Ron Levi, and Ronit Dinovitzer, "The Symbolic Violence of the Crime-Immigration Nexus: Migrant Mythologies in the Americas," *Criminology and Public Policy* 7, no. 1 (2008): 95–112 at 100 (emphasis in original).

15. David Brotherton and Luis Barrios, *Banished from the Homeland* (New York: Columbia University Press, 2009); Corina Graif and Robert Sampson, "Spatial Heterogeneity in the Effects of Immigration and Diversity on Neighborhood Homicide Rates," *Homicide Studies* 13, no. 3 (2009): 242–260; Graham Ousey and Charis Kubrin, "Exploring the Connection Between Immigration and Violent Crime Rates in U.S. Cities, 1980–2000, *Social Problems* 56, no. 3 (2009): 447–473; Alejandro Portes and Alex Stepick, *City on the Edge: The Transformation of Miami* (Los Angeles: University of California Press, 1993); Robert Sampson, Jeffrey Morenoff, and Thomas Gannon-Rowley, "Assessing 'Neighborhood Effects': Social Processes and New Directions in Research," *Annual Review of Sociology* 28 (2002): 4343–4478, doi:28.110601. 141114.

16. My usage of "deportability" differs from that of De Genova, who uses the term only in connection to persons who are undocumented. Nicholas De Genova, "Migrant 'Illegality' and Deportability in Everyday Life," *Annual Review of Anthropology* 31 (2002): 419–447.

17. New York City Department of City Planning, "The Newest New Yorkers: Characteristics of the City's Foreign Born Population," December 2013, http://www1.nyc.gov /site/planning/data-maps/nyc-population/newest-new-yorkers-2013.page. Thomas P. DiNapoli, "A Portrait of Immigrants in New York," November 2016, https://www.osc.state .ny.us/reports/immigration/immigration_2016.pdf.

18. Migration Policy Institute, "Profile of the Unauthorized Population in New York," 2014, http://www.migrationpolicy.org/data/unauthorized-immigrant-population /state/NY.

19. Philip Kasinitz, John Mollenkopf, and Mary Waters, *Becoming New Yorkers: Ethnographies of the New Second Generation* (New York: Russell Sage, 2004); Philip Kasinitz, John Mollenkopf, Mary Waters, and Jennifer Holdaway, *Inheriting the City: The Children of Immigrants Come of Age* (Cambridge: Harvard University Press; New York: Russell Sage, 2008).

20. Christina Boyle, "Mayor Bloomberg: New York Is Most Immigrant-Friendly City in the Country," *New York Daily News*, April 25, 2012.

21. NYC Department of City Planning, *Newest New Yorkers*.

22. NY School of Law, Immigrant Defense Project and Families for Freedom, "Insecure Communities, Devastated Families: New Data on Immigrant Detention and Deportation Practices in New York City," July 13, 2012, http://immigrantdefenseproject .org/wp-content/uploads/2012/07/NYC-FOIA-Report-2012-FINAL.pdf.

23. City of New York, "Municipal ID," NYC Rules, last modified March 10, 2016, http://rules.cityofnewyork.us/tags/municipal-id.

24. Nancy Morawetz and Alina Das, "Legal Issues in Local Police Enforcement of Federal Immigration Law," in *The Role of Local Police: Striking a Balance Between Immigration Enforcement and Civil Liberties*, ed. Anita Khashu (Washington, D.C.: Police Foundation, 2009), appendix B, 69–90.

25. Mary Odem, "Our Lady of Guadalupe in the New South: Latino Immigrants and the Politics of Integration in the Catholic Church," *Journal of American Ethnic History* 24, no. 1 (2004): 25–57.

26. Grant Schellenberg, "Perceptions of Canadians: A Sense of Belonging, Confidence, and Trust," *Canadian Social Trends* 28 (2004): 443–478; Henry Chow, "Sense of Belonging and Life Satisfaction Among Hong Kong Adolescent Immigrants in Canada," *Journal of Ethnic and Migration Studies* 33, no. 3 (2007): 511–520; Jeffrey Reitz and Rupa Banerjee, "Racial Inequality, Social Cohesion, and Policy Issues in Canada," in *Belonging? Diversity, Recognition, and Shared Citizenship in Canada*, ed. Keith Banting, Thomas J. Courchene, and F. Leslie Seidle (Montreal: PQ, 2005), 498–545; Zheng Wu, Christophe Schimmele, and Feng Hou, "Self-Perceived Integration of Immigrants and Their Children," *Canadian Journal of Sociology* 37, no. 4 (2012): 381–408.

27. Schellenberg, "Perceptions of Canadians."

28. Catherine Dauvergne, *Making People Illegal: What Globalization Means for Migration and Law* (Cambridge: Cambridge University Press, 2007).

29. Chow, "Sense of Belonging and Life Satisfaction"; Reitz and Banerjee, "Racial Inequality, Social Cohesion"; Wu, Schimmele, and Hou, "Self-Perceived Integration."

30. Mario Smalls, *Unanticipated Gains: The Origin of Network Inequality in Everyday Life* (New York: Oxford University Press, 2009).

31. Min Zhou and Mingang Lin, "Community Transformation and the Formation of Ethnic Capital: The Case of Immigrant Chinese Communities in the United States," *Journal of Chinese Overseas* 1, no. 2 (2005): 260–284.

32. Deborah Schildkraut, *Americanism in the Twenty-First Century: Public Opinion in the Age of Immigration* (New York: Cambridge University Press, 2015).

33. Smalls, *Unanticipated Gains.*

34. Ibid., 104.

35. Lise Nelson and Nancy Hiemstra, "Latino Immigrants and the Renegotiation of Place and Belonging in Small Town America," *Social and Cultural Geography* 9, no. 3 (2008): 319–342.

36. Cecilia Menjívar and Leisy Abrego, "Legal Violence in the Lives of Immigrants: How Immigration Enforcement Affects Families, Schools, and Workplaces," Center for American Progress, December 2012, https://cdn.americanprogress.org/wp-content /uploads/2012/12/MenjivarLegalViolenceReport.pdf.

37. Robert Cover, "Violence and the Word," *Yale Law Journal* 95, no. 8 (1986): 1601.

38. Cecilia Menjívar and Leisy J. Abrego, "Legal Violence: Immigration Law and the Lives of Central American Immigrants," *American Journal of Sociology* 117, no. 5 (2012): 1380–1421.

39. Johan Galtung, "Violence, Peace, and Peace Research," *Journal of Peace Research* 6, no. 3 (1969): 170–181.

40. David Jacobs, "The Determinants of Deadly Force: A Structural Analysis of Police Violence," *American Journal of Sociology* 103, no. 4 (1998): 837–862; Anya Sarang, Tim Rhoades, Nicholas Sheon, and Kimberly Page, "Policing Drug Users in Russia: Risk, Fear, and Structural Violence," *Substance Use and Misuse* 45, no. 10 (2009): 813–864; Phil Scratton and Jude McCulloch, eds. *The Violence of Incarceration* (New York: Routledge, 2009).

41. Menjívar and Abrego, "Legal Violence."

42. Pierre Bourdieu, *Masculine Domination* (Stanford: Stanford University Press, 1998), 13.

43. This process of internalization can also be linked to Fanon's notion of the processes of colonization and the development of an inferiority complex among the colonized people, who are separated by their individuality and culture. In this case, the colonization would be symbolic as well, as the immigrant comes to the United States with ideas of a better life, which are a product of U.S. imperialism and colonization. Their subsequent mistreatment and eventual acceptance of the increased forms of social control leads to what Fanon describes as an oppressed people, "in whose soul an inferiority complex has taken root, whose local cultural originality has been committed to the grave." Franz Fanon, *Black Skin, White Masks* (New York: Grove, 1967), 2.

44. Menjívar and Abrego, "Legal Violence," 1386.

45. Leisy Abrego and Cecilia Menjívar, "Immigrant Latina Mothers as Targets of Legal Violence," *International Journal of Sociology of the Family* 37, no. 1 (2011): 9–26.

46. Menjívar and Abrego, "Legal Violence," 1385.

47. Ibid., 1416.

48. Bryan Baker and Nancy Rytina, *Estimates of the Lawful Permanent Resident Population Living in the United States: January 2013* (Washington, D.C.: DHS, 2014); Jens Krogstad and Jeffrey Passel, "5 Facts About Illegal Immigration in the U.S.," Pew Research Center, November 19, 2015, http://www.pewresearch.org/fact-tank/2015/11/19/5-facts-about-illegal-immigration-in-the-u-s/.

11. DEPORTED TO TIJUANA

Social Networks and Religious Communities

MARÍA DOLORES PARÍS POMBO, EL COLEGIO DE LA FRONTERA NORTE
GABRIEL PÉREZ DUPEROU, EL COLEGIO DE LA FRONTERA NORTE

Omar was born in Guadalajara, Jalisco, in 1980. When he was only forty-five days old, his mother brought him to the United States. He was never registered, and he never returned to Mexico during the thirty years he lived in California. His parents are U.S. residents; his siblings, his children, and his wife are U.S. citizens. Until his adolescence, he thought he was a U.S. citizen. It was only when he began to have run-ins with the law that he discovered he was not. In September 2010, he was detained and deported for not presenting himself for his immigration court hearing.

Before a judge ordered his deportation, Omar had a family, had a job, and was actively involved in his neighborhood. As a tow-truck operator, he worked with the AAA club and did contract work for the California Highway Patrol. He collaborated with the Santa Ana Police Department on a Christian grassroots program aimed at rescuing youths involved in gang activity. He had a driver's license, a social security card, and a work permit; he paid his taxes and supported his children.

When they think back to the deportation, Omar and his wife, Diana, repeat the word "nightmare." On that day, officers came to detain him at his workplace, removed him from the country, and sent him to Tijuana. He did not know anyone in Mexico, did not speak Spanish well, and did not have a single document of identification; for the first time in his life, he felt like a total stranger. The first few nights, he stayed at the Casa del Migrante (Migrant's House) shelter with many other deportees, all sharing similar experiences. He felt devastated, uprooted, and severed from his most significant ties: those to his wife, mother, and children.

Diana was extremely worried about crossing the border because of all the news about the violence and insecurity in Tijuana. Her sister's mother-in-law had family in the city, and they accompanied her. After finding Omar, these distant relatives gave him a place to live at their house. Diana remained in Orange County to take care of the family, and she would go down to visit on the weekends. Omar started to work at a Christian church, where despite not being paid, he received spiritual support and gained knowledge about Tijuana. This was of great value in informing his next decisions.

After nine months, the couple rented a house in Tijuana. Omar found New Life Church Tijuana. He joined Bible-study sessions and classes, went to Sunday services, and supported congregational activities. Facing obstacles in acquiring his birth certificate and the low wages in Mexico, the couple decided that Diana should work in the United States and that Omar should dedicate himself to the church.

A year after his deportation, the couple decided that their two children should go live with him in Tijuana. So while his wife worked from Monday to Thursday, taking on overtime to increase her income, Omar would be in charge of the children's education through homeschooling. In 2013, the religious leaders of New Life Church asked Omar to assume the leadership of a project of discipleship for men with a history of addiction and family problems. Initially his wife was skeptical about moving to Mexico, but she finally decided to leave her job in Orange County to reunite with Omar and their children and to participate in missionary work.

As of 2016, three years have passed since Omar was placed in charge of this program. The family's social capital, generated in the religious community, has been strengthened. Omar has been able to obtain his birth certificate and identification card. He would like to obtain a visa to cross the border and visit the rest of his family. He and his wife worry about the future of their children's education, and the oldest one has expressed a desire to return to California for high school.

According to Hagan, Leal, and Rodriguez, deportations have separated more than a million families, severely affecting the social ties of spouses and children remaining in the United States.[1] The authors indicate that one of the least-studied effects has been the decrease of social capital in immigrant and Latino communities. Because many of the deported immigrants had lived for such a long time in the United States, they were embedded in family and workplace networks. A generalized fear of raids has resulted in immigrants not going to places such as churches, schools, and hospitals. Likewise, immigration enforcement deters civic and community mobilization, such as participation in unions and religious activities.

In places of forced return or relocation, deportees usually face solitude, depression, and emotional distress due to feelings of loss and abandonment.[2] In one study on deportees in San Salvador, Dingeman-Cerda and Coutin found that despite the legal rhetoric used in the United States, which presents deportation as a return to one's homeland, for many Salvadorans, deportation resembles something akin to exile: "This sense of exile is often reinforced by the reactions of fellow citizens in their countries of origin, who perceive and treat deportees as outsiders, foreigners, and/or violent criminals threatening state security."[3] In the same vein, Kanstroom speaks aptly of "the U.S. deportation diaspora," which consists of "a forcibly uprooted population of people with deep, cohesive social and cultural connections to each other and to the nation-state from which they have been involuntarily removed."[4]

This study analyzes the possible recovery or reconstruction of family and social ties after deportation to Tijuana, Mexico. It describes the role of religious organizations and congregations in providing stability and a social network to deported migrants who decide to settle in this city. It emphasizes how congregations not only constitute a social infrastructure that links deportees to local institutions but also help them and their families cope with economic and emotional hardship. We deal with the role of two Catholic organizations that have traditionally given emergency support to migrants and the poor in Tijuana: the Casa del Migrante and the Desayunador del Padre Chava (Father Chava's Dining Hall). We also study the response of an evangelical congregation (New Life Church Tijuana). We raise the following questions: What kind of social or cultural resources are necessary for deportees to build new networks in Tijuana? How do religious organizations and congregations help buffer migrants against the disruption and isolation caused by their forced return or relocation to this city?

The research on religion and immigration has been principally focused on the processes of adaptation in places of destination. It has been argued that religion can play a major role for immigrants as a bridge to inclusion in their new society, providing a sense of belonging and participation, as well as a familiar cultural environment where immigrants can form new networks and make friends.[5] Religious institutions often provide migrants with a safe haven when they go through economic hardship or political persecution.[6]

As many of the deportees in Tijuana were forcibly expelled to a city that they did not consider theirs, it is likely that the process of social integration and reconstitution of networks might actually be similar to the one experienced by refugees or exiles. Religious congregations might then act as a safeguard, providing necessary ties for the most pragmatic of activities—such as searching for work or housing—in a place that is completely unknown and where there are no prior established networks. Additionally, they might be a space for the reconstruction of important and meaningful ties between family and friends.

DEPORTATION TO TIJUANA AND
FAMILY SEPARATION

Until the 1990s, Tijuana was the main border-crossing point into the United States.[7] The route through Tijuana was not only relatively easy but next to California, where the majority of the Mexican migrants were headed. It was also the main point of forced repatriation.[8] In the second half of the 1990s, the Instituto Nacional de Migracion (National Migration Institute) recorded between 300,000 and 450,000 repatriations each year.[9] Most migrants were apprehended by the border patrol and sent back to Mexico on several occasions before successfully entering the United States.

Since 1994, the border patrol's strategies of containment in the San Diego sector and the construction of the border wall led to Tijuana no longer being the main corridor of undocumented migration; the migratory flows were displaced toward the east. The legislative changes passed by the U.S. Congress in 1996, as well as the Patriot Act of 2002, prompted an increase in deportations and a change in the profile of individuals expelled to Tijuana.[10] This change began to be documented by social organizations, such as the Casa del Migrante. Between 2003 and 2010, the shelter recorded an increase each year in the number of men who had lived more than ten years in the United States and had close relatives there.[11]

París Pombo, Buenrostro, and Pérez Duperou found that migrants deported to Tijuana, in comparison with migrants deported to other cities, are older on average (thirty-seven years old vs. thirty-four), have lived longer in the United States, and are more likely to have children and a spouse in the United States.[12] Such characteristics reflect a long-term process of settlement and social integration of Mexican immigrants in California.

According to a survey on migration administered by El Colegio de la Frontera Norte (Colef), when they are forcibly sent to Tijuana, 38 percent of men and 55 percent of women say their intention is to stay in the city.[13] These decisions are informed by the surveillance of the border in the San Diego region, the social infrastructure for the immediate support of deportees, and the geographical proximity to California, where family and friends are established. Some deportees count on the economic and emotional support of relatives who stayed in the United States. Depending on the strength of these ties and on their immigration status, they can receive visits in Tijuana. But soon, resources are depleted and visits become more infrequent. In other cases, family separation and the weakening of ties precede the deportation; much of this is linked to periods of imprisonment and drug use.

Family disintegration and impoverishment often lead to destitution. This is particularly visible in the zone known as "El Bordo," situated along the canal of the Tijuana River. Over the years, this area has been home to between seven hundred and one thousand people living in extremely poor and unsanitary conditions in excavations, amid sewage, and under bridges. Another study conducted by Colef on the estimation and characterization of the resident population of this zone found that 91 percent had lived in the United States; of these, 92 percent had been deported and 8 percent had returned voluntarily. The overwhelming majority were men (96 percent). The authors of this study also found that the inhabitants of El Bordo were inhibited from entering the labor force because they had no identification documents. The absence of government programs for immediate relief and for long-term aid relegated them to perpetual reliance on civil society organizations. The authors concluded, "The feelings of pain arising from family separation after being deported to Mexico was the beginning of marginalization, which among other factors, included the use of drugs."[14]

As a vast majority of deportees (around 90 percent) are adult males, their removal usually leads to the loss of the principal family income. When their spouse and children live in the United States, it also leads to the forced formation of single-parent, female-headed households. Sometimes all family members will migrate to Mexico to reunite with the deported parent and spouse. More often, the deportee will try to reenter the United States, where he will have more economic opportunities to support his family, even being undocumented. With the door closed to an authorized return, his only chance to get back home is to resort to informal networks for an unauthorized crossing. He will probably have to incur high expenses, and he could put his life in danger. In addition, he will be at risk of new detentions and spending months or years in prison, accused of reentering without authorization. Imprisonment and a second deportation would deteriorate the financial situation of the family even more.

Many deported men speak about the unconditional support received from their mother, and sometimes their wife or ex-wife, in the postdeportation crisis. In the interviews, they emphasize the contrast between the desertion of their friends and the strengthening of the bonds with their mother or partner. On the one hand, their gang *compañeros* and coworkers stop answering their calls, ignoring their pleas for assistance. On the other hand, despite the immediate physical separation from their family and periods of imprisonment, the bond with their mother is not broken. Instead, it is consolidated, as the mother helps with resources and emotional support. For example, David describes his arrival and his mother's appearance at "the line":

> I arrived at night. I remember I arrived to Mexico and they gave us all of our stuff. I do not remember well where we were, which part of the line. I remember only passing through the swing doors and being close to the *puente México*. As I left I remember walking and hearing my name. I turned around and it was my mother, my faithful mother. She said, "Son, I was behind your bus and I knew it was your bus." After that we went to her car and fell asleep in the car.

In other cases, it is the wife who crosses the border to immediately assist or even stay to live with her husband. This is what happened with Octavio. When he was deported in 2013, after having lived in Santa Ana, California, for eighteen years, the hardest thing for him was to see his wife waiting for him in Tijuana.

> To see her when they deported me, that same day, for me was very difficult. Something very hard. . . . I would speak to her from jail, and I would tell her not to wait, not to follow me. I'm going to a country where I don't know anyone. I have no future there. I don't know where I will be taken. I have nothing, and you have everything here.

His wife not only decided to move to Tijuana with their young children, but she also traveled several times to California to retrieve money owed to them and to sell their belongings.

Some deportees also mention receiving visits from family members—especially their children—in the first moments after deportation. Over time, these visits become less frequent. In many cases, deportation implies a long-term separation, and sometimes even a definite family breakdown, leading to greater social exclusion.

EMERGENCY HELP IN THE POSTDEPORTATION PHASE

Tijuana has dozens of organizations dedicated to helping and defending migrants. Most of them were formed during the migration flows prompted by IRCA (the Immigration Reform and Control Act of 1986) and during the strengthening of border control in the 1990s. In 1987, the Scalabrini religious community founded the Casa del Migrante in Tijuana to attend to a large number of men and women from Mexico and Central America who were arriving to cross the border into the United States.[15] In 1990, the Casa YMCA, a shelter for young migrants, was established. In 1994, Scalabrini nuns finished building the Instituto Madre Asunta (Mother Asunta Institute), a home for migrant women and children located close to the Casa del Migrante.

Currently, many deportees and migrants in transit find temporary shelter in Tijuana while planning to cross the border or while recuperating from deportation and deciding their immediate future. Velasco and Coubès calculated that the shelters for migrants house approximately one thousand people each day.[16] Both private and public institutions provide assistance with housing and food, some of them charging two dollars a day. These services offer a certain stability to the deportees. In many cases, the shelters also serve as a way for deportees to access help through public programs that would otherwise be inaccessible given their vulnerability and unfamiliarity with the city of Tijuana.[17]

For the men who are deported and do not immediately return to their home communities, the Casa del Migrante is often the first stop in Tijuana. Aside from lodging, this shelter serves two daily meals and offers other complimentary services, such as phone, Internet, bathrooms, and clothing. It also offers medical, legal, and psychological assistance. Since 2009, deportees have made up the majority of the boarders.

Another organization that serves hundreds of deportees each day is the Desayunador del Padre Chava. This project of the Salesian congregation in Tijuana was originally conceived to give a complete meal once a day to the poor and homeless.[18] It was founded in 1999 in a borrowed warehouse located in downtown Tijuana. In 2009, the organization acquired a piece of land close to El Bordo. There, the Salesians built a shelter with a kitchen, a dining room, a dormitory, bathrooms, and a living room. Currently, the project is run with the work of nearly forty volunteers, and it serves about a thousand people every day. According to a study conducted by Colef, 70 percent of those served by this community kitchen have been deported at some time, and on average, these individuals lived in the United States for around seventeen years. While the Casa del Migrante serves men who were recently deported, the Desayunador receives poor and homeless men and women, most of whom were deported months or years ago, with the majority (55 percent) suffering from problems with addiction.[19]

With the goal of providing an opportunity for deportees to gather social and material resources to settle in Tijuana, the Casa del Migrante has prolonged the time migrants can stay in the shelter to a month and a half. It has also launched a comprehensive job placement program. The program consists of helping deportees obtain a birth certificate and a voting registration card, which in Mexico serves as the main document of identification. According to the director of the program, in 2015 more than 450 jobs were provided in factories, construction, and call centers. Nevertheless, these are mainly precarious and low-wage jobs. Many of the returnees abandon them as soon as they are ready to cross the border again or when they become discouraged by the meager salary.

The Desayunador has also promoted a similar program. Since 2015, it has given shelter to around thirty interns with the aim of securing them employment, allowing them to save money to eventually rent their own apartments. These individuals do not have a time limit on when they must leave the shelter. Furthermore, an area of the Desayunador is currently dedicated to teaching computing, and many deportees participate in workshops in a technical school. Despite these services, the director of the Desayunador still regrets the very limited gains those being helped have made in employment. Many of the deportees lose their jobs because of problems with addiction or because they suffer from emotional distress owing to their solitude and family separation. Others try to reenter the United States.

The strength of Catholic organizations such as the Desayunador and the Casa del Migrante comes from their providing emergency assistance to deportees, which buffers the trauma of deportation. We might even consider that these organizations supplement public repatriation programs, which have limitations and inconsistencies. Nonetheless, the social organizations provide few opportunities for forming social networks. Indeed, in the temporary shelters and in the community kitchens, hundreds of migrants and deportees come together under extremely precarious conditions. They are separated from their families, and the majority lack social ties in Mexico.

The great diversity of migratory, educational, religious, and political experiences of the deportees receiving help from these organizations can be a hindrance to the formation of a sense of belonging and identity. Interviews with priests give an account of how difficult it is to do pastoral work in these shelters. The majority of the deportees converted to different religions or cults in the United States, including "*la Santa Muerte*" (the Holy Death), Islam, and above all various Protestant Christian denominations. The director of the Desayunador considers the greatest obstacles to the work of catechesis to be addiction, family disintegration, and the "deep psychological wounds" suffered by deportees.

LONG-TERM HELP AND RELIGIOUS NETWORK: THE CASE OF NEW LIFE CHURCH TIJUANA

While the Catholic organizations discussed in the previous section have the mission of assisting migrants and the most vulnerable, the Protestant Christian churches provide a favorable social and cultural environment in which deportees can recover a sense of belonging and participation. While the pastor of New Life Church Tijuana did not specify the church's mission as providing material help for deportees, nearly twenty families in this congregation have at least one person who was removed from the United States.

New Life Church Tijuana belongs to an Evangelical movement that began in California, then expanded into various cities in the United States and Latin America during the second half of the twentieth century. The pastor who founded and directs the church in Tijuana arrived twenty years ago from the United States with a group of missionaries, who began working in one of the poorest neighborhoods of this border city. There, they constructed their first church. Eventually they spread and built another church downtown, as well as in other cities in Mexico. They also acquired a ranch in the municipality of Ensenada, where they currently run a spiritual retreat program. Despite not considering it to be a rehabilitation center, the ranch mainly receives recovering addicts, almost all of them deportees.

The congregation consists of around fifty families, all with mixed immigration and citizenship status. Most women were born in the United States or became citizens. Many children and adolescents in the congregation were born in the United States and typically speak English. Only one of the women was deported. She is a single mother whose children stayed with relatives in California when she was repatriated; a few months later, the children were reunited with her in Tijuana.

On weekends, visiting church members often come to New Life Church Tijuana from New Life Church churches in California, especially from the area surrounding Los Angeles. These churches perform cross-border activities with a missionary approach and provide help to communities in Mexico. Thus, religious groups come from California to help build rooms for the church in Tijuana, remodel its atrium, teach biblical interpretation, conduct conferences for youths, and donate food and clothes. Religious services are presented bilingually twice a week. Celebrations and parties, especially those held with the members from California, are also bilingual.

The deportees who attend this church arrived through diverse paths. Some of them belonged to a sister church in California, and when they were deported, they went straight to New Life Church Tijuana in search of material and emotional support. Others converted when they were in jails, prisons, or detention centers in the United States. Some were referred to the pastor and called him after being deported to Tijuana. Finally, many searched for weeks or months for a Christian church where they would feel warmly accepted and, after having tried other congregations, chose New Life Church Tijuana. The church has rooms where it can lodge four men for up to nine months while they search for work to pay for their own place. During those months they are given food and a small stipend. In exchange, they perform maintenance work in the church and participate in biblical studies.

In interviews, deportees and their wives said that they found two fundamental factors for their emotional well-being in this congregation: a new family and a religious purpose. In addition to the church's celebrations and services, about ten families regularly come together for celebrations, barbecues, and holidays such as Thanksgiving. As expressed by Cynthia, the wife of a deportee: "In the church we have found brothers, and it is like a great family because we finally have people to hang out with." In some cases, they consider this new family to be much more united and harmonious than the one they left in the United States. In the congregation, they naturally find a support group. They can identify with many of the families because of shared experiences of deportation and the process of religious conversion.

In contrast to those who go to the Desayunador, many deportees have the economic resources to support themselves in Tijuana. Some of them might have kept a business or have savings in the United States. Others may benefit from a wife "working on the other side." Moreover, with the support of the church and its regular members, the families of the deportees have access to an institutionalized network made up of permanent ties and important material resources. In other words, they have the social capital necessary for settlement in Tijuana.

Through our interviews, we also found that religious faith has allowed for the imputation of meaning into the deportation process. Several deportees declared that they have no intention of returning to the United States, even if the opportunity presents itself. In the words of Carlos: "I don't think I would return to where I grew up. In the *barrio* there is evil, so why would I return there? Now I know that I am with the Lord here and I already know Him."

The church provides multiple opportunities to participate in the religious community. Worshippers get involved in evangelization ministries, visiting the sick in hospices and shelters, feeding the homeless, and biblical studies. Thus, they strengthen their bonds within the communities and proselytize. Omar, whose story is narrated in the introduction, is currently the church's ranch manager in Ensenada. Other deportees have left to construct new churches in various regions of Mexico. This intense level of participation allows them to feel that they belong to a very active community with a collective purpose. In addition, the church has also established civic ties with Tijuana's broader society. For example, with the involvement of a church member who works in the local police department, it has promoted a training program for chaplains.

The deportees repeatedly express that in their congregation they have been able to "connect" with their brothers in faith, with their families, and with God. Luis states, "Being away (from the place where I was raised) has allowed me to focus on my family which is my wife, my daughter and God. It helps me be connected, and be more centered. There I was more disorganized, exposed to things that are not good for anyone."

The number of deportees and their families integrating into the congregation of New Life Church is very low compared to migrants receiving help in Catholic organizations or deportees in severe conditions of exclusion in Tijuana. An array of factors—criminalization, structural violence, harassment by the police, lack of identity documents, and limited help provided by public institutions—usually lead many deportees to precarity and addictions.

TRANSBORDER FAMILIES

Many deportees who attend New Life Church have been reunited with their wives and children or have formed new families in Mexico. From an economic and emotional standpoint, women provide the strategic assistance for social inclusion and settlement. For example, many of them regularly cross to California to buy secondhand goods to subsequently sell in Tijuana's swap meets. Other women commute to work in San Diego. While deportees stay "trapped on the border," their families find themselves forced to develop a cross-border life.[20]

Carolina illuminates this situation. In 2013, her husband, Luis, was deported. After three months, he tried to reenter without authorization and was detained for a year before being deported again. The second time, Carolina arrived in Tijuana with her baby, waiting for her deported husband at the border. Although he had never returned to Mexico before being deported, she had occasionally made trips to Tijuana and Rosarito during her childhood and adolescence. Because of this, she thought that her help could be key for facilitating his navigation through basic aspects of life in Mexico. "For me," she says, "it was like, I have to be with him—to more or less show him, 'oh, this is how you use pesos, this is how we exchange money.' And, for him, everything was completely new. He—his mother brought him when he was five, so he doesn't remember anything."

During her first year of residence in Tijuana, Carolina would regularly cross the border to San Diego to study to become a medical assistant. Now she works there four days a week in a clinic for the elderly. To make it to work on time, she has to leave their house at 4 a.m., and returns at 7 p.m. Meanwhile, Luis is in charge of taking their daughter to school and picking her up. Once a month, Carolina travels to Orange County with her daughter to visit her parents, siblings, uncles, and aunts.

These transborder lives result from the difficulty in attaining a well-paid job in Tijuana. In addition to the emotional and cultural shock when they are expelled to Mexico, deportees are hit by the economic impact arising from the wage gap between the United States and Mexico. To deal with this situation, women have to keep their jobs in California or find one that permits them to cross daily, earning a better salary than those offered in Tijuana.

This is the case of Carlos, who was deported from Los Angeles in 2012 after having lived there for thirty years. During the three years following his deportation, his wife would periodically cross the border so they could see each other. After that, she moved to Tijuana with their two children so that they could be reunited with him. The working conditions and the low salaries meant that the family had to depend on her earnings. She would cross the border daily to work as a nurse in San Diego. Meanwhile, he would stay at home to homeschool the children.

The change in responsibilities transforms the family structure and gender roles. Octavio expresses it succinctly: "I practically became the woman; I was the one who would take care of the kids, wake them up early, make them do their homework on the computer, while she goes to work and makes us dinner." It should be noted that this change of roles does not necessarily mean that men end up being in charge of the housework; this situation places a great burden on the women, frequently resulting in physical exhaustion.

For children, family reunification in Tijuana breaks their school routine. They have to move away from friends and cousins they grew up with. Enrollment in Tijuana's schools is complicated—in many cases impossible—because of the documentation that the school authorities require. Also, many students say they have problems integrating because of social stigmas and language differences. Among our subjects, all of the children were studying in the United States when their parent was deported. In some of the families, children were enrolled in a school in San Diego after reuniting with their father in Tijuana, and their mother would cross the border with them every day. Nevertheless, their wait time at the border was exhausting and had a negative impact in their performance at school. In the case of New Life Church Tijuana, the majority of the children are homeschooled. This means that the only time they have for socializing with others is at the church.

Parents thus become the teachers of their children and are made responsible for their educational advancement. As Octavio explains, "So you have to see that they're doing the work and then you grade them." Diana thus confirms, "We are not teachers, and I would say to Omar, 'How would we teach them if we don't have any preparation to give classes to our children?'"

When the children are adolescents, they often insist on returning to the United States for high school. In some cases, family members who live there offer to take the youths in so that they can study in California and have access to the opportunities offered by their U.S. citizenship. In other cases, parents are reluctant to have their children leave home so young. Finally, several young people have returned to work in the United States, often with the help of their "brothers in faith."

EXPULSIONS AND THE LOSS OF RESOURCES

As most deportees are Latino males, Golash-Boza and Hondagneu-Sotelo refer to a "gendered and racial removal program."[21] The authors mention several associated factors: the war against terrorism, the great recession, and disappearing Latino men's jobs, particularly in construction and building trades. In a broader sense, these mass expulsions are related to neoliberal policies and a degrading of social welfare.[22] The shrinking economic spaces in the United States have thrown many immigrant males out of work and excluded complete families from basic services and goods. This surplus population may also be expelled from the country and forcibly relocated in Third World cities.

Mass deportations have forced the formation of many single-mother households in the United States, making them especially vulnerable to deep poverty.[23] When the family is reunited in Mexico, local socioeconomic conditions—especially the wage gap between the United States and Mexico—are obstacles for economic reintegration.

Mothers' deportation leads to even deeper family crisis and a massive loss of resources for children.[24] Only one member of New Life Church, Mariana, is a deported woman and a single mother. After reuniting with her four children in Tijuana in 2011, she found a job in a maquiladora, where she earned less than $350 a month. In 2016, she was hired by a call center and now works overtime to make ends meet. As her children are homeschooled, the church is their only space of recreation and socialization: "Wednesdays and Sundays are for the church, and sometimes I have also to work on Sundays. Believe it or not, those days I begin at four in the morning and I finish at noon, and those days I go directly to the church. A friend picks my children up and drives them to the church. During the service, I suddenly feel that I am falling asleep."

In an illustrative study on the limits and weakening of networks among Salvadoran immigrants in the United States, Cecilia Menjívar shows that "social networks, particularly those based on kinship, are not infallible and can weaken under extreme conditions of poverty, when too many demands are placed on individuals."[25] She brings to our attention what she calls "structures of opportunity"—the ensemble of structural forces together with the set of resources shared by the particular community. Often coming from poor and divided families, some of them with instances of domestic violence, many deportees depend on a weak structure of opportunity. If they rely on family ties to survive, these become weakened very fast.

In the same vein, Pierre Bourdieu cautions that social capital should be related not only to the density of ties within a network but also—and for the most part—to the quantity of material and symbolic resources available in the network.[26] In this sense, the basic characteristic of social capital—just like any other form of capital, according to the French sociologist—is its convertibility into economic capital. Social capital is based on the totality of resources that the network comprises in its ensemble, and it works as a support for the individuals who belong to the network. In other words, it makes them creditworthy (or not).

New Life Church allows deportees and their families to access a dense and enduring social network that holds important material and symbolic resources. In spite of this, we observed few bridges being constructed between local institutions, employers, and Tijuana's society more broadly. This "closure" hinders access to other types of indispensable resources for social integration. We identified an absence of weak ties (which sociological research has shown is beneficial for integration) that could facilitate deportees' insertion into more diverse labor and educational networks.[27] Their employment opportunities remain limited by the information they exchange within the religious community, and the mutual support between "Christian brothers." Some deportees work temporarily in remodeling the church. Several end up in precarious low-wage jobs because the social capital within the Christian community is not sufficiently bridged with that of the broader civil society.

Family reunification in Tijuana does not mean a break in ties and commitment with relatives remaining in California. In fact, one of the reasons for staying in Tijuana is the proximity of the border. While the men who were deported get trapped in Tijuana, their wives and children develop an intense transborder life, working, visiting family members, vacationing, studying, and assisting sister churches in the United States.

In this sense, deportees' families share some features of the "transnational communities" described and analyzed by multiple scholars since the 1990s. For instance, Basch, Schiller, and Blanc define "transnationalism" as "the processes by which immigrants forge and sustain multistranded social relations that link together their societies of origin and settlement."[28] Peggy Levitt considers that "transmigrants" of Miraflores (Dominican Republic) are "integrated, to varying degrees, into the countries that receive them, at the same time that they remain connected to the countries that they leave behind."[29] As the so-called "transmigrants," deportees keep and even cherish their language, cultural, and religious links to the communities where they grew up. Interestingly, the congregation of New Life Church Tijuana forges such links to California, in the same way that some small and homogeneous churches in the United States symbolically link immigrants to their countries of origin.[30]

However, transnationalism emphasizes the agency and the capacity of migrants to defy state power. From this point of view, physical borders and national boundaries seem to lose relevance. Transmigrants are able to control their movements into and through the borders, contest boundaries, and control their identity.[31] In contrast, deportees in Tijuana are confined to one side of the border. Their movements are constrained by the physicality of the border and by punitive migratory policies. Forced to a place they do not perceive as theirs, deportees express a sense of banishment.[32] Therefore, they resemble more of a diaspora than a transnational community.[33]

According to Kanstroom, "parental deportation can be devastating for children (many of whom are U.S. citizens) who remain in the United States. Such children often must grow up in a family broken by deportation or must move in with other relatives or friends if they wish to remain in the States. In addition, there is the less well-known phenomenon of children who are, in effect, *de facto*, deported along with their parents."[34]

In New Life Church Tijuana we observed that children who are reunited with their deported parents are uprooted from their family and social space. Their "de facto deportation" greatly limits their educational and employment opportunities.[35] It is likely that in the near future, the majority of reunited children—especially those who are U.S. citizens—will return to California to continue their studies or to find employment. To what extent will the return of children, forced to move to Mexico because of their parents' deportation, constitute a new "weak" citizenship, uprooted and greatly damaged by deportation policies?

After being deported to Tijuana, migrants who had been living in the United States for many years usually go through several phases. First, they suffer a shock and overwhelming feelings of total loss. They search for emergency help from social organizations and family networks. During the second phase, they try to cross back into the United States. The failed attempts at reentry, and the new detention periods, result in the progressive dismantling of social networks and chronic depression. This leads in the medium run to marginalization and frequent drug use.

As argued by Ruben, van Hute, and Davids, "The return can only be sustainable when returnees are provided with possibilities to become embedded in terms of economic, social networks, and psychosocial dimensions."[36] In cases of forced returns or deportations, migrants find themselves facing greater challenges, owing to their feelings of a lack of performance and a very low sense of self-esteem. In the case of Tijuana, we found that some congregations can be of crucial help in reconstructing social networks after deportation.

Two Catholic organizations in Tijuana, the Casa del Migrante and the Desayunador del Padre Chava, respond to the postdeportation state of emergency. Recently they have promoted reintegration programs to help fend off greater impoverishment and marginalization of deportees. The historic commitment of these organizations to migrants' rights, and their strong links with public institutions and local civil society, are significant symbolic and social resources that could facilitate their work of assisting the integration of migrants into the city. Nevertheless, the number and diversity of the people the organizations assist on a daily basis, and the conditions of homelessness and poverty the deportees face, make it difficult to build dense social networks and to form bonding social capital.[37]

In this study, we found that New Life Church provides an institutionalized web of persistent relations: religious leaders and established members of the church enjoy prestige and recognition in their community. They facilitate adaptation to a new place and help to reconstruct social networks. However, strong ties within this network constrain the mobility of its members. Employment and educational opportunities, access to housing and medical care, and other elements for sustainable social inclusion are confined to existing resources within a small religious community. Most of the households rely on female work and suffer economic hardship.

Tijuana has long been one of the main ports of forced repatriation to Mexico. In 2016, more than one hundred deportees arrived each day, and nearly half of them stayed in the city for short- or long-term periods. Although as of March 2017 the city had not yet witnessed the massive deportations announced by the Trump administration, thousands of deportees already struggle to integrate in a very poor labor market or to enroll their children in schools. They now compete for scarce emergency resources and for social integration with new international migrants and asylum seekers from Central America, South America, and the Caribbean, stranded at the U.S.-Mexico border by fears of exclusionary migratory and asylum politics.[38] The arrival of these new flows has created a logistical and capacity challenge for social service providers and human rights organizations. More than thirty Christian churches, migrant camps, and improvised shelters have opened their doors to house these newcomers. As border security and racist discourse in the United States escalate, and Donald Trump declares that his administration will deport up to three million immigrants, some communities on the southern side of the border are already overwhelmed.[39]

NOTES TO CHAPTER 11

1. Jacqueline Hagan, David Leal, and Nestor Rodriguez, "Deporting Social Capital: Implications for Immigrant Communities in the United States," *Migration Studies* 3, no. 3 (2015): 370–392.

2. David Brotherton and Luis Barrios, *Banished to the Homeland: Dominican Deportees and Their Stories of Exile* (New York: Columbia University Press, 2011).

3. Catherine Dingeman-Cerda and Susan Bibler Coutin, "The Ruptures of Return: Deportation's Confounding Effects," in *Punishing Immigrants: Policy, Politics, and Injustice*, ed. Charis E. Kubrin, Marjorie S. Katz, and Ramiro Martínez Jr. (New York: NYU Press, 2012), 114.

4. Daniel Kanstroom, *Aftermath: Deportation Law and the New American Diaspora* (New York: Oxford University Press, 2012), 9.

5. Cecilia Menjívar, "Latino Immigrants and Their Perceptions of Religious Institutions: Cubans, Salvadorans and Guatemalans in Phoenix, Arizona," Research Gate, January 2001, https://www.researchgate.net/publication/28137805_Latino_immigrants _and_their_perceptions_of_religious_institutions_Cubans_Salvadorans_and _Guatemalans_in_Phoenix_Arizona; Helen Rose Ebaugh and Janet Saltzman Chafetz, eds., *Religion Across Borders: Transnational Immigrant Networks* (Lanham: Altamira, 2002).

6. Jacqueline María Hagan, *Migration Miracle: Faith, Hope, and Meaning on the Undocumented Journey* (Cambridge: Harvard University Press, 2008).

7. Jorge Santibáñez Romellón, "Características de la migración de mexicanos hacia y desde Estados Unidos," in *Migración y fronteras*, ed. Manuel Ángel Castillo,

Alfredo Lattes, and Jorge Santibáñez (Mexico: El Colegio de la Frontera Norte, Aso-ciación Latinoamericana de Sociología, El Colegio de México, 1998).

8. María Dolores París Pombo, "Procesos de repatriación: Experiencias de las per-sonas devueltas a México por las autoridades estadounidenses (Washington, D.C.: Woodrow Wilson Center, 2010).

9. Unidad de Política Migratoria, "Eventos de repatriación de mexicanos desde Esta-dos Unidos según entidad federativa y punto de recepción 1995–2014," Series históricas, Estadística Migratoria, 2015, http://www.politicamigratoria.gob.mx/es_mx/SEGOB/Series _Historicas.

10. Kanstroom, *Aftermath*.

11. William Becerra, *Revista Migrantes* (Tijuana: Centro Scalabrini, 2011), xvii, 1.

12. María Dolores París Pombo, Diana Buenrostro Mercado, and Gabriel Pérez Dup-erou, "Trapped at the Border: The Difficult Integration of Deportees in Tijuana," in *Deportation and Return in a Border-Restricted World: Experiences in Mexico, El Sal-vador, Guatemala, and Honduras*, ed. Bryan Roberts, Cecilia Menjívar, and Nestor Rodriguez (New York: Springer, forthcoming).

13. El Colegio de la Frontera Norte, *Encuesta sobre Migración en la Frontera Norte de México*, 2016, https://www.colef.mx/emif/.

14. Laura Velasco and Sandra Albicker, "Estimación y caracterización de la población residente en el bordo del canal del río Tijuana," El Colegio de la Frontera Norte, June 14, 2013, http://www.colef.mx/estudiosdeelcolef/estimacion-y-caracterizacion-de-la-poblacion -residente-en-el-bordo-del-canal-del-rio-tijuana/.

15. Originally established in Italy at the end of the nineteenth century, the Scal-abrini are a transnational Catholic congregation of priests, nuns, and laypersons dedi-cated to providing pastoral care to migrants.

16. Laura Velasco and Marie Laure Coubès, "Sobre dimensión, caracterización y áreas de atención a mexicanos deportados desde Estados Unidos," El Colegio de la Frontera Norte, December 2013, http://www.colef.mx/wp-content/uploads/2014/01 /Reporte-Deportos.pdf.

17. París Pombo, Buenrostro Mercado, and Pérez Duperou, "Trapped at the Border."

18. The Salesian missions were historically dedicated to education of youth and train-ing workshops. Also founded in Italy in the nineteenth century, they accompanied migrant workers across the world.

19. Marie Laure Coubès et al., "Estudio sobre los usuarios del Desayunador Sale-siano Padre Chava," El Colegio de la Frontera Norte, Feburary 2015, http://www.colef .mx/wp-content/uploads/2015/03/Reporte-ejecutivo-estudio-desayunador.pdf.

20. París Pombo, Buenrostro Mercado, and Pérez Duperou, "Trapped at the Border."

21. T. Golash-Boza and P. Hondagneu-Sotelo, "Latino Men and the Deportation Crisis: A Gendered Racial Removal Program," *Latino Studies* 11, no. 3 (2013): 284.

22. Saskia Sassen, *Expulsions: Brutality and Complexity in the Global Economy* (Cambridge: Harvard University Press, 2014).

23. Applied Research Center, "Shattered Families: The Perilous Intersection of Im-migration Enforcement and the Child Welfare System," *Colorlines*, November 2011.

24. María Dolores París Pombo and Diana Carolina Peláez-Rodríguez, "Far from Home: Mexican Women Deported from the US to Tijuana," *Journal of Borderland Studies* 31 (2016).

25. Cecilia Menjívar, *Fragmented Ties: Salvadoran Immigrant Networks in America* (Berkeley: University of California Press, 2000).

26. Pierre Bourdieu, "The Forms of Capital," in *Handbook of Theory and Research for the Sociology of Education*, ed. J. Richardson (New York: Greenwood, 1986), 241–258.

27. Mark Granovetter, "The Strength of Weak Ties: A Network Theory Revisited," *Sociological Theory* 1 (1983): 201–33.

28. Linda Basch, Nina Glick Schiller, and Cristina Szanton Blanc, *Nations Unbound: Transnational Projects, Postcolonial Predicaments and the Deterritorialized Nation-State* (New York: Gordon and Breach, 1994), 7.

29. Peggy Levitt, *Transnational Villagers* (Berkeley: University of California Press, 2001).

30. Cecilia Menjívar, "Religious Institutions and Transnationalism: A Case Study of Catholic and Evangelical Salvadoran Immigrants," *International Journal of Politics, Culture, and Society* 12, no. 4 (1999): 589–612.

31. Michael Kearney, "Transnationalism in California and Mexico at the End of Empire," in *Border Identities: Nation and State at International Frontiers*, ed. Thomas M. Wilson and Hastings Donnan (Cambridge: Cambridge University Press, 1998), 124.

32. Brotherton and Barrios, *Banished*.

33. Kanstroom, *Aftermath*.

34. Ibid., 141.

35. Ibid.

36. Ruerd Ruben, Marieke van Houte, and Tine Davids, "What Determines the Embeddedness of Forced-Return Migrants? Rethinking the Role of Pre- and Post-Return Assistance," *International Migration Review* 43, no. 4 (2009): 908–937.

37. Hagan, Leal, and Rodriguez, "Deporting Social Capital," 1–23.

38. From May to December 2016, more than twenty thousand international migrants, most of them Haitian citizens, arrived in Baja California hoping to enter the United States. At the port of San Ysidro, the CBP was systematically sending asylum seekers back to Mexico, allowing about forty to sixty Haitians to cross the border per day. In October, when the U.S. government began to deport numerous Haitian citizens, their family members and friends who were still waiting to cross the border decided to stay in Tijuana.

39. Haeyoun Park and Troy Griggs, "Could Trump Really Deport Millions of Unauthorized Immigrants?," *New York Times*, February 21, 2017, https://www.nytimes.com /interactive/2016/11/29/us/trump-unauthorized-immigrants.html.

12. MEDICAL DEPORTATIONS

Blurring the Line Between Health Care and Immigration Enforcement

LISA SUN-HEE PARK, UNIVERSITY OF CALIFORNIA, SANTA BARBARA

This chapter focuses on medical deportations—the forced removal of chronically ill or disabled immigrants from the United States to other nations. Various terms have been used—"medical removal," "medical repatriation," "medical deportation," "medical rendition," and "international patient dumping"—to describe the practice of forcibly removing low-income, uninsured immigrant patients to other countries in order to avoid the burden of costly long-term care by hospitals. The goal of this chapter is to provide greater detail about this little-known practice, including its historical formation, how it operates, and its larger social implications. Medical deportations serve as important evidence of the increasingly blurred state of health-care provision and immigration enforcement.

Medical deportation is one of the more unique methods among the increasingly varied efforts in immigration enforcement. Medical deportation is similar to other initiatives in which government workers and private citizens are "authorized" to screen individuals for citizenship status. However, there are two central differences. First, the extent of its actions toward law enforcement goes beyond merely reporting an individual's potential status to federal immigration authorities. By orchestrating the deportations, hospitals not only extend the reach of the state but actually supplant the state by engaging in the act of removal in cases in which the state has no interest or has refused to do so.[1] Second, there is no formal authorization by federal or state enforcement agencies to carry out these removals. Federal immigration authorities and local law enforcement play no role in these private repatriations and have remained silent on the issue, thereby allowing for it to continue.[2]

I argue that medical deportation is a combination of an age-old administrative policy of public charge and a new culmination of policies created by a series of federal and state immigration, welfare, and health-care related legislation. This combination has resulted in greater muddling of the role of health-care providers who care for vulnerable immigrant populations. The goal of this study is not only to add to the limited body of knowledge on medical deportation but also to address the larger societal implications of health-care providers operating within conditions of increasingly diffused immigration enforcement practices.

This chapter provides one portion of a larger project on the patchwork nature of health-care access for low-income and uninsured immigrants in the United States. The larger study focuses on metropolitan areas in four U.S. states: Texas, New Mexico, Arizona, and California. Each of these states, which border Mexico, have concentrated populations of immigrants and, in combination, comprise 39 percent of the nation's foreign-born population.[3] And each state has adopted different policy approaches to immigrants and their access to health care. The metropolitan areas include Houston, Texas; Albuquerque, New Mexico; Phoenix and Tucson, Arizona; and San Diego, California.

For the purposes of this chapter, I highlight a specific case of attempted medical deportation that took place in Phoenix in 2011. My primary data sources for this analysis include personal interviews with immigrant advocates and health-care providers, news articles, and policy reports. However, the private, unregulated nature of medical deportations makes systematic documentation difficult. As a consequence, the methods for this study were somewhat exploratory— meaning that flexibility in its sampling and interview structure was required. In May 2014, my research team and I began by identifying safety-net hospitals and clinics in each of the targeted metropolitan areas that serve large numbers of immigrant patients. The selection of key respondents relied on a combination of sampling procedures. Careful literature, media, and Internet searches on immigrant health-care access and medical deportations, along with conversations with knowledgeable policy researchers, helped identify the initial pool of potential interviewees. We contacted key individuals—administrators, health-care providers, and community health advocates—in these hospitals, clinics, and community organizations.

According to media reports, both private and public hospitals have engaged in medical deportations. And given the potentially sensitive nature of this practice, the interviews began with questions regarding the larger issue of health-care access for uninsured immigrants. I then followed with questions specific to long-term-care concerns for this population. Finally, I specifically inquired about their response to medical deportations and whether or not their hospital engages in this practice. This gradual process was successful in eliciting thoughtful responses to potentially uncomfortable questions.

Medical deportations reside at the intersection of multiple and conflicting laws. To address this intersection, this study provides a comparative policy analysis of the various health-care and immigration-related legislation that culminates to produce this phenomenon, as well as interviews with health-care providers and immigrant advocates.

AGE-OLD POLICY: CONTINUING RELEVANCE OF PUBLIC CHARGE

While seemingly an obscure and contemporary phenomenon, medical deportation highlights significant age-old political disputes concerning immigrants and their associated economic and social costs and benefits to the nation. For more than a century, public charge provisions within U.S. immigration law have allowed the forced removal of immigrants, including those with legal residency status, based on a largely discretionary determination of an individual's potential to become a public burden. Immigrants' potential health-care costs are one of the most frequently cited sources of this burden.

Public charge—meaning a public burden—is a political classification used to exclude or deport those immigrants perceived to be or to have the *possibility of becoming* a burden on the state.[4] In its early stage, during the mass migration of Europeans at the turn of the last century (1892–1920), public charge was the most frequently used category of exclusion. According to historian Martha Gardner, "Between 1880 and 1924, 'likely to become public charge' provided a catch-all category of exclusion through which vast numbers of immigrants found themselves deported as potential paupers for moral, marital, physical, and economic deficiencies."[5] And while other administrative laws evolved during the twentieth century, public charge determinations remained in a state of "arrested development" as they moved out of public view, limited largely to the confines of American consulates abroad.[6]

Public charge remains a powerful tool in its strategic ambiguity and quiet location on the outskirts of public notice. It is a statutory provision under the jurisdiction of nonjudicial staff and not subject to oversight by legislatures or courts. Throughout its existence, this law was left largely undefined and vague in its applicability. Public charge law, then, is a key example of "deportability." This concept is one of the most compelling lines of inquiry in understanding the everyday life of immigrants today.[7] Defined as the possibility of deportation— of being removed from the space of the nation-state—deportability highlights the legally vulnerable condition of many contemporary immigrants in the United States, particularly those who are undocumented.[8] In fact, Nicholas De Genova argues that "the legal production of migrant 'illegality' has never served simply to achieve the apparent goal of deportation, so much as to regulate the flow of Mexican migration in particular and to sustain its legally vulnerable condition of deportability."[9] In this way, public charge law in general and medical deportations in particular function as a tool of deportability.

After considerable pressure from immigrant legal advocates to clarify the ambiguous nature of this law, U.S. Citizenship and Immigration Services refined the definition of *public charge* for the first time in 1999. The one-page notice of clarification included this statement: "'public charge' means an individual who is likely to become primarily dependent on the government for subsistence, as demonstrated by either the receipt of public cash assistance for income maintenance or institutionalization for long-term care at government expense."[10] While this clarification allayed some fears regarding the potential reach of public charge law, immigrants who receive cash assistance or long-term care were specifically identified as socially burdensome, heightening their deportability status.

Medical deportations raise significant issues regarding the current-day application of public charge law by explicitly highlighting long-term health care as grounds for immigrant inadmissibility and removal. In the last few years, the U.S. government has formally deported historic numbers of immigrants. Federal immigration authorities deported approximately 400,000 immigrants in 2009 and the same number again in 2011, the highest numbers in the country's history. At the same time, growing numbers of state and county governments have enacted laws that require local government workers and even private citizens to verify the legal status of residents. At the height of these local actions, according to the National Conference of State Legislatures, more than 180 immigration control measures, spanning 43 states, were enacted in 2007 alone. And 92 of these local immigration bills specifically targeted immigrant health coverage.[11]

The act of deportation by hospitals is an important example from which to understand the growing trend toward privatization of immigration law enforcement. Studies have documented the displacement of immigration surveillance to local police, other state officials (e.g., welfare eligibility workers), health-care providers, employers, college admissions officers, and other private citizens.[12] Of particular significance for this study is the parallel increase in more informal or nongovernmental modes of immigrant removal, from privately conducted and largely undocumented forms of repatriation to "self-deportations"—a term describing the strategy of making living conditions so difficult that immigrants "choose" to leave the country without the government having to incur the cost of formal deportation proceedings.

NEW POLICIES:
INTERSECTIONS AND THEIR GAPS

Immigration to the United States has increased significantly since 1970, and it is estimated that nearly one in five Americans will be an immigrant in 2050.[13] This demographic transformation has precipitated intense political debates regarding the social and economic costs and benefits of immigration in the United States. One of the most passionately argued reasons against immigration is the use of health care by those who are undocumented.

In a recent iteration of this debate, researchers at Harvard Medical School found that undocumented and documented immigrants, given their relative young age, contributed far more to Medicare than they received from 2002 to 2009. They argue that immigrants disproportionately subsidize the Medicare trust fund, which supports payments to hospitals and institutions, and thereby contribute significant benefits to the United States.[14] At the same time, hospitals nationwide incur approximately $2 billion in costs every year for treatment of undocumented immigrants.[15] According to the U.S./Mexico Border Counties Coalition, the southwest border region endures a disproportionate burden in providing emergency health-care services to undocumented immigrants. The coalition estimates that the region pays nearly $195 million in uncompensated costs for emergency medical care for undocumented patients.[16] In the midst of this political quagmire, hospitals find themselves falling through gaps in health-care coverage and wading into new and potentially contradictory roles within immigration control as the boundaries between health care and immigration increasingly blur.

The Emergency Medical Treatment and Active Labor Act of 1986 (EMTALA), which was passed in response to public outrage over alarming reports of hospitals "patient dumping" uninsured individuals, is repeatedly cited as one of the leading sources of this funding gap. EMTALA mandates hospitals to "stabilize" an emergency medical condition and restricts the discharge or transfer of patients unless to an "appropriate" medical facility for specialized treatment.[17] This national mandate is required of all hospitals with Medicaid and Medicare funding. To opt out of EMTALA would entail dropping out of Medicare altogether, which would be devastating for most hospitals. However, once stabilized, federal funding to cover uninsured, low-income, unauthorized (meaning undocumented and newly arrived documented) immigrant patients ends. In general, the vast majority of patient-dumping cases involved uninsured minority patients—89 percent were identified as African American or Hispanic.[18]

Contributing further to this funding gap, the 1996 welfare and immigration laws deemed significantly more immigrants ineligible for Medicaid benefits. The federal welfare reform bill (PRWORA—Personal Responsibility and Work Opportunity Reconciliation Act; PL 104–193) and federal immigration legislation

(IIRIRA—Illegal Immigration Reform and Immigrant Responsibility Act; PL 104–208) significantly altered health-care eligibility for immigrants by creating new, more restrictive categories of eligibility for means-tested programs, including Medicaid—a public health insurance program for those who are low income or disabled. Concerns regarding the potentially burdensome costs of health care appear to underpin much of the major legislation affecting immigrants. For instance, PRWORA created new barriers to Medicaid for legal immigrants who entered the country after August 22, 1996, by making them ineligible for public benefits during their first five years in the United States. Remarkably, restrictions on immigrant benefits alone accounted for almost half the total initial federal savings from PRWORA.[19] After PRWORA, the sole means for many unauthorized immigrants to obtain public assistance in medical care became EMTALA.

Undocumented immigrants were already ineligible for most major means-tested entitlement benefits, including Medicaid. However, IIRIRA created the additional requirement that all family-sponsored immigrants who apply for an immigrant visa or adjustment of status after December 19, 1997, must have an affidavit of support (INS Form I-864) from a qualifying sponsor. Without this form, he or she could be found inadmissible as a public charge.

The passage of IIRIRA and PRWORA also facilitated the exchange of information regarding immigration status and the receipt of Medicaid-funded services between states and federal immigration authorities.[20] Hospitals must now verify the immigration status of a foreign-born Medicaid applicant with the Department of Homeland Security if the person applies for a Medicaid benefit that includes federal financial participation.[21] This is a departure from previous policies in states like California, wherein verification of immigration status was required only for those seeking full-scale benefits, and when required, a social security card or birth certificate was sufficient to establish legal immigration status. This additional verification requirement created considerable concern for health-care providers who worried that their hard-won trust with immigrant patients would erode.[22] And as a result of the culmination of gaps in policy, health-care providers scrambled to find alternative funding mechanisms to cover the costs of caring for uninsured and low-income immigrant patients.[23]

The combined effect of these health-care and immigration-related laws significantly reduced potential reimbursements for uninsured immigrant health care. Currently, hospitals are (partially) reimbursed for emergency care for uninsured immigrants but are left with a difficult conundrum after these patients are stabilized but require ongoing medical care. If, as is often the case, the hospital cannot find a nursing home or another appropriate facility to accept the patient, it has little choice but to assume the cost of that care.

More recently, hospitals adjusted to regulations associated with the new federal health-care law—the Affordable Care Act (ACA)—and its intended and unintended effects. For instance, beginning in 2017, the federal government will dramatically reduce Medicaid Disproportionate Share Hospital payments, which are provided to hospitals that care for large numbers of patients who are low income and uninsured. And while millions of previously uninsured patients have become eligible for Medicaid under this new health-care law, undocumented and many newly arrived immigrants have not.[24]

Federal immigrant eligibility restrictions to Medicaid, including the five-year or more waiting period for most lawfully residing, low-income immigrant adults, continue to apply. Undocumented immigrants, on the other hand, are not only ineligible for public health insurance but also restricted from purchasing private health insurance at full cost in state insurance exchanges. They are also ineligible for Medicare, nonemergency Medicaid, and the Children's Health Insurance Program. For undocumented immigrants, health-care access is restricted to emergency care and nonemergency health services at community health centers or safety-net hospitals. Currently, an estimated 21 percent of the 32 million uninsured people in the United States are noncitizens.[25] Of this number, approximately 5.6 million are undocumented immigrants.[26] Most undocumented immigrants have remained uninsured after ACA and now constitute a larger share of the remaining uninsured population in the country.[27] Some policy analysts predict that immigrants will become the largest segment of the population without health insurance after ACA is fully implemented.[28]

Finally, new immigration legislation may bring another layer of complexity. Legislation presented by Congress in 2013 coupled a defined route toward citizenship for undocumented immigrants with increasingly more aggressive methods of homeland security and border enforcement.[29] The bipartisan Senate bill proposed a new wave of border security programs to be initiated before any of the estimated ten million undocumented immigrants could be allowed to apply for citizenship. And proof that an applicant would not become a public charge was explicitly noted as one of the requirements for gaining registered provisional immigrant status, which places undocumented persons on the path to citizenship.[30] This process was expected to take thirteen years. While this bill quickly died after its initial proposal, the current punitive political climate appears favorable for greater use of medical deportations as a cost-effective method of forced repatriation of public burdens.

MEDICAL DEPORTATION

The earliest documented case of medical deportation was reported in 2001, but it was not until a number of detailed investigative stories were published in the *New York Times* in 2008 that this issue received national attention.[31] What little information is available is largely limited to scattered media reports of specific cases and legal analysis of those cases. In one report, Antonio Torres—an uninsured, lawful permanent resident living just outside Phoenix, Arizona—was left comatose with a severe brain injury after a car accident. Two days after he was admitted, St. Joseph's Hospital in Phoenix tried to persuade Torres's family to remove his life support. When they refused, the hospital made plans to transfer the nineteen-year-old Torres to a hospital in Mexicali, Mexico. The hospital placed Torres—unconscious and suffering from an infection—into an ambulance and transported him to the U.S.-Mexico border. He lay there in the summer heat for hours waiting for a local ambulance to transport him to a public hospital in Mexico. Once at the Mexican hospital, there was no bed available, and Torres was left in the emergency ward, where his infection worsened. Fortunately for Torres, Latino community leaders in Arizona organized on his behalf and raised enough money to transport him back to the United States, this time to a charity hospital in California. He arrived in California in septic shock, but he survived and emerged from his coma a few weeks later.[32]

Most of the known cases of medical deportation involve undocumented immigrants, but as Antonio Torres's experience indicates, this is not always the case. Lawful permanent residents (those with green cards), temporary visa holders, and at least one U.S. citizen born to parents who did not have legal documentation status were involuntarily repatriated. Torres's advocates and family were able to bring him back to the United States because he was a documented immigrant, unlike the majority of the cases. There are documented cases of medical deportations to countries around the world, including South Korea, the Philippines, and Poland. However, the evidence suggests that most cases involve immigrants from Latin America. In fact, there is enough demand to sustain at least one company specializing in medical repatriations—MexCare, based in Chula Vista, California. The company offers its services nationwide to transport uninsured immigrants from Latin America to hospitals and treatment centers in their country of origin. The existence of such a business enterprise may signal the beginnings of a growing market and increasing pressure to at least consider the possibility of medical deportation as a cost-saving endeavor, if not to formalize the practice in more institutional ways.

In 2011, near the San Luis port of entry in Arizona, Jose Gutierrez was apprehended by U.S. Customs and Border Protection (CBP) agents for illegal entry. According to border patrol agents, Gutierrez was combative and was consequently "subdued" with an electronic control device (i.e., a Taser). Their report states that he subsequently fell, hitting his head on a rock.[33] His wife, Shena, at home in Woodland Hills, California, received a phone call from the Mexican consulate in Yuma notifying her that Jose was at St. Joseph's Hospital in Phoenix, Arizona. Shena immediately left for Phoenix and went directly to St. Joseph's. When she arrived at the hospital, Shena was told that there was no patient by that name. She called her contact at the Mexican consulate to confirm, and after two hours, the hospital acknowledged Jose's existence. Shena "doesn't scare easily," since she also works in the health-care field; in fact, she is employed by the same hospital network in California.[34] Shena recounted her first impression:

> I am taken to his room and he is unconscious with serious head injuries. There are tubes everywhere and an open wound on his frontal lobe. The nurse tells me that he is basically a vegetable. To demonstrate, the nurse pokes her finger in the open wound in his skull. "See, he can't feel a thing," she says to me. I am absolutely horrified as the nurse keeps pressing her finger into his open wound. I became upset and told her to stop touching him. I leaned down to Jose and told him that I'm here now and that I will take care of him. "He can't hear you," the nurse tells me. By then, I am so upset. I yelled at the nurse to leave him alone.
>
> I was totally outraged by the treatment of everyone at St. Joseph's from the nurses, doctors, to the orderlies. His attending doctor came into the room popping candy into this mouth—just so arrogant and casual. [The doctor] showed such disregard, such disrespect. I couldn't believe it. Jose was repeatedly called a "cockroach" and an "illegal alien" that "needs to go home." The doctor called Jose a "criminal." He said that the hospital will throw in life support equipment that Jose can take with him to Mexico. All of them . . . all they could talk about was deporting him . . . about sending him "home."[35]

Throughout this process, the border patrol and the hospital were at odds about which institution was financially responsible for Jose's care. He was in a coma for 2.5 weeks and then was induced back into a coma after complications arose. Border agents stood guard outside Jose's hospital room twenty-four hours a day.

Shena arrived each morning at 7 a.m. and stayed by Jose until 3 or 4 a.m. She found support from local immigrant health advocates who advised her to not leave Jose alone. She also contacted an attorney to look into how Jose was so seriously injured. And she began to speak with media outlets to bring greater pressure on the CBP to investigate Jose's case. For the five weeks Jose was at St. Joseph's, Shena had to push the hospital and the border patrol to make sure Jose got the care he needed. Shena explained, "They were constantly making plans to get rid of him. I would leave the room for a little while and then come back to find them packing his wounds with ice packs to ready him for transport. It felt like I couldn't leave for a minute."[36]

She recalled a particularly difficult moment:

One night, everything blew up at the hospital. . . . By then I had been at the hospital every day for weeks and everyone knew my schedule. The nurses, doctors, everyone. That night, I really needed to get out of the hospital for a little while. I just needed to get some air. I came back to ICU at 7:50 p.m. to find his door closed and curtain drawn. I thought this was really strange. It's not closed unless they're washing him or changing him and I know it wasn't time for that. I walked in and opened the curtain to find him bent over, squeezing closed his trach[eal] tube. He wasn't breathing and all the machines were beeping and going crazy. He was somehow sitting forward, and he had soiled himself. And, no one was coming. All the machine alarms are going off and no one would come. I start yelling and calling for the charge nurse. She finally comes in and tells me to calm down. That I'm acting ridiculous. I won't lie, I was cursing at this point. I was so upset. Jose could have died. The nurse called security and threatened to have me barred from his room. I took out my phone and started taking pictures and threatened to post everything on the web. The nurse then backed down.[37]

During our interview, Shena said, "I'm so glad you asked about the hospital. People ask about BP [border patrol] but never about the hospital. The hospital is just as bad." In addition to donations, Shena used all their savings and sold their house and cars to hire an attorney. A lawsuit, filed on Jose's behalf against the border patrol, is ongoing, and his deportation has been halted while the case is pending. Shena remains unclear about what exactly happened in the desert five years ago.

Jose Gutierrez, forty-one, was deported to Mexico from Los Angeles on March 21, 2011. His undocumented status was discovered, and he left behind his partner, Shena; his two children; and a job as a film engineer. He had arrived in the United States as a young child and no longer had any connection to Mexico. Nine days after his deportation, he attempted to reenter the United States through Arizona when he was apprehended. During this process, Jose apparently tried to slip away and run back to Mexico. Eleven border patrol agents ran after him and subdued him. After this encounter, Shena reports that Jose ended up at St. Joseph's with Taser marks all over his chest and arms, a broken tooth, two black eyes, cuts and bruises throughout his body, and five parts of his skull removed. Shena vehemently disputed CBP's version of the incident, pointing out that Jose's injuries do not correspond to their narrative. Most damaging is the fact that Jose's head injuries are located in his frontal lobe, and CBP contends that he fell backwards onto a rock after being tased once.

Shena's skepticism is warranted. According to an independent task force report released on March 15, 2016, the system for disciplining abusive or corrupt border patrol agents and officers is fundamentally flawed and does not deter criminal misconduct in the nation's largest law enforcement agency. Co-chaired by William J. Bratton, police commissioner of New York City, the report states:

Because CBP has the largest number of armed, sworn law enforcement officers in the United States, over 44,000, there is a very real potential for the use of excessive and unnecessary force, especially by CBP's Border Patrol given the difficult environment in which it operates. In its brief history, CBP has not been noted for its transparency when it comes to use of force incidents, although this is changing, and given its size, it has never developed a truly CBP-wide process for receiving, tracking and responding to public complaints. Its disciplinary process takes far too long to be an effective deterrent.[38]

What remain largely unexamined in Jose Gutierrez's case are the deportation attempts by the hospital. While Jose was undocumented and uninsured, he had the support of Shena, his wife turned citizen advocate, who was able to successfully prevent his deportation. She went back to Jose's former employer and explained his condition. The company was able to extend COBRA health coverage, which allowed Shena to find a long-term-care facility in California that would accept him. With donations, Shena was able to cover the $75,000 private plane and medical equipment to transport him to California. In addition, Shena made connections with local immigrant activists in Arizona and used media attention to great effect. Each time hospital personnel attempted to deport Jose, Shena notified the media, and activists stationed themselves with their cameras at the hospital exits. Other immigrant patients at St. Joseph's whom Shena met during Jose's stay were not as fortunate. Shena said to me, "People are dying and nobody cares. It is heartbreaking. I'm devastated thinking about the others."[39]

Three years later, Shena reports, "He is not the same Jose. He is not the same man." He continues to experience seizures as a result of his traumatic brain injury. He takes large amounts of medication each day, he has lost his sense of smell, he cannot bend his knee, and he is emotionally fragile. "He goes from happy to sad to angry, just like that. He cannot control his emotions."[40]

In response to Jose's case, St. Joseph's sent a statement to *LA Weekly*:

> St. Joseph's will never move a patient without a safe discharge plan. Our commitment is always to work in collaboration with the family to get their agreement on this plan. St. Joseph's is dedicated to working with patients and their families to provide a safe discharge from its acute care setting to longer term care facilities when a patient needs this.[41]

The sentiments of this statement were very much in line with what was conveyed in my interviews with Sister J, a member of St. Joseph's executive leadership.[42] By far, St. Joseph's has been the most transparent regarding its deportation practices of any of the hospitals and clinics I interviewed in five different metropolitan areas across four states. Interviewees acknowledged the practice and discussed their decision-making process. To be clear, hospital administrators identified this practice as "transfers back to the patient's home country"—terms such as *deportation, repatriation,* or *removal* were never used. Sister J described the decision-making process regarding "charity care" of low-income, uninsured, and undocumented immigrants as "very difficult." She explained further:

> Our decisions regarding transfers depend on where the whole support system is. . . . Is it in their home country or here? They are typically single males and we work with the Mexican Consulate to get them placed near their families back home and pay for their transportation. We've had two cases in the past six months. They are always hard decisions to make. It's hard to really know what's their reality. Do they have support back home? We are always working to refine the process.[43]

St. Joseph's, a not-for-profit hospital founded by the Sisters of Mercy, is a key part of the state's health-care safety net. Given the wide range of health, social, and support services it provides for the poor and underserved, it is the only viable option for health care for many immigrants. And hospital administrators view their care of this population as a "humanitarian effort" that goes beyond their health-care mandate. Instead, immigrant health-care decision making is construed as a matter of doing "what is right." In this way, medical deportation is a difficult moral decision that is in keeping with their Catholic faith. According to Sister J, spending $45,000 for medical transportation to send someone back "home" so that they may die with their family is the charitable, right thing to do.

Medical deportations accentuate the increasingly blurred boundary of the role of health-care providers as they engage in immigration enforcement. Not only are issues of professional medical ethics in question, but also legal obligations to ensure the patient's right to privacy, due process, and informed consent.[44] In 2008, the California Medical Association was the first state medical association to pass a resolution opposing forced deportations of patients.[45] Then, in 2011, the American College of Physicians published a position statement arguing that "access to health care should not be restricted based on immigration status, and people should not be prevented from paying out-of-pocket for health insurance coverage."[46] It stated, "Physicians and other health care professionals have an ethical and professional obligation to care for the sick. Immigration policy should not interfere with the ethical obligation to provide care for all."[47]

In one of the only medical deportation cases to reach trial, *Montejo v. Martin Memorial Medical Center,* jurors in Florida found the hospital's repatriation of a traumatically injured undocumented immigrant to Guatemala "reasonable under the circumstances" and did not find any monetary liability against the hospital despite reiteration by the district court of appeals that deportations are the exclusive province of the federal Department of Homeland Security.[48] While future legal suits challenging medical deportations are expected, it is also anticipated that some hospitals will continue this practice even if they lose these lawsuits. The calculation is that a hospital with a million-dollar verdict may still save millions of dollars in long-term care.[49]

Currently, there is real concern that medical deportations will increase under the new administration of Donald Trump—and perhaps become formalized as accepted U.S. policy. A leaked draft of an executive order dated January 23, 2017, titled "Protecting Taxpayer Resources by Ensuring Our Immigration Laws Promote Accountability and Responsibility," calls for expanding the grounds for inadmissibility and deportability of immigrants based on their use of public benefits.[50] These efforts focus on expanding the definition of "public charge" and are based on the erroneous assumption that "households headed by aliens (legal and illegal) are much more likely than households headed by native-born citizens to use federal means-tested public benefits."[51] While it remains unsigned at the time of this writing, the potential consequences are severe.

This proposed executive order upends current procedure in which public charge determinations are focused on those who are likely to become *primarily* dependent on public cash assistance for income maintenance or institutionalization for long-term care at government expense. In addition, the receipt of these benefits is to be evaluated within a "totality of circumstances" before a determination is made. This new executive order could greatly expand the definition of "public charge" to include documented and undocumented noncitizens who use (or are likely to use) *any* means-tested public benefits, including Medicaid, food stamps, and reduced school lunches. It also instructs the secretary of homeland security "to rescind any field guidance concerning the inadmissibility or deportability of aliens on the ground that they are likely to be or have become public charges, as applicable (public-charge grounds), and replace it immediately with new field guidance consistent with the provisions of this order."

Whether this proposal will be signed in its current form is uncertain at this point. The Trump administration's attempt to initiate a travel ban on six mainly Muslim nations through executive order has been tumultuous, and first attempts to repeal the Affordable Care Act failed. However, immigration restrictions remain high on the administration's list of priorities, and public charge is clearly within its sights as a governmental tool for deportation. Low-income and uninsured immigrants in need of government-funded long-term health care are particularly vulnerable within this increasingly punitive neoliberal moment.

The fact that safety-net hospitals have become an enforcement zone raises serious questions about the increasingly militarized basis of citizenship and the stark separation of people based on nation-state borders. In this regard, immigrants with irregular citizenship status are made to be wholly outside our consideration—to the point that questions of deserving or undeserving immigrants, which weighed heavily in past studies of social welfare, are no longer relevant. The blurring of health-care provision and immigration enforcement within current conditions of neoliberal privatization functions to sharpen the divisions among people. And as I have shown, the question of whether or not an immigrant is a "public charge" has been definitively addressed in the many federal and state health-care, immigration, and welfare policies over the years. The answer is yes. Consequently, it is an extraordinary moral good to care for any immigrant at all, rendering the forced removal of severely injured patients a nonissue in the overall state of immigrant health care. Ethical obligations to provide care for *all* remain intact even as immigrants are defined as being outside the nation-state entirely.

NOTES TO CHAPTER 12

1. Medical deportations also happen in other counties. See Kenyon Wallace, "Family Faces Deportation Over Son's Autism," *Toronto Star*, June 9, 2011, http://www.thestar .com/news/canada/2011/06/09/family_faces_deportation_over_sons_autism.html. However, cases in which hospitals conduct the actual act of removal are uncommon outside the United States.

2. Deborah Sontag, "Immigrants Facing Deportation by U.S. Hospitals," *New York Times*, August 3, 2008, http://www.nytimes.com/2008/08/03/us/03deport.html. This was also supported in my interviews with hospital administrators and Shena Gutierrez.

3. U.S. Census Bureau, *2009 American Community Survey* (Washington, D.C.: U.S. Census Bureau).

4. U.S. Citizenship and Immigration Services, *Fact Sheet: Public Charge*, May 25, 1999, http://www.dhs.gov.

5. Martha Gardner, *The Qualities of a Citizen: Women, Immigration, and Citizenship, 1870–1965* (Princeton: Princeton University Press, 2009), 89.

6. Patricia Evans, "'Likely to Become a Public Charge': Immigration in the Backwaters of Administrative Law, 1882–1933" (PhD diss., George Washington University, 1987).

7. Nicholas De Genova and Nathalie Peutz, eds., *The Deportation Regime: Sovereignty, Space, and the Freedom of Movement* (Durham: Duke University Press, 2010).

8. Nicholas De Genova, *Working the Boundaries: Race, Space, and "Illegality" in Mexican Chicago* (Durham: Duke University Press, 2005), 8.

9. Ibid.

10. U.S. Citizenship and Immigration Services, *Fact Sheet*.

11. National Conference of State Legislatures, "2007 Enacted State Legislation Related to Immigrants and Immigration," January 31, 2008, http://www.ncsl.org/issues -research/immig/2007-enacted-state-legislation-related-to-immigran.aspx.

12. Lisa Sun-Hee Park, *Entitled to Nothing: The Struggle for Immigrant Health Care in the Age of Welfare Reform* (New York: NYU Press, 2011).

13. Jeffrey Passel and D'vera Cohn, *US Population Projections: 2005–2050*, Pew Research Center, February 11, 2008, http://www.pewhispanic.org/files/reports/85.pdf

14. Leah Zallman, Steffie Woolhandler, David Himmelstein, David Bor, and Danny McComick, "Immigrants Contributed an Estimated $115.2 Billion More to the Medicare Trust Fund Then They Took Out in 2002–09," *Health Affairs* 32, no. 6 (2013): 1153–1160.

15. Nabilah Irshad, "Medical Repatriations: Death Sentencing United States Immigrants," *Transnational Law and Contemporary Problems* 20 (2012): 797–824.

16. U.S./Mexico Border Counties Coalition, *Medical Emergency: Costs of Uncompensated Care in Southwest Border Counties*, September 2002, http://sandiegohealth.org/border/bordercounties/medicalemergency.pdf.

17. Ibid., 806.

18. Mitchell Rice and W. Jones, "The Uninsured and Patient Dumping: Recent Policy Response in Indigent Care," *Journal of the National Medical Association* 83 (1991): 875.

19. Thomas MaCurdy and Margaret O'Brien-Strain, *Reform Reversed? The Restoration of Welfare Benefits to Immigrants in California* (San Francisco: Public Policy Institute of California, 1998).

20. Both the 1996 welfare and immigration reforms include provisions that require sharing of information between the state Department of Health and federal immigration authorities. States must now verify the immigration status of a foreign-born Medicaid applicant with Homeland Security if the person applies for a Medicaid benefit that includes federal financial participation. See Ann Morse, Jeremy Meadows, Kristen Rasmussen, and Sheri Steisel, *America's Newcomers: Mending the Welfare Safety Net for Immigrants* (Washington, D.C.: National Conference of State Legislatures, 1998). See also Lisa Sun-Hee Park, Rhonda Sarnoff, Catherine Bender, and Carol Korenbrot, "Impact of Recent Welfare and Immigration Reforms on Use of Medicaid for Prenatal Care by Immigrants in California," *Journal of Immigrant Health* 2, no. 1 (2000): 5–22.

21. Public hospitals seeking federal reimbursement for emergency services provided to nonqualified aliens are required to follow federal procedures regarding verification of immigration status. In this way, public hospitals are forced to verify their patients' immigration status in order to be compensated for their care. See California Legislature Senate Office of Research, *Federal Welfare Changes Affecting California's Immigrants*, (Sacramento: Senate Office of Research, 1996).

22. Park, *Entitled to Nothing*.

23. Ibid.

24. National Immigration Law Center, "How Are Immigrants Included in Health Care Reform?," April 2010, http://www.aapcho.org/wp/wp-content/uploads/2012/01/NILC-How_Are_Immigrants_Included_in_Health_Care_Reform.pdf; Bonnie Jerome-D'Emilia and Patricia Suplee, "The ACA and the Undocumented," *American Journal of Nursing* 112, no. 4 (2012): 21–27.

25. Henry J. Kaiser Family Foundation, "Key Facts About the Uninsured Population," October 5, 2015, http://kff.org/uninsured/fact-sheet/key-facts-about-the-uninsured-population/.

26. National Institute for Healthcare Management, *Understanding the Uninsured: Tailoring Policy Solutions for Different Populations*, Issue Brief, April 2008, http://www.nihcm.org/pdf/NIHCM-Uninsured-Final.pdf.

27. Steven P. Wallace, Jacqueline Torres, Tabashir Sadegh-Nobari, and Nadereh Pourat, "Undocumented and Uninsured: Barriers to Affordable Care for Immigrant Populations," UCLA Center for Health Policy Research, 2013.

28. Irshad, "Medical Repatriations."

29. Julia Preston, "Beside a Path to Citizenship, a New Path on Immigration," *New York Times*, April 16, 2013, http://www.nytimes.com/2013/04/17/us/senators-set-to-unveil-immigration-bill.html?_r=0.

30. National Conference of State Legislatures, "Short Overview of 2013 Senate Immigration Bill," http://www.ncsl.org/issues-research/human-services/short-overview-of-2013-senate-immigration-bill.aspx.

31. Deborah Sontag, "Getting Tough: Deported in Coma, Saved Back in US," *New York Times*, November 9, 2008, A1.

32. Ibid.

33. Simone Wilson, "L.A. Resident Jose Gutierrez, in Coma After Being Tased by Arizona Border Agents, Threatened with Deportation While Still Unconscious," *LA Weekly*, April 15, 2011, http://www.laweekly.com/news/la-resident-jose-gutierrez-in-coma-after-being-tased-by-arizona-border-agents-threatened-with-deportation-while-still-unconscious-2389853.

34. Author's interview with Shena Gutierrez, May 20, 2014.

35. Ibid.

36. Ibid.

37. Ibid.

38. U.S. Department of Homeland Security, Homeland Security Advisory Council, *Final Report of the CBP Integrity Advisory Panel* (Washington, D.C.: DHS, 2016). Accessed from *LA Times*, "Report on US Customs and Border Protection," March 14, 2016, http://documents.latimes.com/report-us-customs-and-border-protection/.

39. Ibid.

40. Ibid.

41. Wilson, "L.A. Resident Jose Gutierrez, in Coma."

42. Sister J is a pseudonym.

43. Author's interview with Sister J, May 18, 2015.

44. Nisha Agarwal and Liane Aronchick, "A Matter of Life and Death: Advocates in New York Respond to Medical Repatriation," *Harvard Civil Rights–Civil Liberties Law Review* 46 (2010): 1–21; Vishal Agraharkar, "Deporting the Sick: Regulating International Patient Dumping by U.S. Hospitals," *Columbia Human Rights Law Review* 41 (2010): 569–600; Kit Johnson, "Patients Without Borders: Extralegal Deportation by Hospitals," *University of Cincinnati Law Review* 78, no. 2 (2009): 657–698; Lori Nessel, "Disposable Workers: Applying a Human Rights Framework to Analyze

Duties Owed to Seriously Injured or Ill Migrants," *Indiana Journal of Global Legal Studies* 19, no. 1 (2012): 61–103; Seton Hall University School of Law's Center for Social Justice and the Health Justice Program at the New York Lawyers for the Public Interest, *Discharge, Deportation, and Dangerous Journeys: A Study on the Practice of Medical Repatriation*, December 2012, http://medicalrepatriation.wordpress.com/our-report/; Stefanie Vincent, "Medical Repatriation: A Fourteenth Amendment Analysis of the International Patient Transferring of Illegal Aliens," *Houston Journal of International Law* 33, no. 1 (2010): 95–135; Jill Winland-Brown and Adam Dobrin, "Medical Repatriation: Physicians' and Nurses' Responses to a Dilemma," *Southern Online Journal of Nursing Research* 9, no. 4 (2009): 1–14.

45. Jennifer Smith, "Screen, Stabilize, and Ship: EMTALA, U.S. Hospitals, and Undocumented Immigrants," *Houston Journal of Health Law and Policy* 10 (2010): 309–358.

46. American College of Physicians, *National Immigration Policy and Access to Health Care* (Philadelphia: American College of Physicians, 2001), 1.

47. Ibid.

48. Lori Nessel, "The Legality and Ethics of Medical Repatriation," *Emerging Issues* 4404 (2009): 5; Daniel Procaccini, "First, Do No Harm: Tort Liability, Regulation and the Forced Repatriation of Undocumented Immigrants," *Boston College Third World Law Journal* 30 (2010): 475.

49. Johnson, "Patients Without Borders," 688.

50. Abigail Hauslohner and Janell Ross, "Trump Administration Circulates More Draft Immigration Restrictions, Focusing on Protecting U.S. Jobs," *Washington Post*, January 31, 2017.

51. Andrew Bremberg, "Executive Order on Protecting Taxpayer Resources by Ensuring Our Immigration Laws Promote Accountability and Responsibility," January 23, 2017, 1, https://www.nafsa.org/uploadedFiles/NAFSA_Dojo/Professional_Resources/Browse_by_Interest/International_Students_and_Scholars/DraftEOtaxprograms.pdf.

13. CITIZENSHIP IN THE GREEN CARD ARMY

SOFYA APTEKAR, UMASS BOSTON

When Lance Corporal Jose Gutierrez[1] became one of the first U.S. soldiers to be killed in Iraq in 2003, many were shocked to learn that this young Marine was not a U.S. citizen. For many Americans, it was a revelation that the soldier heroes dying in Operation Iraqi Freedom were not even technically Americans. As Gutierrez's story unraveled, it turned out that he had crossed the U.S. border without authorization in the mid-1990s and likely falsified his age to avoid deportation to his native Guatemala. The misrepresentation of age would make him deportable had he lived, but being killed by what turned out to be friendly fire in the first three days of the war gave Gutierrez U.S. citizenship—posthumously.[2] Many others have since been naturalized posthumously, and Gutierrez was just the latest in a long line of noncitizens who fought in the U.S. armed forces from the beginning of U.S. history.

Opinions about the participation of noncitizens in the U.S. military do not fall neatly along ideological lines.[3] On one side of the political spectrum, there is suspicion about these immigrants' loyalty and trustworthiness. At the same time, conservatives might see military service as a way to earn national membership and demonstrate allegiance as the ultimate deserving immigrant. Advocates of the DREAM Act, which would establish a path to citizenship for young undocumented immigrants who were brought to the United States by their families, also argue that these immigrants should be allowed to join the military to prove their deservingness and earn their citizenship. And then there are those who point out the exploitation inherent in the military recruiting process—the "poverty draft"—which targets underprivileged youth of color with promises of jobs, education, and a quick path to citizenship while downplaying the serious risks of enlisting.[4]

Political arguments notwithstanding, noncitizens have become an entrenched part of military recruitment strategies. The U.S. military is struggling with recruitment, and military leaders have identified immigrant enlistment as a way to overcome shortfalls in personnel. Under the Obama administration, the Department of Defense and many highly ranked military officials even expressed support for the DREAM Act.[5] Citizenship is a central piece of strategies to recruit an all-volunteer army to fight a war that has dragged on for over a decade. Noncitizen members of the military are now immediately eligible for naturalization. And yet many members of the military have not become American citizens. Like all other noncitizens—but with much higher risks of PTSD, substance abuse, and homelessness—veterans can be deported when they come into contact with the criminal justice system. Once deported, they have no access to veteran benefits aside from eventual burial on American soil.

In this chapter, I review the history of immigrants and naturalization in the U.S. military and describe the role of citizenship and its acquisition in the post-9/11 armed forces. I analyze how the increasingly criminalized and militarized U.S. immigration system plays out for immigrants in the military by considering the deportation of veterans, undocumented immigrants in the military, recruitment of nonimmigrant aliens, and posthumous naturalization. I discuss the ways in which the participation of immigrants in the military and their acts of heroism are used to justify military policies, illustrate American exceptionality, and prove immigrant deservingness.

Throughout the chapter, I draw on recent interview data with immigrant veterans to illuminate the experience of immigrants themselves. I conducted in-depth, semi-structured interviews with immigrant veterans in 2015 and 2016 as part of a research project on citizenship acquisition in the military. Participants were recruited through formal and informal veteran networks, including veteran organizations and veteran services. Varying in country of origin, migration trajectory, and military branch, interviewed veterans enlisted primarily after 9/11, when special citizenship provisions were instituted to attract and reward immigrant military service.

CITIZENSHIP, IMMIGRANTS, AND THE U.S. MILITARY

The history of immigrants in the U.S. military is as old as the history of the nation itself. And for just as long, citizenship, especially in wartime, has been used as a tool to recruit, control, and reward noncitizen soldiers.[6] In the hundred-plus years since 1907, more than 700,000 immigrants naturalized through military service, although many noncitizen soldiers—particularly Asian immigrants—were excluded from naturalization.[7] In addition, colonial populations participated in U.S. war efforts for decades without being able to access U.S. citizenship. In this section, I describe the history of immigrant soldiers and military naturalization.

During the Revolutionary War, state militias used state citizenship to encourage the enlistment of the foreign born.[8] Noncitizens were also recruited during the War of 1812 and the Mexican-American War.[9] The Civil War saw the first national draft, and all males that had filed their intentions to naturalize—a formerly widespread step that gave access to some rights—were included in the draft, making the Union army as much as 25 percent foreign born.[10] Immigrants also fought on the Confederate side.[11] In 1862, the waiting period for citizenship through military service was lowered from five years to one year for those who were honorably discharged.[12]

During World War I, almost 200,000 primarily European immigrants became citizens through military service, which represented approximately 50 percent of all naturalizations at that time.[13] Despite draconian anti-Asian citizenship laws, a few Japanese, Indian, and Filipino veterans were able to get citizenship, not by attempting to claim whiteness, as was then common, but by highlighting their loyalty and allegiance.[14] However, in most of the court cases over Asian eligibility for naturalization, race outweighed military service.[15] Over 100,000 immigrant soldiers primarily from Europe—naturalized during World War II.[16] Meanwhile, the citizenship of thousands of Japanese American soldiers was rescinded, and with their new classification as enemy aliens, Japanese Americans were not eligible for the draft until the end of the war. By the time a segregated Japanese American unit was created in 1944, many interned Japanese Americans chose prison over this demeaning reversal.[17]

Military service has been implicated in U.S. colonial empire as well. One of the largest immigrant groups in the military today are Filipinos, who for many decades could join the U.S. Navy directly from the Philippines, where the United States continues to have a heavy military presence.[18] During World War II, hundreds of thousands of Filipinos fought with the U.S. armed forces, but Roosevelt's promise to give them U.S. citizenship was withdrawn in 1946. When they finally got citizenship in 1990, some of the elderly veterans migrated to the United States.[19] Strikingly, by the 1970s, there were more Filipinos in the U.S. Navy than in the Philippine Navy. Until the 1980s, they were primarily stewards and essentially constituted a racialized segment of the U.S. military.[20] In 2015, I interviewed Proceso, who was among the last to enlist in the navy directly from the Philippines in the early 1990s. Proceso explained that in order to gain permanent legal residency, he had to reenlist for a second six-year commitment. He would not get naturalized until 2003.

NATURALIZATION IN THE MILITARY AFTER 9/11

After the attacks of 9/11 and the consequent invasion of Iraq and then Afghanistan by the U.S. military, immigrant soldiers were some of the first to die. Fifteen years later, about five thousand green card holders join the military each year, and approximately twenty-five thousand noncitizens are currently serving.[21] Altogether, immigrants constitute about 5 percent of the armed forces.[22] As the wars continue, military leadership has struggled to recruit volunteer personnel, and immigrants have come to be targeted more directly, with the promise of citizenship as a recruitment tool.[23] Noncitizens are a particularly desirable demographic group for military recruitment because they are younger than the native born, tend to be less likely to drop out of the military, and have language and cultural skills the military might need.[24] Over 100,000 noncitizens have been naturalized through military service between 2002 and 2016.[25] During these years, multiple changes in policy have facilitated access to U.S. citizenship for noncitizen service members; yet despite this considerable improvement, citizenship is not guaranteed, and some immigrant soldiers do not become naturalized.

Since the launch of the War on Terror, the U.S. government has made several changes that ease access to citizenship for noncitizen soldiers. The president is authorized to waive naturalization requirements for the military in official times of hostilities, which continue in 2017. In 2002, President Bush signed an executive order making noncitizens on active duty on or after September 11, 2001, immediately eligible for citizenship, rather than after one year of honorable service.[26] The National Defense Reauthorization Act of 2004 made naturalization possible outside the United States, which launched the now common practice of all-military naturalization ceremonies on overseas bases. Starting that year, immigrants in the military no longer had to pay the fees required of other naturalization applicants.[27] In 2008, after an immigrant soldier was killed on his way to be fingerprinted, U.S. Citizenship and Immigration Services (USCIS) stopped requiring military applicants for naturalization to submit fingerprints, and began using the fingerprints the applicants submitted upon enlistment.[28]

Noncitizen immigrants who have enlisted in the past several years benefit from the Naturalization at Basic Training Initiative, which was phased in between 2009 and 2013.[29] Now it is common to receive citizenship at graduation from boot camp, with assistance during basic training in filing the naturalization application (although no extra time is given to study for the citizenship exam). Those who fail to become naturalized at basic training can try again during advanced training.[30] Tens of thousands of immigrants have become citizens in this way.[31] While this initiative eases access to citizenship, making it part of basic training also makes it seem compulsory. Some immigrants may not want to naturalize, whether at that point in time or ever, and as Amaya points out, in cases of post-humous naturalization, enlistment does not equal desire to naturalize.[32]

In 2013, USCIS instituted a parole-in-place policy for military families. This means that on a case-by-case basis, relatives of service people can adjust their status, offering relief for the undocumented as well as those waiting in long lines for family reunification.[33] Part of the rationale for this policy is that it assists with military readiness because soldiers need family support and become distracted by deportations of loved ones.[34] Under the intensified deportation regime of the Trump administration, it is likely that more soldiers are going to have to worry about their immigrant family members. At the same time, parole in place is an administrative policy that can be easily reversed. As of the writing of this chapter, the policy's future was uncertain under the general direction of Trump-appointed DHS secretary John Kelly that parole programs be "exercised sparingly."[35]

Naturalized immigrant soldiers gain the right to vote, easier international travel, an improved ability to sponsor the migration of family members, and protection from deportation. In addition, many jobs within the military and outside it require citizenship.[36] David, a Haitian immigrant and navy veteran, explained that citizenship was necessary for his military career: "All of a sudden, when you reach a certain level . . . Even though I was enlisted, I wanted to become a Naval Officer, [so] I had to be [a] U.S. citizen." A quick pathway to citizenship for immigrant soldiers benefits the military as well. Occupation specialties that are closed to noncitizens create inefficiencies and internal personnel shortages. Commanders need active-duty soldiers with security clearances, which are contingent on citizenship. Naturalization during basic training reduces work absences.[37]

Before naturalization was made easier, immigrant soldiers had considerable difficulties applying for U.S. citizenship.[38] The requirement to be physically present on U.S. soil was onerous for soldiers undergoing multiple deployments, and the frequent changes of address meant repeatedly missing communications and deadlines. In other words, the requirements of immigration authorities were a spectacularly poor fit for the realities of military life. I interviewed a Mexican American veteran, Diego, who enlisted the day after he married a U.S. citizen and ceased being undocumented. It took him six years to finally get permanent legal residency. Diego recalls camping out outside the Los Angeles immigration offices overnight just to learn that his case was once again closed because his changes of address—due to deployments—were not entered into the system. Diego was not able to naturalize until he left the military. In some cases, veterans think they became U.S. citizens through their service; in fact, my interviews with immigrant activists indicate the possibility that some immigrants erroneously believe that naturalization happens automatically.[39]

Despite the new provisions that undoubtedly make naturalization easier for many immigrant members of the military, the military cannot guarantee citizenship. Just as with the civilian population, not everyone who applies for citizenship becomes a citizen. A recent Al Jazeera America Freedom of Information Act (FOIA) request revealed that between 2003 and 2014, 7,255 naturalization applications from immigrant soldiers were denied, while over 88,000 were approved, a denial rate slightly lower than that for the civilian population.[40] These figures do not take into account cases that were administratively closed; thus, the true rejection rate is likely higher.

The FOIA data reveals causes of denial for over four thousand service members. The most common category was poor moral character (over 1,500), which means one or more in a long list of moral shortcomings, from lying to committing crimes to being part of the Communist Party. Crucially, immigration officials exercise a wide discretion and can determine lack of good moral character even if the applicant does not fall into any of the categories on the list.[41] Civilian naturalization denials are less than half as likely to have been due to poor moral character. Kao reports on a case of an immigrant soldier whose permanent legal residency based on a marriage to a U.S. citizen was approved but whose subsequent application for naturalization was denied out of a lack of good moral character, due to earlier notes officials wrote questioning the validity of the marriage.[42]

Other noncitizen service members were denied citizenship because they did not respond to a request for more information, which can happen when USCIS does not keep up with military transfers and deployments.[43] Still others left the military too early: immigrants who naturalize through the military have to have five years of honorable service or face losing their citizenship.[44] The FOIA data lists many other reasons for denying naturalization to service members, including missing special requirements, already having citizenship, missing the citizenship interview, and failing the civics and history exam. Fourteen of these four-thousand-plus applicants were denied because they died while their applications were being processed. Interestingly, 124 of the denials were because the applicants turned out not to have been lawfully admitted to permanent residency or had been found deportable in the past.[45] This confirms the tendency of USCIS to treat naturalization as the last chance to find deportable immigrants, even among members of the military.[46]

DEPORTED VETERANS, UNDOCUMENTED SOLDIERS, AND MAVNI

The past two decades have seen a militarization of U.S. borders, criminalization of immigrant populations, increased emphasis on surveillance and screening of immigrants, and securitization of the boundaries around citizenship.[47] Some of these changes came directly after 9/11, including the reorganization of the Immigration and Naturalization Service from the Department of Justice to the new Department of Homeland Security. Others, such as mass detentions and deportations of hundreds of thousands of immigrants each year, stem from legislation that predates 2001, particularly the Illegal Immigration Reform and Immigrant Responsibility Act of 1996. The fates of immigrant service members and veterans are caught up in this increasingly criminalizing and militarized system. In the previous section, I explained how the scrutiny of immigrants at the point of naturalization results in denial of military applicants. The story is not complete without addressing the plight of deported veterans, considering how undocumented immigrants and nonimmigrant aliens fit in the military, and wrestling with the meaning of posthumous naturalization.

Over two million immigrants were deported during the Obama administration.[48] Soon after the 2016 elections, Trump vowed to quickly deport two to three million immigrants.[49] Veterans who are not U.S. citizens have faced deportation alongside civilians. There are over 500,000 foreign-born veterans in the United States, constituting about 3 percent of all U.S. veterans. Of the foreign-born veterans, approximately 18 percent have not naturalized and thus can be deported.[50] Deported veterans tend to be permanent legal residents, but due to a brush with the criminal justice system—sometimes decades prior—they face removal to their countries of birth. There are no special provisions in immigration courts for veterans. In an era of mass incarceration and widespread use of plea bargains, in which the accused are pressured to plead guilty to a lesser crime, immigrant veterans are particularly vulnerable. Disproportionately affected by substance abuse and homelessness, immigrant veterans who plead guilty to aggravated felonies— which range from minor crimes to murder—are often not told and do not themselves realize that this places them at risk for deportation:

> They sentenced me to 16 months in prison for possession, for a possession. It wasn't a possession for sales, it was just for my own use. And when they sentenced me, they never advised me that if I pleaded guilty there would be a chance that I would get deported. . . . They never advised me. The public defender never told me . . . if you are going to plead guilty, you know that you are deportable? . . . I told the judge that I was a Vietnam Era veteran. And he said, no, you know what, we are going to deport you.[51]

Deported veterans do have a right to return to the United States: they are guaranteed a spot in a military cemetery. It is nearly impossible for most of them, however, to access their Veteran Administration benefits once deported.[52]

Deported veterans began to gain visibility in 2015, in part due to the efforts of deported veterans themselves. Hector Barajas, who runs the Deported Veteran

Support House in Tijuana, enlisted right after high school and left the army six years later, in 2001, with an honorable discharge. After serving a short sentence for discharging a firearm, he was deported to Mexico. Barajas is in touch with dozens of deported veterans across the globe, and coordinates assistance for deported veterans in Mexico. Some have been deported because of drug possession charges, including Howard Bailey, a navy veteran now living in Jamaica. Bailey was not placed in deportation proceedings until he applied for naturalization, highlighting the criminalization of naturalization itself.[53] In fact, Diego, the veteran whose change-of-address forms had been repeatedly lost, wanted to naturalize in order to protect himself from being deported:

> Now if I commit a felony, they still can't deport me. Which is a joke. But that's the reality. I have two cousins who have been deported. . . . Feeling secure if whatever reason, I can't be deported anymore. Some people, they get into car accidents, DUIs, they get deported for making mistakes. That was always a fear of mine: what am I going to do in Mexico? . . . And to this day, I fear going to prison. Even though I don't do anything wrong, this is America, innocent people go to prison. That's one of my biggest fears: go to jail or getting deported. For me, it was a huge relief knowing that no matter what, I will never have to leave this country.

Given the criminalization of black and Latino Americans and the mass deportations, even veterans with exemplary service records can be afraid of losing their foothold in the United States.

At the same time as veterans with legal status are being deported, it is indeed possible for undocumented immigrants to serve in the armed forces. According to the Code of Federal Regulations (8 USC §1440), "aliens and noncitizen nationals" who are on active duty during an official period of hostilities can become naturalized, regardless of their immigration status. Plascencia points out that this means that a person who can be apprehended and deported in civilian life would instead become a citizen if he or she served in the military, and refers to this phenomenon as "no-card soldiers."[54] In a high-profile case soon after the U.S. invasion of Iraq, an immigrant soldier was revealed to have presented fraudulent documentation to enlist. Juan Escalante was an undocumented Mexican immigrant who came to the United States as a child and used a low-quality fake green card to enlist. The military decided not to discipline Escalante, and he became a U.S. citizen soon after.[55]

I interviewed Adolfo, an Ecuadorian immigrant who had trekked over multiple borders to arrive in New Jersey, where he enlisted in the army using a fraudulent stamp in his passport that indicated he was about to get a green card. Through considerable luck and skill, and despite several close calls, he managed to leave the military six years later without having been detected. Years later, and living once again as an undocumented migrant, Adolfo learned that he qualified for U.S. citizenship because he had enlisted a month before the First Gulf War ended and thus during an official period of hostilities:

> I went from illegal to citizen. I never had a green card. . . . I said: this is like getting me out of jail. Seventeen and a half years I've been without papers. . . . My mother and father died and I couldn't be at their funerals.

In addition to those who enlist with fraudulent documents, the military can authorize the enlistment of noncitizens—bypassing the normal requirements that enlistees be citizens or permanent residents—if they decide that these recruits are vital to the national interest. The determination of vital national interest is up to the U.S. Department of Defense (DOD) and has not been interpreted by the courts.[56] Using these powers, DOD created the Military Accessions Vital to the National Interest (MAVNI) recruitment program in 2009. Until it was suspended in 2016, the program attracted people on temporary nonimmigrant visas who had medical skills or "special languages and culture backgrounds." Fifty languages have been deemed of vital national interest, including Chinese, Russian, and Czech, as well as Arabic and Pashto. Interestingly, DOD drew an explicit parallel to the enlistment of Philippine nationals between 1952 and 1991, framing MAVNI as a descendant of that practice.[57]

MAVNI resulted in the enlistment of over ten thousand people, primarily of noncitizens on student visas, refugees, and those with temporary protected status.[58] Many successfully became U.S. citizens through the program, skipping permanent legal residency.[59] Margaret Stock, the architect of both MAVNI and the Naturalization at Basic Training initiative, received a MacArthur "genius grant" for her work. Despite the popularity and perceived success of MAVNI, some soldiers who were recruited through this program were not able to obtain citizenship.[60] As with other immigrant soldiers, citizenship may be used as an incentive, but it is not guaranteed. Moreover, since 2016, many of those who became naturalized through MAVNI have been singled out for enhanced security screenings that handicap their careers. The program itself has been suspended to deal with the new screening requirements, and there are indications that the Pentagon will cancel MAVNI enlistment contracts of those who are in the delayed entry program and have not yet gone through basic training. It is estimated that as many as a thousand of these enlistees have had their immigration status lapse while waiting. A cancellation of their contracts with the military will make them deportable.[61]

While many service members may never see frontline action, military service carries considerable risk to life and limb. By February 2017, there had been 6,896 military casualties in the various operations constituting the War on

Terror.[62] Pursuant to the Immigration and Naturalization Act, noncitizens who die in combat can be granted posthumous citizenship.[63] Since 2004, surviving spouses of those granted posthumous citizenship become eligible for citizenship. In addition, foreign spouses; parents; and children of citizens, legal permanent residents, and other immigrants who were posthumously naturalized can receive special adjustment-of-status benefits.[64] Over a hundred noncitizens have been naturalized in this way, including Jose Antonio Gutierrez, whose story opened this chapter.[65] Surviving family members, who may get little help with the process, are responsible for initiating the posthumous naturalization process within two years.[66] If the application is successful, the deceased is considered to have been a citizen at the time of death.[67] With the Naturalization at Basic Training program in place, it is hoped that posthumous naturalization will be less prevalent.[68] Regardless, turning noncitizen soldiers into citizens, particularly those who are undocumented, helps hide the contributions of this otherwise reviled social group to the security of the nation.[69] Naturalizing immigrant soldiers before and after their death supports dominant narratives of the U.S. military and its heroic volunteer labor force, as well as feeds into deservingness discourses around immigration reform, as I discuss in the next section.

LEGITIMATING THE MILITARY AND NATION, AND DEFENDING IMMIGRANT DESERVINGNESS

Recruitment of immigrant soldiers helps relieve the critical personnel shortages after a decade of war amidst the political impossibility of a draft. But their enlistment and subsequent work perform the additional duties of legitimating the U.S. military and the American nation. Their service helps preserve the image of the military as a volunteer force of heroes, and their choice to enlist—however constrained in reality—reaffirms dominant narratives of the nation. Even more apparent, military service of immigrants is used in the politics of deservingness, especially in the struggles over the DREAM Act.

There has not been a draft in the United States since the Vietnam War, and despite the shortage of soldiers, a draft is not politically feasible. The U.S. military is firmly entrenched in the American imagination as an all-volunteer force of patriot warriors: "Army Strong"; "America's Navy"; "the Few, the Proud, the Marines." The targeting of minority and immigrant communities in recruitment supports the image of the military as an inclusive, equitable, and modern institution that represents racial progress and color-blind meritocracy. And using naturalization to attract immigrants further relieves the pressure to institute a draft.[70] Moreover, the military needs its immigrant soldiers to be U.S. citizens in order to support narratives about loyalty and sacrifice to the nation. At a naturalization ceremony in Harlem in 2007, Congressman Charlie Rangel welcomed new citizens and spoke to the family members of Juan Alcantara, a Dominican-born soldier, who were receiving a certificate of posthumous citizenship. Rangel had served in the same division as Alcantara during the Korean War:

> Your son, your brother, your father, your child, wore the same uniform that I wore in 1950. . . . On November 30, 1950, I was at the northern border of North Korea. . . . We were overrun by tens of thousands of Chinese. And 90 percent of those people in the 2nd infantry division did not come home. I was one of the few that did. When I think about Juan not coming home, I wonder what would have happened if Sergeant Rangel did not come home on November 30, 1950. Would people be saying that I had been fighting the wrong war? Would they have condemned President Truman for sending me there? Would they have condemned the United Nations because I was there? I would hope not.
>
> I would hope that they would say that the late Sergeant Charles B. Rangel was a proud member of the 2nd infantry division. He was not a politician, he could not decide where my division was stationed on the border of North Korea or, these days, Iraq, . . . He took an oath that said when his Commander in Chief ordered him to defend the flag, he was to defend it for you, and for you, and for me, and for generations that follow. He took an oath that he was not going to challenge the political wisdom of where he was but that we could depend on him to defend this country as I would hope they would have said about me, if I didn't come home. . . . These are strong people, that risk their lives, that don't have the political opportunity to determine whether certain wars are right or wrong. They pledge their allegiance to the flag, they pledge their allegiance to this country, they pledge their allegiance to the armed forces and they do it to make our lives safer.[71]

When immigrant soldiers die while on active duty, making them citizens posthumously confirms that they died for a country that was theirs. Posthumous naturalization allows a particular set of meanings to attach to their death, one that benefits the U.S. military and does not disrupt dominant narratives of the War on Terror. The alternative is imagining the military as being staffed by foreigners—whether mercenaries or exploited—because few "real" Americans are willing to fight for their country. Instead, service in the military is reframed as the American Dream worth dying for.[72]

The service of immigrants in the armed forces, including stories about their disproportionate receipt of Medals of Honor, helps support narratives of the U.S. military as a vital force driven by mythical American patriots.[73] At the same time, it legitimates the American empire and U.S. military invasions. After all, the immigration trajectories of many immigrant soldiers can be traced to U.S.

invasions of their countries, not least in the case of the Philippines, as described earlier in this chapter.[74] In the current conflicts, the catastrophic costs of U.S. military invasions to citizens of Iraq and Afghanistan can be supplanted by the heartwarming stories of how quickly translators and "cultural experts" can receive U.S. citizenship.

The very spectacle of naturalization ceremonies that now take place on overseas bases is a powerful tool of nation building. Dozens of racially diverse soldiers, all in the same uniform, swear allegiance to the American nation. Some of them came to the United States as children, and others may have arrived a few months before the ceremony, but all together they reaffirm the high price of U.S. citizenship as something worth the ultimate risk. When these soldiers are praised for their service, the exploits of the U.S. military are implicitly supported and praised as well:

> I would like to take this moment to thank you. You are sacrificing much to protect the very freedoms that your soon to be adopted country cherishes and loves. I am proud to soon call you my fellow Americans. You are all heroes in the war on terror. Know that the United States is behind you, and that we support you—completely. One Team, One Fight![75]

Even in many post-9/11 civilian citizenship ceremonies that I observed for an earlier project, military members in uniform were placed in the front row and distinguished repeatedly for their contributions.[76] Their very presence, as people who were willing to die for the United States without even being full members, demonstrated the value and worth of U.S. citizenship.

Immigrant soldiers are a powerful symbol that supports the U.S. military and empire. They are also used to make arguments in defense of immigrant deservingness. The stories of heroic immigrants who risk their lives in battle rebuke the nativist images of free-riding immigrants and criminal illegals.[77] Immigrant service members can avoid the stereotypes of unskilled immigrants or immigrants who take Americans' jobs. Veterans for Immigration Reform, for instance, uses the "Nation of Immigrants" narrative by connecting today's immigrant soldiers to those who served in the world wars, with all the positive connotations of heroism and patriotism. Advocates claim a right for immigrants to serve, and a position as equals in lobbying for immigration reform: "We stand here together today under the red, white and blue not to threaten or to beg, but to participate in the democratic process and to ask our members of Congress to do the right thing."[78] They argue for deservingness not as supplicants or menaces but as equals. Their arguments are supported by the perception of the military as an institution of integration and assimilation, not only for immigrants but for domestic minorities as well.[79]

In addition, military service is the ultimate way of *earning* citizenship and proving one's worth to the United States. Of course, it is not always enough. Richard Avila, a deported Marine, bemoaned the unfairness of what happened to him:

> If there is one thing I could say to the secretary of the Veterans Administration, it would be that regardless if you were drafted or not—I enlisted myself—that in itself shows loyalty. It's insistent that to be a U.S. national, you have to have permanent allegiance to the United States. And what better way of showing your allegiance to the United States than by enlisting.[80]

Avila strongly links the *choice* to enlist with allegiance to the United States. The reduced naturalization eligibility periods for members of the military are politically palatable in part because military service so effectively proves allegiance to the United States.[81]

Immigrant soldiers have become formidable rhetorical figures in arguing for immigrant rights. At the same time, immigration reform is increasingly militarized.[82] As noted previously, DOD actively supports the DREAM Act legislation, which would provide a path to citizenship for undocumented youth who go to college or enlist in the military. From the perspective of the military, these undocumented youth are an attractive population because, unlike foreigners, there is more information about their backgrounds, and they have attended U.S. schools. Mariscal even calls this proposed legislation the "Recruiter's DREAM."[83] (Deferred Action for Childhood Arrivals, instituted in 2012 and not providing a path to citizenship, does not allow undocumented youth to enlist except for those who qualified for MAVNI due to special skills.)[84]

Were the DREAM Act to pass, more young immigrants would choose the military as a path to citizenship over college. College is more costly, and barriers to it are higher than for enlisting. Research on undocumented youth indicates that many see the military as not only the more realistic strategy for getting citizenship but also the one that better proves their loyalty and gratitude.[85] Those who go to college and those who enlist would be required to complete two years before becoming eligible for permanent residency. The key difference is that military contracts are much longer than two years.[86] It is clear, then, that the U.S. military would benefit tremendously from the passage of the DREAM Act, which would legalize over a million immigrants.[87] The benefits to immigrants themselves have to be weighed alongside studies that show that as people of color, Asian, Latino, and black soldiers are more likely to experience combat and more likely to exhibit symptoms of posttraumatic stress disorder.[88] As immigration reform becomes militarized, the promise of citizenship is tied to participation in a continuous and bloody war overseas.[89]

There is a long history of immigrant participation in the U.S. military, as well as the use of citizenship to recruit and control immigrant soldiers. In recent years, barriers to naturalization through the military have been lowered, although citizenship remains elusive for too many vulnerable veterans. Naturalization through the military fits within the larger frameworks of securitization and militarization of the immigration system. The use of naturalization to entice immigrants to join the military is ironic given the concern about immigrants seeking naturalization for the wrong reasons, such as to access welfare or bring over multiple relatives, rather than out of allegiance to the United States.[90] In this case, it appears that it is the U.S. government and its military that are using naturalization instrumentally—that is, to meet personnel shortages in the armed forces.[91]

The militarization of naturalization improves access to citizenship and the rights and security that go with it for many immigrant soldiers. But the intersection of military and immigration systems creates multiple gaps through which immigrants might fall. Deemed good enough to enlist by the military, they may not be deemed good enough to receive citizenship by the immigration authorities. An already marginalized population, they assume tremendous risks in order to have a chance of gaining a foothold on full membership in society. By building naturalization into basic training, the option to carefully weigh the risks and benefits of the citizenship acquisition process may become less available.

NOTES TO CHAPTER 13

1. Jose Gutierrez as referred to in this chapter is a different person from the Jose Gutierrez whose story is the focus of chapter 12.

2. Rebecca Leung, "The Death of Lance Cpl. Gutierrez: Simon Reports on Non-Citizen Soldiers," CBS News, April 23, 2003, http://www.cbsnews.com/news/the-death -of-lance-cpl-gutierrez/; Luis Plascencia, "Citizenship Through Veteranship: Latino Migrants Defend the US 'Homeland,'" *Anthropology News* 50, no. 5 (2009): 8–9.

3. Jorge Mariscal, "Immigration and Military Enlistment: The Pentagon's Push for the Dream Act Heats Up," *Latino Studies* 5, no. 3 (2007): 358–363; Cara Wong, "Who Fights: Substitution, Commutation, and 'Green Card Troops,'" *Du Bois Review* 4 (2007): 1–22.

4. Jorge Mariscal, "No Where Else to Go: Latino Youth and the Poverty Draft," *Political Affairs*, September 23, 2004.

5. Catherine Barry, "New Americans in Our Nation's Military: A Proud Tradition and Hopeful Future," Center for American Progress, 2013; Mariscal, "Immigration and Military Enlistment"; Veterans for Immigration Reform, "On the Front Line: The Impact of Immigrants on Military Force Readiness," National Immigration Forum and National Immigration Forum Action Fund, 2014, http://www.vets4reform.org/wp -content/uploads/2014/06/OnTheFrontLine.pdf.

6. Barry, "New Americans"; Darlene Goring, "In Service to America: Naturalization of Undocumented Alien Veterans," *Seton Hall Law Review*, no. 30 (2000), http://digitalcommons.law.lsu.edu/faculty_scholarship/267; Plascencia, "Citizenship Through Veteranship"; Wong, "Who Fights."

7. Barry, "New Americans in Our Nation's Military."

8. John Whiteclay Chambers, *To Raise an Army: The Draft Comes to Modern America* (New York: Free Press, 1987).

9. James Jacobs and Leslie Anne Hayes, "Aliens in the U.S. Armed Forces: A Historico-Legal Analysis," *Armed Forces and Society* 7, no. 2 (1981): 187–208; Chambers, *To Raise an Army.*

10. Barry, "New Americans"; Chambers, *To Raise an Army.*

11. Mae M. Ngai, *Impossible Subjects: Illegal Aliens and the Making of Modern America* (Princeton: Princeton University Press, 2014).

12. Michael LeMay and Elliott Barkan, *U.S. Immigration and Naturalization Laws and Issues: A Documentary History* (Westport: Greenwood, 1999); Wong, "Who Fights."

13. Barry, "New Americans"; Deenesh Sohoni and Amin Vafa, "The Fight to Be American: Military Naturalization and Asian Citizenship," *Asian American Law Journal* 17 (2010): 119–151.

14. Ngai, *Impossible Subjects*; Sohoni and Vafa, "The Fight to Be American."

15. Sohoni and Vafa, "The Fight to Be American."

16. Catherine Barry, "Being All They Can Be? U.S. Military Experience and the Earnings of Young Adult Immigrants" (paper presented at the American Sociological Association Annual Meeting, Boston, August 2008).

17. Ngai, *Impossible Subjects.*

18. Barry, "New Americans"; Jeanne Batalova, "Immigrants in the U.S. Armed Forces," Migration Policy Institute, 2008, http://www.migrationpolicy.org/article/immigrants-us-armed-forces.

19. Gay Becker, Yewoubdar Beyene, and Leilani Canalita, "Immigrating for Status in Late Life: Effects of Globalization on Filipino American Veterans," *Journal of Aging Studies* 14, no. 3 (2000): 273–291.

20. Proceso James Paligutan, "American Dream Deferred: Filipino Nationals in the US Navy and Coast Guard, 1947–1970" (PhD diss., University of California, Irvine, 2012), http://gradworks.umi.com/35/43/3543831.html; Yen Le Espiritu, "Colonial Oppression, Labour and Importation and Group Formation: Filipinos in the United States," *Ethnic and Racial Studies* 19, no. 1 (1996): 29.

21. U.S. Department of Defense, "Military Accessions Vital to National Interest (MAVNI) Recruitment Pilot Program Fact Sheet," 2015, http://www.defense.gov/news/mavni-fact-sheet.pdf; Joanna Kao, "Good Enough to Fight for the US but Missing the Mark for Citizenship," *Al Jazeera America*, May 8, 2015, http://america.aljazeera.com/multimedia/2015/5/good-enough-to-be-soldier-but-not-citizen.html.

22. Barry, "New Americans"; Veterans for Reform, "On the Front Line."

23. Barbara A. Bicksler and Lisa G. Nolan, "Recruiting an All-Volunteer Force: The Need for Sustained Investment in Recruiting Resources—an Update," Strategic Analysis, December 2009, http://prhome.defense.gov/Portals/52/Documents/RFM/MPP

/Accession%20Policy/docs/Bicksler%20Recruiting%20Paper%202009.pdf; Barry, "New Americans"; Tracy Lachica Buenavista, "Citizenship at a Cost: Undocumented Asian Youth Perceptions and the Militarization of Immigration," *AAPI Nexus: Asian Americans and Pacific Islanders Policy, Practice and Community* 10, no. 1 (2012): 101–124.

24. Anita Hattiangadi, Aline Quester, Gary Lee, Diana Lien, and Ian MacLeod, "Non-Citizens in Today's Military: Final Report," Center for Naval Analyses, 2005, https://www.cna.org/CNA_files/PDF/D0011092.A2.pdf; Omer Senturk and Lynn O'Neill, "Noncitizens in the U.S. Military" (master's thesis, Naval Postgraduate School, 2004), https://calhoun.nps.edu/handle/10945/1640.

25. U.S. Citizenship and Immigration Services, USCIS Policy Manual, vol. 12, Citizenship & Naturalization, Part D—General Naturalization Requirements, chap. 7—Attachment to the Constitution, 2016, https://www.uscis.gov/policymanual/HTML/PolicyManual-Volume12-PartD-Chapter7.html.

26. U.S. Department of Defense, "MAVNI Fact Sheet," https://www.defense.gov/news/mavni-fact-sheet.pdf.

27. Barry, "New Americans."

28. Associated Press, "Mother Uses Son's Iraq Death to Change Law, Help Soldiers Get Citizenship," *New York Daily News*, June 27, 2008, http://www.nydailynews.com/latino/mother-son-iraq-death-change-law-soldiers-citizenship-article-1.295840.

29. Associated Press, "Army, Navy Add Citizenship Option to Boot Camp," *Boston Globe*, April 21, 2011, http://archive.boston.com/news/nation/articles/2011/04/21/army_navy_add_citizenship_option_to_boot_camp/; Barry, "New Americans."

30. Associated Press, "Army, Navy Add Citizenship Option."

31. Buenavista, "Citizenship at a Cost."

32. Hector Amaya, "Dying American or the Violence of Citizenship: Latinos in Iraq," *Latino Studies* 5, no. 1 (2007): 3–24.

33. U.S. Citizenship and Immigration Services, Policy Memorandum, Parole of Spouses, Children and Parents of Active Duty Members of the U.S. Armed Forces, the Selected Reserve of the Ready Reserve, and Former Members of the U.S. Armed Forces or Selected Reserve of the Ready Reserve and the Effect of Parole on Inadmissibility Under Immigration and Nationality Act §212(a)(6)(A)(i) PM-602-0091, 2013, https://www.uscis.gov/sites/default/files/USCIS/Laws/Memoranda/2013/2013-1115_a_in_Place_Memo_.pdf.

34. Veterans for Immigration Reform, "On the Front Line."

35. U.S. Department of Homeland Security, "Implementing the President's Border Security and Immigration Enforcement Improvement Policies," Memo, February 20, 2017, https://www.dhs.gov/sites/default/files/publications/17_0220_S1_Implementing-the-Presidents-Border-Security-Immigration-Enforcement-Improvement-Policies.pdf.

36. Sofya Aptekar, *The Road to Citizenship: What Naturalization Means for Immigrants and the United States* (New Brunswick: Rutgers University Press, 2015); Associated Press, "Army, Navy Add Citizenship Option."

37. Associated Press, "Army, Navy Add Citizenship Option."

38. Barry, "New Americans."

39. Susan Cooper Eastman, "U.S. Citizenship Given to Cuban-Born Man Who Thought 1975 Army Enlistment Made Him Citizen," Reuters, May 21, 2014, http://www.reuters.com/article/2014/05/21/us-usa-florida-immigration-idUSBREA4K13Z20140521.

40. Kao, "Good Enough to Fight."

41. Sofya Aptekar, "Constructing the Boundaries of US Citizenship in the Era of Enforcement and Securitization," in *Citizenship, Belonging and Nation-States in the 21st Century*, ed. Nicole Stokes-Dupass and Ramona Fruja (New York: Palgrave-MacMillan, 2016); Kevin Lapp, "Reforming the Good Moral Character Requirement for U.S. Citizenship," *Indiana Law Journal* 87, no. 4 (2012).

42. Kao, "Good Enough to Fight."

43. Ibid.

44. Associated Press, "Army, Navy Add Citizenship Option."

45. Kao, "Good Enough to Fight."

46. Aptekar, "Constructing the Boundaries."

47. Ibid.

48. Marc Rosenblum and Doris Meissner, "The Current Record on Deportations: What Underlies the 'Eye of the Beholder' Dynamic?" Migration Policy Institute, April 2014, http://www.migrationpolicy.org/news/current-record-deportations-what-underlies-eye-beholder-dynamic.

49. Haeyoun Park and Troy Griggs, "Could Trump Really Deport Millions of Unauthorized Immigrants?," *New York Times*, February 21, 2017, https://www.nytimes.com/interactive/2016/11/29/us/trump-unauthorized-immigrants.html.

50. Jie Zong and Jeanne Batalova, "Immigrant Veterans in the United States. Spotlight," *Migration Information Source*, Migration Policy Institute, October 13, 2016, http://www.migrationpolicy.org/article/immigrant-veterans-united-states.

51. Oscar Leyva, featured in DPC Vets, *Honorably Discharged, Dishonorably Deported*, documentary film, 2015, https://www.youtube.com/watch?v=xGK48Ky6hHw.

52. ACLU, "Discharged, Then Discarded: How US Veterans Are Banished by the Country They Swore to Protect," ACLU California, July 2016, https://www.aclusandiego.org/wp-content/uploads/2017/04/DISCHARGED-THEN-DISCARDED-fixed.pdf.

53. Julia Alsop, "War Veteran Smokes Pot, Faces Deportation," NPR, November 13, 2015, http://latinousa.org/2015/11/13/war-veteran-smokes-pot-faces-deportation/; James Clark, "Desperate to Return Home, Deported Veterans Face Exile," *Task and Purpose*, December 17, 2015, http://taskandpurpose.com/desperate-to-return-home-deported-veterans-face-exile/.

54. Plascencia, "Citizenship Through Veteranship."

55. Chris McGann, "Soldier's Medal of Honor Is Citizenship," *Seattle Post-Intelligencer Reporter*, February 11, 2004, http://www.seattlepi.com/local/article/Soldier-s-medal-of-honor-is-citizenship-1136838.php; Plascencia, "Citizenship Through Veteranship."

56. Bryant Jordan, "Lawyer Says Immigration Military Recruitment Legislation Unnecessary," Military.com, May 20, 2015, http://www.military.com/daily-news/2015/05/20/lawyer-says-immigration-military-recuitment-legislation-unneeded.html.

57. U.S. Department of Defense, "MAVNI Fact Sheet."

58. Alex Horton, "The Pentagon Promised Citizenship to Immigrants Who Served. Now It Might Help Deport Them," *Washington Post*, June 26, 2017, https://www.washingtonpost.com/news/checkpoint/wp/2017/06/26/the-pentagon-promised-citizenship-to-immigrants-who-served-now-it-might-help-deport-them/.

59. Barry, "New Americans"; U.S. Department of Defense, "MAVNI Fact Sheet."

60. Kao, "Good Enough to Fight."

61. U.S. Immigration and Customs Enforcement, "MAVNI Program Status for Fiscal Year 2017," https://www.ice.gov/doclib/sevis/pdf/bcm-1612-02.pdf; Horton, "Pentagon Promised Citizenship."

62. U.S. Department of Defense, U.S. Casualties of Operations Iraqi Freedom (OIF), Enduring Freedom (OEF), and New Dawn (OND), 2017, http://www.defense.gov/casualty.pdf.

63. Sohoni and Vafa, " Fight to Be American."

64. Margaret Stock, *Essential to the Fight: Immigrants in the Military Eight Years After 9/11* (Washington, D.C.: American Immigration Council, 2009).

65. Batalova, "Immigrants in the Armed Forces."

66. Buenavista, "Citizenship at a Cost."

67. Amaya, "Dying American."

68. Stock, *Essential to the Fight*.

69. Plascencia, "Citizenship Through Veteranship."

70. Wong, "Who Fights."

71. Charles Rangel, Remarks made at naturalization ceremony, City College, City University of New York, July 3, 2007, transcribed from recording and notes made by author.

72. Amaya, "Dying American."

73. Barry, "New Americans"; Wong, "Who Fights."

74. Buenavista, "Citizenship at a Cost."

75. Eduardo Aguirre, Director of USCIS, Remarks at a naturalization ceremony at Camp Victory, Baghdad, October 2004.

76. Aptekar, *Road to Citizenship*.

77. Wong, "Who Fights."

78. Veterans for Immigration Reform, "On the Front Line."

79. Barry, "New Americans"; Ngai, *Impossible Subjects*; Wong, "Who Fights."

80. DPC Vets, *Honorably Discharged, Dishonorably Deported*.

81. Sohoni and Vafa, " Fight to Be American."

82. Buenavista, "Citizenship at a Cost."

83. Mariscal, "Immigration and Military Enlistment."

84. U.S. Department of Defense, "MAVNI Fact Sheet."

85. Buenavista, "Citizenship at a Cost"; Mariscal, "Immigration and Military Enlistment."

86. Mariscal, "Immigration and Military Enlistment."

87. Pew Research Center, "Up to 1.4 Million Unauthorized Immigrants Could Benefit from New Deportation Policy," Pew Research Center, 2012, http://www.pewhis

panic.org/2012/06/15/up-to-1-4-million-unauthorized-immigrants-could-benefit-from -new-deportation-policy/.

88. Buenavista, "Citizenship at a Cost"; Mariscal, "No Where Else to Go"; Mariscal, "Immigration and Military Enlistment"; Peter Nien-chu Kiang, "About Face: Recognizing Asian and Pacific American Vietnam Veterans in Asian American Studies," *Amerasia Journal* 17, no. 3 (1991): 22–40.

89. Buenavista, "Citizenship at a Cost."

90. Aptekar, *Road to Citizenship.*

91. Amaya, "Dying American."

14. THE PRODUCTION OF NONCITIZEN EXCLUSIONS
UNDER H-1B AND L-1 VISAS

PAYAL BANERJEE, SMITH COLLEGE

Vir, an Indian software engineer in the United States working on an H-1B visa, received a phone call late one evening from his employer. This employer was a labor subcontractor whose employees—like Vir—were placed on various clients' projects on term contracts across the country. The conversation quickly escalated into an altercation, in which the point of contention was Vir's salary. The employer had bluntly announced his decision to increase the share of his own "cut" out of Vir's billing rate (the billing rate is the dollar amount that the end client, a large investment firm on the East Coast, was paying hourly for Vir's work).

Vir objected vehemently; this sudden move seemed arbitrary, with no indication in their initial mutual decision about the 20 percent commission that the employer would take out of Vir's billing rate. Now the rate was to be increased to 30 percent. Vir's resistance cost him dearly: not only was he fired on the spot, but the termination of his employment added to various other travails. Vir was told that his H-1B visa would be canceled the next morning and that he should immediately vacate his apartment, which his company rented out to employees like him. Vir did not want to attract any more trouble or precipitate a confrontation, distraught as he now was without a job, his housing, and his visa status. He packed quickly, left the apartment, and went to a friend's house nearby. He was not sure what he would have done at that hour had he not had that friend to turn to for refuge.[1]

Vir and others who participated in this research represent the much larger population of Indian IT workers who have been inducted into the U.S. economy on H-1B visas in numbers that have crossed tens of thousands since the late-1990s. Throughout the course of my research and interviews, I came across dozens of narratives that closely resembled or resonated with the incident just described. A central message was at their core: the protections of work visa–based documented status are fragile, particularly conditional, and very easily intercepted. Vir's account also gave me pause, as it jolted me into recollecting another incident I came across in the early 2000s, during the course of fieldwork for a project on a restaurant in upstate New York run by Indian immigrants. Manpreet, the niece of the owners of this restaurant and herself a noncitizen then in her teens, would often share with me the details of the struggle her undocumented father, Navjot, had faced in the United States. These included finding work at restaurants and grocery stores, paying rent, and putting in countless hours in multiple jobs to bring the rest of his family from India to the United States. She narrated an event that conveyed an uncanny similarity with Vir's experience:

> My father worked at his friend's store. When he first arrived, his friend behaved very well and helped him begin his life here. My father used to stay with his friend's family and also have his meals with them. . . . But after a while, they began to misbehave with him. Once they asked him to get out of their house, and it was snowing heavily that night. He had no shoes on. He did not have his work papers yet, so he was quite helpless.

One of the many in a series of hardships that Navjot had endured, this particular event attests to what we already know about the structural reasons that unleash the indignities, exploitations, and asymmetries of power associated with undocumented immigration status. However, a juxtaposition of the ways in which both Vir and Navjot could be thrown out into the streets and pushed deeper into the recesses of status threat overnight—despite notable differences in immigration status, class, and occupational placement—makes visible how work visa–based legal standing has been constituted by conditional protections, circumscribed heavily within the essential impulses of immigrant exclusions and deportability.

To be sure, having market-average salaries and visas stamped on passports— particularly visas like the H-1B, which are explicitly reserved for college-educated "skilled workers"—does confer certain social and economic privileges.[2] They reinforce a class-based identity for their bearers, for example, simply on account of being classified as white-collar workers in a professional field. Further, so long as the visa is current—that is, the noncitizen's employment is not terminated— individuals on the H-1B can reenter the country, petition for dependent visas for spouses and children, get a social security number, set up bank accounts, and obtain a driver's license with relative ease. Most of these privileges, however, are of limited durability and entirely conditional on the validity of status attached to the work visas, which, as will be elaborated on, define and institutionalize for noncitizens a highly unstable legal status upon whose duration these workers have little control. As a result, noncitizens on these visas make many accommodations to keep their jobs, for it is their affiliation with an employer that serves as the only means for them to preserve their legal status as well as the only official endorsement of their capacity to reside in the United States.

Thus, when the exploitation and marginality of those on work visas apportioned for the so-called specialty occupations are read alongside the experiences of noncitizens of color working in farms, factories, grocery stores, or restaurants, often navigating the state's surveillance and a mass-scale deportation regime, what becomes visible is a more comprehensive spectrum of immigration control and racialized exclusions in the current age of punishment.[3] This chapter takes a closer look at how the ever-present specter of status loss and deportability, encoded deep within the parameters of documented status defined by law under the terms of the work visas, has structured the disciplinary mechanisms that firmly emplace noncitizens within the administrative ambit of immigration enforcement. Having emerged in part from the legal genealogy of the exclusion-based exploitation of Asian immigrant labor, and therefore reflecting the long arc of the racialized development of American capitalism and global hegemony, these work visas today are endowed with important specifications suitable for the state's current immigration control and racial management strategies, designed to sustain the U.S. empire's transnational security regime and economic dominance.[4]

NONCITIZEN LABOR INCORPORATION, WORK VISAS, AND THE TECHNOLOGIES OF EXCLUSIONS

Amar graduated from an engineering college in India with a degree in computer programming in the early 2000s, a time when a large number of Indian- and U.S.-based companies had already streamlined an aggressive hiring strategy for IT positions all over the United States. Amar and his cohort, however, were beginning to confirm what they had already heard from "seniors" in college: that almost all the jobs on offer represented short-term and contractual employment with consulting companies or labor subcontractors and not with the end client. Eager to minimize in-house expenses and accompanying commitments associated with retaining employees on direct payroll, companies in the United States had already started to externalize their IT labor needs to consulting firms, which in turn had begun to rely on labor vendors to access workers on temporary contracts. As a result, the vast majority of Indian IT workers found themselves in the lower tiers of the subcontracting hierarchy in the United States, as employees of labor vendors or the so-called body shops.[5]

However, the materialization of this racialized labor flexibility, with access to the necessary workers and a vast, multilayered, intricate support system, depended on the social production of certain interrelated and specific conditions of capital and immigrant labor incorporation: (1) the institutionalization of a set of transnational linkages between India and the United States to forge a pathway for accessing labor from the global South; and (2) the convenience of a visa, one whose terms would render this labor docile, deportable, and vulnerable under the radar of immigration enforcement writ large—that is, visa terms that were amenable to the production of flexible workers for capital and temporary noncitizens for the state. As the cost of skilled labor began to escalate with the growing salience of IT in business processes since the 1970s, advanced capitalist economies of the global North sought sources of cheaper and more flexible labor, in the form of both noncitizen workers and offshore labor based in countries with an appropriate workforce, such as India and Ireland. A number of companies, including the tech giants based in the United States, took advantage of India's recent economic liberalization, specifically in software and IT. Thus, they invested heavily in these sectors in anticipation of high growth and revenue, as well as access to a skilled workforce at pay rates that represented a remarkable advantage compared to similar costs in the United States. Many multinationals in banking, finance, and management followed this trend. These processes mobilized the flow of investment capital from the United States and, by the 1990s, had integrated the two countries' IT sectors via the links of trade in software for U.S. clients, use of offshore labor in India, and the establishment of an extensive network of corporate branches and subsidiaries in both countries.

In this structural context, U.S. companies' growing need for skilled labor mobilized the recruitment of Indian IT workers and their incorporation of noncitizen labor on the H-1B since the late-1990s.[6] As an employer- and employment-dependent temporary work visa, the declared function of the H-1B is to enable companies in the United States to hire skilled foreign nationals for employment in "specialty occupations," defined as positions that "require the theoretical or practical application of a body of highly specialized knowledge, including but not limited to scientists, engineers, or computer programmers."[7] The visa requires at the bare minimum a bachelor's degree (or an equivalent degree or experience). The visa, however, enforces rigid restrictions on who can be employed and in which occupations under this program: the applicant's educational credentials and experience must match the specialized field of the position and the specific content of the job (e.g., someone with a BA in economics is unlikely to be granted a visa to work in the position of an accountant). In the late-1990s, the IT industry's demands for an increased supply of high-skilled labor on the H-1B visa resulted in a series of evaluations and congressional hearings, after which the U.S. Congress increased the annual cap set at 65,000 visas. The American Competitiveness and Workforce Improvement Act of 1998, and later the American Competitiveness in the Twenty-First Century Act of 2000 increased the quota to 195,000 for each year through 2002. The number of applications per year for this visa, despite two phases of economic downturn (in the early 2000s and again post-2008), continuously outstripped the supply of these visas throughout the late 1990s and into the twenty-first century (with a few exceptions). The H-1B visa—in one instance dubbed the "workhorse of the IT industry"—has since the late 1990s enabled the recruitment and placement of hundreds of thousands of Indian IT workers, predominantly male, on IT projects across all sectors in the U.S. economy.[8]

As noted, the corporate sector in the United States was unwilling to take on the task of hiring this workforce as direct employees, preferring instead the convenience of completing their projects with contingent workers on temporary contracts. As a result, Indian IT workers have continued to encounter a unique proposition: the H-1B visa requires a U.S. employer by legal mandate; the end clients, however, are not interested in hiring, even though it is their labor demand that fuels the recruitment of this noncitizen workforce. In this scenario, subcontractors have been entrusted with the task of assembling the components necessary for sustaining the flexibility that capital has required—that is, hiring the workers, legitimizing their employability in the United States by processing their visas, and keeping on hand a labor-ready workforce prepared to be deployed at clients' sites at short notice.[9]

When Amar was offered a job by a U.S.-based vendor and reached the United States as its employee, he joined the ranks of thousands of Indian noncitizen "contract workers" hired under the auspices of the term-bound H-1B visa. Coca-Cola, Microsoft, and General Electric, among others, represent the spectrum of clients for which some of the interviewees in this research were working as subcontracted labor. Although placed on projects with companies that represent the highest echelons of global capitalism, the majority of the IT workers revealed that their work experience in these spaces of accumulated wealth and power conferred no sense of entitlement, affiliation, or long-term career prospects, defined as they were by their non-belonging. As temporary, externalized, and highly disposable subcontracted workers, they were categorically marked by their noncitizen visa-dependent status on the H-1B. As the following section elaborates, employers' need for flexible workers corresponded with the U.S. state's priorities in keeping noncitizens' status temporary, which has been achieved through their placement within a legal framework in which status can be terminated at any given moment, making noncitizens vulnerable to removal proceedings at any time.

TEMPORARY AND CONTRACT BASED

Milind had worked on several projects with different clients in New York, New Jersey, Texas, Arizona, and Virginia. His longest client tenure was about seven months; the shortest, just over a month. One did not have to be told that he felt tired of having to move around as a contract worker. But there was another fear that compounded his insecurity:

> It is the visa, you know. Being on the H-1B means that your status is always on the line. I have this job now, my employer [a subcontractor] is good. I have had clients back-to-back, so he doesn't complain, he makes his money [commission]. But there is no telling. If anything happens tomorrow and I get fired, I have lost my visa. To stay here, have a job, have status, I have to start again by looking for an employer who will agree to do [process] my visa. On this visa, it is hard, so hard. The status can go, vanish in an instant.

The increasing reliance on nonimmigrant-category temporary work visas, like the H-1B, to access migrant labor is not just emblematic of corporate preference for labor flexibility. It is an equally potent marker of the U.S. state's resolve to implement various forms of immigration exclusions, disentitlements, and impermanence in such a way that the needs of capital are served while the noncitizens are kept as far removed as possible from a more permanent and secure status. In the post–World War II era, the demand for skilled labor necessary to sustain U.S. economic and political expansion was met in part by the Hart-Celler Act (1965) reforms, which established mechanisms to integrate much-needed labor under the "occupational preference system"—one of the two primary avenues toward achieving immigrant status or legal permanent residency. This option provided work authorization to those deemed skilled workers (contingent upon meeting certain labor criteria) and offered a fairly permanent and stable immigration status, conducive to settlement and future citizenship. Despite the limitations of country-specific annual green card quotas, which particularly affect applicants who are citizens of countries like China and India, the occupational-preference system-based work authorization and legal permanent residency (long-term and renewable legal status) still remains an option and admits a large number of new noncitizens each year.[10]

Since the 1990s, however, a different approach toward inducting noncitizens started to gain ground—one that has decidedly turned away from extending to noncitizens the interrelated prospects of long-term settlement and autonomous labor status, replacing them with short-term employment- and employer-based entry. The H-1B is generally issued for an initial term of three years, during which it remains valid only so long as the employment criteria and all other labor conditions are met. A visa stamp bearing a three-year validity does not therefore automatically guarantee the noncitizens' right to enter or live in the United States for the specified duration. During this time, whether the visa will remain current and usable is determined by employment status. The stipulated parameters that render a visa current and valid can be expanded, contracted, nullified, or terminated, either by the employer or by the state, without the consent of the noncitizen. After the first three years, the H-1B can be renewed following a formal application for another three years, pending the same conditions. When a noncitizen uses up the six years, continuing and maintaining work status comes with additional hurdles. Unless there is an employment-based green card application in place and beyond a certain stage of advancement, which allows short-term extensions of stay, the noncitizen needs to exit the country for one year before a fresh H-1B can be processed. This visa has now been made "portable," which means that immigrants can change employers, but only if a prospective company agrees to process a visa as the new petitioning employer on the noncitizen's behalf.

DEPENDENT AND DEPORTABLE

The H-1B, though explicitly designed for employment, does not confer to noncitizens ("aliens," according to the U.S. Citizenship and Immigration Services) any independent work authorization. Instead, one needs to remain at the behest of an employer in order to be authorized to work and be in the United States, from which other aspects of embodied life might follow. In the following excerpt, Ajay's insider view underscores how employer dependence—the foundational clause of the H-1B—enforces noncitizens' subordination to capital while ensuring that noncitizens' enterprise and productivity flow into the U.S. political economy:

> So this is how the visa governs you. I managed to find a project. A large client, I know the finance industry well, and the consulting company managing the project was keen to put me on board. We had talked, gone over my resume and experience. And the billing rate was good too and I knew that my employer will be fine with it, as he would make a good margin. But see on the H-1B, I cannot actually sign anything or make promises. I have to first approach my employer. Explain everything, about the client, the project, the consulting firm, what they are willing to pay for me. And then only hope that he would agree and do the contract for me with that management firm. Paperwork has to be "corp to corp," [agreement between corporations or companies] and I, as an employee *on the H-1B*, have no authorization that allows me to get into

the project without my employer's permission and agreement with the other company. Although I found the project, I have to now step back and let him take over. Also, I cannot quit to get into that project as an independent consultant, because then, *who is my employer? Where is my visa status?* To keep my status, I have to work *through* an employer. And I have to keep doing that, to keep my visa, and agree to the employer's requirements.

Because the absence of an employer divests "aliens" of both legal status and work authorization, the H-1B, by law, has produced a category of noncitizens whose existence in the United States can continue within the space of the temporary period authorized so long as they remain subordinate, compliant, and productive (generating "good margins" for visa-holding employers and clients). As the following reflections further reveal, the reach of this visa-dependent status cuts across to subsume aspects of the labor experience that on the surface might appear to have nothing to do with the visa itself.

By placing on employers the power to determine documented status—and therefore its integral and immediate corollary, deportability—the visa has activated a field of disciplinary technologies to control noncitizens. Abhi's description of what transpires when noncitizen contract workers are out of projects, or "on the bench," articulates how deportability serves, in part, as a template against which the many variants of documented status, along with the economic and social possibilities therein, find material expression:

> As a contract worker, you don't always have projects. You hope that you will get another client right after you finish one project, but that is rare. No guarantees. Sometimes there is a gap of a few weeks, sometimes months between projects. And that "bench" period is totally scary if you are on the H-1B. Since you are not working for a client, you are not generating any revenue for the guy who holds your H-1B. So the longer you wait for your next project, the more worried you get, for he can fire you any time. This time it took me a while to find a new project. The employer knew I was so desperate to get back on the project, to start my billing cycle, so he hiked his commission on my billing rate. He called me late the night before I was joining the client and said, "Look, I think we should split sixty and forty." Before it used to be seventy and thirty. I had no choice. I agreed. He knew I would, for he holds my visa. If I quit this company, I'd have to go and find another one like him. And he would do the same, right?

Given that the continuity of their dependent status is the only collateral against deportability, noncitizens make many accommodations in order to defer to their employers' priorities rather than their own in matters that bear heavily on quality of life and career. Throughout the interview transcripts, references to being "tagged," "bound," "tied," and "governed by employers" articulated how the experience of this mode of control was inflected with specifications that carried distinct psychic and embodied costs. Ashish, as we will see, summarized one of the core themes that resonated in every interview: how the H-1B could, and does, plunge into and dictate the intricate recesses of noncitizens' everyday navigations for survival, while aligning this workforce's productivity and tractability in favor of capital:

> If your bench period exceeds a few weeks or a month has passed, it causes a lot of stress! You are not on a client's project and so your employer is not making any revenue from commissions during this time. With every passing day you begin to feel this intense pressure. Because if you are not on a project for too long, your employer will fire you. And you know what that means? You have no visa, no job. And you cannot let that happen. So even before one projects wraps up, I start to worry and begin to look for the next client. I have found over five out of the seven that I have worked on. It is not uncommon for your employer to pay half of your salary or nothing if the bench continues for a long time. But this way you keep the job at least. It is not legal, but it happens a lot, because guys on the H-1B have to keep their status.

Unmitigated anxieties about safeguarding their legal status and paychecks force these noncitizens to take on the responsibility of finding projects while accommodating a range of disembodying work conditions. Placed on temporary contracts of unpredictable duration, these noncitizens move from one client project to another, at whichever region of the United States it might be, without any assurances of consecutive projects, job security, or steady pay. Frequent relocations, short-term stays in hotels, expensive short leases, and "bunking up" with other immigrant colleagues present a very rough shorthand of what it takes for these noncitizens to sustain the demands of their work life. Other means of dealing with the challenges of repeated unemployment/salary cuts and recurring—and generally unreimbursed—relocations include the adoption of frugal lifestyles and keeping possessions to a minimum. Based on experience, one family, with two small children, had established a rule to cope with the many long-distance moves: they would limit their personal items to what they could fit in the trunk of their car. Given that these workers are almost exclusively from the global South, the proliferation of this set of interceptable, dependent, and temporary status categories reflects the U.S. state's historical stakes in reproducing whiteness as an authentic marker of cultural belonging, political citizenship, labor autonomy, and economic entitlement within the national sphere.[11]

EXCLUSIONS' OTHER REINFORCEMENTS:
L-1 AND B-1 VISAS

The U.S. Citizenship and Immigration Services reported in April 2016 that 236,000 H-1B petitions were filed for 85,000 available visas under the program's visa caps for that year. A computer-generated lottery system has been used over the last few years to cope with such high demand.[12] As previously noted, with the exception of a short period in the early 2000s, the demand for H-1B visas has always outstripped supply, which has meant that tens of thousands of applications get rejected each year. The restrictions placed by the annual quota, a very high refusal rate, and the H-1B's lengthy processing time have prompted subcontractors and consulting firms to seek alternatives, such as the L-1 and, in much fewer cases, the B-1 visa. Abhay, like several others interviewed, had first been sent to the United States on the L-1 visa, so that the U.S. client's labor demand could be met expediently:

> At the time, I was based in the Kolkata branch of the consulting firm, which as you know has branches and site offices in the US, and in Europe too. They had just got a huge client in the US, a big insurance company, and the project had to start almost right away. Our US branch office sent the client's project requirements to us here. My manager put me in that team that was being sent to the client's site. Some members of that team were already in the US finishing projects at other client sites. I and some others were in India. I didn't have any US visas yet. There was not enough time for an H-1B—that could take many months it seemed. And the company had to move fast. So they processed the L-1. The engineers like us didn't know what all these visas were. For me, it was my overseas deputation and we had to get the job done well. Anyway, I was told that they would process an H-1B for me, but for then I had to leave as soon as the L-1 came through.

The L-1 visa classification is designed to facilitate the entry of intracompany transferees or overseas employees of multinational companies with branch offices, affiliates, or subsidiaries in the United States, or vice versa.[13] Many IT consulting firms with such branches in the United States have supplemented their use of the H-1B with those under L-1 categories (most typically, the L-1B Intracompany Transferee Specialized Knowledge visa). Not limited to the annual cap, these visas are valid for one to three years and come with the option of renewal for up to five or seven years depending on the L-1 visa type. Formally categorized as employees of the overseas branches under the precepts of the L-1 visa, people like Abhay in the United States are not subject to the prevailing wage requirement. Neither are their employers required to file the Labor Condition Application to procure authorization from the U.S. Department of Labor.[14] It was not uncommon for interviewees on the L-1 to experience a general lack of clarity as to which U.S. labor protections law applied to them or how they might be implemented.

In a similar vein, the handful of interviewees in this research who had been sent to the United States on the B-1, as a stopgap measure before their H-1B could be processed, faced many uncertainties surrounding their labor entitlements. The B-1 business visa allows short-term entry (six months) to individuals or representatives of companies abroad seeking to establish corporate ties with U.S. companies or explore investment opportunities. People on the B-1 can engage in activities that count as business purposes but are barred from employment and cannot receive a salary during their stay in the United States. This stipulation thus makes the question of employment authorization or fair wages irrelevant. The immediacy of U.S. clients' extensive need for flexible labor, however, has prompted many consulting firms to send Indian workers on the B-1 visa. This practice thus placed interviewees at particular risk of being exposed and generated deep concerns about the legitimacy of their status. Indeed, these individuals knew that no matter how short the duration of each subcontracted project, they were working at the client sites on a visa that does not permit them to undertake such work. In terms of payment, the general practice in place was that their Indian scale–based salaries, along with a small "foreign deputation allowance," would get deposited directly into their accounts back home. Employers also added a supplementary amount to cover certain expenses in the United States. The interviews suggest that there is no established standard that dictates these rates, and employers are at liberty to decide how much is sufficient to cover expenses. One interviewee in particular had been going through "a terrible battle," as he described it, to make his employer reimburse the expenditures he had incurred while on two previous projects in different states. This overhead included the cost of travel, extended stay in a hotel, a lease penalty, and other miscellaneous items that the employer had agreed to cover. Underpaid, vulnerable, and denied the social designation of "workers" who put in labor in the United States, these Indian IT workers encountered still other structural barriers because of how the B-1 constructed their immigration status. The visa's six-month validity and employment ban often meant that these noncitizens on "foreign deputation" could not get social security numbers, which placed severe limitations on their ability to access important services that rely on this identification number, such as banking. Unable to open bank accounts or get checkbooks to pay the security deposits for housing, these noncitizens then had to turn to colleagues with access to such basic facilities.

Philip Kretsedemas and David Brotherton put it rather aptly in their introductory chapter of this volume that "the quotidian subject of the current migration regime is now the guest worker, not the permanent settler."[15] Throughout the dozens of interview transcripts, the phrase "that's life as H-1B workers"—repeated in many variations by the current immigration regime's "quotidian subject"— acquired an idiomatic quality that signaled not only the commonplaceness of socioeconomic insecurities and status precarity these noncitizens deal with, but also the manner in which the source code of deportability has been factored into the terms of the visa (documented status). What remains obscured from the formal descriptions of the H-1B, however, is how the visa encodes deportability without explicitly naming it as such and, more specifically, how noncitizen workers' status under the visa falls squarely within the overarching purview of deportability in socio-juridical, material, and symbolic terms. Official delineations of this nonimmigrant work visa center around the primary concern of allowing U.S. companies access to skilled workers on the basis of certain criteria demanded of both foreign workers and their U.S. employers: for instance, the prevailing wage clause, which purports to ensure pay parity between noncitizens and citizens so that the latter may be protected from any unfair wage competition that can arise from lower salaries paid to noncitizens; and the portability clause, which now grants the prospect of changing employers when certain conditions are met (this option was not allowed until very recently). The H-1B visa, it should be added, is one of the extremely few under the nonimmigrant category that allows what is called "dual intention," meaning that the visa holder is eligible to apply for a green card while still on the visa, pending certain conditions. Unlike foreign students seeking an F-1 visa, H-1B applicants are not subject to the requirement of marshaling persuasive proof, such as family ties or economic affluence back home and the pull of such bonds and privileges, to satisfy visa officers of their firm intention to return to their sending countries. All told, the H-1B descriptions can read like a more or less fair compendium of clauses and conditions that bear in mind the needs and interests of multiple constituencies: the state; the American employer and citizen; and, in a more limited sense, the foreign worker. What is more, consular officers who approve and grant the H-1B hand out to successful applicants an information pamphlet titled *Know Your Rights*, which outlines a set of protections that a worker, regardless of visa status, can expect against labor exploitation in the United States.[16] The tangible lives of Indian IT workers on the H-1B, however, show that the scope and durability of documented status provisioned under the visa extend only up to a point and do not necessarily allocate meaningful rights. As we have seen, the conditional demarcations of their status serve as a juridical mechanism that ensures a noncitizen's disadvantageous placement within a field of power asymmetries; for example, the worker on the H-1B is dependent on the employer by definition, and it is this dependence that determines, as a precondition, the longevity and viability of the worker's documented status. Meanwhile, the preservation of legal status for those on the H-4 visa—the "dependent visa" reserved for spouses of

H-1B holders—is contingent on *double* dependence: dependence on married partners who are, to begin with, employer dependent by mandate. Moreover, although employment-based visas are supposed to confer the legitimacy and documented status necessary for a measure of stability, the experiences discussed in this chapter reveal how those on visas are often left without the means to access necessities that pertain to the sustenance of their own and their families' embodied lives, such as health care, driver's licenses, bank accounts, and social security numbers. Restricted by their employment- and employer-dependent status and concentrated in the lower tiers of the subcontracting hierarchy, these noncitizens get exposed to a range of disciplinary and exploitative practices.

Though documented status and deportability can be construed as more or less antonymous, what we see throughout the narratives in this research is that they have been bound together, operating as an integrated dyad: documented status has been made conditional and interceptable, whose termination can activate the state of deportability at any given time. Thus, even in the absence of experiencing the actual fact of detention or deportation, these workers find themselves emplaced unequivocally within immigration enforcement's socio-juridical ambit of deportability precisely because visa-based documented status is defined and circumscribed by it. Across visas, such as the H-1B as we have seen here or the L-1, B-1, H-4, H-2B, F-1, or F-4, the most overwhelming and common denominator is deportability. The specificities that distinguish one visa from another classify "nonimmigrant aliens" into different status categories of productivity and disciplinary control but without destabilizing the larger common core of deportability and dependence (on employers, universities, or spouses/parents).

To put it rather simply, nonimmigrant visas suspend "aliens" in an ongoing state of deportability in which maintaining status is another name for avoiding deportation one day, a few months, or one client at a time. In the context of the present racialized immigration enforcement regime, this divalent calibration of what might be called the *documented-deportable dyad* intended for noncitizens has resolved (1) neoliberal demands for a tractable, self-motivated, and productive workforce that actually works the subcontracting system on its own volition to avoid deportation; and (2) in light of the global security regime, the U.S. state's ability to exclude, criminalize, detain, deport, and control noncitizens of color and, to the extent possible, slot this population into various categories of non-belonging but without foreclosing the avenues that produce surplus.[17] The labor flexibilization and status precarity that noncitizen workers on H-1B visas experience are not distinct from but an integral part of the overarching socio-juridical and symbolic domain of immigration enforcement. Their experiences, determined by the ever-present specter of deportability, underscore how the conduits of enforcement, as expansive and excessive as they already are, have been installed and bolstered beyond "the social fact of mass deportation."[18]

NOTES TO CHAPTER 14

1. Vir managed to find another employer, also a subcontractor, within a month of this event.

2. The law requires that workers on the H-1B be paid "prevailing wages" of the industry, commensurate with education and experience. This condition is meant to protect American workers from any wage depression and competition that might arise if noncitizens are paid lower salaries.

3. Payal Banerjee, "The Insecuritization of Immigrant Labour: Asian Indians in the United States," *Man in India* 93, no. 4 (2014): 521–539. See also Nicholas De Genova, "The Legal Production of Mexican/Migrant 'Illegality,'" *Latino Studies* 2, no. 2 (2004): 160–185.

4. For an in-depth understanding of the Asian American critique of U.S. immigration and an analysis of Asian exclusions as a method of racialized and gendered subordination of noncitizens on the basis of status exclusions, see Lisa Lowe, *Immigrant Acts: On Asian American Cultural Politics* (Durham: Duke University Press, 1996); Mae Ngai, *Impossible Subjects: Illegal Aliens and the Making of Modern America* (Princeton: Princeton University Press, 2014); Evelyn Nakano Glenn, *Unequal Freedom: How Race and Gender Shaped American Citizenship and Labor* (Cambridge: Harvard University Press, 1986); Joan Jensen, *Passage from India: Asian Indian Immigrants in North America* (New Haven: Yale University Press, 1988); Ronald Takaki, *Strangers from a Different Shore: A History of Asian Americans* (Boston: Little, Brown, 1989). In evaluating the impact of H-1B visa policies on IT workers, the relevance of this framework lies in one of its central theses: that since the late nineteenth century, the U.S. state's anti-Asian immigration, citizenship, property, and family reunification laws have structured Asian migrants' exclusions from political entitlements. Moreover, this socio-legal production of Asians' subordination to capital and the state ensured their prolonged vulnerability to capitalist exploitation. The denial of property rights, for instance, prohibited Asians' class mobility during the exclusion era, which ensured the continuity of their position as wage laborers dependent on employment. Likewise, laws prohibiting Asian women's entry into the United States prevented the viability of families, which further facilitated the accumulation of surplus value: employers could pay Asian men low wages, relocate them easily and quickly, and fire them during periods of lean production. The entire corpus of anti-Asian legislation spanning citizenship to property laws thus helped sustain the development of modern American capitalism (see Lisa Lowe, *Immigrant Acts*). For a comparative analysis of the similarities between the racialized experiences of Asian American labor rendered highly exploitable in the Asian exclusion era and the specific experiences of contemporary Indian IT workers under the terms of the H-1B visa and flexible production, see Payal Banerjee, "Indian Information Technology (IT)

Workers in the U.S.: The H-1B Visa, Flexible Production, and the Racialization of Labor," *Critical Sociology* 32, no. 2–3 (2006): 427–447.

5. These intermediaries are of varying sizes and strength, whose range includes well-established consulting companies in India (such as Tata Consulting Services or TCS), those in the United States that branched out into recruiting from India, and the very small brand-new companies in the United States that have emerged on the horizon to take advantage of U.S. clients' need for IT labor. See Payal Banerjee, "Flexible Hiring, Immigration, and Indian IT Workers' Experiences of Contract Work in the United States," in *People at Work: Life, Power, and Social Inclusion in the New Economy*, ed. M. DeVault (New York: NYU Press, 2008), 97–111; Banerjee, "Indian Information Technology (IT) Workers in the U.S."

6. Banerjee, "Indian Information Technology (IT) Workers in the U.S."

7. U.S. Citizenship and Immigration Services, "H1-B Fiscal Year (FY) 2017 Cap Season," https://www.uscis.gov/working-united-states/temporary-workers/h-1b-specialty -occupations-and-fashion-models/h-1b-fiscal-year-fy-2017-cap-season.

8. Kristen Ayers and Scott Syfert, "U.S. Visa Options and Strategies for the Information Technology Industry," *International Quarterly* 14, no. 4 (2002): 535–565 at 540.

9. Although citizens and residents are also subject to contingent work arrangements via labor market intermediaries, they do not have to rely on employers for their legal status and therefore tend to be employed with larger consulting firms, which deal directly with clients.

10. In this case, immigrants gain the authorization to work in any position, regardless of occupational sector, and are not restricted to jobs or rank that correspond with their educational credentials. The H-1B, as the reader will recall, does not confer this freedom.

11. Yen Espiritu, *Asian American Women and Men: Labor, Laws, and Love* (Thousand Oaks: Sage, 1997); Evelyn Nakano Glenn, *Unequal Freedom: How Race and Gender Shaped American Citizenship and Labor* (Cambridge: Harvard University Press, 2002); Bill Hing, *Making and Remaking Asian America Through Immigration Policy, 1850–1990* (Stanford: Stanford University Press, 1993); Lisa Lowe, *Immigrant Acts*; Mae Ngai, *Impossible Subjects*; David Roediger, *How Race Survived US History: From Settlement and Slavery to the Obama Phenomenon* (London: Verso Books, 2008); Patricia Williams, *The Alchemy of Race and Rights* (Cambridge: Harvard University Press, 1991).

12. Patrick Thibodeau, "U.S. Gets 236,000 H1-B Visas, a New Record: On-Going Demand for Visas Won't Change the Well-Worn Debate," *Computer World*, April 12, 2016, http://www.computerworld.com/article/3055028/it-careers/us-gets-236000-h-1b -petitions-a-new-record.html?token=%23tk.CTWNLE_nlt_computerworld _dailynews_2016-04-13&idg_eid=99d9b4c5dc71a5f13cc7345e4a760d51&utm_source =Sailthru&utm_medium=email&utm_campaign=Computerworld%20First%20 Look%202016-04-13&utm_term=computerworld_dailynews#tk.CW_nlt_computerworld _dailynews_2016-04-13.

13. There are two subcategories within the L-1 visa. The L-1A enables a U.S. employer "to transfer an executive or manager from one of its affiliated foreign offices to one of its offices in the United States. This classification also enables a foreign com-

pany which does not yet have an affiliated U.S. office to send an executive or manager to the United States with the purpose of establishing one." See U.S. Citizenship and Immigration Services, "L-1A Intracompany Transferee Executive or Manager," 2016, https://www.uscis.gov/working-united-states/temporary-workers/l-1a-intracompany -transferee-executive-or-manager. The L-1B nonimmigrant classification "enables a U.S. employer to transfer a professional employee with specialized knowledge relating to the organization's interests from one of its affiliated foreign offices to one of its offices in the United States. This classification also enables a foreign company which does not yet have an affiliated U.S. office to send a specialized knowledge employee to the United States to help establish one." See U.S. Citizenship and Immigration Services, "L-1B Intracompany Transferee Specialized Knowledge," 2016, https://www.uscis.gov /working-united-states/temporary-workers/l-1b-intracompany-transferee-specialized -knowledge.

14. The Labor Condition Application (LCA) is a document in which employers of prospective H-1B workers must attest that they will adhere to the required labor standards as specified in the H-1B program. The LCA is submitted for authorization and approval to the Department of Labor. See U.S. Department of Labor, "E-Laws—H1-B Advisor," 2016, http://webapps.dol.gov/elaws/h1b/glossary.aspx?word=lca.

15. See page 2 in the editors' introductory chapter in this volume.

16. See U.S. Department of State, Bureau of Consular Affairs, "Rights and Protections for Temporary Workers," 2016, https://travel.state.gov/content/visas/en/general /rights-protections-temporary-workers.html.

17. Tanya Golash-Boza, *Due Process Denied: Detentions and Deportations in the United States* (New York: Routledge, 2012); Tanya Golash-Boza, *Immigration Nation: Raids, Detentions, and Deportations in Post-9/11 America* (New York: Routledge, 2015); Philip Kretsedemas, *The Immigration Crucible: Transforming Race, Nation, and the Limits of the Law* (New York: Columbia University Press, 2012); Sunaina Marr Maira, *Missing: Youth, Citizenship, and Empire After 9/11* (Durham: Duke University Press, 2009); Sunaina Marr Maira, "Surveillance Effects: South Asian, Arab, and Afghan American Youth in the War on Terror," in *At the Limits of Justice: Women of Color on Terror*, ed. S. Perera and S. Razack (Toronto: University of Toronto Press, 2014), 86–106; Shoba Sivaprasad Wadia, *Beyond Deportation: The Role of Prosecutorial Discretion in Immigration Cases* (New York: NYU Press, 2015).

18. For a detailed analysis of this point, see Kretsedemas and Brotherton's introductory chapter in this volume. The phrase is quoted from page 2 of the chapter.

15. THE PRECARIOUS DEPORTEE AND HUMAN RIGHTS IN THE DOMINICAN REPUBLIC

YOLANDA C. MARTÍN, CUNY

Florencio Flores was forty-seven at the time of his deportation hearing in April 2014. A green card holder for more than forty years, he could not even remember his homeland, the Dominican Republic. Yet he was placed in removal proceedings when, at the urging of his wife, he applied for U.S. naturalization. In 1994, Florencio pled guilty to a felony drug charge, serving a one-year suspended sentence. Upon his release, Florencio became a professional welder; married his current wife, Elisa; had a son and daughter; and became a loving stepfather to Elisa's daughter from a previous marriage. He never committed any further crimes, so he could not comprehend why he faced deportation.

My field notes record that Florencio firmly believes he must have been arrested by mistake, in place of a "real criminal." "I'm going nuts," he tells me before we enter the courtroom, "at the idea of Elisa and the kids going on welfare." Florencio has been diagnosed with depression and suffers from severe insomnia, now exacerbated by worries that his adolescent son, who has autism, might grow up without him; he has lost forty-five pounds since his ordeal began. I am asked to serve as an expert witness, describing assassinations of deportees by Dominican police. The courtroom is full of relatives and friends, most in tears as they listen to my testimony.

A pro bono immigration attorney had contacted me to assist in a waiver of removal request under the Convention Against Torture (CAT). Florencio's hearing had already been postponed for two years, and we would wait nine additional months for a final hearing. Eventually, our argument that Florencio's deportation would constitute a form of torture prevailed, and he was allowed to stay in the United States with his family.

My five most recent cases serving as expert witness (2012–2016) have been granted CAT withdrawal of removal proceedings. All the individuals facing deportation proceedings suffered from various comorbid mental health conditions (e.g., chronic depression and bipolar disorder) or cognitive disabilities. All barely remembered their "homeland," having been U.S. residents since early childhood and forming strong family and community roots in this country. Though only examples, these cases suggest that New York City's immigration courts are increasingly sympathetic to the CAT argument against immigrant removal.

For seven years I have studied immigrants deported from the United States on criminal grounds. My ethnographic and research findings document the suffering that immigrant returnees experience postdeportation. This chapter highlights the human rights violations the United States is committing in the name of national security and border control, as well as the emotional and physical abuse military and law enforcement officers commit against deportees. I advocate that on deportation, the poorest, darkest-skinned individuals face the most extreme abuse, which qualifies as a form of torture under CAT criteria.

Withdrawals of immigrant removal under CAT are rare, but they are gradually becoming a real possibility. The Convention Against Torture mandates that signatory states shall not return a person to a country in which there is a substantial likelihood that he or she will be tortured.[1] Incorporated into the Foreign Affairs Reform and Restructuring Act of 1998, the convention protects U.S.-resident noncitizens from deportation.[2] To obtain relief, applicants must show that it is more likely than not that they would be tortured if returned to their home country. CAT definitions are broader for the purpose of withholding deportation than for seeking asylum. In removal cases, torture need not involve persecution due to race, religion, nationality, membership in a particular social group, or political opinion. Rather, any intentional, unlawful infliction of extreme physical or mental abuse, acknowledged and condoned by a public or government official in order to intimidate, extract a confession, or commit blatant discrimination, may count as torture. I have witnessed and recorded firsthand accounts of such abuse against deportees.

I advocate for an approach to justice that eschews narrowly defined conceptions of the rule of law for natural law—definitions of justice based on universal values such as community well-being and human rights.[3] I question traditional interpretations of territoriality and de facto citizenship privileges that can be stripped away arbitrarily even under the rule of law. Human rights have become a lingua franca of global politics; whether a government embraces or rejects human rights ideals, they are the standard by which we evaluate the living conditions of the individual—not the rights of citizens but the person by virtue of being a human as such, regardless of gender, race or ethnicity, or religious background.

Linda Bosniak's concept of the "alien citizen" refers to individuals who are excluded from formal citizenship status yet allowed to exercise the same basic rights formally granted by citizenship, such as political engagement and self-identity as full-fledged members of society.[4] The corollary of the alien citizen concept, therefore, would be the phenomenon of the deportee as citizen alien. Deportees in the Dominican Republic, particularly those who grew up in the United States, did not maintain family ties to the island and do not speak Spanish. They may have membership owing to birthright but are treated as outcasts, permanently barred from the rights, privileges, and protections that come with their citizen status. Deportees are forcefully brought in, expelled from the country in which they have established social ties, and sent to a country that excludes them from de facto citizenship freedoms. They are national aliens in their own country of birth.

A body of legal scholarship argues strongly that the rule of law may lead to morally questionable outcomes; our current laws and their enforcement are causing more harm than good, and they must be changed for humanitarian reasons.[5] U.S.-resident noncitizens—particularly those from Central and South American and Caribbean countries—exemplify what Gibney has defined as "precarious residents": "people living in a state that possess few social, political or economic rights, are highly vulnerable to deportation, and have little or no option for making secure their immigration status."[6] Ironically, deportees returned to the Dominican Republic frequently become "precarious disenfranchised citizens," facing worse odds than they had in the United States, despite their Dominican citizenship. Deportees are rendered highly vulnerable—even de facto stateless— by the systematic denial of basic protections. Unwelcomed second-class citizens, they live in constant fear of institutional and structural abuse.

BACKGROUND

Immigration and Customs Enforcement annual statistics show that between fiscal years 1997 and 2015, more than 5,066,413 noncitizens were deported from the United States.[7] Forced repatriations rose from 30,039 in 1990 to 188,047 in 2000 and to a record 409,849 in 2012. Among Caribbean countries, the Dominican Republic receives the highest number of deportees, averaging more than 2,450 annually.

The mass deportation phenomenon was triggered by the Illegal Immigration Reform and Immigrant Responsibility Act (1996), exacerbated after September 2001 by the Patriot Act (2001), which intertwined immigration with criminal enforcement. President George W. Bush institutionalized this relationship in 2003 by converting the Immigration and Naturalization Service into the Department of Homeland Security, responsible for overseeing both immigration control and counterterrorism. The message of this restructuring was obvious: immigrants are a threat to the United States, even though all available data indicate that immigrants are less likely to commit crimes than U.S. citizens.[8] Other key legislation has also dramatically affected immigrant groups. Until 1996, an immigrant who faced deportation on criminal charges could apply to an immigration judge for a waiver of deportation (a 212(c) waiver) if the individual could demonstrate long-term residence, strong ties to the community, family commitments, military service, or economic hardship on dependents. The Anti-Drug Act of 1996 amendments to the immigration laws eliminated the 212(c) waiver. "Aggravated felony" legislation was enacted in 1988 to mandate automatic deportation for murder and federal drug and firearms trafficking crimes. Today this category is applied under 8 USC §1101(a)(43) to more than thirty types of offenses that need not be either aggravated or felonies: simple battery, theft, and failure to appear in court can all now trigger deportation.

VALIDITY OF CAT IN DEPORTATION CASES

Based on more than 180 primary interviews; ethnographic research conducted among deportees in Santo Domingo, Dominican Republic (2009–2016); and secondary law enforcement sources, I conclude that deportation to the Dominican Republic should be considered torture. My reasons fall under two broad categories: (1) social isolation, stigma, severe economic deprivation, and lack of social services; and (2) police brutality toward deportees.

Deportees from the United States arrive every other Wednesday at Las Américas Airport in Santo Domingo. Dominican law enforcement officials meet the plane, and U.S. marshals hand over the deportees' criminal files. Deportees are usually interrogated that day. They are booked and fingerprinted on the spot, and many are placed in detention until the police have time to review their records. These detention facilities are notorious for inhumane conditions—lacking beds or toilets, disease ridden, overrun by rodents, and so on. Many detainees have not eaten in days when they are released.

I interviewed many deportees who struggled to reconcile their personas with the stigma of deportation, ashamed of their lost social and moral status and their new role as social outcasts. Some internalized the stigma so deeply that they considered themselves worthless and subsequently initiated high-risk behaviors. The stigma against deportees extends throughout Dominican society, hindering their reinsertion to the country.[9]

The deportation experience produces multiple mental health issues (e.g., depression and anxiety), and my ethnographic observations revealed multiple cases of posttraumatic stress disorder (PTSD). Common symptoms are anxiety and panic attacks, hyperarousal (irritability, inability to sleep), avoidance of or lack of response to social interaction, and paranoia. In some cases these symptoms were visible immediately after deportation; in other cases their onset was delayed until months after their arrival in Dominica. Medical literature has amply documented the PTSD–substance abuse connection, in which people "self-medicate" to relieve PTSD-related symptoms. My interviewees experienced overwhelming feelings of isolation and frustration, driving them to find solace in mind-state altering substances, from alcohol or marijuana to heroin. They all had tried to "pass" as nondeportees, hoping to avoid stigmatization, but few had succeeded.

To understand the synergistic processes that push a large percentage of deportees into depression and serious health conditions, we need to recognize the deportation process as a deeply traumatic turning point in an individual's life. Most of the deportees I interviewed had arrived in the United States as children, had not returned to the Dominican Republic in decades, had little knowledge of Dominican customs, and had limited ability to speak Spanish on their removal. As in the United States, lower-class individuals in the Dominican Republic are deemed undeserving of full-fledged citizenship.

Compounding these problems, the Caribbean region is one of the most violent nonwar zones in the world. Violence and crime are at an all-time high in the Dominican Republic, with the most homicides in the Caribbean region, at a rate of 22.1 per 100,000 inhabitants in 2012 (2,472 in total), up from 12.7 in 1995. By comparison, the murder rate in Haiti in 2012 was 10.2 per 100,000 (a total of 1,033).[10] There is a widespread stereotype in public opinion, in the media, and among officers of the law that deportees are all violent criminals and are to blame for the surging violence. In consequence, even those deportees with family ties in the Dominican Republic find that their relatives often deny them housing or assistance because they "bring shame into the family." It is worth noting that in reality, from 2000 to 2010 only 2.8 percent of all deportees had any recidivism records.[11]

Deportees are easily identifiable because of their "Americanized" clothes, demeanor, and accents. In fact, all the aspects of U.S. culture that deportees once adopted to fit into the United States prevent their reintegration into Dominican society. These habits now signal difference, suggest a deportation history, and label them as likely criminals. As a result, deportees have very limited opportunities for social interaction with the general population, leading them to "cluster" in marginal living and social spaces and aggravating their risk for poverty, violence, and disease.

As stated previously, stigma not only prevents numerous deportees from finding stable jobs but is also a major cause of risky health behaviors. Stigma, or shame, is directly connected to social prestige, understood as one's standing in society.[12] Shame lowers one's social capital, limiting access to material and emotional support, as well as to financial resources needed to access Dominican public health services. Stigma creates a pathway to negative health risk outcomes through the systematic denial of prestige-driven social benefits. The participants in my study, like many other deportees, reported that carrying the deportee stigma led to poor nutrition, sleep deprivation, housing instability, unemployment, poverty, exposure to street violence, mood disorders, depression, a high risk of disease, and adoption of self-destructive behaviors (alcoholism, substance dependency, and even self-mutilation). Once they became ensnared in substance abuse, structural violence limited their physical and mental capacity to seek and access health services or adhere to a treatment regimen, creating a recipe for disaster.

At the Las Américas branch of Hogar Crea (a rehabilitation center) in Santo Domingo, I interviewed a man in his mid-forties who complained about his loss of social capital upon return:

> Jobs? This is not like the US. There, if you have your papers, your green card, you can get a job. If you can't speak in English, then it's a bit more difficult, but if you do, you can always find a job. Here it's different . . . you need to have contacts, friends who own small businesses or know of someone who could hire you. Here it's all about connections. Still, there will be times when they find out that you are a deportee and they won't want to hire you. I have suffered a great deal. Do you remember when the twin towers fell? That is exactly how I felt when I was deported. Everything fell apart, for my family and me.[13]

Similarly, a thirty-year-old female returnee blamed her difficulty in getting a job on her deportee status:

> It's very hard for me to get a job. I'm full of tattoos, the way I talk . . . everybody is like, "Shit, this girl scares me." I have a degree in literature from Florida International University. I have a degree in business administration from Florida State University . . . so I'm not dumb . . . but all they see is my tattoos and the way I dress. I can't get a job. I have a different outlook.[14]

Furthermore, because they are frequently ignorant of local Dominican regulations and laws, returnees are at high risk of inadvertently breaking the law. Their expectations of Dominican society based on cultural representations of Dominicanness and interpretations of their parents' worldview may not correspond to the reality they encounter upon arrival in their "homeland." Anomie and alienation driven by culture shock exacerbate the propensity for physical and mental health problems.[15]

In 2013, the Dominican District Attorney's Office created a new deportee reintegration initiative. Yet based on my interviews and direct observations, this office is severely underfunded and understaffed. As a developing country, the Dominican Republic cannot afford to provide the level of assistance that those who have experienced deportation trauma would require. Indeed, in 2015, about 41.1 percent of the urban population lived under the poverty level.[16] The only services for mentally ill adults are private clinics, available only to those with the means to pay. Adequate facilities, trained personnel, and medication are scarce throughout the country. Even community clinics require patients to pay for intervention materials and prescription medication. But even if grossly inefficient in its goals to secure job training and actual employment, the Unidad de Reinserción de Repatriados (Reintegration Unit for Returnees) is sending an important message to the wider society: it acknowledges that these men and women are worthy of a second chance as members of the state.

Structural violence is a form of violence that major social institutions perpetrate against subordinated populations, such as the poor and working classes, people of color, women, and sexual minorities. Conceptually it refers to constraints on human potential imposed by prevailing political and economic structures, such as unequal access to (1) resources needed to sustain life or provide a reasonable quality of life; (2) political power; (3) education and acquisition of helpful information; and (4) legal status, housing, and other aspects of daily life. "The idea of structural violence is linked very closely to social injustice and the social machinery of oppression."[17]

Unlike physical violence, structural violence remains socially invisible because it is incorporated into the daily functioning of public institutions. Structural violence is indirectly condoned and therefore goes unpunished. Furthermore, because structural violence is unrecognized, its consequences are normalized and perceived as failures on the part of its victims. Paul Farmer defines structural violence as "a host of offenses against human dignity: extreme and relative poverty, social inequalities ranging from racism to gender inequality, and the more spectacular forms of violence that are uncontested human rights abuses."[18] Sometimes referred to as "social suffering," it is a form of sanctioned violence that encompasses relations of inequality that greatly exacerbate human suffering and damage human well-being.[19] Examples include denying health care to the lower classes, excluding certain groups from decent housing due to their social class or ethnicity, or limiting life options through a two-tiered educational system. The specific expressions of structural violence overlap (e.g., the effects of poverty and of ethnic discrimination are usually interconnected).

Structural violence leads to what Loic Wacquant terms "suffusive spatial stigma," or the normalized discrediting of residents in marginal neighborhoods.[20] When the media and public opinion come to perceive certain areas as "hellholes," with high rates of crime and social disorganization, the residents begin to internalize that stigma. Poverty is treated as synonymous with criminality and drug use, and public shame diminishes potential manifestations of resistance in the barrios. Social ties are eroded, neighbors feel compelled to retreat to their houses, and a chain of self-fulfilling prophecies is set in motion.

In addition, there are several effects on health. Structural violence and interpersonal victimization often go hand in hand because certain individuals are given to understand that their lives are worth less than others' lives and that they are dispensable.[21] Chronic stress is another major contributor to disease in people subjected to structural violence. Unlike short-term stress responses (i.e., fight-or-flight reactions) that release energy to the muscles in times of perceived threat, the chronic stress caused by prolonged exposure to such social ills as discrimination or marginalization is highly destructive and can lead to immune system damage.

The series of intertwined factors of structural marginalization that overlap and mutually interact with one another, resulting in wider and more severe medical outcomes in society, is the phenomenon that Merrill Singer has termed "syndemics."[22] As a World Health Organization report states, a "growing body of evidence accumulated over the last 20 years . . . shows that people who live in disadvantaged social circumstances are more prone to illness, distress and disability and die sooner than those living in more advantaged circumstances."[23] Social inequality is a primary stressor and cause of syndemics in that it reduces access to basic necessities, such as residential stability and appropriate medical care. Additionally, incarceration, disproportionately inflicted on poorer classes, often leads to the spread, concentration, and interaction of severe physical and mental health conditions.[24]

Pablo Mella—professor at the Juan Montalvo Center, a Jesuit university in Santo Domingo—describes how structural violence manifests against the poorer classes in the Dominican Republic:

> [The government] has responded to the growing problem of violence in the neighborhoods with militarization and "social assistance" programs. However, we keep ignoring the issue of structural violence. . . . And we must ask ourselves: isn't it violence that a neighborhood like La Zurza has a 16 percent illiteracy rate? Isn't it violence that in Domingo Savio, with 4,600 youths of middle-school age, there is no school serving that level? Isn't it violence that 39.51 percent of residents in the north zone of Santo Domingo live in overcrowded conditions? Isn't it violence that, of a total of 358,068 persons of working age, more than 60 percent work in the informal economy? Should we ignore the fact that this 60 percent lacks health insurance and hence is excluded from health-care services?[25]

The interactions between structural violence and health were not lost on my interviewees. Pan Quemado, one of the participants in the study, frequently used illness metaphors in reference to deportees' housing conditions and their extremely desperate situation:

> I remember asking Pan one day: "What happened to the door? It wasn't like that last year." "It has cancer. The door has cancer. Illness is falling upon us." That was his response, with a witty smile on his face as he pointed at it.[26]

The Dominican police are known for widespread use of violent tactics and extrajudicial killings, which are hardly ever prosecuted. Even the U.S. embassy in Santo Domingo has expressed concern about extrajudicial killings by police, noting that "most of these killings, which generally are in connection with criminal activities in the poorer districts, receive minimal further investigation of note."[27] Yeni Berenice Reynoso, a top prosecutor in the Dominican Republic, has publicly denounced widespread corruption among the military and the police, who she claims are involved in some 90 percent of all organized crime cases. Between June 2013 and March 2014, more than three thousand members of the national police were discharged for engaging in illegal activities. And in January 2015, the head of the antinarcotics police (DICAN) and several officers were indicted for diverting and selling 1.2 tons of cocaine, running the agency as an organized drug cartel.[28] There have been some efforts to professionalize Dominican law enforcement agencies with better training and higher salaries. However, these initiatives have only affected the most elite agencies. Regular police officers receive the equivalent of $200 per month, not enough to maintain a family. Furthermore, police officers fired for misconduct are typically eventually hired back, either as officers or as private security guards.

In this corrupt system, deportees are particularly vulnerable. All deportees, criminal or not, come into contact with the police the day they arrive at the airport, where they are sometimes held while the authorities check their history. There are no official statistics on the frequency of physical attacks during this initial detention, but more than half the people I interviewed spontaneously mentioned having suffered physical beatings and mistreatment at the airport. The motivations for such acts ranged from stealing their belongings to randomly exerting power and control. Matters only get worse once the deportees are released and begin trying to rebuild their lives. Police frequently stop deportees in the streets without probable cause, simply because they are perceived as a constant threat to Dominican society. Police officers also routinely use physical abuse and intimidation to obtain false confessions from detained deportees for crimes the officers or their associates have in fact committed.

Making the situation worse, the Dominican government is increasingly using the military to perform routine law enforcement duties, especially in the marginalized neighborhoods where deportees tend to concentrate. Dominican military personnel are infamous for their regular use of violence against disempowered populations.

Rafael, a Dominican male in his late thirties, offers a telling example not only of police brutality but also of the interconnections among institutional, interpersonal, and structural violence. Rafael moved from the Dominican Republic to Puerto Rico with his parents in early childhood. Diagnosed with bipolar disorder, he had problems finishing high school. Around age eighteen, he moved to the Bronx to live with an uncle, hoping to get a job in the service industry. Because of his lack of health insurance, however, Rafael did not get adequate treatment for his mental illness and was unable to hold any job for more than a few months. At nineteen, he and some friends joined the neighborhood informal economy, selling marijuana for an African American gang. Rafael was arrested twice and charged with drug possession but was merely fined.

He moved to Boston for a while, where he lived with some family friends who helped him get his life in order. When he was thirty-three, Rafael's mother was hospitalized in the Dominican Republic for severe respiratory complications. Rafael visited her for a couple of months, the first time he had been in that country for more than twenty years. Upon his attempt to reenter the United States, customs officers in Miami detained him, and he was deported due to his drug-related criminal record. Rafael's mother passed away shortly after his deportation, and he has no other close relatives to assist him. His parents had divorced, and his father was still living in Puerto Rico. In Santo Domingo, Rafael had been using heroin for a few years despite several failed attempts to quit.

One day I received a phone call from the police, who had detained Rafael. When I arrived to pick him up, he was broken inside and out. He told me the story:

> I was just outside La Nacional [supermarket]. One security guard calls me in. He says he knows me, that he's seen me before. He then calls up other security staff. They take me to a storage room. They start kicking me right away. The first kick was in the mouth. They grabbed a stick to beat me. They tied me up and threw water on my face, holding me up. They dropped me to the floor. Hit me with a stick in my private parts. When I almost fainted, they threw some more water at my face, and then continued hitting me. They kept accusing me of working in tandem with one employee from the supermarket, stealing liquor for him to sell. They left me on the floor for a while, coming back a bit later. I was blindfolded, with my head inside a bag, so I couldn't identify their faces. They were really enraged now, beating me on my chest. I began pleading with them to stop, saying they were going to kill me. I overheard one of them telling the other: "I'm going to kill this criminal garbage." He continued until he heard some police officers arrive. It seems a cashier had called the police, knowing what was happening to me.[29]

Rafael had no drugs and no store merchandise on his person.

During my fieldwork in the Dominican Republic, I heard many other accounts of police and military brutality against noncriminal deportees. I have reviewed and retained relevant medical reports and have personally observed a range of physical injuries from police torture:

- the loss of an eye after a beating with baseball bats
- near asphyxiation caused by a plastic bag being placed over the victim's head during interrogation
- burns from cigarette butts
- disfigurement of victims' faces and various parts of their bodies from assaults
- beatings resulting in the victim bleeding from her nose and mouth
- two ribs broken and one molar lost during a beating
- gang rapes against women

These kinds of violent attacks against deportees usually go unreported. Because of the stigma attached to the deportee label, victims lack the social standing and credibility to prevail in an official complaint. They are more likely to experience retaliation than vindication from law enforcement agencies if they protest. Overall, this makes them "safe" targets for police abuse. Corrupt Dominican officials have found in the deportee community the perfect scapegoat to deflect attention away from themselves—or to abuse in order to obtain information about rival organizations. Deportees are a criminalized collective who lost credibility and moral standing even before their arrival in the Dominican capital. They are rendered invisible for the most part, except when violence erupts, leading the media to blame them for a broad array of social ills.

In fact, however, government officials themselves contradict the image of deportees as a highly criminalized element. During an informal interview I conducted at the Ministry of Interior and Police, government officials acknowledged that in 2010 there were more police officers than deportees serving prison sentences (6 vs. 3 percent of the Dominican prison population, respectively).[30] Given that the vast majority of crimes committed by law enforcement officers are never investigated, those police officers serving prison sentences reflect only the small percentage who were prosecuted due to the exceptional severity or visibility of their particular crimes.

When I interviewed Virgilio Almánzar, president of the Dominican National Committee for Human Rights, he framed the experience of deportees in terms of human rights violations, beginning from the moment their plane lands in the Dominican Republic:

> The problem of the deportees is not a criminal justice issue. It's a human rights issue. These individuals have already paid for their crimes, yet we're treating them like criminals as soon as they arrive here. We need to come up with reinsertion programs,

not with measures that will stigmatize them even further. Both U.S. and Dominican societies are failing to take advantage of these repatriates' professional and personal skills. We're failing to treat them as equal members of our communities. We have heard about a case in which a deportee was killed by a police officer only because the police officer liked the deportee's car and wanted to take it away. Since the victim was a deportee, no investigation was ever done. The presumption of guilt is always on the side of the deportee. We should drop the label of the "deportee" altogether. We need to find a way to do that, because they're being discriminated against as soon as they're identified as such, even if they behave as law-abiding citizens. We were hoping that with Leonel things would change, because he was supposed to be the president "of the people." But our president moved radically to the right and now is more concerned with pleasing large corporations than helping the masses.[31]

Drug trafficking is a fairly new development in the Dominican Republic that also has significant implications for deportee suffering. Widespread heroin consumption in the country is a relatively recent phenomenon, appearing as the Caribbean became a major corridor for drugs destined for the United States or Europe.[32] As more drugs have stayed on the island, widespread availability and fairly low prices for heroin (as well as powdered cocaine and marijuana) have fueled domestic consumption. (My interviewees report that one vial bag of heroin costs about US$7.) Many deportees were already involved in using or dealing drugs in the United States, but even those who were not find drugs and drug-related crime a pervasive trap that is very difficult to avoid.

Organized drug cartels are fully aware of the limited life options available to deportees because of the stigma against them, and traffickers frequently take advantage of this social marginalization to recruit them. Deportees are perceived as a constantly available army of low-level drug mules that can easily be exploited, abused, and later replaced by newly arriving deportees. Men become involved in the drug trade more often than do women, in part because of societal expectations for men to be breadwinners, on top of the fact that the large majority of deportees are male. A deportee who is recruited by a trafficking organization for low-level, "discreet" drug dealing will generally be left alone by the police as long as he pays them off on a weekly or monthly basis. However, once either the deportee fails to make the required payment to the police or the drug trafficking activity becomes more public, the situation changes dramatically. The police will target that deportee for all crimes committed by the drug-trafficking network or by the police themselves. This is when deportees are at the highest risk of being victimized or even killed by the police.

Based on my research, I believe all deportees to the Dominican Republic, and particularly those lacking in education or job skills and with no family willing or able to help them, are at high risk of being severely physically abused by the police. I anticipate that any newly arriving deportees with such profiles will suffer frequent physical abuse to the point of physical torture (which is usually employed to obtain false incriminatory confessions) and even death within a few months post removal. Moreover, the horrendous abuses of deportees that I witnessed in the Dominican Republic are only a small proportion of the abuses deportees suffer around the world, as they are sent to conflict areas and subjected to extrajudicial killings by the military or the police in such countries as Guatemala, El Salvador, and Honduras, to name a few.

Until fairly recently, federal immigration courts have been reluctant to approve any waiver requests on the grounds of torture, perhaps for fear of opening the gates to a flood of such petitions. Now that the courts are sometimes granting waivers based on CAT requests, we must seize the moment to make this a viable alternative for vulnerable immigrants like Florencio Flores, who do not pose a realistic criminal threat to the United States. Forced removals from the United States have increased beyond any conceivable threat and are wildly out of proportion to the deportation rates in previous years. CAT is aligned with the recognition of basic human rights protecting the mental and physical integrity of the individual, and it should be used aggressively, on a wide scale, and combined with media attention to change policy as well as public opinion regarding the plight of nonviolent deportees.

One could argue that a human rights approach is inherently problematic. Treaties of this nature are the result of ratifications by nation-states, while states are themselves part of the problem due to their role in the enforcement of border control, which denies the right of free movement for all persons. The state is also responsible for fulfilling the legal obligations of fully sanctioned citizenship based on jus soli, yet we see the gross gap in compliance that the Dominican state manifests toward repatriated men and women. The question at hand is, How do you achieve a de facto human rights position by a government that has an inherently antihuman rights position, as seen through their treatment of Dominicans of Haitian descent?[33] This is a complex issue that calls for a multipronged solution but one that must be rooted in bottom-up organizing of affected members from the deportee community.

NOTES TO CHAPTER 15

1. Article 3 of the Convention on Torture, G.A. Res. 39/46, U.N. Doc. A/RES/39/46 (December 10, 1984).

2. P.L. No. 105–277, div. G, Title XXII, 2242(b), 112 Stat. 2681–2822 (1998).

3. I subscribe to a "thick" definition of the rule of law, in line with the International Bar Association's resolution of 2009, upholding its basic elements as the following: "An

independent, impartial judiciary; the presumption of innocence; the right to a fair and public trial without undue delay; a rational and proportionate approach to punishment; a strong and independent legal profession; strict protection of confidential communications between lawyer and client; equality of all before the law." International Bar Association, *Resolution of the Council of the IBA on the Commentary on Rule of Law Resolution September 2005*, October 8, 2009, London.

4. Linda Bosniak, *The Citizen and the Alien: Dilemmas of Contemporary Membership* (Princeton: Princeton University Press, 2006).

5. Onora O'Neill, *Bounds of Justice* (Cambridge: Cambridge University Press, 2000); Zygmunt Bauman, *Society Under Siege* (Malden: Blackwell, 2002); Will Kymlicka, "Territorial Boundaries: A Liberal Egalitarian Perspective," in *Boundaries and Justice: Diverse Ethical Perspectives*, ed. David Miller and Sohail Hashmi (Princeton: Princeton University Press, 2001), 249–277; Matthew Gibney, "Precarious Residents: Migration Control, Membership and the Rights of Non-Citizens," United Nations Development Programme, Human Development Reports, 2009, http://hdr.undp.org/en/content/precarious-residents.

6. Matthew Gibney, "Is Deportation a Form of Forced Migration?," *Refugee Survey Quarterly* 32, no. 2 (2013): 116–129.

7. U.S. Immigration and Customs Enforcement, "FY 2015 ICE Immigration Removals," https://www.ice.gov/removal-statistics.

8. Ruben Rumbaut and Walter Ewing, "The Myth of Immigrant Criminality and the Paradox of Assimilation: Incarceration Rates Among Native and Foreign-Born Men," American Immigration Law Foundation, February 21, 2007, http://www.immigrationpolicy.org/sites/default/files/docs/Imm%20Criminality%20%28IPC%29.pdf.

9. David Brotherton and Luis Barrios, *Banished to the Homeland: Dominican Deportees and Their Stories of Exile* (New York: Columbia University Press, 2011); David Brotherton and Yolanda Martin, "The War on Drugs and the Case of the Dominican Deportees," *Journal of Crime and Justice* 32, no. 2 (2009): 21–48.

10. One could argue that crime statistics in Haiti are unreliable and, most likely, underreported. However, the same could be said about the Dominican Republic. One of the main causes of the high rates of homicide in the Dominican Republic is easy access to guns. Haitians for the most part do not have access to guns, except for the elite (based on a personal interview of a police officer in Port au Prince, Haiti; June 2, 2016); UN Office of Drugs and Crime, "Global Study on Homicide 2013," March 2014, http://www.unodc.org/documents/gsh/pdfs/2014_GLOBAL_HOMICIDE_BOOK_web.pdf.

11. A Dominican newspaper reported a consistently low recidivism rate among deportees of 2–3 percent in 2000–2010. Ramón Urbáez and Ramón Cruz Benzán, "Sólo 3% de los deportados a RD es reincidente," *Listin Diario*, December 21, 2010, www.listin.com.do/la-republica/2010/12/21/170953/Solo-3-de-los-dominicanos-deportados-son-reincidentes.

12. Erich Goode, *Deviant Behavior*, 8th ed. (Upper Saddle River: Prentice Hall, 2014).

13. Interview, March 2010.

14. Interview, June 2010.

15. Émile Durkheim, *The Division of Labor in Society* (New York: Free Press, 2014 [1893]).

16. World Bank, Dominican Republic Data, 2016, http://data.worldbank.org/country /dominican-republic.

17. Paul Farmer, Bruce Nizeye, Sara Stulac, and Salmaan Keshavjee, "Structural Violence and Clinical Medicine," *PloS Medicine* 3 (2006), box 1, doi:10.1371/journal .pmed.0030449.

18. Paul Farmer, *Pathologies of Power: Health, Human Rights, and the New War on the Poor* (Berkeley: University of California Press, 2003), 1.

19. Philippe Bourgois, Mark Lettiere, and James Quesada, "Social Misery and the Sanctions of Substance Abuse: Confronting HIV Risk Among Homeless Heroin Users in San Francisco," *Social Problems* 44, no. 2 (1997): 155–73, doi:10.1525/sp.1997.44.2.03x0220l.

20. Loic Wacquant, *Deadly Symbiosis: When Ghetto and Prison Meet and Mesh* (Hoboken: John Wiley & Sons, 2010).

21. Merrill Singer, *Introduction to Syndemics: A Critical Systems Approach to Public and Community Health* (San Francisco: Jossey-Bass, 2009).

22. Merrill Singer, "AIDS and the Health Crisis of the US Urban Poor: The Perspective of Critical Medical Anthropology," *Social Science and Medicine* 39, no. 7 (1994): 931–948.

23. Candace Currie et al., eds., *Inequalities in Young People's Health: HBSC International Report* (Copenhagen: World Health Organization, 2008), www.euro.who.int /__data/assets/pdf_file/0005/53852/E91416.pdf, 2. See also Bruce Link and Jo Phelan, "Social Conditions as Fundamental Causes of Disease," *Journal of Health and Social Behavior* 35 (1995): 80–94.

24. Singer, *Introduction to Syndemics*.

25. Personal interview, February 19, 2010.

26. Field notes, March 3, 2010.

27. Wikileaks Public Library of US Democracy, "Subject: Police Under Spotlight Following Death of Two Suspects in High-Profile Kidnapping Case," cable from U.S. embassy, Santo Domingo, October 28, 2009, www.wikileaks.org/plusd/cables /09SANTODOMINGO1257_a.html.

28. Loren Riesenfeld, "Police Involved in 90% of Dominican Republic Organized Crime Cases," InSight Crime, March 20, 2015, www.insightcrime.org/news-briefs/90 -percent-police-organized-crime-dominican-republic.

29. Interview, March 24, 2010.

30. Interview, February 15, 2010.

31. Interview, October 17, 2009, my translation from Spanish.

32. Leah Blumenfeld, "Trading Democracy for Security? The Effects of the International Drug War on the Quality of Democracy in the Dominican Republic, 1996–2008" (PhD diss., Florida International University, 2010).

33. More than 210,000 Dominicans of Haitian descent have been denationalized, after the Constitutional Tribunal Sentence 168–13 of 2013, which retroactively scaled back birthright citizenship, or jus soli, to 1939. This constitutes severe violations of international human rights treaties and principles, and has led to an outcry against the government of Dominican president Danilo Medina.

CONTRIBUTORS

Sofya Aptekar is Assistant Professor of Sociology at the University of Massachusetts Boston. She studies immigration, race and ethnicity, and urban neighborhoods. Dr. Aptekar is the author of *The Road to Citizenship: What Naturalization Means for Immigrants and the United States* (2015). Her research has also been featured in several journals, including *Ethnicities, Ethnic and Racial Studies,* and *Citizenship Studies.*

Payal Banerjee is Associate Professor at the Department of Sociology, Smith College. Her research focuses on globalization, the political economy of migration and immigrant experiences, and the centrality of state policies in sculpting the structures of labor incorporation. Dr. Banerjee's work on Indian immigrant IT workers in the United States has appeared in *Critical Sociology; Race, Gender, and Class; International Feminist Journal of Politics; Irish Journal of Anthropology; Women's Studies Quarterly; Social and Public Policy Review; Man in India;* and in other edited volumes.

Carolina Sanchez Boe is a post-doctoral researcher at Aalborg University, Denmark, and currently teaches sociology and anthropology at Université Paris V and Columbia Global Centres, Paris. She is the author of *The Undeported: The Making of a Floating Population of Exiles in France and Europe* (forthcoming 2018). She has conducted research on migration, penal institutions, and deportation for numerous organizations, among them the National Human Rights Consultative Commission (CNCDH), the American Friends Service Committee, and Amnesty International Denmark. Dr. Boe worked as a paralegal lawyer for French nonprofit Cimade for four years, defending foreign-national prisoners with deportation orders, and she frequently serves as an interpreter in asylum and deportation cases.

David C. Brotherton is Professor of Sociology, Urban Education, and Criminal Justice at the John Jay College of Criminal Justice and the Graduate Center of the City University of New York, and Visiting Professor at the Universities of Kent and Suffolk, UK. He is the editor of Studies in Transgression (Columbia) and codirector of the Center for Work, Culture and Technology (Graduate Center, CUNY). Dr. Brotherton's research on social exclusion and resistance through critical ethnography has led to over fifty academic books, peer-reviewed articles, and chapters. He has received numerous academic awards, and his current projects include crime control in Ecuador; juvenile justice reform in Washington, D.C.; and the sociology of vindictiveness in U.S. immigration hearings.

Deirdre Conlon is a Lecturer in Critical Human Geography at the University of Leeds. Her research examines tensions around immigration management practices and immigrants' everyday experiences. Dr. Conlon's recent publications include articles in *Annals of the Association of American Geographers* and *Race and Class*, as well as the coedited books *Carceral Spaces: Mobility and Agency in Imprisonment and Migrant Detention* (with Nick Gill and Dominique Moran; 2013) and *Intimate Economies of Immigration Detention: Critical Perspectives* (with Nancy Hiemstra; 2016). Her current research and writing focus on the internal infrastructure and dynamics that gird immigration detention in the United States.

Gabriel Pérez Duperou is a Research Assistant at El Colegio de la Frontera Norte. He received his MA in Regional Development in 2012 at El Colegio de la Frontera Norte. He has worked in nongovernmental organizations defending the rights of migrants from Mexico and Central America. His research interests are immigration policy and human rights, social networks in international migration, and risks and vulnerabilities of undocumented migration.

Matthew B. Flynn is an Assistant Professor of Sociology and International Studies at Georgia Southern University. His interests include globalization, development, immigration, and global health. Dr. Flynn's most recent book, *Pharmaceutical Autonomy and Public Health in Latin America: State, Society, and Industry in Brazil's AIDS Program* (2015), analyzes the impact of intellectual property regimes and access to high-cost medicines in Brazil. His work on immigration detention includes the coedited book *Challenging Immigration Detention: Scholars, Activists and Policy-makers* (with Michael Flynn; 2017), coediting the Working Paper Series at the Geneva-based Global Detention Project, and a publication in *Contemporary Readings in Law and Social Justice*.

Michael Flynn is the Executive Director of the Global Detention Project in Geneva, Switzerland. He holds a BA in Philosophy from DePaul University and an MA and PhD in International Studies from the Graduate Institute of International and Development Studies. Dr. Flynn previously worked as a project director at the Institute for

Policy Studies in Washington, D.C.; as a project coordinator at the Graduate Institute's Programme for the Study of Global Migration; and as an associate editor of the *Bulletin of the Atomic Scientists*. He is coeditor, with Matthew Flynn, of the book *Challenging Immigration Detention: Scholars, Activists and Policy-makers* (2017).

Tanya Golash-Boza is a Professor of Sociology at the University of California, Merced. She is the author of five books, including *Deported: Immigrant Policing, Disposable Labor and Global Capitalism* (2015) and the textbook *Race and Racisms: A Critical Approach* (2015). Dr. Golash-Boza has published over a dozen articles in academic journals and has won awards for her research and public service. She also writes on contemporary issues for many outlets, including *Al Jazeera*, the *Boston Review*, the *Nation*, *Counterpunch*, the *Houston Chronicle*, and the *Chronicle of Higher Education*.

Graham Hudson is Associate Professor of Criminology at Ryerson University. His current research interests include security studies, crimmigration, sanctuary cities, and legal pluralism. Graham is a member of several research teams, including the Canadian Network for Research on Terrorism, Security and Society's SSHRC Partnership Grant and an SSHRC Insight Grant on the intersection of security, irregular migration, and asylum. He is also conducting a socio-legal study of the "sanctuary city" movement in Canada.

Philip Kretsedemas is Associate Professor of Sociology at the University of Massachusetts Boston. His research has examined how noncitizens are constructed as racial others and the politics of immigration and social policy, with a focus on neoliberalism. Dr. Kretsedemas has published several academic research articles and book chapters and has coedited three books on migration and immigration policy, including *Keeping Out the Other: A Critical Introduction to Immigration Enforcement Today* (2008), with David Brotherton. He is also the author of *The Immigration Crucible: Transforming Race, Nation, and the Limits of the Law* (2012) and *Migrants and Race in the US: Territorial Racism and the Alien/Outside* (2013).

Shirley Leyro is an Assistant Professor of Criminal Justice at Borough of Manhattan Community College, CUNY. A critical criminologist, Dr. Leyro's research focuses on deportation effects, including the impact of the fear resulting from the vulnerability to deportation. Her research interests include immigration, legal violence, social disorganization, and crimmigration. She is coeditor of *Outside Justice: Immigration and the Criminalizing Impact of Changing Policy and Practice* (with David Brotherton and Daniel Stageman; 2013), as well as a contributor to the same volume. She is also a member of the Leadership Team for the Latina Researchers Network.

Greg Martin is Associate Professor of Socio-Legal Studies in the School of Social and Political Sciences at the University of Sydney, Australia. Dr. Martin has published widely in socio-legal studies, criminology, policing, and law, including in the *British Journal of Sociology*; *Crime, Media, Culture*, the *Journal of Law and Society*; *Policing and Society*; and the *Sydney Law Review*. He is the author of *Understanding Social Movements* (2015) and coeditor of *Secrecy, Law and Society* (with Rebecca Scott Bray and Miiko Kumar; 2015). He is an Editor of *The Sociological Review*, Associate Editor of *Crime*

Media Culture, and a member of the Editorial Advisory Board of *Social Movement Studies.*

Yolanda C. Martín is a critical criminologist who holds a PhD in Sociology from the Graduate Center of the City University of New York. Dr. Martin's research has been published in the *International Journal of Criminology, Radical History Review,* and *Latino Studies.* She is currently a member of the Editorial Board of the American Sociological Association journal, *Contexts.*

Lisa Sun-Hee Park is a Professor of Asian American Studies at the University of California, Santa Barbara. Dr. Park's interdisciplinary research focuses on the politics of migration, race, and social policy. Her latest publications include two books: *Entitled to Nothing: The Struggle for Immigrant Health Care in the Age of Welfare Reform* (2011) and *The Slums of Aspen: Immigrants vs. the Environment in America's Eden* (co-authored with David N. Pellow; 2011). Dr. Park is working on a new project on medical deportations of low-income immigrants in need of long-term care.

María Dolores París Pombo is a Professor and Researcher in the Cultural Studies Department at El Colegio de la Frontera Norte. She is the author of *La historia de Marta: Vida de una mujer indígena por los largos caminos de la Mixteca a California* (2006) and editor of *Migrantes, desplazados, braceros y deportados: Experiencias migratorias y prácticas políticas* (2012). Dr. Pombo's research has also been featured in several migration-themed publications, including the *Journal of Borderlands Studies, Migrations Société,* and *Latin American Perspectives.*

Claudia Tazreiter is Associate Professor of Sociology at the University of New South Wales, Australia. Her research focuses on forced and irregular migration, human rights, the role of nongovernmental organizations and civil society in social change, and gender in migration. Dr. Tazreiter is co-author of *Fluid Security in the Asia Pacific: Transnational Lives, Human Rights and State Control* (with Sharon Pickering, Leanne Weber, Marie Segrave and Helen McKernan; 2016); author of *Asylum Seekers and the State: The Politics of Protection in a Security-Conscious World* (2004, 2006); and coeditor of *Globalisation and Social Transformation in Two Culturally Diverse Societies: The Australian and Malaysian Experience* (with Siew Yean Tham; 2013). She is managing editor of the *Australian Journal of Human Rights* and an associate of the Australian Human Rights Centre.

Sarah Tosh is a PhD candidate in Sociology at the Graduate Center of the City University of New York. She is a Predoctoral Fellow at the Behavioral Science Training in Drug Abuse Research program at the National Research Development Institute, and a Research Fellow with the Vera Institute of Justice's Center on Immigration and Justice. Her work centers on the intersection of punitive immigration and drug policy in the United States.